FORGOT HOOSIERS

AFRICAN HERITAGE

IN

ORANGE COUNTY, INDIANA

Coy D. Robbins

HERITAGE BOOKS
2011

HERITAGE BOOKS

AN IMPRINT OF HERITAGE BOOKS, INC.

Books, CDs, and more—Worldwide

For our listing of thousands of titles see our website
at
www.HeritageBooks.com

Published 2011 by
HERITAGE BOOKS, INC.
Publishing Division
100 Railroad Ave. #104
Westminster, Maryland 21157

Copyright © 1994 Coy D. Robbins

Other Heritage Books by the author:

Forgotten Hoosiers: African Heritage in Orange County, Indiana

Indiana Negro Register, 1852-1865

Reclaiming African Heritage at Salem, Indiana

CD: Indiana African Heritage

International Standard Book Numbers
Paperbound: 978-0-7884-0017-9
Clothbound: 978-0-7884-8652-4

We write in celebration of those
who came before us,
and survived.

CONTENTS

LIST OF TABLES

LIST OF MAPS AND CHARTS

PREFACE

This book highlights the history of people of African descent who were among the early American settlers in southern Indiana. Although their story has never been included in our history books, these brave, courageous souls were among the pioneers -- both as free and enslaved persons.

My pursuit of early African history in Indiana evolved gradually with my growing interest and skills in genealogical research, and the realization that public records created long ago in county courthouses contained the chronicles of *all* Americans and "not just white folks." A dogged curiosity compelled me to learn about early Africans in the Hoosier state: who were they, where did they come from, and what happened to them and their children.

Paoli is only fifty miles south of Bloomington, and during the years I had lived here, I never knew of any African Americans in Orange County. In fact many Hoosiers seem to regard Paoli as being an all-white town whose residents harbored strong feelings against outsiders, especially those of a different race.

During the early 1970s when tensions between races were extremely high in this nation, I first heard about the "Little Africa" Cemetery from one of my Bloomington neighbors. He thought I might be interested in researching the colored persons who were buried near his hometown, Paoli. I did not take to the idea, explaining that if I ever found the time to pursue historical research as a hobby I would prefer to focus on Hamilton County, my home community in central Indiana. Nothing more came of the idea at that time.

Meanwhile, inspired in 1976 by Alex Haley and the publication of his book, *Roots*, I started spending weekends and vacations doing research on my family history in Indiana. Continued success in uncovering ancestral roots in central Indiana and Ohio as well as in Guilford County, North Carolina helped me gain a working familiarity with the numerous African American historical and genealogical collections in several state libraries, archives, and local repositories of public documents.

When I made my first historical research trip to Paoli in 1981, I felt well prepared to explore the legend of African Americans who once lived in Orange County, to determine what happened to them, and to discover how and when their pioneer cemetery now incorporated into the land of Hoosier National Forest ever acquired the name of "Little Africa." Additionally, I carried with me the names of all free people of color listed as Orange County residents in the 1830 U. S. Census.

A bit apprehensive over the kind of racial reception I might encounter in Paoli, I stopped first at the small, red brick Carnegie Public Library on the northeast corner of Courthouse Circle. The librarian, Carol Vance, responded cordially and acquainted me with their genealogy and local history holdings as we chatted about the "Little Africa" cemetery and her lack of familiarity of any colored people who lived in the area.

Thus my introduction to Orange County was a friendly one. The ambience remained the same as I returned there many times over the next twelve years to uncover its African heritage. During this project, I gradually became acquainted with other residents in addition to Mrs. Vance, and they were friendly and seemed truly interested in the progress of my research and always willing to direct me to possible sources of local "colored" history.

During 1982-83 I authored several articles based upon my tentative findings and primarily to acquaint others with the fact that Africans had been contributors to Indiana's pioneer history. The first writing, "Lick Creek Settlement: An Early Black Community in Orange County", appeared in 1982 as a two-part series in *Black History News & Notes*. In 1986 I published three additional articles in *The Journal of the Afro-American Historical and Genealogical Society*, Washington, D. C.: "Negro Register: Orange County, Indiana (1853-1861)," "Freedom Papers Found in Orange County, Indiana," and "Orange County, Indiana: African Americans Enumerated in the 1850 U. S. Census."

Publication of these writings eventually got me involved locally in a nation-wide controversy which flourished in the mid-1980s. The dispute centered on the conservation of our national forests, methods of tree harvesting, and the recreational use of public land. In southern Indiana the Hoosier National Forest served as one of the arenas where opposing groups directed their energies. To support its stance, one state-wide citizens group chose as its goal the preservation of the "Little Africa" cemetery and have it placed on the Register of National Historic Sites. Other conservation groups demanded that off-road recreational vehicles and motorcyles be outlawed from the forestry land in order to curb the severe soil erosion developing in recent years.

It turned out that my few published writings were the only detailed documentation available on the "Little Africa" historic site. Reporters from the regional press and television medias contacted me for interviews and personal opinions, as did members of various ad hoc conservation groups and representatives of the lumber industry, school teachers, historians, genealogists, free lance writers, and concerned citizens who sought my immediate support of their particular point of view on these matters.

Not all callers to my home during this controversy were amicable. Several challenged truculently the accuracy of my research on "Little Africa," or at least their understanding of it based upon the newspaper accounts they had read. Some would not accept my evidence that free African Americans ever lived in Orange County before the Civil War. Others insisted that those county residents I found were only a few slaves or runaways, and several callers contended adamantly that there were never any "colored people" in Orange County. Furthermore, they suggested that the "Little Africa" story was really a hoax perpetrated by some government officials determined to keep the young people from enjoying life and doing as they pleased in the public forests. "After all, this government land belongs to us, the people."

The number of requests coming to me for information about Orange County persisted, and in 1990 I decided to publish a compilation of my earlier writings to help handle some of these inquiries. However, due to writing commitments which I had made to the Indiana African American Historical and Genealogical Society, I was unable to make any extensive revisions on these articles at the time.

In early October 1990, this reprinting effort came to a sudden halt after I experienced a cerebral hemorrahagic stoke which left me paralyzed on the entire left side of my body. Weeks of hospitalization and months of outpatient therapies enabled me to walk again, to use my left arm, and to resume normal daily independent activities, including the driving of a car and using my computer.

Throughout my illness I remained strongly motivated to get well as soon as possible so that I could complete my family history research and move ahead with this publication. Even greater determination to regain my former health resulted several weeks after I returned home from the hospital and found several lengthy reports in the mail from Rocco Gibala of Hoosier National Forest Office in Paoli.

Mr. Gibala and I had met briefly the previous July when he guided me and a friend of mine from Gary, Indiana to see the "Little Africa" cemetery site. During this trip we talked about my past research efforts on the cemetery, and some of my unanswered questions about the Lick Creek Settlement. He volunteered to help me by examining old deed record files in their office containing copies of all legal documents pertaining to the land purchased by the federal government in the 1930s to form the Hoosier National Forest. All that he would need to start the search was a list of some African Americans who formerly resided in Orange County. Hopefully the results would identify the specific landowners, and also reveal how many of them lived in the vicinity of the "Little Africa" cemetery.

I supplied him immediately with a copy of my *master list* of names, and several months after my stroke he mailed me the preliminary reports of his findings. Reading the tremendous amount of excellent work he had accomplished was exciting, and the results greatly exceeded my initial expectations (see details in Chapter IV and Appendix C). Just studying the reports kept me busy for days, and his new data expanded greatly so many dimensions of my earlier research. More library and field work in Orange County was needed before incorporating his material. Consequently, this publication is a blending of materials from my earlier articles with the results of subsequent research I pursued during my recuperative period.

Here, I wish to recognize my indebtedness to Mr. Gibala, who is now with the United States Forestry Service, Lexington, Kentucky, for his generous contributions to the study of land records. In addition, he read a manuscript draft and offered some helpful suggestions about the Lick Creek Settlement land ownerships described in Chapter IV. Also I am grateful for the courtesy shown by the staffs of the Hoosier National Forest, United States Department of Agriculture, Paoli, Bedford and Brownstown, Indiana offices when sharing copies of maps and other pertinent research materials used in this publication.

Genealogical and historical studies are rarely ever finished. Unfortunately, the researcher can never learn everything about past events and their effect upon human lives, no matter how diligently he tries. So I've been forced to interrupt this research process in order to put some of my findings into a publication. This writing is done with great hopes that the results will help some readers to discover to what extent the real story of African Americans in Indiana has in the past been excluded from our history books. More importantly, however, may it serve to inspire others to become interested in researching the history of their African American ancestors in Indiana, and perhaps in the process they will discover that some of the Orange Countians mentioned on these pages were their ancestors. I will always be glad to hear from any readers who are especially interested in the family genealogies discussed so briefly in Chapter XV.

Acknowledgements

Several residents of Orange County were very helpful to me with this research endeavor. In addition to those previously mentioned, I am grateful to three African American families who welcomed me into their homes and participated freely in this study: Rev. and Mrs. Robert H. Bennett and Mr. and Mrs. William E. Norris of Paoli, and Mr. and Mrs. Artie Smith of West Baden Springs. Each family seemed to have deep personal roots into the total community, and I appreciated their warmth, friendliness and willingness to contribute what they could to my research.

Thanks to the staff in the County Clerk and County Recorder offices who assisted me in locating and duplicating old records. Special recognition is due to Robert and Rita Carnes, Janet S. Padgett, and Grant M. Rutherford, now retired.

Acknowledgements also go to Wilma and Everett Davis. Both are delightful people, busy retirees, and active participants in commmunity life. She is a dedicated genealogist who became the Orange County Historian in 1990, and she was extremely helpful to me in locating obituaries and newspaper articles about the twentieth century residents.

Also to Donald L. Mauger, President, Orange County Genealogical Society, who provided me with copies of old Paoli photographs from his personal collection; Marjorie Lapping, President, Orange County Historical Society; James Babcock, Principal, Paoli High School; Valerie Moon, Paoli News-Republican newspaper; Mrs. Aaron Parks and Delores York, Melton Public Library in French Lick; and to Lin Wagner of French Lick.

I appreciated the willingness of Patricia Clements, widow of Attorney Harry Clements, to share with me copies of his personal records generated by the 1970 Boy Scout Troop project to restore the "Little Africa Cemetery." Special thanks to Mr. and Mrs. Gerald Stout, Bloomington, Indiana, my former neighbors who facilitated the meeting with Mrs. Clements.

Others who aided me in some way with this research included: Rev. Elizabeth B. Bridgwaters, Blooomington, Indiana; Roger Peterson, Spencer, Indiana; Joe H. Burgess, Hamilton County (Indiana) Historian; Wilma Gibbs, Indiana Historical Society; Robert Horton, Indiana State Archives; Staff of the Genealogy Department, Indiana State Library; Curt B. Witcher and staff of the Genealogy Department, Allen County Public Library, Fort Wayne, Indiana; Mrs. Jacqueline Brown, Wilberforce University (Ohio) Archives; Dr. Jessie Carnes Smith and staff, Fisk University Library and Archives; Staff, North Carolina State Archives and Library, Raleigh, N. C.; Arlie C. Robbins (deceased) and staff, Raleigh Township Centennial Museum, North Buxton, Ontario, Canada.

A special indebtedness is due my wife and best friend, Jean Johnson Robbins, for her constant loyalty and unflagging support, encouragement, and generous contributions to this book in countless ways. Also to our daughter, Linda D. Robbins Atwood, who furnished computer expertise, consultation, and technical guidance throughout the completion of this manuscript. Thanks to our son-in-law, Larry G. Atwood, for his caring, understanding, and cooperation.

Finally, I trust sincerely that Orange County residents will soon discontinue use of the outdated prejudicial label of "Little Africa" and replace it with the name selected by the original inhabitants for their pioneer farming community -- the *Lick Creek Settlement*. Such act would constitute an honest, timely and respectful tribute to the memory of those gallant settlers of African ancestry, both the free-born and captive people, who first migrated into this region of the state more than one hundred and seventy years ago.

Coy D. Robbins

May 20, 1993
Bloomington, Indiana

CHAPTER I

INTRODUCTION

Genealogy and History Go Together

Since starting my family history research fifteen years ago, I've gone through countless stacks of books and public records seeking genealogical information about my African ancestors. This search has exposed me to a multiplicity of local, state and national public documents, such as population censuses, vital, land and probate records. Continued success with this research has helped me to realize that although I am still not able to trace my roots to progenitors on the continent of Africa, I have unearthed, nevertheless, an American heritage that is distinctive, meaningful, illustrious, captivating and also extremely enigmatic.

In this same process I determined ultimately that what I was learning about people of African descent who were among the pioneers in Indiana had rarely ever been embodied into the traditional historical literature. Even more amazing to me was the finding that the genealogical literature also tended to exclude much data about African Americans.

These painful discoveries helped me to realize again the extent to which earlier writers, historians, and genealogists have ignored, disregarded or deliberately misinterpreted the presence and contributions of racial minorities. Even though the original public documents which I was now studying oftentimes contained racial references, as given in state and federal population censuses, white compilers and indexers frequently eliminated these designations in their publications. As a result the readers naturally assumed that the historical documents pertained only to white Americans. The practice to publish only what the white majority was interested in reading has left Americans until very recently wholly ignorant of the "real" history.

Without any substantial body of historical and genealogical literature about persons of African ancestry in Indiana to draw upon, I was forced to research everything, being guided primarily by a deep-seated desire to recover the "forgotten" history of my people as preserved long ago in Hoosier county records. Since no one knows for certain how many old documents of this nature actually exists, I am never certain that I have exhausted the research potentials of any particular county.

More Than Two Primary Themes

Each day as my work progresses I'm amazed over how much about African Americans in Indiana has been omitted from the history books. Undoubtedly the Euramericans felt justified to create and perpetuate "a white man's history" in America, even though doing so required that they ignore their presence or malign the contributions of Native Americans, Africans and other racial minorities.

These days it is becoming less difficult to locate realistic information about African Hoosiers than it was only a few years ago. Within the past decade significant public repositories, such as the Indiana Historical Society, the Indiana State Library and Archives, and the Allen County Public Library started expanding their ethnic collections. Until the 1970s, there was no major historical society, library, archive, or academic program supported by taxes and staffed by professionals dedicated to the gathering and preservation of significant state-wide historical documents pertaining to racial minorities in this state.

From the collected material about African Americans, the bulk of it seemed to fall broadly within two classifications: slavery and the underground railroad. Restricting collections to these general subjects was not only a common practice in Indiana but throughout our nation. It subsisted on the need for many white Americans to construct a historical reality compatible to their perceived role as the dominant cultural group, and to provide a brief explanation of why there was a visible racial minority in this country. Mounting evidence accumulated in these narrowly defined collections was used to repudiate the creditability of any protestors who insisted that their ancestors failed to fit the sterotypical roles assigned to them in the white history.

The first theme about slavery purported that the only persons of African descent to ever participate in early Indiana history were either slaves or indentured servants. They never arrived here on their own. Instead they were brought into the state by white southerners who were wealthy and sought excitement and their fortunes up North. The concept that "free people of color" migrated into Indiana before the Civil War is wholly incomprensible to proponents of this theme.

Local storytellers embellished the slavery theme. They dreamed up colorful, romantic tales about the happy days on the plantations which often left the reader to wonder why anyone, and especially the slaves, ever wanted to leave such a blissful tranquility for the Indiana wilderness. These fanciful legends are deeply treasured by some Hoosier families and passed on to succeeding generations who cherish proudly their southern ancestors, especially those who were the "good" slaveholders. For so many these stories blended ultimately into a singular historical fact: the only Africans to ever be in Indiana until after the Civil War ended were slaves, or runaway slaves, the property of white folks.

If these Hoosiers had been familiar with the federal and Indiana laws of the era, they would have realized that any slave-holding ancestors in Indiana were actually lawbreakers. As early as July 13, 1787, the United States government prohibited slavery in the Northwest Territory out of which the state Indiana was eventually carved, and the state's first constitution adopted in 1816 incorporated similar anti-slavery provisions.

For those Hoosiers whose European ancestors arrived on American shores within this century, the prevailing myth was readily accepted. No legitimate voice ever contradicted the accuracy of the one-race version of American history. Furthermore, rarely was there an opportunity for them to view members of racial minorities any differently from the sterotypical images put forth in the daily press, educational, governmental and political media. For most Americans the myth was was believable; afterall, the races continued living apart as each succeeding generation struggled toward becoming more Americanized.

The second theme to gain widespread acceptance about African heritage sprang from the stories of the "underground railroad." It is closely related to the first theme and became deeply embedded in America's popular culture toward the end of the nineteenth century.

Hoosiers, like many Americans, were led to believe that all Africans in this country were slaves. They were not humans but animals destined to be owned, sold and controlled by Euramericans or their descendents. Therefore, if anyone expressed a firm knowledge of African Hoosiers before the Civil War, they usually reasoned that these were merely runaway slaves who were traveling surreptitiously through the state via the "underground railroad."

For many, especially whites, the real history of Africans in Indiana began and ended with the legends of the "underground railroad." The term is synonymous with African Hoosier history. I have discovered that during any serious discussions of my research in this state, someone will eventually ask me about the "underground railroad" if I did not comment on the subject in my presentation. Some wish to determine if I am familiar with the many historic sites dedicated to their ancestors who labored to rescue the "poor black slaves from the South." These Hoosier myths abound in minutiae about the unusual hiding places, clever identifying signals, sharing warm food and clothing, and displaying compassion for the sick, elderly and wretched slaves being passed secretly through the state to ultimate freedom in Canada by a complex system maintained by friendly white people.

Rarely do these family tales include any information of note concerning the "railroad's" human passengers. In these dramatic vignettes the African characters were nebulously presented, without any real substance or character, black in color (they all look alike), an odd kind of mystical being who traveled only at night and often wore disguises. If these travelers had names, they were only first names since everyone knew slaves never had surnames. They waited patiently without emotion for the kind conductors to take them to the next safe haven.

On the other hand, the "underground railroad" literature in Indiana was filled with lengthy accounts of the exploits of white Hoosiers, usually males and listing their full names and family histories, who generously assisted the runaways. These legends gave no logical explanation why the Africans who had been enslaved and cruelly mistreated by whites in the South would suddenly conclude that some whites living in Indiana were of a different species, that they were trustworthy, and that they would protect them in a racially hostile environment. Few historical writers of the times ever point out that while these humanitarian rescues were taking place, the nation was reaping immense profits and economic benefits (slaves were taxable property) from the enslavement of captive Africans.

For too many Hoosiers these themes represent the extent of their knowledge of African Americans in the state before the Civil War. These myths have continued to spread for various reasons, including the fact that their authenticity has rarely been challenged. Some attempts are now being made to study and reappraise our historical past from a more democratic perspective, one which includes all Americans who actually participated in the events, regardless of racial, ethnic, religious, original country of origin, wealth or social class. Such efforts may help us to overcome one day the pervasive ignorance of the realities of African experiences which exist in this state, a condition which hampers any serious understanding of the complete history of Hoosiers.

Project Research Methods

No easy method has yet been devised for doing African American genealogical and historical research.[1]

It remains an extremely slow, laborious, and time-consuming process. For the faithful researcher, nonetheless, the payoffs come from the small and unexpected breakthroughs after months or even years of routine busy-work: the personal feelings of gratification after locating the name of an ancestor who lived in the 18th century; the weed-grown location of a long-deserted "colored" cemetery; finding the land records proving that a free man of color, such as John Williams, from Tennessee once owned and operated a 160-acre farm near Salem, Indiana for almost thirty years before the Civil War started.

Without a written guide for collecting the pioneer history of Africans in the several Indiana counties, I learned through repeated trial-and-error efforts that the first place to begin this kind of historical research was the local library. Typically their collections, especially when I began my research in the 1980s were very meager at best, although several county libraries, historical and genealogical societies had started to collect some materials on African Americans and to set up special displays for Black History Month in February.

Once I familiarized myself with the local holdings on the subjects of "Colored People," "Slavery," "Negroes and Blacks," I usually proceeded to the second step in the research process. It involved the tremendous task of patiently gathering copies of the written data on all African Americans enumerated as living in the particular county under study when the United States decennial population censuses were conducted between 1790-1910. This task today should include also the 1920 census information which was first opened to the public in March, 1992. Names and full census data was copied, often by hand, of all county residents labeled racially as colored, Black, mulatto or Negro. These essential data provide unquestionable documentation of the African presence in the state, the exact number of persons found within a certain time frame, and enables the researcher to develop some initial familiarity with the principal family groups and surnames for more individualized study in the future.

The decision about where to start the census research was made after evaluating several factors not readily known to the novice genealogist. Ideally, its the 1850 census because this is the first federal population census which includes the names, sex, and ages of *all* persons in the household. All decennial censuses through 1840 listed by name only the head of the household. I followed this plan for the Orange County research and eventually -- over the period of several years -- I completed this arduous task for censuses between 1820 and 1910 (Appendix B).

These data were used later to devise a *master list* containing in alphabetical order each surname and given name along with the each year the person was listed in a census as living in Orange County, Indiana. This *master list* soon became my primary research tool. I used it frequently to confirm as African Americans the names of persons and family groups discovered when checking out the local public documents, e.g., marriages, deed and land records, etc. The genealogical collection in the local public library became suddenly relevant for my research, for now I had a list and approximate period of time persons of African ancestry lived in the county. As my research efforts exhausted the local library holdings, I went to the specialized historical collections in and outside the county (the courthouse and county administrative offices, Indiana University Libraries, Indiana State Library and Archives, Indiana Historical Society) seeking additional leads to further research.

At first, my greatest number of finds came from the county's vital records: marriage, birth and death. Data from these sources established the pace for my unearthing copies of the "certificates of freedom" recorded in the deed records books more than one hundred and fifty years ago. And in this process the "Negro Register" compiled in the 1850s and secured in the vault of the County Clerk was brought for my inspection. Additional names and family data found in its contents were added to the *master list*.

The mass of statistics about African families grew at a varying pace as I used my vacations to search other courthouse records, such as land, deeds, wills, probate court, apprenticeship, miscellaneous and commissioners reports. Churches, schools, and cemetery records were important but did not become useful until this project was well underway. Interspersed between infrequent periods of field research were the many hours spent in my office translating the handscript in old documents, sorting and examining them for proof that they actually pertained to the people of color.

The final stage of this research process involved the early publication of results. Even though much might still be unknown, I found it important to publish the genealogical data as quickly as possible. Since there was so little in print about the early presence of Africans in Indiana, others were eager to read about my research. For some African Hoosierss, my writings stimulated them to consider seriously looking for their ancestors in Indiana's pioneer history. As we launch on the search for our African ancestors, we are realizing that "things aren't necessarily the way they were written up in history books."

Definition of Color

Every writer in African American history is soon confronted with the dilemma of what racial terminology to use.[2] Americans as a whole have never reached an unanimous decision about racial labels, except that the majority of Euramericans appear satisfied with the "white" race designation although it really denotes anything significant about their personkind although its use has persisted for generations.

On the other hand, minorities in this country were never consulted regarding their preferences for racial designations. Even if asked today, many would probably prefer to be in a democratic society where there was never a need for racial tags. People are more than a mere classification based upon the lack of skin pigmentation, and true understanding of another is based upon many factors including sex, language, education, language, country of ancestral origin, marital status, skills, achievements, acceptance of others.

Labels do exist, however, and they are used every day in our society. Historically, a variety of racial epithets became official for designating persons of African ancestry. Some labels were extremely negative and degrading, willfully employed by those who felt superior simply because they were descendants of pale Europeans without any dark skinned African ancestors.

The height of absurdity was reached when legal codes adopted the "one drop rule" to prevent any person of African descent from contaminating the blood of pure Americans.[3] Laws defined "Negroes" and "mulattoes" for the purpose of granting or denying them privileges in our society as well as to discourage miscegenation. Oddly enough, to the best of my knowledge, there has never been any legal definition of "whites" or Euramericans.

Indiana, like most northern states at the time, followed the common practice and adopted early in its history a legal definition of "Negro": *any person having one-eighth part or more of Negro blood*. In others words, regardless of one's physical appearance, skin and eye colors or hair texture, any person who had seven white (European) grandparents but *one* grandparent of African descent was legally classified as a "Negro." This law remained on the books until 1965!

In my study and writing I have tried to use consistently the racial designations as I found them reported in the U. S. Population censuses: "free people of color" or "free colored persons" in decennial reports through 1840, and "black," "mulatto," "Negro" labels for the ensuing census years. To my *master list* I added from time to time any names I found of individuals identified in vital records, courthouse documents, obituaries and cemetery records, and newspaper articles as "colored", "Negro," "black," or "Afro-American." All of these words are utilized interchangeably in this book with the word "Black" to refer to any person having at least one African ancestor.

Today, I prefer personally to use the label of "African American" or "person of African descent or ancestry." For years our society has commonly employed similar terms to ethnic groups from Europe and Asia in recognition of their different cultural backgrounds. At the same time I remain fully cognizant of the fact that not all of my readers, regardless of their skin color or racial identity, may feel comfortable seeing any literature which venerates our African heritage. This may be particularly true of the those who are completely unaware of the sizeable number of persons of African ancestry and predominately European appearances and demeanor who regularly "crossed over" the racial lines and are assimilated in this country as white Americans.

Antebellum Migratory Patterns

Despite their status as "free" persons and the fact that certain individuals were financially able to relocate, free Africans in the United States had more difficulty moving about than slaves. In no southern state could free Africans migrate as they wished, and in some northern communities it was dangerous to try because of the risk of being mistaken for a fugitive slave.

Conditions in the North were not greatly dissimilar to racial conditions in the South. The overwhelming majority of white Americans wherever they lived held a firm belief in the superiority of the white race and that this nation was a white man's country.

The treatment of free Africans in the North was not always pleasant. Northern whites might refrain from showing unusual hostility to those who were already living in their midst, but they did not welcome any immigration which would increase the size of the African population and make it an important force in the community.

Indiana, as other northern states, formulated anti-immigration statutes and other "Black laws" to discourage African settlers from coming into the state and to prescribe the citizenship rights of those already living within its boundaries.

Hostility and prejudice confronted the African traveler everywhere in the state. Outsiders generally were regarded suspiciously by the local residents, but an African stranger, especially in villages and sparsely populated areas, could provoke threats of immediate expulsion, severe bodily harm, and imprisonment.

In spite of misgiving over the personal dangers involved Africans traveled both in and out of Indiana. Worsened economic conditions caused them to move on seeking elsewhere "a better tomorrow." Congenial designations within the state were limited and restricted to those rural and urban African communities where the population had not yet reached the number that would be intolerable to sympathetic whites.

For African pioneers to survive in a racially offensive environment, it was essential for them to keep close ties with friends and relatives living in other scattered settlements. Networking was achieved through occasional visits, shared holiday celebrations, social and church activities, such as revivals, camp meetings and homecomings. Marriages of their offspring often cemented the bonds between unrelated families.

Very little is known about the intrastate movement of free Africans in Indiana during the antebellum period. Genealogists are discovering that there are many families with African ancestors who were reportedly born or resided in this state prior to the mid-1800s. Documenting such legends, however, can be difficult since there are few studies identifying the names of African families residing within the regional areas of Indiana, such as the southern, east central, western and urban parts.

To date my research experiences in Indiana point out that the African pioneers did move often about the state and regional areas (Chapter III). As the number of surnames increased on the *master list* in Orange County, I recognized the names of some families whose descendents live today in central and northern Indiana counties.

Records of the Roberts, Scott, Thomas and Newby family histories summarized in Chapter XV identify some of the places descendants moved outside of Orange County: Washington, Martin, Daviess, Greene, Monroe, Owen, Vigo, Marion, Rush, Hamilton, Howard, Wayne Counties in Indiana--as well as to the states of Kentucky, Ohio, Michigan, Illinois and Canada.

NOTES

1. Some references to basic genealogical research include Val D. Greenwwod, *The Researcher's Guide to American Genealogy*, (Baltimore, MD: Genealogical Publishing Co., Inc., 1973), Gilbert H. Doane, *Searching For Your Ancestors*, (New York: Bantam Books, 1974); Donald L. Jacobus, *Genealogy as Pastime and Profession*, 2nd ed. rev. (Baltimore: Genealogical Publishing Co., 1968); and Emily A. Cromm, *Unpuzzling Your Past: A Basic Guide to Genealogy* 2nd ed. (White Hall, VA: Betterway Publications, Inc. 1989).

For African American genealogy: Coy D. Robbins, *Source Book: African American Genealogy in Indiana* (Bloomington, IN.: Indiana African American Historical and Genealogical Society, 1989); Charles L. Blockson, *Black Genealogy* (Englewood Cliffs, NJ: Prentice-Hall, Inc., 1977); Sandra M. Lawson, *Generations Past: A Selected List of Sources for Afro-American Genealogical Research* (Washington, DC: Library of Congress, 1988); David H. Streets, *Slave Genealogy: A Research Guide With Case Studies* (Bowie, MD: Heritage Books, Inc., 1986); and Curt C. Witcher, *A Bibliography of Sources for Black Family History in the Allen County Public Library Genealogy Department* (Ft. Wayne, IN: 1983).

2. The classic study on this subject is Edward B. Reuter, *Race Mixture: Studies in Intermarriage and Miscegenation*, (New York: Whittlesey House, 1931; reprint Negro Universities Press, 1969), especially the essay, "Racial Amalgamation in the United States", pp. 27-57.

3. Excellent discussion by F. James Davis in his book, *Who is Black? One Nation's Definition* (University Park, PA., The Pennsylvania State University Press, 1991).

MAP: Indiana Counties and Selected Cities

(Adapted from map in *Illustrated Historical Atlas of the State of Indiana*, 1876)

CHAPTER II

AN OVERVIEW: AFRICAN HERITAGE IN INDIANA

Hoosiers today accept the historical fact that Native Americans were the original inhabitants of this region. And of course, all are acquainted with the lengthy narratives about the Euramericans and their contributions to Indiana's history. But what is generally unknown or forgotten is that Africans were also among our pioneers.

Several factors may explain why writers, historians and publicists have failed to include the African presence in early Indiana. When the Euramericans entered this area they carried with them the prevailing racist attitudes toward non-whites. For many generations the European societies had nutured the belief that they were superior to anyone unlike themselves, and particularly persons with dark skins from Africa.

It was no happenstance that newly arrived white immigrants with their diverse languages and customs were soon molded into a certain way of thinking by the concept of "Americanism." Early colonists totally surrounded by the Native Americans found that skin pigmentation formed a different reality in their daily existence. As this nation expanded skillful leaders manipulated the prejudicial feelings of their followers. Rallying calls went forth "to create a white man's country." With their highly prized white skins, European immigrants were welcomed into this infant nation. The newcomers in their zeal to become "Americans" accepted the frontier challenges, eager to grab a share in the fabled wealth of the New World. Under the banner of a white supremacy, they battled westward to claim the lands already occupied.[1]

Yet, West Africans were in Ancient America long before the Europeans. Their arrival as early as 800 to 700 B.C. has been confirmed by recent archaelogical data.[2] Our traditional literature reports nothing of these African navigators or the men in the Mali expeditionary fleet who came to South America, Caribbean islands, and to Mexico in 1310. We understand now that among the natives who greeted Christopher Columbus in the West Indies were persons with Negroid-African features, dark brown and copper skin, kinky hair, and broad noses. The influence of ancient Black-Africans on the early Mexican cultures was considerable. Portuguese and Spanish explorers in the New World were astonished to find some Native Americans who venerated black gods with African physical features. The manner in which these Native Americans assimilated the Africans and persons of African ancestry into their cultures is still to be studied.[3]

In time the Europeans labeled all non-white strangers they met as "Indians," and failed to note among them any racial or cultural traits attributable to Black-African civilizations. Instead, they recorded detailed financial reports about the millions of enslaved Africans they treated as "subhumans" and used as forced labor to develop this continent's agrarian and natural riches.[4]

Columbus himself was said to be the first to initiate slavery in the Americas, even against the wishes of the Spanish Sovereigns. By 1501, however, the Spaniards were importing captive Africans into their West Indies colonies. Over the next one hundred years many enslaved Africans worked the sugar fields and gold mines in Cuba, Panama, Mexico and South America. Some revolted, and managed after gaining their freedom to remain as free people in the same colonies.

Oddly enough, the first Africans brought into the English colonies on the North American continent were not slaves. The twenty of them who arrived in 1619 at the Jamestown settlement in Virginia were actually indentured servants. After their term of service ended, these Africans purchased land and were able to remain in the colony as free persons.[5]

Slavery soon flourished, nevertheless, in the English colonies. By 1700 the Boston traders engaged in a highly profitable business of supplying enslaved Africans to the New England settlements as well as those in Virginia. The English settlers dealt harshly with enslaved Africans under their control.

On the other hand, slavery in French North America was markedly different from that in the English colonies.[6] Soon after landing on Santo Domingo (later Haiti) in 1641, French men purchased African females from slave traders or abducted them from the Spanish and nearby settlements. Many of these mixed-blood families were legalized and the children educated by sending them to schools in France. In 1685 the French government adopted the *Code Noir* or "Black Code" to regulate slavery and to bring a sense of organization and order to a system of colonial exploitation.

In 1716, the French introduced African slavery at New Orleans in their Louisiana Territory. Slaves imported from the French West Indies accompanied the explorers, fur traders and missionaries up the Mississippi River Valley into the Old Northwest. By the mid-1700s African slaves dwelled with their French owners in the settlements at Fort de Chartres and Cahokia in Illinois along the Mississippi River and at Fort Saint Vincennes on the Wabash River in what eventually became the state of Indiana.

At Saint Vincennes, Father Sebastian Louis Meurin began as early as 1755 to make references to enslaved Africans in his Catholic Church records. These Jesuit fathers themselves owned both "negre et rouge esclaves." Records in the church archives today still affirm the baptisms, confirmations, marriages and deaths of African and "Indian" slaves along with those of other parish members.[7]

Free men of African-French descent were among the early fur traders who traveled throughout the Mississippi and Ohio River Valleys. Frequently they entered the Indiana country via the Wabash River, before heading northward to Detroit and Canada. Among these French traders was a Jean Baptiste Pointe Du Sable (or Point de Sable), the son of a French father and an African woman from St. Domingue. DuSable (1745-1818) is credited with starting a fur trading post which eventually became the city of Chicago.[8]

In the Treaty of Paris, 1763 which ended the Seven Years' War in Europe and the French and Indian War on this continent, the French surrendered all territory east of the Mississippi and south of the Hudson Bay country, except Florida, to England. The paucity of Africans in the

Northwest Territory soon changed as the English greatly increased the use and number of slaves in all of their colonies.

By 1774 the estimated total population of the English North American colonies was 2,600,000, of whom 2,100,000 were whites and 500,000 Africans, with the largest number of slaves in Virginia (165,000), South Carolina (110,000), Maryland (80,000), and North Carolina (75,000).

Shortly after the Revolutionary War began, Lord Dunmore, the deposed Governor of Virginia, promised freedom to those slaves who would fight with the Loyalists against the rebelling Americans. Thousands of Africans deserted their owners and joined the British Forces. The enormity of these events compelled General George Washington in 1775 to reverse his ban on African enlistments in the Continental Army. Between 8,000 and 10,000 Africans, both free persons and former slaves, served in various capacities. Approximately 5,000 of them were regular soldiers.[9]

Vermont in 1777 was the first state to abolish slavery. Over the next ten years several other states enacted manumission laws. Gradually the number of free Africans in America increased in both northern and southern states. Those living in the North were usually freeborn. Some enterprising slaves were able to save enough money to buy their freedom. Thousands of others subjugated in both the North and South became free by simply running away.[10]

When the Revolutionary War ended, America had trouble taking possession of the western lands they had won from the English. For several decades afterwards the Native Americans fought to protect their lands against the advance of Euramerican settlers. By the time Indiana attained its statehood in 1816, Native Americans still controlled one-third of the region's land.

In 1787 the United States Congress passed the Northwest Ordinance. It contained a clause prohibiting slavery throughout the new lands east of the Mississippi and north of the Ohio Rivers. The first territorial Governor, Arthur St. Clair, was a former Virginian and he contended that this clause did not apply to those slaves already held in the territory prior to the edict. For many years thereafter whites tried unsuccessfully to circumvent the law and to make slavery legal in the Northwest Territory.[11] As the frontier lands opened for settlement, free Africans, undoubtedly encouraged by the anti-slavery provisions, joined the whites in the Northwest Territory.

African Americans remained only a small fraction of the area's total population. In 1800, during the Indiana Territorial years, there were 298 Africans (163 free people of color and 135 slaves) who represented slightly more than five percent of the total population.[12] Ten years later in 1810 the 630 Africans (237 slaves and 393 free people of color) represented less than three percent of its total population.[13]

When Indiana adopted its first state Constitution in 1816, it contained prohibitions against both slavery and involuntary servitude. Nevertheless vestiges of these illegal practices lingered on in the state for many years. The total number of enslaved Africans in Indiana, however, remained extremely small. By 1840, *only* three slaves were counted in the state when the U. S. Population Census was completed. Later enumerations had none.

It must be emphasized here again that free people of African ancestry were among the early settlers in Indiana. Like their white counterparts, they came primarily from Kentucky and the eastern states of Maryland, Virginia and North Carolina. Often they were free born in the states where they formerly lived. Old public records usually classified them as "free people of color," "free colored persons," or "colored people."[14]

Among the pioneers who sought haven in Indiana were also the recently emancipated slaves. Restrictive laws in states where they had been enslaved required the newly freed persons to leave the state within a certain period or to face reenslavement. Fugitive or runaway slaves also arrived with the early settlers.

By 1820 Indiana had 1,230 "free colored persons." By the eve of the Civil War, there were ten times the original number or 11,428 Blacks and mulattoes listed in the 1860 census. They lived by then in *all* but four of the ninety existing Indiana counties, and the largest concentrations were in Wayne, Randolph, Marion and Vigo counties.[15]

The African pioneers in Indiana were not much better off economically than their enslaved brothers and sisters. The financial depression of the 1830s, the mass waves of immigrants from Europe, and the resulting competition for available jobs produced chaos nationally. Under these conditions, only a smattering of African Americans were ever able to achieve any significant degree of economic stability.

Most Africans in early Indiana were farmers. They lived in rural settlements on their own or rented land. Some of their rural communities lasted for only a few decades, but several did survive into the twentieth century. Among the Indiana African American settlements known to have been established before the Civil War were:[16]

> (1) Graysville Settlement (Jefferson County)
> (2) Greenbrier Settlement (Decatur County)
> (3) Lick Creek Settlement (Orange County)
> (4) Roundtree and Lyles Station (Gibson County)
> (5) Beech Settlement (Rush County)
> (6) Lost Creek and Underwood Settlements (Vigo County)
> (7) Weaver Settlement (Grant County)
> (8) Roberts Settlement (Hamilton County)
> (9) Cabin Creek Settlement (Randolph County)
> (10) Greenville Settlement (Randolph County)
>   and Darke County, Ohio)

Just as the presence of persons of African ancestry in Indiana's early history has been ignored, so has their involvement in the early white churches. Religion played an important role in the lives of the settlers, irregardless of their race. Because their church histories today contain no indication of any non-white members, we have assumed that congregations in the pioneer churches were Euramericans.

Yet, during the first half of the nineteenth century religion in America was in turmoil. The evangelical revival with its emphasis on the individual's spiritual experience appealed more to the pioneers than the traditional Anglo-Protestant churches of colonial America. As the protestant religious movement reached Indiana, we discovered that African Americans were also members of the early white Methodist Church in Paoli (see Chapter IX on Religion and Churches).

The growing practices of racial segregation within these churches, however, caused some Africans to withdrew and start their own church. Often it was a solitary log cabin structure consecrated as a "Church of God" which served as center of the settlement's religious, educational, cultural and social activities. The earliest African American churches in Indiana were probably of the Baptist denomination, much like the one in Rush County which dated to 1831.[17]

The African Methodist Episcopal (A.M.E.) Church system reached Indiana in the mid-1830s. It began in Philadelphia as a racially separated organization in 1816 and gradually expanded westward as the settlements of free people of color grew in Ohio and Indiana. Soon there was a sufficient number of A.M.E. congregations in the Hoosier State to justify the organization of a new church conference. Indiana became the sixth conference of the A.M.E. Church when it was established on October 2, 1840 at the Beech Settlement Church in northern Rush County. Both the national church group and the Indiana Conference are still functioning.[18]

Another fact left out of the history books pertains to persons of African ancestry who fought in every one of our nation's military conflict since the War of Independence.[19] It was not until the Civil War, however, that these soldiers were racially segregated into a specially created unit with the Union Army called the *United States Colored Troops*. At least 1,390 Africans from Indiana served in the Colored Troops, and the vast majority were volunteers. Additional study is needed, however, to determine how many were actually drafted, as Simon Locust was in Orange County, how many served in the U. S. Navy and Merchant Marines, and how many Africans, either free and enslaved, fought with the military forces of the Confederacy.[20]

All Indiana pioneers suffered hardships, but African Hoosiers had to endure additional ones never experienced by any white settlers. Racial barriers to restrict their citizenship rights and individual freedom, similar to those found in adjoining northern states and in the South, dated to the colonial and earliest territorial days.

Euramericans dominated interactions between members of the two races, irrespective of social or economic status. They believed deeply in their racial superiority, and rarely allowed it to be challenged. While some white Americans oppose and fought against slavery, only a few ever tolerated a non-white as an social equal and to live in their midst, except as a servant.

Beginning in 1800, the so-called "Black Laws" in Indiana greatly hampered the liberty of African citizens. These laws placed tremendous political, legal, educational and social restrictions on non-whites, and created an environment as racially segregated as those in the deep South. The Indiana Territorial Legislature patterned its earliest "Black Laws" after those existing in Kentucky and Virginia.[21] Some modifications resulted from subsequent legislative acts and new regulations added after Indiana achieved statehood. These combined directives which were never codified as "Black Laws" controlled for many years the rights of only African citizens."[22]

Examples abound. Africans were required to post bonds before they could settle in *any* Indiana town. These surety bonds which usually amounted to $500 or more could be forfeited if the insured was ever guilty of disturbing the peace or if they became public charges.[23] Unlike other citizens, African Hoosiers when traveling always carried a copy of their certificate of freedom or manumission papers as protection against any unexpected accusations of being a runaway slave simply because of color of their skin.[24]

Other Indiana laws compelled the African landowners to pay school and sometimes poll taxes, even though other laws denied them benefits from either. The right for colored children to attend public schools in Indiana was not legal until 1869.[25] And Negro males did not acquire the right to vote in any election until 1881, long after the Civil War was over.

African citizens could not testify against whites in courts or serve on juries until 1885.[26] And, the right to serve in the state militia and the Indiana National Guard were granted finally in 1936.[27]

During certain periods of its history, Indiana refused African Americans the right to sign contracts, to purchase land, and to engage in certain occupations. Until well into this century they were denied or had restricted use of public accommodations, such as eating in restaurants, staying in hotels, and using rest rooms. Marriages between the races in Indiana remained illegal until 1965.[28]

Enforcement of these "Black Laws" was erratic, and highly dependent upon the transitory moods of white Hoosiers. Regardless of how strictly they were enforced, "Black Laws" served effectively to intimidate the African minority and "kept them in their place."

The 1850s became a perilous decade for free Africans throughout the nation. Intersectional political strife over the slavery issue was slowly mounting. In 1850 the total African American population was 3,638,808 or 15.7 percent of all Americans. 435,495 or 11.9 percent of these were free citizens, and over one-half of them lived in the southern slave states. A prime slave field hand sold for approximately $1,600, and the main products of slave labor in this country -- cotton, tobacco, sugar cane, hemp, rice, and molasses -- totaled over 136 million dollars. Abolitionists and their sympathizers were relentlessly pressing for slavery to end, and slaveowners worried over the loss of their runaway slave property. The average American family, white or African, struggled financially to survive.

As a condition for acceptance of the 1850 Compromise, the United States Congress enacted the more stringent fugitive slave law demanded by the southerners to curb runaway slaves. This new law allowed any claimants of a runaway slave to take possession upon establishing proof of ownership before a federal commissioner. No safeguards, such as a jury trial or judicial hearing for the accused, were included in the law. In other words, the imputed citizen could not assert his right of habeas corpus or to testify on his own behalf against the accuser.

This new law at once made all the African citizens of Indiana, even the native-born, subject to kidnapping and being sold into slavery.[29] Many fled the state and sought sanctuary in Canada from the added dangers confronting them if they remained in their native land. Some became Canadian citizens and never returned to America.

As if coping with the "Black Laws" and the constant threat of legalized kidnapping were not disabling enough, African Hoosiers received an additional racial blow in November, 1851. The Indiana voters approved at that time the following provision of Article XIII in the second State Constitution, one which remained in effect for thirty years:

> "No negro or mulatto shall come into or settle in the state, after the adoption of this constitution."

In spite of the exclusionary law, the number of African Hoosiers increased slowly after the Civil War ended. The slavery issue nationally was settled. Africans, for the first time in this country's history, were granted national citizenship. Included in these new federal rights was the freedom to travel anywhere without the fear of kidnapping, possible enslavement, or the need to carry official passes. Some of the former slaves came northward into Indiana, escaping the chaotic aftermath of the war and the devastated market economy in the South. Urban industries expanded from the war economy received them as laborers.

By 1870 the African American population in the Hoosier state reached 24,560 or 1.5 percent of the total. By 1900 there were 57,505 persons of African ancestry living in the state. Nation-wide, as well as in Indiana, non-whites converged mainly in the urban-industrial areas where racial discrimination forced them to accept menial jobs and to live with the poor in overcrowded, segregated residential communities.

NOTES

1. Winthrop D. Jordan, *White Over Black: American Attitudes Toward the Negro 1550-1812*, (Chapel Hill: University of North Carolina Press, 1968), especially the final chapter, "Toward a white man's country."

2. Ivan Van Sertima, *They Came Before Columbus*, (New York: Random House, 1976).

3. William Loren Katz, *Black Indians: A Hidden Heritage*, (New York: Athenum, 1986). One of the best well-known African-Native Americans was Chief Osceola, who led the Seminoles in Florida war of 1835-37; Lorenzo J. Greene, *The Negro in Colonial New England*, (New York: Athenum, 1969); 19, 127, 160.

4. Saunders Redding, *They Came in Chains: Americans from Africa*, (New York: J. B. Lippincott Co., 1950), 1-27.

5. John Hope Franklin, *From Slavery to Freedom: A History of Negro Americans* (New York: Alfred A. Knopf; Fifth Edition, 1980), 54-57. In the census counts of 1623 and 1624 the 20 Africans were identified as "servants." As late as 1651 some Blacks whose terms of service had expired were being assigned land in much the same way as it was being assigned to whites who had completed their indentures. Nevertheless, by 1640 some Africans in Virginia became bondsmen for life. In 1624, William Tucker, the first African born in the English North America, was baptized in Jamestown.

6. Charles J. Balesi, *The Time of the French in the Heart of North America, 1673-1818*, (Chicago: Alliance Francaise Chicago, 1992), pp. 248-250. For more on this subject, see chapters on "The Indians" and "The Blacks."

6. "Pre-1900 Baptism, Confirmation, Marriage and Burial Records," (unpublished), The Old Cathedral, Basilica of St. Francis Xavier in the Archives, The Brute Library, Vincennes, Ind. Several baptism and death entries written in French refer to Agatha and Etienne, children of Alexander and Dorothee, African slaves owned by the Jesuit priests. Many entries in these early church records contain racial designations, such as "black" or "mulatto" and "Negro" or "colored" for 19th century members.

7. DuSable was born in 1745 in the West Indies, the son of a wealthy Frenchman and a slave woman. He was educated in Paris, eventually came to New Orleans, Louisiana to earn his fortune in the new world. In 1790 he opened a trading post on Lake Michigan shores that came to be known as Chicago. *The Role and Contribution of American Negroes in the History of the United States and of Illinois, A Guide for Teachers and Curriculum Planners* (Springfield, IL: Office of Superintendent of Public Instruction, 1970), 94-95.

8. John Hope Franklin, *From Slavery To Freedom* , 87; Benjamin Quarles, *The Negro In the American Revolution* (Chapel Hill: University of North Carolina Press, 1961); William C. Nell, *The Colored Patriots of the American Revolution* (Boston: Robert F. Wallcutt, publisher, 1855; reprint 1986); Sidney Kaplan, *The Black Presence in the Era of the American Revolution: 1770-1800* (Washington, D.C.: Smithsonian Institution Press, 1973); Philip S. Foner, *Blacks in the American Revolution* (Westport: Greenwood Press, 1976); Jack D. Foner, *Blacks and the Military in American History* (New York: Praeger Publishers, 1974). Of the 300,000 soldiers who served the cause of independence, approximately 5,000 were Blacks. Many served in the navy as well as in the Continental army.

9. Carter G. Woodson, *A Century of Negro Migration* (Washington, D.C. The Association for the Study of Negro Life and History, 1918).

10. Emma L. Thornbrough, *The Negro in Indiana* (Indianapolis: Indiana Historical Bureau, 1957), 6-7. For an academic discussion of the ordinance, see *Pathways to the Old Northwest: An Observance of the Bicentennial of the Northwest Ordinance* (Indianapolis: Indiana Historical Society, 1988), especially Paul Finkelman, "A Constitution for an Empire of Liberty," 1-18 and Malcolm J. Rohrbough, "Diversity and Unity in the Old Northwest," 71-88.

11. Daniel M. Johnson and Rex R. Campbell, *Black Migration in America* (Duke University Press, second printing, 1982), 37.

12. U. S. Bureau of Census, Department of Commerce, *Negro Population 1790-1915* (Washington, D.C.: Government Printing Office, 1918), Table 13, 43-45 and Table 15, 51. Census reports prior to 1820 lumped all free colored persons in a classification, "All other Free Persons except Indians, not taxed" or "All others, etc. etc" thereby leaving the reader with the impression that slaves were the only persons of African descent found in the population.

13. Some excellent general references on free African Americans in the antebellum era include the following: Benjamin Quarles, chapter 4 "The Nonslave Negro (1800-1860) in *The Negro in the Making of America* (New York: Collier Books, revised edition 1969); J.

Jacque Voegeli, *Free but Not Equal: The Midwest and the Negro in the Civil War* (Chicago: University of Chicago Press, 1967); Ira Berlin, *Slaves Without Masters: The Free Negro in the Antebellum South* (New York: Vintage Books, 1976; Eric Foner, *Nothing But Freedom: Emancipation and Its Legacy* (Baton Rouge: Louisiana State University Press, 1983); and Leon F. Witwack, *North of Slavery: The Negro in the Free States, 1790-1869* (Chicago: University of Chicago Press, 1961).

14. Based upon U. S. Population Censuses for years indicated.

15. Compilation of research data from author's private collections. Most of these settlements have been identified in local histories and newspaper articles. Coy D. Robbins, "Lick Creek Settlement: An Early Black Community in Orange County," *Black History News & Notes*, 2 parts in February and May, 1982.

16. Thornbrough, *The Negro in Indiana*, 156-157. Historians have not agreed on the place of the first independent Black Baptist church in America. Some cite the First Colored Baptist Church, Savannah, Georgia which was organized January 22, 1788 by Andrew Bryan. However, the Silver Bluff Baptist Church, Aiken County, South Carolina was also established in 1788 by David George, a slave convert of Rev. George Liele. Leroy Fitts, *A History of Black Baptists*, (Nashvillle, Tenn.: Broadman Press, 1985), 33-39.

17. Coy D. Robbins, "Sesquicentennial of the Indiana A. M. E. Church: 1840-1990," *Ebony Lines*, Indiana African American Historical and Genealogical Society quarterly newsletter, Fall and Winter, 1990. Much of issue was devoted to this subject and early Black history in Rush County, Indiana. General references on topic: Carter G. Woodson, *The History of the Negro Church* (Washington, D.C.: The Associated Publishers, 1921); Milton Sernett, ed., *Afro-American Religious History: A Documentary Witness* (Durham: Duke University Press, 1985).

18. Data about Indiana African American soldiers can be found in the Civil War, Spanish-American War, and World Wars I and II, Korean War Records, Indiana State Archives, Commission on Public Records, Indianapolis. Some excellent references on Blacks in the Civil War are: Benjamin Quarles, *The Negro in the Civil War*, (Boston: Little Brown and Co., 1969); Dudley Taylor Cornish, *The Sable Arm: Negro Troops in the Union Army, 1861-1865* (New York: W. W. Norton & Co., 1966); Jack D. Foner, *Blacks and the Military in American History*, (New York: Praeger Publishers, 1974, Chap. 3 "Blacks in the Civil War"); Robert Ewell Greene, *Black Defenders of America, 1775-1973* (Chicago: Johnson Publishing Co., 1974).

19. Coy D. Robbins, comp., *African American Soldiers from Indiana with the Union Army in the Civil War 1863-1865* (Bloomington: Indiana African American Historical and Genealogical Society, 1989).

20. "Laws for the Government of the Indiana Territory, Adopted at Their Fourth Session...Adopted from the Virginia and Kentucky codes and published at Vincennes the twentieth day of September, one thousand eight hundred and three, by William Henry Harrison, governor and Thomas T. Davis and Henry Vander Burgh, judges in and over said territory." (Indianapolis: Indiana Historical Collections Reprint, 1931), 40, 42-46; 136-139, 452-453, 463-467.

21. A law of 1803 "concerning servants," borrowed from Virginia,--a law which in fact referred only to black servants--was the first of the "Black Laws" of Indiana. George W. Williams, *History of the Negro Race in America 1619-1880* 2 vols. (New York: G. P. Putnam's Sons, 1883; Arno Press reprint 1968), 119-122. Early U. S. Congressional legislation frequently excluded free Blacks from federal rights and privileges. For example, in 1790, Congress limited naturalization to "any alien, being a white person." In 1792, it organized the militia and restricted enrollment to "each and every free, able-bodied white male citizen." In 1810, it excluded Blacks from carrying the U. S. mails. In 1820, it authorized the citizens of Washington, D.C., to elect "white" city officials and "to adopt a code governing free negroes and slaves." Leon F. Litwack, "The Federal Government and the Free Negro, 1790-1860," *The Journal of Negro History* (1958), 43-261-2.

22. "An Act concerning Free Negroes and Mulattoes, Servants and Slaves" approved by the Indiana Assembly, February 10, 1831. *The Revised Laws of Indiana...* (Indianapolis: Printed by Douglas and Maguire, 1831), 375-376.

23. Throughout the antebellum era, every man of color living in a slave state was by law presumed to be a slave. South Carolina law of 1740 stated "...it shall always be presumed that every negro, Indian, mulatto, and mestizos is a slave, unless the contrary be made to appear." Similar laws existed in all slave states except North Carolina where it was confined to negroes of whole blood, while with mulattoes, etc., the presumption was in favor of freedom. Undoubtedly, these laws sensitized all Americans to determine free Blacks by the color of their skin: "colored people." Quoted in article, "Condition of the Free Colored People of the United States" in *The Christian Examiner* (Boston: The Proprietor, 24 Bromfield St., 1859), 5th Series, Vol. IV (Jan, Feb, and Mar), 256-7.

24. Practice was commonplace in the North. Carter G. Woodson, *The Education of the Negro Prior to 1861*. (Washington, D.C., The Association for the Study of Negro Life and History, second edition, 1919).

25. *Indiana Laws of 1817, Chap. 3, sec. 52*. The provision in the 1831 law which banned Blacks to testify against whites also gave a legal definition of a negro: "Every person having one fourth or more of negro blood or any one of whose grandfathers or grandmothers shall have been a negro, shall be deemed a mulatto." *The Revised Laws of Indiana*, 1831; Sec. 37, p. 407.

26. *Civil Rights Laws in Indiana*, (Indianapolis: Indiana Civil Rights Commission Publication, 1965), 4-5.

27. *The Revised Statutes of the State of Indiana* (Indianapolis: Dowling-Cole State Printers, 1843), chap. 35, art. I, sec. 4 reads: "No white person shall intermarry with a negro or mulatto, and no insane person or idiot shall be capable of contracting marriage."

28. Charles H. Money, "The Fugitive Slave Law of 1850 in Indiana," *Indiana Magazine of History*, 17 (1921), 159-297; Emma L. Thornbrough, "Indiana and Fugitive Slave Legislation," *Indiana Magazine of History*, L-3 (Sept 1954), 201-228.

CHAPTER III

POPULATION, 1820-1990

In 1815 the Indiana Territorial Government formed Orange County, a narrow strip of land embracing what soon became Lawrence, Monroe and Orange Counties. After Indiana achieved its statehood in 1816, the Legislature created Lawrence and Monroe Counties within the strip to the north, and left Orange County within its present day boundaries.

Five counties surround Orange: Lawrence on the north, Washington on the east, Crawford to the east and south, and Martin and DuBois on the west. The southern, western and central parts of the county are hilly and broken land, but the northeast portion contains prairie land excellent for farming. Patoka and Lost Rivers and their many branches are its principal streams. The county's southeastern boundary is only fifteen miles from the Ohio River and the state of Kentucky.

Without a doubt, free men of color were pioneers in Orange County. Land records contain the earliest affirmation of their presence. On August 5, 1817 William Constant and Charles Goin purchased 160 acres in Section 27, Township 2 North, Range 1 East of South East Township.[1] This property was in the midst of what later became the Lick Creek Settlement.

There are several local traditions that persons of African descent were among the earliest settlers in the county, but these stories are difficult to confirm today. According to one legend they arrived as early as 1812. Another account states that they were actually the first inhabitants of Jackson Township. Reportedly these settlers were "fugitive slaves who mixed with the Indians ... and [who] became a race half Indian half negro." If this chronicle is valid, then the African Americans came several years before the European Americans who did not acquire land in Jackson Township until June 5, 1815.[2]

Their Presence in the County

Our primary source for obtaining numerical information about African Americans in Orange County was the decennial United States population census reports (Table 1).

These data proved to be quite meaningful. First of all, they validate the fact that people of African descent have lived continuously in Orange County since 1820. Secondly, they confirm that the total number of African Americans in the county has always remained exceedingly small and fairly constant. Over the past one hundred and seventy years, the number of Blacks ranged from sixty-three to the 482 in 1930, the largest number ever enumerated. By 1990 there were twice as many persons of African descent living in Orange County as there had been when the first census was completed following Indiana's statehood in 1816.

Only eleven families were identified in the 1820 census. The sixty-three individuals consisted mostly of children who resided in households headed by Jonathan Broady, Lewis Burnett, Judah Canon, Darcus Constant, Hazel Cummins, David Dugged, Charles Goings, Claiborne Goings, Simeon

Goings, Richard Potridge and Bryant Thomas. Clearly this limited information indicates nothing about where these families actually lived in the county. However, from the deeds of land transactions we can pinpoint the possible location of the Constant and Goings households who owned real estate in South East Township.

Ten years later the population almost doubled to a total of 112. In 1840, there were 124 free persons of color in the county--a small increase over 1830. By 1850 their number was twice that of the previous census. In 1860 on the eve of the Civil War, the total number of African Americans in the county reached 260, the peak figure for the antebellum era.

TABLE 1: African American Population of Orange County, 1820-1990

Year	Total		Year	Total
1820	63		1910	359
1830	112		1920	264
1840	124		1930	482
1850	251		1940	217
1860	260		1950	161
1870	159		1960	145
1890	127		1980	214
1900	184		1990	127

Source: U.S. Population Census Reports

Following the Civil War in 1870, the non-white population decreased sharply by nearly sixty percent. This dramatic reduction in those who remained living in Orange County may have related to changes generally in migration patterns as Hoosiers flocked from the farms to urban areas, taking advantage of the increased employment opportunities created by the war economy. Unlike most of the migrants, however, Africans leaving their rural settlements were free for the first time in our nation's history to travel about the state and countryside without the compelling fear of being arrested as runaway slaves.

Where They Lived

Surviving documentary evidence has added much to our understanding of the Lick Creek Settlement. By chance, are there any indications that African Americans ever resided outside of this single settlement? Were many able to live elsewhere, or did the majority stay in South East and Paoli Townships? Did any townships seem exclusively for the white residents? In other words, how much racial segregation was involved in the county's residential patterns?

Population statistics was the available source which provided answers to some of these questions. Data gathered by townships for the years 1850 through 1910 clearly show that Africans lived in every part of the county--at one time or another (Table 2). They tended nevertheless to cluster primarily in the eastern and northern townships: Paoli, South East, Stampers Creek, North West and Orleans. Social and economic factors probably contributed to the residential clusters revealed by the census data, but no attempt was made to hypothetize about these results.

By 1850 Blacks were enumerated in sixty percent of the county's townships. The largest number of them, however, were living in Paoli and South East Townships within the well established Lick Creek Settlement. Small numbers were in the French Lick, North West, Orleans and Stampers Creek Townships. Concerning the overall location of non-whites in the county, we discover that when the number enumerated in Stampers Creek is combined with those in the adjoining Paoli and South East Townships, over ninety percent of the Africans reported in the 1850 census dwelled in the Lick Creek community.

TABLE 2: African American Population of Orange County Townships, 1850-1910

Township	1850	1860	1870	1880	1890	1900	1910
French Lick	4	10	9	1	N	124	325
West Baden Town					O		(111)
French Lick Town					T		(214)
Greenfield	0	4	0	0		0	0
Jackson	0	0	1	0	A	1	0
North East	0	1	0	0	V	0	0
North West	11	14	4	18	A	0	1
Orangeville	0	16	17	7	I	1	2
Orleans	8	15	20	12	L	16	7
Orleans Town	0	0	(20)	(12)	A	0	0
Paoli	101	95	75	67	B	42	24
Paoli Town	(27)	0	(31)	0	L	0	0
South East	117	74	16	5	E	0	0
Stampers Creek	10	31	17	30		0	0
Total	251	260	159	140	0	184	359

Source: U.S. Population Census reports for the years indicated.

Ten years later in 1860, Africans lived in all but one of the county's ten townships. The largest number was in Paoli Township, but still many resided in South East Township. The Black population in Stampers Creek Township had tripled over the past decade. Such growth probably centered around the Moses Locust family, who were the long time landowners in this township. One interesting finding in 1860 is that nearly twenty percent of the African American population lived on the north side of the county in North West, Orangeville and Orleans townships.

A comparison of the total figures for the African population between 1850 and 1860 discloses that there was a modest increase over the previous decade. This slight growth seems to have occurred in spite of the negative impact generally which the Federal Fugitive Slave Law and the exclusionary provisions in Indiana's constitution had on African migration.

A marked change in the number of minority inhabitants took place by 1870. Africans continued to live in most townships, but now they concentrated in Paoli and its surrounding township.

MAP: Townships of Orange County, Indiana

Lawrence County

| North West | Orangeville | Orleans ● Orleans | North East |

Martin County

Washington County

French Lick
● West Baden Springs
● French Lick

Paoli
★ Paoli

Stampers Creek

Chambersburg ●

Dubois County

Jackson | Greenfield | South East
Lick Creek Settlement

Crawford County

(Map by author)

The number in the South East Township dropped precipitously, and the decline noted ten years earlier in the Lick Creek Settlement population continued.

The residential pattern shifted significantly around the turn of this century. Prior to the 1890s the majority of non-whites lived in the southeastern quadrant of the county. By 1900, however, things were entirely different. Not only were there more Africans than ever living in the county, but a large number of them dwelled in the Springs Valley area of French Lick Township. Situated in the midst of rocky hills on the county's western edge, they lived only ten miles west of the county seat. The remaining residents were in or around the two towns of Paoli and Orleans.

The phenomena responsible for these changes were expanding mineral springs water and resort industries. Abruptly increased in popularity, these attractions brought in thousands of annual visitors for therapeutic baths, gambling in the casinos, and recreational pleasures. Ten years later in 1910, ninety percent of the county's non-white population was located in the towns of French Lick and West Baden Springs.

TABLE 3: African American Population of Orange County Townships in 1960 and 1990

Township	1960	1990
French Lick	130	122
Greenfield	1	0
Jackson	1	1
North East	0	0
North West	0	0
Orangeville	2	0
Orleans	5	0
Paoli	6	3
South East	0	0
Stampers Creek	0	0
Total	144	127

Source: U.S. Population Census reports for years indicated.

Township distribution of the county's Black population after 1910 has been difficult to locate. Data from the 1960 and 1990 censuses, nonetheless, are summarized in Table 3. These demonstrate that African Americans have continued over the past ninety years to live almost exclusively in French Lick Township.

African American Population in Adjoining Counties

At any one time Africans have represented only a fraction of the total population in Orange County. Many locals envisioned that these early settlers were restricted by law or custom to live outside of Paoli in the rural "Little Africa" sector, racially and physically isolated in an existence much like the urban ghetto of today.

But were there any historical facts to verify this local legend? Were these families actually as racially isolated from others of their own kind as their small number suggested? Were there enough Africans living in surrounding counties to constitute a broader, regional community?

Once again we turned to the census data for some possible answers. A tabulation was completed of the total number of Africans living in the five counties surrounding Orange: Lawrence, Martin, Washington, Crawford, and Dubois (Table 4). Irrefutable results show that persons of African ancestry lived in each of these counties during the antebellum era. Orange County had the largest number in the area, with the 260 residents in 1860. Crawford and Dubois had the smallest populations.

TABLE 4: African American Population in Counties Adjoining Orange: 1820-1860

			Census Year		
County	1820	1830	1840	1850	1860
Crawford	0	0	12	1	0
Dubois	8	0	7	21	12
Lawrence	15	59	106	94	118
Martin	4	11	23	96	52
ORANGE	96	124	158	251	260
Washington	59	206	193	252	187
Total in Area	182	400	499	715	629
Total in Indiana	1,230	3,629	7,168	11,262	11,428

Source: U. S. Population Census Reports for years indicated.

Additionally, these data reveal that in 1820 nearly one half of the aggregate population of minority residents in the region was living in Orange County. Ten years later in 1830, however, almost one-half of all African Americans in the region were now in Washington County, not in Orange County.

Washington County continued to have the largest number of non-white inhabitants for both the years of 1840 and 1850. In the ensuing decade, its number declined noticeably while in Orange County there was an increase in 1860. No logical explanation for these reversals has yet been determined.

The people of this region in 1830 represented collectively only eleven percent of Indiana's total African American population. By 1860, this ratio had dropped to less than six percent.

African Americans in Southern Indiana

Black residents of Orange County were even less socially isolated when consideration is given to the total non-white population in the southern part of the state. Data presented in Table 5 underscore the fact that a sizeable number of free people of color once lived in the region, from Jeffersonville and New Albany on the southeast, to Vincennes and Terre Haute on the west; from Madison on the Ohio River and Richmond in the east central to Indianapolis, the state's capitol.

Members of the African communities in this region held more in common than their race. Many were blood relatives with close and extended family bonds. Others were old friends and

TABLE 5: African American Population, Select Counties of Southern Indiana

	Census Year				
County (Seat)	1820	1830	1840	1850	1860
CLARK (Jeffersonville)	138	243	388	582	520
DAVIESS (Washington)	32	44	25	44	74
FLOYD (New Albany)	69	265	402	574	757
HARRISON (Corydon)	69	123	89	91	114
JACKSON (Seymour)	36	120	190	214	179
JEFFERSON (Madison)	115	245	429	568	512
KNOX (Vincennes)	166	437	561	530	449
MARION (Indianapolis)	0	73	258	650	825
VIGO (Terre Haute)	26	123	425	748	706
WAYNE (Richmond)	66	417	626	1036	870

Source: U. S. Population Census reports for years indicated.

acquaintances who had migrated originally from the same locale in the eastern and southern states. Some became acquainted quite by chance when they met during stopovers in Ohio and Kentucky to rest and gather strength and resources before traveling further. These families shared common cultural, social and religious experiences. They endured the same racial prejudice irregardless of their native states or whether they were born free or formerly enslaved. As a group united by their African heritage, they suffered individually and collectively the insults and indignities heaped upon them daily by white Hoosiers. Here they watched impotently as the white voters denied to them the full rights of citizenship which at the same time they granted so freely to the white immigrants freshly arrived from Europe.

It was never any happenstance that Africans became the "forgotten" citizens of Indiana.

NOTES

1. *Tract Book 3*, Orange County Recorder's Office, 89. These same two men were identified as early land holders in Goodspeed's, *History of Orange, Lawrence and Washington Counties*, (1884), 27. The 1820 census identifies a Darcus <u>Constant</u>, female, as a Free Colored Person, age range over 45 years, and head of a household made up of two individuals. No listing found for William Constant. The same census contained three different colored men with the <u>Goings</u> surname. One, Charles Goings, was in the age range 26-44, and heading a household consisting of eight persons. The purchased land was sold on December 28, 1831 to Harrison Cornwell by Charles Goin and Elizabeth, his wife, and William Constant. It is unknown about the relationship between this William Constant and Darcus Constant.

2. Correspondence from Jerrold H. Finley, Orange County Historian, to the Indiana Historical Society "Survey of County History Information" in 1987; *History of Orange, Lawrence and Washington Counties*, 47.

CHAPTER IV

LANDOWNERS

Rocco Gibala, Assistant District Ranger, United States Department of Agriculture Forest Service, Hoosier National Forest, Paoli, Indiana collected the land records data used in this chapter (See Appendix C).

Earliest Landholders of Color

The first purchase of land in Orange County by Americans of African descent was on August 5, 1817. William Constant and Charles Goin obtained a patent deed from the United States for 160 acres in Section 27, Township 2 North, Range 1 East. Situated in Paoli Township near Syria, this property was about four miles due north of Chambersburg and actually outside of what became the Lick Creek Settlement. Fourteen years later in 1831, Constant and Goin sold their acreage to Harrison Cornwell, presumably a white man.

Lick Creek Settlement Area

Throughout the antebellum era, the largest number of African American landholders were south of Chambersburg in the northwest portion of South East Township. As early as the War of 1812 Quakers were settled in this region where they established their first church two miles west of Chambersburg in 1813. Rebuilt on two different occasions near the site of the original, the Quaker Lick Creek Church and cemetery survive today.

Mathew Thomas was the first man of color to obtain land in the area. On May 21, 1831, he purchased 80 acres about three-quarters mile northeast of present day Chambersburg.[1] Other men of color soon followed. Between September and November, 1832, Benjamin Roberts, David Dugged, Peter Lindley and Elias Roberts, all recent migrants from North Carolina, each purchased from the United States of America (patented) 40 acres of land in the area. David Dugged bought land about one mile north of Chambersburg, but the other three men acquired land in the hills south of Chambersburg where the African Americans quickly developed their Lick Creek Settlement. It seemed logical for these early Hoosiers of color and the Quakers to use the same name for their settlements since each was established on the upper branches of Lick Creek, a small stream which meanders westward through the region toward Paoli, the county seat.

The Period of Expansion

Other African American families soon arrived in the county, bought land nearby, and expanded the settlement. Their farm acquisitions were primarily in four different but contiguous sections -- 22, 27, 28 and 33 in the South East Township. Although they tended to buy property from the government land office or other persons of color, the community was never racially segregated. At least during the early years, Blacks and whites were often adjoining landholders.

Mathew Thomas sold his original 80 acres northeast of Chambersburg in late 1833, and he replaced them with two 40 acres (patented) purchases of land in 1834 and 1835 from the United States of America. During the same time period, Benjamin and Elias Roberts each added 40 acres to their original land holdings, and Isaac and Martin Scott, probably brothers, each acquired 40 acres in the area. All six of these purchases were patents from the United States of America, and all six tracts were located south of Chambersburg. In 1835 David Dugged also added 40 acres to his earlier purchase north of Chambersburg.

In 1836 and 1837, Mathew Thomas, and Isaac and Martin Scott each added 40 acres to their original purchases as four new landowners joined the settlement. Ishmael Roberts obtained 80 acres, and Ishmael Roberts Jr., probably his son, acquired 40 acres. Jordon Thomas purchased 40 acres and Calvin Scott obtained 20 acres. All but Calvin Scott's purchase were patents from the United States of America and all tracts were located south of Chambersburg.

By 1840, these ten men of color (Peter Lindley died in 1836) had accumulated a total of 780 acres in the Lick Creek Settlement. But this growth did not stop. Five years later in 1845, eleven Hoosiers of color held title to a total of 940 acres. At the end of the next five years, they had amassed a total of 1440 acres. By 1855, the settlement reached its maximum size in terms of the accumulated total acreage owned by its residents--1557 acres--as shown by the data provided in Table 6.

TABLE 6: Total Accumulated Acreage Owned by African Americans
in the Lick Creek Settlement 1840-1870

Year	Acreage
1840	780
1845	940
1850	1,440
1855	1,557
1860	1,190
1865	734
1870	604

Source: Land Transactions (1817-1905) in Appendix B.

The decline in the number of Black landholders started after the 1850s. Owners engaged in a rapid disposition of their farmlands between 1860 and 1865, selling out often to other African Americans who remained in the settlement.

The Exodus: September, 1862

One of the unusual findings from studying these land transactions was the discovery that seven African Americans disposed of their farms in the Lick Creek Settlement during the month of September, 1862. What seems to make the event so unusual is that it occurred when the Civil War was in progress and no period of racial strife was reported in the local history.

Regardless of the motivating factors, these sales were transacted in the South East Township:

1. Jarmon A. Rickman sold 60 acres on September 10, 1862 to Lee Hazlewood.
2. Joseph Scott sold 40 acres on September 10, 1862 to Lee Hazlewood.
3. Jonathan Thompson sold 40 acres on September 10, 1862 to Lee Hazlewood.
4. Harmon Lynch sold 80 acres on September 13, 1862 to Alfred Atkinson.
5. Alvin Scott sold 80 acres on September 16, 1862 to Alfred Atkinson.
6. Solomon Newby sold 79 acres on September 17, 1862 to Jesse Thompson.
7. Isaac Scott sold 180 acres on September 29, 1862 to David Lindley.

A total of 559 acres of farm land was sold in one month. Solomon Newby sold his land for almost one-half of the original purchase price, which meant that his economic loss was severe in view of the improvements made on the property over his sixteen years of ownership. If the other sellers experienced a similar financial loss, then we must conclude today that these men of color felt under extreme duress when they hastily departed from their farms and settlement.[2]

MAP: Total Acreage Owned in 1855 by African Americans in
Lick Creek Settlement and now in Hoosier National Forest.

(Courtesy Forest Service, U. S. Department of Agriculture)

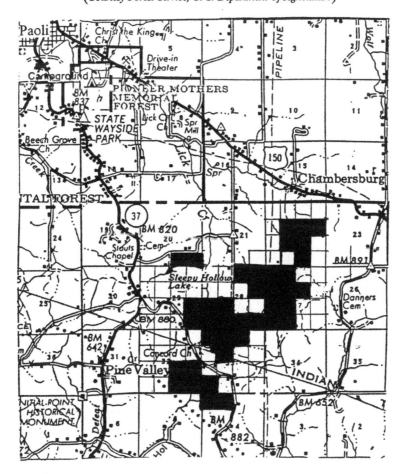

The Declining Years

By 1870, Mathew Thomas, who earlier had purchased land from his departing neighbors, was still the largest landowner. Others among the greatly diminished rank of farm owners included Nancy Roberts, Eli Roberts, Eliza Jane Roberts, Banister Chavis, and persons tilling the ground belonging to the unsettled estate of Elias Roberts, who died in 1866 while holding title to 304 acres of land.

Ten years later in 1880, only Banister Chavis, Eli Roberts, Eliza Jane Roberts, and Thomas Thompson were owning acreage in the area. Additionally there were the properties still remaining from the unsettled estate of Elias Roberts, and the lands belonging to the heirs of Mathew Thomas, who died in 1870 while holding title to 322 acres.

In 1890, William Thomas, son of Mathew Thomas, was the only working African American farmer left in the region. Additional holdings were yet tied up in the estate settlements of Banister Chavis, Eli Roberts and Thomas Thompson, all of whom were now deceased.

The last surviving resident, William Thomas, disposed of his 204 acres on March 18, 1902 and moved his family to a farm south of Paoli and several miles west of the old settlement boundaries. For all intent and purpose, the Lick Creek Settlement of African Americans in Orange County no longer had residents. Only the cemetery endures to remind us today of the early Black Pioneers who once were a part of this county.

Locust Hill in Stampers Creek

Simon Locust was regarded as a member of the African American community and buried in the Lick Creek Settlement Cemetery. His family, however, owned land located about three miles northeast of Chambersburg near Millersburg in Stampers Creek Township.

Moses Locust, the patriarch of this pioneer family, obtained three 40 acre-patent-deeds from the United States of America on August 20, 1832, June 14, 1836 and October 2, 1838--a total of 120 acres. Moses and his family had migrated from North Carolina, and evidently they lived in Orange County for several years before making their first land purchase.[3] Locust Hill, which was named for this family, marks today the location of the farm near the junction of Indiana highway 56 and Tater Road east of Paoli.

Simon Locust acquired ownership of the family's farm after his father died, actual date unknown. By 1880 an increased number of African Americans was living in Stampers Creek Township. The census data list five different households comprised of thirty individuals headed by (1) Simon Locust and his son, (2) William Locust, (3) William Mays, (4) Joseph O'Bannon, and (5) Lewis McClendon. These families may or may not have been kin of the Locusts.

In 1870 Simon Locust, after his military stint in the Civil War, purchased 173 acres in Section 23 several miles southwest of the Locust homestead in Stampers Creek. Seventeen years later on April 19, 1887 he bought an additional 200 acres located in Section 14, not too distant from his land in Section 23.

Simon Locust died in 1891. Four years prior to his death, 200 acres of his land was sold at a public auction on February 16, 1887 for non-payment of debt. Six years after his death, 200 more acres were sold at public auction on March 22, 1897 for non-payment of a Common School Fund Mortgage taken out in 1887. Disposition of the farm land around Locust Hill is still cloaked in mystery. What eventually happened to the original Locust lands is not readily ascertained from the deed transactions included in Appendix C.

Landowners in Other Townships

Research questions came to mind as the land transactions by Africans in the Lick Creek Settlement were studied. Were African Americans able to purchase real estate in other parts of Orange County? Did they own property in towns as well as in rural areas? In what townships did they own land? Were they landowners in those townships surrounding South East where persons of color settled initially? Did they own land in French Lick Township before the mineral springs and resort industries reached peak operations around the turn of this century?

One available resource contained data which helped to answer some of these questions.[4] Enumerators for the 1850, 1860 and 1870 United States Population Censuses collected information about value of real estate (land) and personal estate (buildings, household goods, livestock, equipment etc.) owned by the heads of households. While some census data are known to be grossly unreliable, they can, nevertheless, provide some general factual information to help fill in missing gaps about the pioneer history of African Americans in Indiana.

A compilation was made of all persons who reported owning real estate for the census years of 1850-1870 (Table 7). Although these findings did not provide conclusive answers to our earlier questions, they did confirm that Africans owned land outside of the Lick Creek Settlement area.

According to the 1850 census reports, for example, they possessed land in North West and Orleans Townships, in addition to Paoli and Stampers Creek Townships which are adjacent to South East Township. Thirty years after her husband's estate was probated on August 24, 1834, Penelope Bond, widow of Reuben Bond, and her children still held the farm land in Orangeville Township. Pearson Todd had a small holding in Orleans Township. Jeremiah Hawkins was the solitary landowner in the Town of Paoli. There were five landowners in Paoli Township and some of their real estate in the eastern and southern parts of the township could also have been in the Lick Creek Settlement.

Elias Roberts, of Paoli Township, reported owning land valued at $1000, an amount which exceeded by far the values given by other owners for 1860.

Ten years later, Blacks retained real estate in Orangeville Township. By 1860, however, Elias Lindley and Oliver Burnett were landowners in addition to the Bond family. Pearson Todd continued to occupy his land in Orleans Township, and the remaining property holders were in Paoli, South East and Stampers Creek Townships. Zachariah Roberts, in South East Township, reported owning real estate valued at $4,000--an amount several times larger than the holdings of Elias Roberts and Mathew Thomas, who lived in Paoli Township.

The number of landowners in 1870 was exactly half the total found ten years earlier. Reductions resulted in all townships, but the drop in South East Township owners is most striking. Down to one! Isaac Irvin was a new property owner with land worth $1,400 in Stampers Creek. He joined Simon Locust, whose real estate was now valued at $1,900.

TABLE 7: Value and Location of Real Estate Reported by African Americans in Orange County, 1860, 1870, and 1880

Township	1860 No.	1860 Value	1870 No.	1870 Value	1880 No.	1880 Value
North West	1	$300	-	-	-	-
Orangeville	-	-	3	$1880	1	$1200
Orleans	1	210	1	300	-	-
Paoli	5	1850	6	3700	4	5600
Paoli Town	1	500	-	-	2	450
South East	12	2780	9	6650	1	1000
Stampers Creek	1	700	1	700	2	3300
Totals	21	6340	20	13230	10	11550

Source: Data from U. S. Census Reports for years indicated in Appendix B.

Thomas Burnett just barely topped this figure, with reported real estate in Paoli Township worth $2,000. Others who indicated possessing real estate assets of $1,000 or more were: Oliver Burnett, Orangeville Township, $1,200; Nancy Roberts, Paoli Township, $1,600; and Mathew Thomas, Paoli Township, $1,500.

In 1880 both Enoch Burnett and John Wilson owned property in the Town of Paoli. The real estate owned by African Americans as given in the census for this year totaled $11,550.

One question raised previously about non-white ownership of real estate in French Lick Township can be now answered in the negative. At least census reports until 1880 failed to show that people of color owned land in the Springs Valley area of French Lick Township.

NOTES

1. Mathew Thomas, an orphan of color who was apprenticed to a local Quaker family, obtained 80 acres from Zachariah and Margaret Lindley on May 21, 1831. The south half of the northwest quarter of Section 14, Township 1 North, Range 1 East, this land was located in Stampers Creek Township, located a short distance northeast of Chambersburg. (Family history details in Chapter XV, 141-146)

2. Secret societies, such as the *Knights of the Golden Circle* and *Sons of Liberty*, operated in Orange County between 1861-1865. One of their expressed goals was to drive all people of color from Indiana (Goodspeed, *History of Orange County*, 522-23). Isaac Scott, Solomon Newby, and Harmon Lynch families migrated to Kent County, Ontario, Canada. Further research might reveal other families who sold their lands in 1862 also moved to Canada. It is unknown how some families, such as members of the Roberts and Thomas families, managed to remain in the township after other families of color left the county.

3. Locust listings in 1850 U. S. Census report (Appendix B); Civil War military and pension records of Simon Locust.

4. Obtaining more accurate data about African American land ownership involves searching all deed records books. Difficulties arise, however, because these records rarely indicate the race of participants. Even when using a master list of the names of African Americans found in public documents (e.g., census reports, marriage records, etc.) to be living in the county at a particular time period, the researcher may not be able to determine accurately the race of persons identified in specific land transactions. The greatest challenge comes from the fact that individuals with the same Christian and surnames but of different races frequently resided in the same county.

CHAPTER V

CERTIFICATES OF FREEDOM

Many Africans who settled in Indiana during the antebellum era were "free persons of color" who migrated from the states of Maryland, North Carolina and Virginia.[1] These pioneers left their home states to escape the punitive laws and restrictions placed upon Black citizens by their state legislatures following the slave rebellions.[2]

Free People of Color in the South

Increasingly slavery became an intolerable system of human exploitation as the industrial revolution progressed in the South. The enslaved persons used riots and insurrections to emphasize their sufferings. Slaveowners lived in constant fear of riots and were highly distrustful of any free Blacks who lived in their neighborhoods. The final event which struck the greatest terror in the hearts of the slaveholders was the slave rebellion led by Nat Turner in the Tidewater area of southern Virginia in 1831.

Three southern states had sizeable populations of both slaves and free persons of color dating from colonial days. Beginning in the early 1830s, they resorted to various legislative acts to handle the growing fears whites held of African Americans and slave riots. Maryland, for example, endeavored to get rid of its free Black citizens by passing a law in 1831-1832 providing for them to voluntarily be shipped to Liberia, Africa. At the same time Maryland excluded more free Blacks from coming into the state, and also imposed legal disabilities on the resident free people of color trying to force them to leave Maryland.[3]

Another southern state, Virginia, responded in 1830-31 with legislation prohibiting any meetings for the purpose of teaching free Negroes to read and write. The following year it passed a law denying free Blacks and slaves the right to preach, and it restricted the right of free Black citizens to purchase and permanently own land.[4]

North Carolina, the third southern state with a substantial number of African Americans, expanded its legal campaign to curb the privileges of free Blacks by enacting a law in 1831 to prohibit them from preaching. This law was soon followed by the adoption of a new state constitution in 1835 which, for the first time, limited the right to vote to white men only. Intermarriages between whites and free persons of color to the third generation were declared invalid after 1838. Later restrictions on free Blacks took away their rights to own a gun, a mare, a dog or any intoxicating liquor--and they could not move from one county to another without permission from the government.[5]

Only a trickle of African Americans migrated westward into the former Northwest Territory, but the number increased significantly in the 1830s and early 1840s. Like other migrants, they sought the cheap government land and the income to be earned as farm and day laborers. In this period of history, Indiana needed a lot of labor to clear its forests and to work on its public improvement projects such as the National Roadway across central Indiana and an intrastate canal system. Most migrating families, white or Black, hoped they could purchase land and enjoy the opportunities to "pursue life, liberty, and happiness."[6]

The Quakers

Early African settlers in Indiana tended to establish their homes in or near Quaker communities. They had become acquainted with some members of the Society of Friends who were their neighbors and employers in North Carolina. A small number of Quakers from North Carolina did assist some Black families to come to Indiana. There are numerous legends in Orange County about the activities of the Quakers in the "underground railroad."[7]

Additionally some sympathetic Quakers probably counseled early Black settlers on coping with the racial environment they encountered in this state and with the crises resulting from discriminatory laws. In some Indiana localities the Quakers allowed Black children to attend their subscription schools after Indiana legislation excluded them from the public schools.[8]

Emancipation, Manumission and Free Papers

One legal document carried by the Black settlers was a copy of their certificates of freedom or their "free papers" as they were customarily called. This document, oftentimes, was little more than a few, handwritten statements on a single sheet of paper. Usually a local public official, such as a justice of the peace or a county clerk, wrote them.

Most certificates provided some identifying information, such as age, birthdate and place of birth, physical characteristics and skin coloring, and the last place of residence. In the more elaborate instances, they included statements from white citizens about the African's parentage, special skills and integrity. Some certificates of freedom included declarations about the bearer's previous state of servitude and about the process involved in achieving his/her freedom.

Oftentimes writers have used the words "emancipation" and "manumission" interchangeably. While both words do relate to granting freedom to enslaved people, their legal meanings and the process for accomplishment are somewhat different, depending on the historical period and the particular state in which the event took place.

"Emancipation" was the act of freeing a person from bondage, and it took place *immediately* or by a date specified in the document. At certain periods in the history of slavery in this country, the slave holder wanting to free slaves had to first obtain approval from a court or special commission which established the requirements to be met before the act was legal. An excellent example is President Lincoln's Emancipation Act signed in 1863.

"Manumission" was a formal release from slavery or servitude. A majority of the states in the South proscribed manumission by last will and testament stating freedom would be granted upon the owner's death. Additionally, certain stipulations might need to be met eventually before the actual freedom became final. Such provisos were usually specified in wills, whereby the slave might receive freedom upon reaching majority, or upon the widow's death, etc.[9]

The use of manumissions declined in the nineteenth century because an increase in the number of free Blacks alarmed many whites and after sustaining a long period of prosperity the Southern economy had a greater reliance on slave labor. Certificates of freedom were legal documents where the signer attested to the current free status of the bearer. Free born persons or slaves, who gained freedom by either emancipation or manumission, were supplied with *certificates of freedom*, commonly referred to as "free papers." Conversely, a "bill of sale" or a sworn statement that a person was born to a slave in the owner's possession was satisfactory legal proof of human bondage.

Genealogists, unaware of the history of free Blacks in this nation, have assumed automatically that the term, "free papers," found in courthouse records, meant that the bearer described was recently enslaved. This might not necessarily be true. As examinination of the documents found in Orange County reveal, some certificates of freedom clearly attested that the bearers were "born free."

States laws in the North and South required Africans to prove their freedom status. An attitude commonly held by whites was that "all Black people are slaves--unless they could prove otherwise." Legislation often reinforced these racial attitudes.

Free African Americans were required by law in many states to have a copy of their certificate of freedom whenever traveling beyond the boundaries of their home communities. Indiana laws required Blacks to register at the county clerk's office in order to settle in its communities, but enforcement varied. In many cases, it is believed that free Blacks took the initiative to have a copy of their certificates filed locally as protection against fire, theft or damage to the original. Legends handed down in Black families emphasized the importance of "freedom papers" to their ancestors. Having them at hand in a crisis could amount to a matter of life or death.

Many certificates of freedom found in Orange County were obtained originally as the families prepared to migrate northward (Benjamin Roberts, Thomas Roberts, and Isaac Scott). From the sworn statements of the white attesters, several bearers of the "free papers" were from families known to have been "free persons" over several generations in North Carolina (Newby and Roberts). And, some certificates verified that the holder was formerly enslaved and had been granted his freedom (Clements, Guthrie, and Margy).

"Freedom papers" were easily counterfeited, and often whites were very suspicious of traveling Blacks. They subjected these transients to all sorts of delays, investigations, and/or imprisonments as they questioned the validity of their papers and their right to travel. Racial harassment generally characterized the daily experiences of any Black who ventured beyond the boundaries of his home community, even here in Indiana.[10]

Certificates of Freedom in Orange County

Thus far, twenty copies of "certificates of freedom" were found. They had been filed between 1823 and 1851 at the county recorder office in Paoli, Indiana.[11]

These documents were not easy to locate. For a small legal fee they were transcribed into the Deed Record Books, just as many non-property legal papers were recorded in this period of history. Indices to Deed Books classified the certificates several ways: (1) under the last name of one witness, usually the first one mentioned in the document, (2) under the first or last name of the bearer, (3) in the C's under "certificates," or (4) under the F's for "freedom" or "free papers." Inconsistencies in labeling and indexing these public documents augment the researching time. With no method to determine in advance how many certificates were filed in Orange County over the years, it is impossible to guarantee that all were actually found.

Dates show that a majority of the certificates were filed in the 1840s. These certificates originated from six different locations: six from Orange County, Indiana; one, Franklin County, Missouri; six, Chatham County, North Carolina; one, Cumberland County, North Carolina; five, Orange County, North Carolina; and one from Wake County, North Carolina.

Birthplaces of the bearers were provided in all located documents and the following tabulation summarize the findings: 2 were born in Orange County, Indiana, 1 in Missouri, 16 in North Carolina, and 1 in Virginia.[12]

Some certificates did contain significant historical and pertinent genealogical data. Without a doubt, they confirm that free Africans lived in Orange County before the Civil War, and that some of these pioneers lived as "free" people long before they migrated to Indiana.

Abstracts of Certificates of Freedom

Certificates of freedom found in Orange County were handwritten. Each was photocopied and its contents later transcribed, edited and abstracted. Persons seriously interested in these historical documents should consult the original records on file in the courthouse.

The first document is printed below in its entirety typed from the original handscript without punctuation or minor editing.

1. WILLIAM TURNER ARCHEY

"State of North Carolina Chatham County William Turner Archey a free man of colour son of John and Elizabeth Archey about twenty seven years age five feet three inches high spare made rather dark that also he is free born of free parents in this County and lived most of his time in this neighborhood we the undersigned are well acquainted with said Archey he has conducted himself honest and peaceable sober and tolerable industrious cane make a common good shoe and is well acquainted with farming we hope that none will impose upon him but expect and trust that all protect his rights as free man and trust him as a free man should be treated as his future conduct may deserve this fifth day of December in the year of our Lord one thousand eight hundred and forty four and sixty ninth year of the independence of the United States of America.

Wm Lindley J P

Wm Lay
Sampson Allen
Jacob Hadley

[Clerk's Certificate]

State of North Carolina
Chatham County   : I William P. Taylor Clerk of the Court of Pleas and
quarter sessions for Chatham County do hereby certify that Wm Lindley and
William Lay whose names appear to the foregoing free papers are acting
Justices of the Peace for the County of Chatham and that the foregoing
signatures are genuine and full faith and credit are due all of their acts as
such and that Sampson Allen and Jacob Hadley are respectable citizens of this
County and their names are genuine also. In testimony whereof I have
hereunto set my hand and affixed the seal of office at Pittsboro 14th day of
Sept A.D. 1849
          W.P. Taylor, C.C.C. (LS)
          [Clerk Circuit Court, Legal Seal]
Filed for Record June 24th 1853
10 O'clock Am Recorded July 18th 1853
Josiah Hazelwood ROC [Recorder Orange County]
[*Deed Book 15*, page 449]

2. BANISTER CHAVIS

Dated 11 September 1838, this certificate was signed by two justices of the peace, John
Stafford and James A. Gray. They attested that Bannister Chavis, "a man of colour about twenty
years of age," was free born and had resided in Orange County, North Carolina since early infancy -
- "and has a right to pass as a free citizen." Recorded in Orange County, Indiana on August 31, 1853.
Deed Book 15, page 472.

3. FRANCIS CLEMENTS

Document was written in Orange County, Indiana on January 24, 1846. Five persons --
Thomas Clements, James Clements, John Clements, Robert Montgomery, and Amelia Roberts --
certified that Francis Clements, the bearer, was a free man of color. They stated that they
understood that he was originally purchased as a slave in Virginia by their father, Jesse Clements, who
brought him to Kentucky. There he remained a slave until Jesse Clements died and in his will he
gave Francis to their mother during her natural lifetime. Upon her death, he was set free in
accordance with the father's will.

The certificate indicated also that Francis got his freedom about seventeen years prior to the
date of this certificate, and that since that time he lived in Indiana "and enjoyed all the rights,
privileges and immunities secured by the laws of this state to free persons of color. . . ." Filed for
record on February 8, 1847. *Deed Book K*, page 312.

4. DILLY COPLEY

This certificate originated in Orange County, North Carolina on October 25, 1843. The
bearer was identified as the wife of Peter Copley. Attesters had known her since she was a small
child and stated she was born of free parents and has "always passed as a free woman in Orange
County..." Paper signed by John W. Hancock and Frederick Maize, both justice of the peace. Filed

for record in Orange County, Indiana on August 5, 1845. *Deed Book J-10*, page 413.

5. PETER COPLEY

Document follows the above one and also came from Orange County, North Carolina but originated on May 3, 1841. The affiant, John Taylor, was Clerk of Orange County Court of Pleas and Quarter Sessions, who described the bearer as "a mulatto man about 22 years" and raised in the county. It was also filed for record in Indiana on August 5, 1845.

6. JAMES GUTHRIE

This certificate was completed in Orange County, Indiana on November 28, 1842, by Thomas Newlin. James Guthrie was born a slave in North Carolina and was owned by Clabourn Guthrie. Later he was sold to Nathaniel Newlin, who desired to free him but was unable to do so according to the laws of North Carolina.

Thereafter, Nathaniel Newlin sold the slave to Thomas Newlin, Orange County, Indiana, with the understanding that James Guthrie would be given his freedom in Indiana. Thomas Newlin does "to all intents and purposes forever absolutely and unconditionally release, discharge, manumit, and set free the said James Guthrie." Filed for record March 15, 1847. *Deed Book K*, pages 369-370.[13]

7. ELIAS LINDLEY

Initiated in Orange County, Indiana, on September 7, 1843, this certificate was signed by nineteen subscribers who swore that Elias Lindley, "a colored man about twenty years of age, of a stout, robust figure with a cracked joint on the second finger and a small knot of protuberance on the third finger of the right hand and about six feet high," was born of free parents and raised in Orange County, Indiana. Filed for record March 27, 1847. *Deed Book K*, page 380.

8. MARGY'S CERTIFICATE

No surname was provided. Document was completed in Franklin County, Missouri, by D.C. and Rachel K. McDonald, who swore that Margy, a colored woman now living with them, was a free woman. She never did belong to the McDonalds, but she was believed to have been set free "by her rightful owner" in 1834. The couple certified further that Margy lived in Indiana with the knowledge and consent of "her rightful owner" until she could claim freedom "by the laws of the State of Indiana."

When the McDonalds decided to move from Indiana to Missouri, Margy "chose them for her lawful agent" and accompanied them to Missouri where she continued living with the family. The reason given for Margy's choosing them to be her agent was the fact that people (in Indiana) "threatened to send her to Liberia." It was her choice to live with the McDonalds "as one of the family rather than go to Liberia."

They declared that Margy was a free person "and ought so to be considered by every one." Original papers were recorded in Franklin County, Missouri, March 5, 1847, and filed for record in Orange County, Indiana, November 9, 1849. *Deed Book 13*, page 97.

9. STANFORD MEANS

Certificate was executed in Orange County, Indiana, on October 4, 1849. The five citizens who signed it attested that they had known the bearer, a free man of color, for 15 or 20 years, that he had lived that long in the area, and that all the subscribers recognized him as a free person of color. Stanford Means was described as about five feet eight inches high, 29 years old, and having a scar on the inside of his right hand near the end. Josiah Hazelwood, the county recorder, was one of the certifiers. Filed for record October 4, 1849. *Deed Book 13*, page 58.

10. SOLOMON NEWBY

This instrument was made in Orange County, North Carolina, on September 5, 1840. J.W. and Mary Long stated that they were acquainted with the parents of Solomon Newby and his wife, Margaret, and that the parents of each were free persons of color "at the time Solomon and Margaret were born and ever afterwards." The children of Solomon and Margaret Newby were: Lucinda, age 9, and Emiline, age 2 years. Both children were also free persons. Filed for record in Orange County, Indiana, January 7, 1843. *Deed Record K*, page 268.

11. BENJAMIN ROBERTS

Document was issued in Chatham County, North Carolina, on November 24, 1824. Thirty-one subscribers affirmed that the bearer, a free man of color, his wife Sally, and three children, Serena, Ishmael, and Archibald, had been raised in and were longtime residents of Chatham County. Benjamin Roberts and his family were about "to remove to the State of Indiana." The subscribers regarded the bearer and "an orderly, moral, and peaceable man entitled to civil treatment from persons in a strange [land]."

The lengthy list of subscribers names and titles was most impressive and it included the names of three persons using the initials "J.P." (Justice of the Peace) after their signatures. In addition, the certifying justice of the peace for the document added at the bottom a personal statement emphasizing the positive character of the bearer. Filed for record in Orange County, Indiana, January 7, 1833. *Deed Book D*, page 43.

12. ELIAS ROBERTS

Document was completed in Chatham County, North Carolina on February 10, 1823. Six persons certified that they had known Elias Roberts and his wife, Nancy, for a long time. Further, they stated that the fathers of Elias and Nancy, Ishmael Roberts and Thomas Archie, had resided in Chatham County for 23 years, and that both fathers were soldiers in the Revolutionary War.[14]

They attested "that there can be no doubt that the bearers of this certificate -- Elias and Nancy -- although persons of Couler, are free and entitled to all the rights and privileges of white persons..." The paper indicates that Elias and Nancy have three daughters: Mary, Candice and Nancy.

Certificate was recorded in Orange County, Indiana on February 20, 1833. *Deed Book D*, pages 432-433.

13. THOMAS ROBERTS

This document came from Chatham County, North Carolina, where it was certified on September 2, 1836. Two justices of the peace swore that Thomas Roberts, "a dark mulatto man," was born of free parents, Ishmael and Cusa [Lucinda] Roberts, who were said to be living in Indiana at the time these papers were prepared in North Carolina. Statements declared further that Thomas Roberts was married "to a free bright mulatto girl named Matilda."

Furthermore, one of the justices, William Lindley, stated that Thomas had been "bound" to his father in Chatham County, and that Thomas faithfully served the time until he reached 21 years of age.[15]

"Said Thomas Roberts and his wife, Matilda, have conducted themselves as honest people and are believed to be honest and industrious and persons in whom confidence may be relied on. We hope they will be treated by all with humanity and respect as their future conduct may deserve." Filed in Orange County, Indiana, May 24, 1842. *Deed Book H*, page 312.

14. WILEY ROBERTS

These papers originated at Fayetteville, Cumberland County, North Carolina, on March 21, 1829. Fourteen subscribers indicated they were personally acquainted with Wiley Roberts, a colored man, "for some time past." Bearer was described as 21 or 22 years old, about five feet seven inches or six feet high, "and rather stout in form." His parents were free persons "who have always been respected, acknowledged and permitted the rights and privileges of citizenship." Filed for record in Orange County, Indiana, December 24, 1832. *Deed Book D*, pages 427-28.

15. ZACHARIAH ROBERTS

This document emanated from Chatham County, North Carolina, where it was written on December 20, 1847. Nine citizens certified that they had known Zachariah Roberts, a free man of color, "a considerable time." In his section at the bottom of the document, Nathan A. Stedman, the certifying county clerk in North Carolina, contributed a physical description of all family members:

Zachariah Roberts was about 47 years old, had a scar on his breast caused by a burn and a scar on the right side of his face. His wife, whose first name was not provided, was said to be about 45 years old, "somewhat yellow complexion and cross eyes with strait hair."

Names, ages, and markings of their children: James, about 19 years old with a scar over his left eye caused by a fall from a horse; Zachariah, about 18 years old, weighing 175 pounds; Sylvania, about 16 years old; Martha, 11 years old; John, about 3 years old with a dark mark near his left shoulder. Filed for record in Orange county, Indiana, August 23, 1848. *Deed Book 12*, pages 252-53.

16. ISAAC SCOTT

Certified in Wake County, North Carolina, on February 7, 1835, by seven subscribers, these papers state that the bearer, his wife, Jemimah, and their four children were all free persons of color. Isaac Scott, born on November 27, 1801, was about five feet ten inches high, and had "a rather light complexion." His wife, Jemimah, was reported to be born in 1828, and described to be of light complexion, five feet four inches high, and had two small scars on her forehead, "and her hair inclined to be long and black."

Their eldest son, Alfred M. Scott, was born October 5, 1828, and was "a brighter color than his father." William F. Scott was born in 1831 and was said to be "of a lighter color than Alfred." Joseph K. Scott was born in 1833 and was "of a darker color." Elizabeth Scott was born in 1835 "and is a light complexion." A statement in this document revealed that the family was about to move west "or to some other county," and applied for a recommendation before leaving Wake County, North Carolina. Document filed in Orange County, Indiana, September 4, 1844. *Deed Book J*, pages 136-37.

17. MATHEW THOMAS

Affidavit completed in Orange County, Indiana by sixteen subscribers who declared on October 19, 1833 that they had known the bearer, a man of color, during the previous 8 to 10 years "as a free man . . . [who] always conducted himself civilly, honestly and industriously." They affirmed that this document was being executed at this particular time to save Mathew Thomas "from the molestation of those who might probably apprehend him as a slave. . . We are well appraised that he was free born."

Added to the original certificate was a statement signed by John G. Clendenin and five other citizens who swore that Mathew Thomas was "bound to me by his mother, then a widow, to learn the art of farming." Mathew served the term of indenture until reaching the age of 21 years, and the attester concluded with the comment, "I have at all times found him honest and a boy of truth."

These papers were not filed for record in Orange County, Indiana until August 28, 1853, nearly twenty years after they were written. *Deed Book 15*, page 471.

18. JOHN B. THOMPSON

Papers initiated on August 21, 1845 at Chatham County, North Carolina. The bearer was 35 years old, a free man of color, and the son of free parents, Samuel and Elizabeth Thompson. His physical description indicated that he was "of a light black color, weighing one hundred and forty-eight or fifty pounds."

This certificate was obtained so that John and Mary Thompson could travel to Indiana. The wife, Mary, the daughter of John and Elizabeth Archey, was free born "and very fleshy." Couple was traveling with their seven children: Elizabeth, Martha, Mary, Thomas, Sally, John and an unnamed infant. Filed for record in Orange County, Indiana on November 7, 1851. *Deed Book 14*, page 298.

19. LEWIS TINON

Two citizens, Daniel Ray and Jonathan Whitman of Orange County, Indiana, avowed on September 7, 1846 that they had been acquainted with Lewis Tinon, a man of color, "from his childhood to present time." He was born of free parents in Orange County, North Carolina and his family emigrated to Indiana when the bearer was about six years old. Lewis Tinon was described as five feet ten or eleven inches tall, "spare made and very black," and about 29 years old. Filed for record in Orange County, Indiana on July 30, 1847. *Deed Book K*, page 501.

Original certificate was prepared in Orange County, North Carolina on September 7, 1840. Two justices of the peace, Richard Thompson and Isaac Holt, swore that the bearer was a free man of color who was free born and raised in their immediate neighborhood. "We know him well and certify that he is a free man and of good character." Filed for record in Orange County, Indiana on December 29, 1845. *Deed Book J*, page 541.

NOTES

1. An earlier version of this chapter appeared in the Fall 1986 issue of *The Journal of the Afro-American Historical and Genealogical Society*, Volume 7, Number 3.

2. Carter G. Woodson, "Brief Treatment of the Free Negro" in *Free Negro Heads of Families in the United States in 1830...* (Washington, D.C.: The Assn. for the Study of Negro Life and History, 1925), v-lvii.

3. James M. Wright. *The Free Negro in Maryland, 1634-1860.* New York: Columbia University, 1921, 476-78. Maryland's total population in 1830 was: Slave, 102,994; Free Colored, 52,938; and White, 291,108.

4. John M. Russell, *The Free Negro in Virginia, 1619-1865*, Series XXXI, No. 3, John Hopkins University Studies in Historical and Political Science (Baltimore, 1913), 361; laws which changed status of free people of color in Chapter II, "The Origin of the Free Negro Class," 16-41. Population figures in 1820 for Virginia were: Free Colored, 36,875; Slave, 425,148; and White, 603,381.

5. John Hope Franklin. *The Free Negro in North Carolina, 1790-1860.* (Chapel Hill: University of North Carolina Press, 1943), 18. Population figures for North Carolina in 1830 were: Free Negro, 19,575; Slave, 245,601; and White, 472,823. Also, David Dodge, "The Free Negroes of North Carolina," *Atlantic Monthly*, VVII (1886), 20-30; R. H. Taylor, *The Free Negro in North Carolina* (Chapel Hill: North Carolina Historical Society, 1920), 5-28.

A 1992 genealogical publication on this subject is *Free African Americans of North Carolina* by Paul Heinegg (Self-published). The author researched and included in his book the family histories of more than eighty percent of those counted as "all other free persons" in the 1790 and 1800 U. S. Census. Most striking is his discovery that most of North Carolina's free people of color of African ancestry originated in Virginia where they became free in the early seventeenth and eighteenth century. Some had never been slaves. When their ancestors arrived in Virginia, they were treated much like white servants and were freed upon completing their indentures. Heinegg writes that "chattel slavery and racism developed in the United States after these free families were established in Virginia."

6. John W. Lyda, *The Negro in the History of Indiana*, (Coatesville, Ind.: Hathaway Printery, 1953), 18.

7. Ibid., 36-39 section on "Kidnapping." Also, Emma Lou Thornbrough, *The Negro in Indiana Before 1900*, (Indianapolis: Indiana Historical Bureau, 1957), 92-118. More detailed description on man-stealing and its legal consequences is included in the article by Charles H. Money, "The Fugitive Slave Law of 1850 in Indiana," *Indiana Magazine of History*, XVII, 1921, 159-98 and 257-97; Goodspeed's *History of Orange, Lawrence and Washington Counties*, "Underground Railroad," 385.

8. Richard G. Boone, *A History of Education in Indiana* (New York: D. E. Appleton and Co.; reprint, Indiana Historical Bureau, 1941), "Education of Negroes," 237-240. This prohibition was not changed by the Indiana Assembly until after the Civil War when in 1869 a system of racially segregated schools was initiated. Hiram H. Hilty, *Toward Freedom For All: North Carolina Quakers and Slavery* (Richmond, IN. Friends United Press, 1984); chapters on "Slaves Given Freedom," and "Relocation in the West and North" describe the negative reception the freed Blacks received in Indiana communities.

9. Marion Roydhouse, "Manumission" in *Dictionary of Afro-American Slavery* edited by Randall M. Miller and John David Smith (Westport: Greenwood Press, 1988), 214-216.

10. Thornbrough, *Negro in Indiana*, 92-118.

11. Certificates were located during research in 1980 and later summarized in the article by Coy D. Robbins, "Lick Creek Settlement: A Rural Pre-Civil War Black Community in Orange County, Indiana," *Black History News and Notes*, Indiana Historical Society Library, (February 1982, No. 8) 8-12; May 1982, No. 9, 10-12.

12. Only a small number of certificates were recorded in Orange County, Indiana although the African American population during the antebellum era ranged from 96-260 persons between 1820 and 1860.

13. Hilty, *Toward Freedom For All*, p.79, provides additional background on this event which involved a person known to the Quakers as "Black Jim." Nathaniel Newlin, a Quaker, purchased Jim at a sale in Alamance County, North Carolina, in 1842. The seller was Claiborne Guthrie, Nathaniel's brother-in-law. Newlin's purpose in buying the slave was to set him free, and this he undertook to do by deeding him to his brother, Thomas Newlin, from Indiana who was visiting in North Carolina at the time. Thomas agreed to bring Jim with him to Paoli, Indiana, and once there he proceeded to manumit him. According to the certificate, this was done on November 28, 1842 but it was nearly five years before James Guthrie had the paper filed for record at the courthouse. Hilty's source of this story was *The Newlin Family, Ancestors and Descendants of John and Mary Pyle Newlin* by Algie I. Newlin (Greensboro, 1967) n.p. 57-58.

14. An Ishmael Roberts also came to Orange County, Indiana and was buried in the Lick Creek Cemetery. It is not known if Thomas Archie, the other Revolutionary War soldier mentioned in this certificate, migrated also to Indiana.

15. The fact that Thomas Roberts was "bound out" until he was 21 years old confirms that he was not a slave but rather a dependent child or orphan who was apprenticed for training by the "overseers of the poor" in North Carolina.

CHAPTER VI

NEGRO REGISTER

In 1851 the Indiana General Assembly enacted the second state constitution. Among its provisions was one which excluded African Americans from settling in the state. The great majority of white voters in the state adopted the new constitution the following year.[1]

An ordinance passed by the Indiana Assembly to enforce the exclusionary provisions of "Article XIII Negroes and Mulattoes" required all African Americans who resided in Indiana prior to November 1, 1851 to register with the clerk of the respective county circuit court.[2]

Ledger-size books entitled *Register of Negroes and Mulattoes* were printed and used by county officials to comply with the law.

Location of Negro Registers Today

No accurate count has yet been determined of the number of Indiana counties which actually established Negro Registers. Not every county obeyed the law. For example, whites in Randolph County which had a relatively large number of African Americans voted against Article XIII, and later they refused to comply with the Negro Register requirement because so many of its citizens believed the regulations were harsh and discriminatory.

Nor is it known how many of the established registers survived. County Clerks are mandated by law to keep track of their governmental records, but as the years passed many became unaware of what happened to the Negro Registers. Several counties deposited their registers with the local historical society or public library. Today the books are available for viewing in the Washington County Historical Society in Salem, the Martin County Historical Society in Shoals, and the Knox County Records Library in Vincennes.

Several registers were turned over to the Indiana State Library or the Indiana State Archives in Indianapolis. Collections in both facilities are incomplete and contain either the original books or microfilm copies from the following counties: Floyd, Franklin, Jackson, Jefferson, Jennings, Ohio, Orange, and Switzerland.

Certainly these registers hold a wealth of genealogical and historical data. Any family researcher who locates an ancestor listed in one of these registers will be quite fortunate indeed, especially if the entry contains a detailed description of the progenitor's physical appearance.

The Orange County Register

The Orange County ledger is stored in the locked vault of the county clerk's office.[3] An antiquated cloth-covered book weathered to a dark gray color, it has double-pages, approximately fifteen inches long and twenty-one inches wide. Each double-page is ruled into six columns with printed headings. Each registrant gave the following information: (1) Name, (2) Age, (3) Description, (4) Place of Birth, (5) Place of Residence, and (6) Names of Witnesses who validated the right of each Black citizen to continue living in Indiana. Only about one-third of the total printed pages in the book were required for persons registered.

It is not known when this register was established, but it was probably by mid-summer, 1853, when the first registration was actually entered in the book. At least one Orange County newspaper printed a public notice addressed "To Free Negroes and Mulattoes" about the requirements they had to meet in order to remain living legally in the state (see Appendix A).

There was a total of 141 registrations entered in the book between June 24, 1853 and June 10, 1861. Ninety percent of the enrollers signed up during a five month period between June 24, 1853 and November 18, 1853 (see Table 8). The peak registration was forty-two individuals on Thursday, September 1, 1853. The second largest number was twenty-four registrants on Saturday, August 27, 1853. For the most part the registrations were completed for family groups identified generally by a single adult, often the male head of the household. Two enrollers were current residents of other Indiana counties: Aisley Husbands, Daviess County, and Jonathan L. Roberts, Howard County.

Table 8: Tally of Registrations by Year Enrolled

Year	Count
1853	127
1854	11
1856	2
1861	1
Total	141

Registrations continued irregularly for eight years after 1853. Whether the late enrollers had been longtime county residents who finally got around to complying with the registration law or were recent arrivals in the community is unclear. Nothing has yet been located in public records to suggest that any Orange County citizen was ever punished for violating the 1852 registration laws.

It seems possible that not all African Americans in Orange County signed up, judging from their total population figures in the 1850 and 1860 censuses: 251 and 260, respectively. A comparison between the population figures and the total of 141 names found in the register indicates the possibility that almost fifty percent of the African descendants in the county did not register.

Studying the Contents

By the mid-nineteenth century an increasing number of African citizens in Indiana were ative-born. No longer were migrants from southern states coming to Indiana's settlements. Data reported in the Orange County Negro Register substantiated these facts. More than half of all registrants stated they were born in Indiana. In other words, this population was stable and composed of families with at least one generation of native born citizens. The percentage of people of color who were born in Indiana appeared approximately the same as the proportion of Americans from Europe who were born in the state: in 1850, 525,732 out of 988,416 Hoosiers were native born.[4]

Table 9 shows the distribution of birthplaces reported in the Register. Not only was the largest number in Indiana but ninety-three percent of the Indiana births was in Orange County. For birthplaces outside the state, the largest number or about thirty-five percent of the total was born in North Carolina.

Only scanty numbers reported birthplaces in the states of Kentucky, Maryland, Missouri, South Carolina and Virginia. The small number of registrants with Kentucky birthplaces is surprising, since so many Indiana migrants during the antebellum period came from this older, neighboring state.

TABLE 9: Distribution of Birthplaces Reported in the Negro Register

Place of Birth		Number
Indiana		74
Orange County	69	
Washington County	1	
Vigo County	4	
State of Indiana	1	
Kentucky		5
Maryland		1
Missouri		1
North Carolina		49
Franklin County	1	
Granville County	1	
Orange County	1	
State of NC	46	
South Carolina		1
Virginia		7
Amherst County	1	
Pittsylvania Co	1	
State of Virginia	5	
Unspecified		2
Total Registrants		141

Some general characteristics of the persons listed in the Register were studied such as the range in ages, whether newly formed families with small children or if they included adolescents and young adults.

The distribution of ages is shown in Table 10. The youngest person signed up was a baby girl seven months old, Sabine Baxter, and the oldest was Thomas Butler, who was born in Maryland and reportedly eighty six and a half years old.

Seventy percent of the registrants were under thirty years old, indicating that this was a young group. Children under fifteen years accounted for forty-four percent of the total. Only five percent, or seven persons, was over sixty-one years old.

TABLE 10: Distribution of Ages Given in the Negro Register

Range of Ages	Number
Up to 5 years old	20
6 - 15 years old	42
16 - 30 years old	38
31 - 45 years old	19
46 - 60 years old	14
61 - 86 1/2 years old	7
No age reported	1
Total Registrants	141

What follows is a transcript of the entire register. As much as possible the style, language and spelling found in the original have been retained. Only minimal editing was done to insure its clarity and readability. Undoubtedly the original contained errors. These may have resulted when copiers duplicated the handwritten notes made initially as enrollers were interviewed. Clerks received a small fee from the County Commissioners for each person registered. Such payments may have been in addition to any money collected from the registrants.

REGISTER OF NEGROES AND MULATTOES IN ORANGE COUNTY, INDIANA

Names	Age	Description	Place of Birth	Residence	Names of Witnesses	Date Registered
Archie, Wm. L.	36	Rather dark mulatto, 5 ft and 3 ins. high, very curly hair, high forehead	Orange Co, NC	Orange Co, IN	Hiram Lindley (of Wm)	24 June 1853
Burnett, Thomas	46	Rather dark mulatto, 5 ft 10 ins; curly hair, rather prominent cheek bones; finger on left hand crooked forward caused by a cut.	Orange Co, NC	Orange Co, IN	Henry Miller	24 June 1853
Archie, Martha	32	Rather light negro woman about 4 ft. 9 1/4 in high	Pittsylvania Co, Va.	Orange Co, IN	William Morris	24 June 1853
Cosley, Lucy Ann	5	Quite light colored mulatto about 3 ft 6 1/2 ins. high	Franklin Co, MO	Orange Co, IN	William Morris	24 June 1853
Roberts, Elias	64	Mulatto, 5 ft 9 ins high, gray hair, heavy set, weight 185 or 190 lbs.	NC	Orange Co, IN	William G. Chambers	27 Aug 1853
Roberts, Nancy	54	Light mulatto, gray hair, heavy set, height 165 lbs, 5 ft 4 ins.	NC	Orange Co, IN	William G. Chambers	27 Aug 1853
Roberts, Zachariah	19	Mulatto 5 ft 11 ins, curly hair, well built	Orange Co, IN	Orange Co, IN	William G. Chambers	27 Aug 1853
Roberts, John	14	Mulatto 5 ft high, curly hair, large scar left arm above wrist	Orange Co, IN	Orange Co, IN	William G. Chambers	27 Aug 1853
Roberts, Eliza J.	7	Mulatto 3 ft 8 ins.- fair	Orange Co, IN	Orange Co, IN	William G. Chambers	27 Aug 1853
Thomas, Samina A.	15	Mulatto 4 ft 11 1/2 in high	Orange Co, IN	Orange Co, IN	William G. Chambers	27 Aug 1853
Thomas, Nancy	14	Dark mulatto 5 ft high	Orange Co, IN	Orange Co, IN	William G. Chambers	27 Aug 1853
Thomas, Elias W.	9	3 ft 8 in high, dark mulatto	Vigo Co, IN	Orange Co, IN	William G. Chambers	27 Aug 1853
Chavis, Banister	35	Light mulatto 5 ft 10 1/2 ins	NC	Orange Co, IN	William G. Chambers	27 Aug 1853
Chavis, Henry	10	Light mulatto 4 ft 4 1/2 ins	Orange Co, IN	Orange Co, IN	William G. Chambers	27 Aug 1853
Chavis, Nancy	9	Light mulatto 4 ft 1 1/2 ins	Orange Co, IN	Orange Co, IN	William G. Chambers	27 Aug 1853

45

Name	Age	Description	Birthplace	Residence	Witness	Date
Chavis, Rachel	5	Light mulatto 3 ft 6 ins high	Orange Co, IN	Orange Co, IN	William G. Chambers	27 Aug 1853
Chavis, Riley	4	Light mulatto 3 ft 3 1/2 ins	Orange Co, IN	Orange Co, IN	William G. Chambers	27 Aug 1853
Chavis, Thomas	2	Light mulatto 2 ft 7 ins high	Orange Co, IN	Orange Co, IN	William G. Chambers	27 Aug 1853
Chavis, Sarah	32	Mulatto 5 1.2 ft high	NC	Orange Co, IN	William G. Chambers	27 Aug 1853
Thomas, Mathew	45	5 ft 3 in high, quite dark	NC	Orange Co, IN	William G. Chambers	27 Aug 1853
Thomas, Mary	37	5 ft 4 1/2 in, light mulatto	Orange Co, IN	Orange Co, IN	William G. Chambers	27 Aug 1853
Thomas, Joseph	18	5 ft 5 in, dark mulatto	Orange Co, IN	Orange Co, IN	William G. Chambers	27 Aug 1853
Thomas, Mary A.	14	4 ft 11 in high, mulatto	Orange Co, IN	Orange Co, IN	William G. Chambers	27 Aug 1853
Thomas, Sarah A.	12	4 ft 7 in high, mulatto	Orange Co, IN	Orange Co, IN	William G. Chambers	27 Aug 1853
Thomas, Jeremiah	9	4 ft high, dark mulatto	Orange Co, IN	Orange Co, IN	William G. Chambers	27 Aug 1853
Thomas, William	7	3 ft 9 in high, dark mulatto	Orange Co, IN	Orange Co, IN	William G. Chambers	27 Aug 1853
Thomas, John H.	4	3 1/2 ft high, mulatto	Orange Co, IN	Orange Co, IN	William G. Chambers	27 Aug 1853
Thomas, Adaline S. E.	2	2 ft 8 1/2 in high, mulatto	Orange Co, IN	Orange Co, IN	William G. Chambers	27 Aug 1853
Husbands, Aisley	24	Full blooded negro 5 ft 1 in (Resident of Daviess Co, Indiana)	NC	Daviess Co, IN	J. Wilson	29 Aug 1853
Lingle, Dudley A.	27	About 5 ft 7 1/2 ins, full blooded negro, 2 scars on right wrist, underside of arm and a small piece off left ear	KY	Orange Co, IN	Newton Wright	30 Aug 1853
Lynch, Harmon	38	About 6 ft 2 ins high, mulatto, heavy beard, scar on top of left arm	NC	Orange Co, IN	Alfred McVey	1 Sept 1853
Roberts, Benjamin	17	About 5 ft 3 ins, bright mulatto	Indiana	Orange Co, IN	Henry Thompson	1 Sept 1853
Clemens, Francis	66	Very black negro 5 ft 4 1/2 in	Amherst Co, VA	Orange Co, IN	Josiah Hazlewood	1 Sept 1853
Clemens, Nancy Ann	45	Very dark complexion 5 ft 3 1/2 ins.	VA	Orange Co, IN	Josiah Hazlewood	1 Sept 1853
Clemens, Martha A.	21	Very dark complexion 5 ft 1 in.	Orange Co, IN	Orange Co, IN	Josiah Hazlewood	1 Sept 1853
Clemens, Sarah J.	19	Very dark complexion 4 ft 9 ins.	Orange Co, IN	Orange Co, IN	Josiah Hazlewood	1 Sept 1853

Name	Age	Description	Origin	Registrant	Place	Date
Clemens, Mary E.	14	Very dark complexion	Orange Co, IN	Josiah Hazlewood	Orange Co, IN	1 Sept 1853
Clemens, Wm.	18	Very dark complexion	Orange Co, IN	Josiah Hazlewood	Orange Co, IN	1 Sept 1853
Clemens, Maria	10	Very dark complexion	Orange Co, IN	Josiah Hazlewood	Orange Co, IN	1 Sept 1853
Newby, Solomon	53	Dark mulatto, 5 ft -- ins.	NC	Josiah Hazlewood	Orange Co, IN	1 Sept 1853
Newby, Margaret	38	Dark mulatto, 5 ft 2 1/2 ins.	NC	John Cotes	Orange Co, IN	1 Sept 1853
Newby, Lucinda	22	Dark color 4 ft 4 1/2 ins.	NC	John Cotes	Orange Co, IN	1 Sept 1853
Newby, Emaline	16	Dark colored mulatto	NC	John Cotes	Orange Co, IN	1 Sept 1853
Newby, James	9	Very dark mulatto	Orange Co, IN	John Cotes	Orange Co, IN	1 Sept 1853
Newby, Geo. J.	3	Very dark mulatto	Orange Co, IN	John Cotes	Orange Co, IN	1 Sept 1853
Newby, Moses W.	1	Dark mulatto	Orange Co, IN	Leanid Lindley	Orange Co, IN	1 Sept 1853
Baxter, Amos	42	Dark mulatto 5 ft 6 1/2 in.	KY	John Cotes	Orange Co, IN	1 Sept 1853
Baxter, Allen C.	29	Dark mulatto 5 ft 4 1/2 in.	Orange Co, IN	John Cotes	Orange Co, IN	1 Sept 1853
Baxter, Sab[i]ne	7	Light mulatto	Orange Co, IN	Leanid Lindley	Orange Co, IN	1 Sept 1853
Chandler, Samuel	55	Mulatto 6 ft 1 1/2 in. high.	NC	John Cotes	Orange Co, IN	1 Sept 1853
Chandler, Martha	49	About 5 ft 8 1/2 ins. high, light mulatto	NC	John Cotes	Orange Co, IN	1 Sept 1853
Chandler, Leanid	14	Very light mulatto	Orange Co, IN	John Cotes	Orange Co, IN	1 Sept 1853
Chandler, Sina J.	13	Light mulatto	Orange Co, IN	John Cotes	Orange Co, IN	1 Sept 1853
Chandler, David	14	Very light mulatto	Orange Co, IN	John Cotes	Orange Co, IN	1 Sept 1853
Chandler, Martha A.	8	Bright mulatto	Orange Co, IN	John Cotes	Orange Co, IN	1 Sept 1853
Chandler, Joyce A.	7	Bright mulatto	Orange Co, IN	John Cotes	Orange Co, IN	1 Sept 1853
Sweat, Nancy	29	Bright mulatto 5 ft 9 ins.	NC	John Cotes	Orange Co, IN	1 Sept 1853

Name	Age	Description	Place 1	Place 2	Recorder	Date
Sweat, Mary Ann	9 mos.	Light mulatto	Orange Co, IN	Orange Co, IN	Oliver Lindley	1 Sept 1853
Weaver, Clemenda	6	Bright mulatto	Orange Co, IN	Orange Co, IN	John Cotes	1 Sept 1853
Roberts, Lucretia	65	Mulatto 5 ft 4 1/2 ins.	NC	Orange Co, IN	John Cotes	1 Sept 1853
Roberts, Umphrey	26	Dark mulatto 5 ft 10 1/2 ins	NC	Orange Co, IN	John Cotes	1 Sept 1853
Roberts, Lucretia (II)	6	Mulatto	Orange Co, IN	Orange Co, IN	John Cotes	1 Sept 1853
Roberts, Anna	24	Light mulatto, 5 ft 4 1/2 ins.	NC	Orange Co, IN	John Cotes	1 Sept 1853
Roberts, James	1	Light mulatto	Orange Co, IN	Orange Co, IN	James Danner	1 Sept 1853
Roberts, Sarah C.	8	Light mulatto	NC	Orange Co, IN	John Cotes	1 Sept 1853
Roberts, Archie	5	Light mulatto	NC	Orange Co, IN	John Cotes	1 Sept 1853
Roberts, Alice	4	Bright mulatto	Orange Co, IN	Orange Co, IN	John Cotes	1 Sept 1853
Dungill, Wright	26	Light Mulatto, 6 ft high	NC	Orange Co, IN	John Cotes	1 Sept 1853
Dungill, Betsy	19	Light Mulatto, 5 ft high	Orange Co, IN	Orange Co, IN	John Cotes	1 Sept 1853
Roberts, James	25	Dark Mulatto, 6 ft 1/2 inch high	NC	Orange Co, IN	James Danner	1 Sept 1853
Roberts, Unity	26	Mulatto, 5 ft 1 inch high	NC	Orange Co, IN	Albert Johnson	1 Sept 1853
Roberts, Martha M.	2	Mulatto	Orange Co, IN	Orange Co, IN	James Danner	1 Sept 1853
Clark, Henry	20	Mulatto	Orange Co, IN	Orange Co, IN	Jeremiah Wilson	5 Sept 1853
Roberts, Wiley	50	About 5 ft 5 1/2 ins, light mulatto	NC	Orange Co, IN	J. S. Merritt	5 Sept 1853
Roberts, Mary	40	About 5 ft 5 high, light mulatto	NC	Orange Co, IN	J. S. Merritt	5 Sept 1853
Roberts, Jnoth P.	14	Light mulatto	Orange Co, IN	Orange Co, IN	J. S. Merritt	5 Sept 1853
Roberts, Allen	12	A light mulatto	Orange Co, IN	Orange Co, IN	Jonathan P. Chambers	5 Sept 1853
Roberts, Bryant	9	Light mulatto	Orange Co, IN	Orange Co, IN	Jonathan P. Chambers	5 Sept 1853

Name	Age	Description	Birthplace	Residence	Registered by	Date
Roberts, Mary C.	7	Light mulatto	Orange Co, IN	Orange Co, IN	Jonathan P. Chambers	5 Sept 1853
Clark, Frederick	18	Light mulatto about 5 ft 5 high	Orange Co, IN	Orange Co, IN	John C. Albert	5 Sept 1853
Roberts, Sarah	60	Dark mulatto 5 ft 4 ins.	NC	Orange Co, IN	Hiram Braxton	7 Sept 1853
Guthrie, James	56	Full blooded African 6 ft high	NC	Orange Co, IN	Jnoth. L. Jones	7 Sept 1853
Clark, Lucy	50	Full blooded negro 5 ft 1/2 in.	NC	Orange Co, IN	Jeremiah Wilson	9 Sept 1853
Johnson, Lovina	31	Mulatto 5 ft 5 ins. high	NC	Orange Co, IN	Jeremiah Wilson	9 Sept 1853
Johnson, Andrew J.	13	Dark mulatto	Orange Co, IN	Orange Co, IN	Jeremiah Wilson	9 Sept 1853
Johnson, Catharine	11	Dark mulatto	Orange Co, IN	Orange Co, IN	Jeremiah Wilson	9 Sept 1853
Johnson, Sarah E.	9	Dark mulatto	Orange Co, IN	Orange Co, IN	Jeremiah Wilson	9 Sept 1853
Johnson, Wm. H.	7	Dark mulatto	Orange Co, IN	Orange Co, IN	Jeremiah Wilson	9 Sept 1853
Johnson, Jno. W.	5	Dark mulatto	Orange Co, IN	Orange Co, IN	Jeremiah Wilson	9 Sept 1853
Means, Fanny L.	17	Dark mulatto	Orange Co, IN	Orange Co, IN	Jer. Wilson	9 Sept 1853
Hawkins, Jer	60	Mulatto, heavy built, 5 ft. 5 ins.	VA	Orange Co, IN	Jer. Wilson	9 Sept 1853
Hattaway, John	30	Light mulatto 5 ft 10 ins.	Orange Co, IN	Orange Co, IN	Jer. Wilson	10 Sept 1853
Scott, Alvin	37	Quite light mulatto 5 ft 5 1/2 ins.	NC	Orange Co, IN	Benjn M. Pritchard	10 Sept 1853
Scott, Elizabeth	16	Dark mulatto	NC	Orange Co, IN	Benjn M. Pritchard	10 Sept 1853
Scott, Sarah A.	10	Very light mulatto	Orange Co, IN	Orange Co, IN	Benjn M. Pritchard	10 Sept 1853
Scott, Berry	9	Light mulatto	Orange Co, IN	Orange Co, IN	Benjn M. Pritchard	10 Sept 1853
Scott, Ruel	5	Light mulatto	Orange Co, IN	Orange Co, IN	Benjn M. Pritchard	10 Sept 1853
Thomas, Jordan	37 1/2	About 3/4 negro blood, 5 ft 5 1/2 ins high	NC	Orange Co, IN	Simon Dixon	15 Sept 1853
Thomas, Candis	36 1/2	Light mulatto 5 ft 5 1/2.	NC	Orange Co, IN	Simon Dixon	15 Sept 1853

Name	Age	Description	Birthplace	Witness	Residence	Date
Thomas, Mary E.	13	Mulatto	Vigo Co, IN	Jnoth P. Chambers	Orange Co, IN	15 Sept 1853
Thomas, Benjamin T.	11	Dark mulatto	Vigo Co, IN	Jnoth P. Chambers	Orange Co, IN	15 Sept 1853
Thomas, Wm. A.	6 1/2	Dark mulatto	Vigo Co, IN	Jnoth P. Chambers	Orange Co, IN	15 Sept 1853
Scott, Alfred	24	Mulatto, almost white, very fair, 5 ft 5 in high	NC	James Hallowell	Orange Co, IN	17 Sept 1853
Scott, Martha J.	16 1/2	Mulatto, almost white, very fair, 5 ft 5 in high	VA	James Hallowell	Orange Co, IN	17 Sept 1853
Todd, Pearson	43	About 5 ft 8 1/2 in high, full blooded negro	KY	Henry R. Williamson	Orange Co, IN	19 Sept 1853
Todd, Malvina	32 1/2	Mulatto, about 5 ft 1 in high	Ky	Henry R. Williamson	Orange Co, IN	19 Sept 1853
Todd, Morris B.	--	Near full blooded African	Orange Co, IN	Henry R. Williamson	Orange Co, IN	19 Sept 1853
Todd, Amanda J.	9 1/2	Mulatto	Orange Co, IN	Henry R. Williamson	Orange Co, IN	19 Sept 1853
Todd, Wm. P. Q.	8	Mulatto	Orange Co, IN	Henry R. Williamson	Orange Co, IN	19 Sept 1853
Todd, Hiram H.	6	Mulatto	Orange Co, IN	Henry R. Williamson	Orange Co, IN	19 Sept 1853
Todd, John E.	3 1/2	Mulatto	Orange Co, IN	Henry R. Williamson	Orange Co, IN	19 Sept 1853
Walker, Charles	68 1/2	Negro 5 ft 7 1/2 in high	VA	Elizabeth Taylor	Orange Co, IN	19 Sept 1853
Walker, Jane	68	Negro 5 ft 6 in high	KY	Elizabeth Taylor	Orange Co, IN	19 Sept 1853
Taylor, Hiram	16	Mulatto	--	Elizabeth Taylor	Orange Co, IN	19 Sept 1853
Bonds, Penelope	50	Negro five feet high	NC	Davey Clendenin	Orange Co, IN	23 Sept 1853
Bonds, Jno W.	24 1/2	Mulatto 5 ft 4 ins. high	SC	Davey Clendenin	Orange Co, IN	23 Sept 1853
Bonds, Monroe	14	Mulatto	Orange Co, IN	Davey Clendenin	Orange Co, IN	23 Sept 1853
Butler, Thomas	86 1/2	5 ft 7 1/2 high, full blooded Negro	MD	Arthur J. Simpson	Orange Co, IN	4 Oct 1853
Lynch, Martha	39	5 ft 1 in high, mulatto with European blood	NC	Arthur J. Simpson	Orange Co, IN	8 Oct 1853
Lynch, Mila	18	Dark color with Indian blood	NC	Vincent Moore	Orange Co, IN	8 Oct 1853

50

Name	Age	Description				Witness	Date
Husbands, Laura	21	5 ft 2 1/2 ins, almost full blooded negro, part Indiana	NC		Orange Co, IN	Arthur J. Simpson	8 Oct 1853
Scott, Martin Sr.	75	Mulatto, half white blood, about 5 ft 8 3/4 in high, scar on left breast.	NC		Orange Co, IN	Cornelius White	4 Nov 1853
Scott, Joseph	37	Mulatto, 3/4 white blood, about 5 ft 5 in high, mole on neck in front.	NC		Orange Co, IN	Cornelius White	4 Nov 1853
Scott, Isaac	52	About half white blood 5 ft 10 ins.	NC		Orange Co, IN	Aaron Andrew	10 Nov 1853
Roberts, Giliann	14 1/2	Mulatto of slender form	NC		Orange Co, IN	Benjn. M. Pritchard	17 Nov 1853
Roberts, Jno. L.	28	About 5 ft 11 ins, mulatto	NC		Howard Co, IN	Benjn. M. Pritchard	17 Nov 1853
Burnett, Enoch	18	Light mulatto	NC		Orange Co, IN	Josiah Hazlewood	17 Nov 1853
Roberts, Wm. R.	22	Light mulatto 5 ft 10 1/2 ins		Orange Co, IN	Orange Co, IN	Charles McVey	11 March 1854
Scott, John M.	12	Light mulatto rather slender		Orange Co, IN	Orange Co, IN	William Hill	2 Aug 1854
Scott, Daniel I.	10	Light mulatto		Orange Co, IN	Orange Co, IN	William Hill	2 Aug 1854
Scott, Jemima	46	Light mulatto high cheek bones 5 ft	NC		Orange Co, IN	Oliver Lindsey	3 Aug 1854
Scott, Joseph K.	21	Mulatto 5 ft 8 1/4 in high	NC		Orange Co, IN	Oliver Lindsey	3 Aug 1854
Scott, Elizabeth	20	Mulatto 5 ft 2 3/4 in high	NC		Orange Co, IN	Oliver Lindsey	3 Aug 1854
Scott, Zachariah L.	18	Mulatto		Orange Co, IN	Orange Co, IN	Oliver Lindsey	3 Aug 1854
Scott, Sanders J.	16	Dark mulatto slender made		Orange Co, IN	Orange Co, IN	Oliver Lindsey	3 Aug 1854
Scott, Needham L.	14	Light mulatto		Orange Co, IN	Orange Co, IN	Oliver Lindsey	3 Aug 1854
Scott, Doctor F.	7	Light mulatto		Orange Co, IN	Orange Co, IN	Oliver Lindsey	3 Aug 1854
Scott, Mary A.	3	Mulatto spine disease		Orange Co, IN	Orange Co, IN	Oliver Lindsey	3 Aug 1854
Wright, Edmund	57	Full blooded African		Franklin Co, NC	Orange Co, IN	Jesse Field	Nov 1856

Name	Age	Description	Birthplace	Residence	Surety	Date
Hart, John O.	20 1/2	Light mulatto 5 ft 11 inches	Granville Co, NC	Orange Co, IN	James Butler	17 Nov 1856
Goins, Sinajane	19	A mulatto 5 feet and 5 ins, small scar on the upper lip and left cheek.	Washington Co, IN	Orange Co, IN	Elias Lindley	10 June 1861

NOTES

1. Earlier version of material in this chapter was published in *The Journal of the Afro-American Historical and Genealogical Society*, 1986 (Summer), 7-2, 88-94.

2. "An Act to enforce the 13th article of the Constitution," approved June 18, 1852, in *The Statutes of the State of Indiana*, James Gavin and Oscar B. Hord, eds., (Indianapolis, Second edition, 1870), I, 443-44. Further provisions of Article XIII voided all contracts made with a person coming into the state in violation of the Article, subjected persons who employed such Negroes or encouraged them to stay in the state to fines ranging up to $500, and provided that money collected from such fines should be used to colonize Negroes already in the state. Emma Lou Thornbrough, *The Negro in Indiana*, 55-91.

3. Tentative findings from this research were published by Coy D. Robbins, "Lick Creek Settlement: An Early Black Community in Orange County," *Black History News and Notes*, 8 (February 1982), 8; 9 (May 1982) 8.

4. Barnhardt and Carmony, *Indiana from Frontier to Industrial Commonwealth*, I, 414-15.

52

CHAPTER VII

CIVIL WAR SOLDIERS

Persons of African descent fought in every American war before the outbreak of the Civil War. They battled in the colonial wars (1528-1774), in the Revolution (1775-1783), in the War of 1812 (1812-1815), and in the Seminole Wars (1816-1842).

Until the Civil War, however, they were never a part of the official military establishment of the United States. Africans helped out in times of crisis, but after the crisis they reverted to what they had been before: slaves or free colored persons. The regular army was closed to them. States laws, as in Indiana, excluded Blacks from joining the militia because militiamen bore arms.

It was during the Civil War that Africans permanently won the right to fight for America. Since then they became an official part of the regular army and have served in the militia in some states. The end of segregated service in the several branches of the armed forces of the United States, nevertheless, was not achieved until the Korean War in 1951.[1]

Until very recent years the presence of Africans as soldiers in the Civil War remained an obscure chapter in American history. Early literature treated this subject obliquely, rarely mentioning their military participation and exploits. As a result the general public harbored much misconception, misunderstanding, and misinformation about Black soldiers and sailors. The true story of their involvement in the Nation's war efforts has oftentimes been either forgotten, or badly twisted, distorted and mutilated. Standard history books and some of the revered specialized studies of the Civil War made no more than a passing reference to the African soldiers.

Official War Department military reports showed that over 180,000 African Americans served in the Union Army and over 30,000 more served with the Union Navy during the Civil War. While the bulk of these soldiers and sailors came from the three and a half million enslaved Africans in Southern states, free men of African descent living in both the North and South also served in the Civil War.[2] In addition, free and enslaved Africans in the South wore the military and naval uniforms of the Confederate States of America.

28th Infantry Regiment, U. S. Colored Troops

African American males from seventy-three Indiana counties served in the Union Army during the Civil War. The majority were in the Twenty-Eighth Regiment of the United States Colored Troops (U.S.C.T).

It was not until November 30, 1863 that the War Department authorized Indiana to start recruiting colored soldiers. Soon military personnel in Indianapolis organized six companies totaling five hundred and eighteen enlisted men. Thirty-nine white officers were in charge of these companies

MAP: Civil War Travels of Indiana U. S. Colored Soldiers

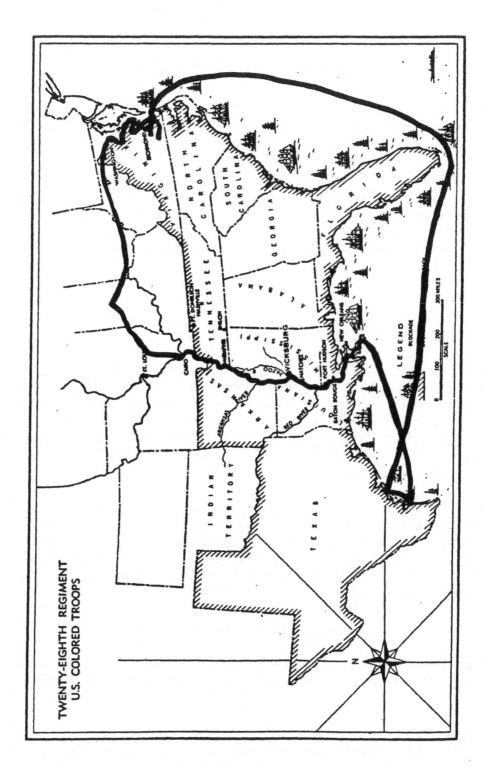

(Map reprinted, by permission, from Joe H. Burgess, *Hamilton County and the Civil War*, Noblesville, IN, 1967)

which formed a battalion of the Twenty-Eighth Regiment, U. S. Colored Troops. An Indianapolis resident, Lieutenant Colonel Charles S. Russell, headed the battalion when it left for Washington, D. C. on April 24, 1864.[3]

Men later recruited in Maryland brought the 28th to full regimental strength. They spent several weeks encamped near Alexandria, Virginia while the new recruits underwent military drills and preparations for active field service.

The 28th Regiment had its first engagement with the enemy starting in June, 1864. At what was called the "White House" battle in eastern Virginia, the regiment suffered severe losses. Afterwards while assigned to the Ninth Army Corps, it fought during the summer and fall of 1864 in the military campaign against Petersburg. Nearly half of its men died in the "Battle of the Crater" or from battlefield injuries.

Under the quota calls of July and December, 1864, some colored men in Indiana were accepted as substitutes for drafted white men. These men joined the colored regiments already operating in the field.[4]

The 28th Regiment also engaged the enemy at Hatcher's Run, and it performed duties with the Quartermaster's Department at City Point, Virginia. Here it remained until the final siege against the Confederates in Richmond. The 28th Regiment was among the first military units to enter that city after its fall.

When peace came the regiment was a part of the Twenty-Fifth Army Corps. They went by sea to Texas and disembarked at Brazos Santiago on July 1, 1865. They remained in Texas until November 8, 1865 when the men mustered out of service. The 28th Regiment returned home as an unit to Indianapolis, via New Orleans, Louisiana and Cairo, Illinois.

Its original strength was 950 enlisted men plus a 1,624 additional recruits. Losses were by death: 218, by desertion: 87, and unaccounted for: 865.

Men from Indiana served in other units of the United States Colored Troops besides the Twenty-Eighth Regiment. These included the Eighth, Thirteenth, Fourteenth, Seventeenth, Twenty-Third and Sixty-Fifth Infantry Regiments, and the Fourth Heavy Artillery Regiment.

Outside the state, African men from Indiana fought also with the First Michigan and the Fourteenth Rhode Island U. S. Colored Troops, as well as in the Massachusetts Fifty-Fourth Regiment. The 1990 Hollywood motion picture production, *Glory*, dramatized the military experiences of Black soldiers in the Massachusetts famous Fifty-Fourth and Fifty-Fifth Regiments who fought at Fort Wagner, South Carolina.

It should never be forgotten that Black men possessed an extraordinary amount of courage to join the Union Army during the Civil War. In addition to enduring the usual hardships of military regimen, they received unequal pay, unfair work duties, inadequate equipment, inferior medical care, and severely limited opportunities for military advancement.[5]

Black soldiers oftentimes faced constant racial slurs from white officers and enlisted men whenever they shared the battlefield to fight a common enemy. More significant yet were the gruesome realities of what would happen to them in event of capture by the Confederates. Unlike their white counterparts, Blacks were rarely held captive in southern prison camps. After surrender, they were frequently shot to death by captors on the battlefields, even though the submission was under the direct orders of their white army officers.[6]

Orange County Men in the U.S.C.T.

The rosters of enlisted men in the United States Colored Troops found in the State Archives, Indiana Commission on Public Records contained information about twenty five soldiers from Orange County. All held the rank of private at the time of discharge and most were assigned to Companies D (12), E (5), and F (3).[7] Data copied from these files appear below.

BURDEN, HENRY

Rank: Private. Company F, 28th Regiment. Enrolled: March 20, 1864 at Grant Co, IN. Mustered in: March 31, 1864 at Indianapolis by Lt. Thatcher. Age: 19. Eyes: Grey. Hair: Black. Height: 5'7" Complexion: Light. Nativity: Grant Co, IN. Occupation: Farmer. Single. Residence: Orange Co. Died September 2, 1864 at Alexandria, VA consumption.

BURNETT, ARCHEY

Rank: Private. Company D, 28th Regiment. Enrolled: January 6, 1864 at Paoli. Mustered in: January 15, 1864 at Indianapolis by Lt. Melburn. Age: 21. Eyes: Black. Hair: Black. Height: 5'6" Complexion: Black. Nativity: Orange Co, IN. Occupation: Teamster. Single. Residence: Paoli, IN. Mustered out: November 8, 1865.

CALHOUN, MIKE

Rank: Private. Company and Regiment: Not reported. Enrolled: October 26, 1864 at Jeffersonville, IN by Capt. Meriwither for one year. Mustered in: October 26, 1864 at Jeffersonville. Age: 18. Eyes: Black. Hair: Black. Height: 5'3" Complexion: Black. Nativity: Georgia. Occupation: Laborer. Comments: Substitute for Andrew Wilson drafted from Orangeville Township, Orange Co., IN. No mustered out date given in record, but a note indicated that pay for this soldier was sent to Orangeville, Orange Co., IN.

CHAVERS, HENRY

Rank: Private. Company F, 28th Regiment. Enrolled: January 4, 1864 at Orange Co., IN. Mustered in: March 31, 1864 at Indianapolis by Lt. Thatcher. Age: 19. Eyes: Black. Hair: Black. Height: 5'10" Complexion: Black. Nativity: Orange, IN. Single. Residence: Orange Co., IN. Mustered out: November 8, 1865.

CLARK, FREDERICK

Rank: Private. Company E, 28th Regiment. Enrolled: January 27, 1864 at Indianapolis. Mustered in: February 5, 1864 at Indianapolis by Lt. Mills. Age: 29. Eyes: Brown. Hair: Black. Height: 5'7" Complexion: Light. Nativity: Orange Co., IN. Occupation: Farmer. Married. Residence: Indianapolis. Mustered out: November 8, 1865 at Corpus Christi, TX.

CLARK, HENRY

Rank: Private. Company E, 28th Regiment. Enrolled: January 27, 1864 at Indianapolis. Mustered in: February 5, 1864 at Indianapolis. Age: 30. Eyes: Brown. Hair: Black. Height: 5'6" Complexion: Light. Nativity: Orange Co., IN. Occupation: Farmer. Married. Residence:

Indianapolis. Mustered out: November 8, 1865 at Corpus Christi, TX.

COOK, HEZEKIAH

Rank: Private. Company D, 28th Regiment. Enrolled: January 7, 1864 at Richmond, IN. Mustered in: January 15, 1864 at Indianapolis, IN. by Capt. Thatcher. Age: 24. Eyes: Black. Hair: Black. Height: 5'9" Complexion: Brown. Nativity: Mariette, OH. Occupation: Farmer. Single. Residence: Paoli. Mustered out: November 8, 1865 at Corpus Christi, TX.

EVANS, PLEASANT

Rank: Private. Company D, 28th Regiment. Enrolled: January 4, 1864 at Paoli, IN. Mustered in: January 15, 1864 at Indianapolis, IN. by Lt. Melburn. Age: 21. Eyes: Black. Hair: Black. Height: 5'7" Complexion: Black. Nativity: Washington, IN. Occupation: Farmer. Married. Residence: Paoli, IN. Mustered out: November 8, 1865 at Corpus Christi, TX.

EVANS, SAMUEL

Rank: Private. Company D, 28th Regiment. Enrolled: January 4, 1864 at Paoli. Mustered in: January 1, 1864 at Indianapolis, IN. by Lt. Melburn. Age: 25. Eyes: Black. Hair: Black. Height: 5'6" Complexion: Black. Nativity: Washington, IN. Occupation: Farmer. Married. Residence: Paoli. Mustered out: November 8, 1865 at Corpus Christi, TX.

GUTHRIE, WILLIAM

Rank: Private. Company D, 28th Regiment. Enrolled: January 4, 1864 at Paoli. Mustered in: January 15, 1864 at Indianapolis, IN. by Lt. Melburn. Age: 18. Eyes: Black. Hair: Black. Height: 6'1" Complexion: Black. Nativity: Orange Co., IN. Occupation: Farmer. Single. Residence: Paoli. Mustered out: November 8, 1865 at Corpus Christi, TX.

HARDEN, WILLIAM

Rank: Private. Company D, 28th Regiment. Enrolled: January 4, 1864 at Paoli. Mustered in January 15, 1864 at Indianapolis, IN. by Lt. Melburn. Age: 36. Eyes: Black. Hair: Black. Height: 5'11" Complexion: Brown. Nativity: TN. Occupation: Farmer. Single. Residence: Paoli. Died September 13, 1865 in hospital, New Orleans, LA.

HENRY, CHARLES

Rank: Private. Company D, 28th Regiment. Enrolled: January 4, 1864 at Paoli. Mustered in January 15, 1864 at Indianapolis, IN. by Lt. Melburn. Age: 22. Eyes: Black. Hair: Black. Height: 5'7" Complexion: Black. Nativity: Jefferson Co., IN. Occupation: Laborer. Single. Residence: Paoli, IN. Died January 23, 1864 in hospital, Indianapolis, IN.

IRVIN, ISAAC

23rd Regiment, U. S. Colored Troops. Mustered in February 20, 1865 and mustered out May 22, 1865. Residence: Orange Co., IN.

LOCUST, SIMON

Rank: Private. Company E, 13th Regiment Infantry. <u>Drafted</u> from Orange Co., IN on September 23, 1864 for one year. Mustered in October 15, 1864 at Jeffersonville, IN. by Capt. Meriwether. Age: 40. Eyes: Black. Hair: Black. Height: 5'9" Complexion: Black. Nativity: Orange Co., IN. Occupation: Farmer. Mustered out: October 18, 1865 at Nashville, TN. expiration of term of service. Discharged to Stampers Creek, Orange Co., IN.

PORTER, JAMES

13th Regiment, Infantry, U. S. Colored Troops. Sent as a substitute from Orange Co., IN. Mustered in April 4, 1865 and mustered out May 23, 1865. Residence: Orange Co., IN.

REED, PETER

Rank: Private. Unassigned Recruits, U. S. Colored Troops. Enrolled: October 12, 1864 at Jeffersonville, IN. as a substitute for Alexander Smith, who was drafted in Northeast Twp., Orange Co., IN. Mustered in October 12, 1864 at Jeffersonville, IN by Capt. Merriwether for one year. Age: 29. Eyes: Age: Black. Hair: Black. Height: 5'4" Complexion: Black. Nativity: KY. Occupation: Laborer. Residence: Orange Co., IN.

ROPER, JOHN

Rank: Private. Company D, 28th Regiment. Enrolled: January 4, 1864 at Paoli. Mustered in January 15, 1864 at Indianapolis, IN. by Lt. Melburn. Age: 27. Eyes: Black. Hair: Black. Height: 5'6" Complexion: Black. Nativity: Lawrence Co., IN. Occupation: Laborer. Single. Residence: Paoli, IN. Mustered out: November 8, 1865 at Corpus Christi, TX.

SHIRLEY, WILLIAM

Rank: Private. Company E, 28th Regiment. Enrolled: January 27, 1864 at Indianapolis, IN. Mustered in February 5, 1864 at Indianapolis, IN. by Lt. Mills. Age: 19. Eyes: Black. Hair: Black. Height: 5'6" Complexion: Black. Nativity: Orange Co., IN. Occupation: Farmer. Single. Residence: Indianapolis. Died June 29, 1864 at Alexandria, VA.

SMITH, LEWIS

Rank: Sergeant. Company F, 28th Regiment. Mustered in March 31, 1864. Residence: Orange Co., IN. Mustered out: November 8, 1865 at Corpus Christi, TX.

THOMPSON, THOMAS M.

23rd Regiment, Infantry, U. S. Colored Troops. Mustered in February 20, 1865. Residence: Orange Co., IN. Mustered out: May 22, 1865.

TOLIVER, GEORGE W.

Rank: Private. Company D, 28th Regiment. Enrolled: January 1, 1864 at Paoli, IN. Mustered in January 15, 1864 at Indianapolis, IN. by Lt. Melburn. Age: 27. Eyes: Black. Hair: Black. Height: 5'5" Complexion: Black. Nativity: Spencer Co., IN. Occupation: Laborer. Single. Residence: Orange Co., IN. Died February 12, 1865 in hospital, City Point, VA.

WALDEN, JOSEPH

Rank: Private. Company D, 28th Regiment. Enrolled: December 31, 1864 at Paoli, IN. Mustered in January 15, 1864 at Indianapolis, IN. by Lt. Melburn. Age: 25. Eyes: Black. Hair: Black. Height: 5'6" Complexion: Black. Nativity: Spencer Co., IN. Occupation: Laborer. Married. Discharged on October 31, 1864 on Surgeon Certificate of Disability.

WASHINGTON, GEORGE

Rank: Private. Company D, 28th Regiment. Enrolled: January 1, 1864 at Paoli, IN. Mustered in January 15, 1864 at Indianapolis, IN. by Lt. Melburn. Age: 25. Eyes: Black. Hair: Black. Height: 5'8" Complexion: Black. Nativity: Spencer Co., IN. Occupation: Laborer. Single. Residence: Paoli, IN. Discharged February 26, 1865 from hospital, Alexandria, VA.

WASHINGTON, THOMAS

Rank: Private. Company D, 28th Regiment. Enrolled: January 11, 1864 at Paoli, IN. Mustered in January 15, 1864 at Indianapolis, IN. by Lt. Melburn. Age: 25. Eyes: Black. Hair: Black. Height: 5'8" Complexion: Black. Nativity: Madison, IN. Occupation: Laborer. Single. Residence: Paoli. Died February 26, 1864 in hospital, Indianapolis, IN.

WILSON, JOHN

Rank: Private. Company E, 28th Regiment. Enrolled: January 8, 1864 at Indianapolis, IN. Mustered in February 5, 1864 at Indianapolis, IN. by Lt. Mills, Age: 22. Eyes: Dark. Hair: Dark. Height: 5'6" Complexion: Dark. Nativity: Wayne Co., IN. Occupation: Laborer. Residence: Orange Co., IN. Deserted on April 20, 1864 at Indianapolis, IN.

What Happened to These Veterans?

At least five of these soldiers died or were killed in battle during the Civil War: *Henry Burden, William Harden, Charles Henry, George W. Toliver,* and *Thomas Washington.*

In the course of this research information was gathered about other soldiers. *Archibald Burnett* returned to Orange County, married Mary Sweat, and they lived in Paoli where he worked as a teamster (Census data, Marriage records). He died there on September 23, 1900 and is buried in the Friends (Quaker) Newberry Cemetery, two miles west of Paoli.

Pleasant Evans married Clorinda Weaver during the war, and afterwards they settled in Owen County, Indiana. After barbering for four years in Spencer, he joined a barber shop in Bloomington, Indiana around 1884. Eventually he headed the shop and bought the downtown building where it was located. Following Clorinda's death in 1892, Pleasant married Mary Edith PORTER of Indianapolis and they continued to live in Spencer, Indiana. He died in 1927 after working over forty years as a Bloomington barber. He was buried in Riverside Cemetery in Spencer. (Pension records) Pleasant had at least seven children and some of his descendants are known to be living in Bloomington, Indiana and Chicago, Illinois.

Simon Locust returned to his farm in Stampers Creek Township, Orange County. He died there on September 24, 1891 and is said to be the last person buried in the Lick Creek Settlement cemetery near Chambersburg. Following the death of his first wife around 1882, Simon remarried and his widow continued to receive his pension. (Pension records).

After the Civil War ended, *John Wilson* married Rebecca Burnett and they remained in Paoli where he worked as a laborer. In the 1870s the family which by now consisted of several children moved to Bloomfield (Greene County), Indiana. Several years later they settled in Spencer (Owen County), Indiana where he died on January 30, 1884. He is buried in what is known today as the Wilson Cemetery, several miles west of Spencer. (Marriage and pension records).

Black Soldiers from Nearby Counties

At the same time African descendants in Orange County were sending their sons, brothers, husbands, fathers and boy friends to the Civil War, others in surrounding counties did likewise as indicated by the tabular summary in Table 11. Thirty-five percent of the Black Civil War soldiers came from Orange County, followed by the twenty-four percent from Washington County and the twenty-two percent from Harrison County.

TABLE 11: Distribution of Soldiers by Residences
in Counties Surrounding Orange

Crawford	1
Dubois	10
Harrison	16
Lawrence	2
Martin	2
ORANGE	25
Washington	18
Total Number of Soldiers from Area	74

It can only be speculated why the military contingent from Orange County exceeded in number those from other counties. One possible explanation may relate to the distribution of the adult Black males living in these counties during the Civil War period.

Contrabands or Citizens?

The commitment of Northern Blacks to Civil War military service was most impressive. More than 34,000 men of African descent from northern states served in the Union Army--over fifteen percent of the entire free Black population in 1860--an extremely high rate.

National Black leaders led by Frederick Douglass supported the war vigorously. They urged Black men to join the Union Army to aid their downtrodden brothers and to preserve the union. Many responded, believing such participation would greatly benefit their race and nation.[8]

Once the national government decided finally in 1863 to recruit African American soldiers, Blacks in the North became subject to military draft and could serve as substitutes for Northern whites, frequently for less money than the white substitutes.

The presence of Indiana's African American soldiers with the Union Army has been discounted by some historians who called these men "contrabands." Early in the Civil War northern generals employed this term to identify large numbers of enslaved persons, both males and females, who escaped into the Union lines or who came freely into their camps as the military troops advanced into the Confederacy.[9] Long after the fighting ceased, prejudiced historians exploited the term to play down the involvement of African Americans in the war efforts.

An example of the "contraband" labeling is found in Charles Blanchard's 1884 history of Morgan County, Indiana. He reported accurately that thirty-three colored men from Washington Township in Morgan County were with the Union troops in the Civil War. The account continued by reporting that local citizens hired these men at $100 each to represent the county. Supposedly, only four or five of them actually came from Morgan County and the others were "partly countrabands from the South."[10]   Recent research findings in the county discredited this longstanding local history statement.

TABLE 12

Distribution of Nativity Report by Soldiers
From Orange County, Indiana

County or State	Number
Orange County, Ind	9
Daviess County, Ind	1
Spencer County, Ind	3
Lawrence County, Ind	1
Jefferson County, Ind	2
Grant County, Ind	1
Wayne County, Ind	1
Ohio (Mariette)	1
Kentucky	1
Georgia	1
Not reported	4
Total	25

In case similar myths also endured in Orange County, the nativity or birthplace data reported in archival records for the above soldiers were tabulated to determine how many of them were native Hoosiers (Table 12).

Over sixty percent of these soldiers were born in Indiana and could never be classified as "contrabands." Distribution of findings by counties shows further that thirty-six percent of them were born in Orange County, and another twenty-eight percent in nearby Indiana counties. The vast majority, without a doubt, were born in the North. Only two reported birthplaces in the slave states of Kentucky and Georgia, and both men could have been free Indiana residents before they entered military service.

The contraband labeling of Black soldiers was unjust. It represented another deliberate attempt to distort the role in history of Indiana's minorities. It served successfully to help create the false impression that free African Americans in the North did not fight in the Civil War. Furthermore, by implication, it helped to sustain the common myth that African Americans did not come into Indiana until after 1863 when Lincoln freed the slaves, another historical event which was immensely romanticized and inaccurately reported in the history books.

Discovering these historical inaccuracies is troublesome today. We may eventually learn how they were used effectively to influence Hoosiers in overlooking the courage required for free Black men in the state to volunteer and fight in the segregated Union Army. By the way Simon Locust from Orange County never volunteered--actually he was drafted.

NOTES

1. Robert Ewell Greene, *Black Defenders of America, 1775-1973: A Reference and Pictorial History*, (Chicago: Johnson Publishing Co., 1974), Jack D. Foner, *Blacks and the Military in American History*, (New York: Praeger Publishers, 1974), and Department of Defense, *Black Americans in Defense of our Nation* (Washington, DC., U. S. Government Printing Office, 1985).

2. Enrollment figures in the U. S. Colored Troops for selected states: Indiana, 1,537; Ohio, 5,092; Illinois, 1,811; Iowa, 440; Kansas, 2,080; Michigan, 1,387; Kentucky, 23,703; and Missouri, 8,344. Taken from George W. Williams, *History of the Negro Race in America from 1619 to 1880* II, 300.

Additional writings on subject include Benjamin Quarles, *The Negro in the Civil War* (Boston: Little, Brown & Co., 1969); Thomas Wentworth Higginson, *Army life in a Black Regiment* (Boston: Beacon Press, 1869; 1970 edition); Dudley Taylor Cornish, *The Sable Arm: Negro Troops in the Union Army, 1861-1865*, (New York: W. W. Norton & Co., 1956; Norton Library edition, 1966); James M. McPherson, *The Negro's Civil War* (Urbana: University of Illinois Press, 1982); Margaret Leech, Chapter XII "Black, Copper and Bright" in *Reveille in Washington 1860-1865* (Alexandria, Va., Time-Life Books, Inc., 1980).

3. William H. H. Terrell, *Report of the Adjutant General of the State of Indiana*, III (Indianapolis: Samuel M. Douglas, State Printer, 1866), 379-383; Coy D. Robbins, "Civil War Letters (1864-1865)," *Ebony Lines*, IV-3, Fall-Winter, 1992, 20-26.

4. Terrell, *Report of the Adjutant General*, vol. I; reprint,*Indiana in the War of the Rebellion* (Indianapolis: Indiana Historical Bureau, 1960), 98-100 on recruiting practices for colored troops; 77-78 on bounty payments.

5. Joseph T. Glattharr, *Forged in Battle: The Civil War Alliance of Black Soldiers and White Officers* (New York: Free Press, 1990; reprint Meridian Books, 1991), Chap. 5, "Coping with Racism," and Chap. 9, "Prejudice in the Service."

6. Ibid., Chap. 8, "Leaving Their Mark on the Battlefield," 155-159. Wartime atrocities against colored soldiers were commonplace. One famous massacre was in April, 1864 at Ft. Pillow, on the Mississippi River north of Memphis, Tenn. Later U. S. Congressional investigations concluded that the colored troops who surrendered to the Confederates were butchered.

7. Terrell, Report of the Adjutant General, VII (1867) 668-671. Data provided for each company member were: name and rank; residence; date of muster, 1864; and remarks. Non-commissioned officers were African Americans, but none were from Orange County.

8. Frederick Douglass, former Maryland slave, edited and published the *Douglass' Monthly* at Rochester, New York. In a lengthy May, 1861 editorial, "How to End the War,' he urged the Lincoln Adminstration to "LET THE SLAVES AND FREE COLORED PEOPLE BE CALLED INTO SERVICE, AND FORMED INTO A LIBERATING ARMY, to march into the South and raise the banner of emancipation among the slaves." III, 451, as quoted in Dudley Taylor Cornish, *The Sable Arm*, 5.

9. Benjamin Quarles, *The Negro in the Civil War*, 58-77; Dudley Taylor Cornish, *The Sable Arm*, 1-28.

10. Charles Blanchard, ed., *Counties of Morgan, Monroe and Brown, Indiana* (Chicago: F. A. Battey & Co., 1884), 65.

CHAPTER VIII

MARRIAGES

Early Marriages

When Michael Mavity, justice of the peace, married Moses Archey and Polly Roberts on November 15, 1829, it became the first African American marriage on record in Orange County.

Early marriage records rarely show the race of participants. Such was the case in Orange County. The Archey-Roberts' marriage record does not contain any indication that the groom and bride were of African ancestry.

Racial confirmation, nevertheless, was found in other public documents. Data in the 1830 census identified Moses Archey as a free colored male in the age range of 36-55 years, and heading a household with four persons.

Additional early marriages in the county included: (1) Wiley Roberts, who obtained a license to marry Mary Thomas on August 21, 1830, (2) Francis Clements and Annis Martin, who were married by Rev. William W. Martin on September 28, 1831, (3) Reubon Bond to Penelope Hill by Lewis Byram on June 7, 1832, (4) Mathew Thomas, who secured a license to wed Polly Roberts on December 10, 1834, (5) Frederick Bonds and Sarah Means, who were married on November 11, 1835, (6) Elias Washington and Sabrina Roberts, who married on November 26, 1837, and (7) Jordon Thomas and Candiss Roberts on January 11, 1838.

Marriage Records Are History

When the list of marriages was accumulated, a number of research questions emerged. Did the number of marriages vary significantly during any particular decade? For instance, did marriages decline during the 1850s when state-wide efforts were made to exclude non-whites from Indiana? Were there any marriages after the 1890s when, according to one local legend, "colored people" vanished from Orange County?

Data collected in Table 13 provided answers to some questions. The peak of marriages during the antebellum period was highest in the decades of the fifties and the sixties, suggesting that in spite of the racial exclusionary efforts, marriages between African Americans continued in Orange County. The rate of marriages declined eventually during and after the Civil War. However, they never ceased after the 1890s and affirmed that the Black population did not disappear from the county.

Tabulation of the years marriage licenses were issued revealed that the frequency rate varied from one to three applications annually. For the twenty year period between 1850 and 1870, at least one marriage license was issued to a couple of African ancestry every year except in 1855, 1864, 1868 and 1869 when no applications were made.

An overall decline in the annual marriage rate started after the Civil War and continued steadily into the decades of the seventies and eighties. In the period between the years 1885 and 1907 there was a single marriage between non-whites in 1892. The rate increased slowly through the years of the first World War, and the five applications in 1915 was the largest number for any year. Participants in practically every marriage of the twentieth century lived in the West Baden Springs-French Lick resort area.

TABLE 13

Distribution of Marriage Dates
1829-1920

1820s	1
1830s	8
1840s	11
1850s	17
1860s	16
1870s	8
1880s	4
1890s	1
1900s	5
1910-1920	15

African American Marriages in Orange County

The following list was accumulated from entries in the Works Project Administration (WPA) indexes to the county's marriage records. These indexes compiled between 1939-1941 covered the period from 1829-1920 and they are available in the Orange County Clerk's Office at the Court House.

Racial designations given for entries in these indexes were validated by comparison with the names on the research *master list* before merging in this report. Data provided in brackets are from entries found in the WPA indexes.

Every effort was made to assure the accuracy of this information. Serious researchers, however, are urged to check further with the official marriage records in the Court House.

Grooms

ABEL, James R. [birthdate: July 11, 1879] to Pearl BROWN on September 18, 1907 [colored].
    Book C-12, Page 80.
ABLE, Francis M. to Sarah E. SHIRLEY on September 3, 1865. Book C-5, Page 189.
ALLEN, Laurie [birthdate: April 26, 1885] to Lillian WILLIAMS on December 25, 1913. [colored].
    Book C-16, Page 103.

ARNOLD, Rizzie [birthdate: November 3, 1886] to Nannie P. HOWARD on April 1, 1918 [colored]. Book C-18, Page 267.

ARCHEY, Moses to Polly ROBERTS on November 15, 1829. Book C-2, Page 24. Married by Michael Mavity, JP.

ARCHEY, William T. to Martha MCDONALD on October 17, 1851. Book C-3, Page 386.

BARTON, John to Frances A. SHOAF on November 18, 1877. Book C-6, Page 520.

BAXTER, Amos to Lucinda ROBERTS on September 26, 1850. Book C-3, Page 330.

BAXTER, Amos to Ellen WHITE on March 24, 1852. Book C-3, Page 408.

BEACHAM, William [birthdate: February 10, 1879] to Ella BLAINE on December 2, 1915 [colored]. Book C-17, Page 158.

BLACK, John to Nannie BASS [birthdate: October 27, 1892] on April 12, 1915 [colored]. Book C-17, Page 42.

BLACKWELL, Arthur [birthdate: December 27, 1879] to Alice GARRETT on September 11, 1907. Book C-12, Page 78.

BLACKWELL, William [birthdate: April 2, 1883] to Gertrude FRYE on May 7, 1909 [colored]. Book C-13, Page 104.

BOARDS, Robert [birthdate: September 23, 1885] to Helen BELL on January 1, 1909 [colored]. Book C-11, Page 262.

BOND, Reubon to Penelope HILL on June 7, 1832. Married by Lewis Byram. Book C-2, Page 43.

BONDS, Frederick to Sarah MEANS on November 11, 1835 by A. Micham, JP (people of color). Book C-2, Page 66.

BONDS, Monroe to Mary A. THOMAS on October 29, 1863. Book C-5, Page 57.

BONDS, Osmand to Mary GUTHRIE on August 4, 1853. Book C-3, Page 488.

BOWMAN, Henry to Martha A. BROWN on February 22, 1856. Book C-4, Page 161.

BOWMAN, Oscar to Allie BURNETT on November 10, 1885. Book C-7, Page 513.

BRIGGS, James [birthdate: May 27, 1880] to Corvella JACKSON on [no date given] [colored]. Book C-14, Page 73.

BROWN, Richard to Ella WHITE on February 5, 1865. Book C-5, Page 149.

BRYANT, C. J. [birthdate: April 24, 1876] to Rowena TODD on April 14, 1915 [colored]. Book C-17, Page 43.

BURNETT, Aaron to Charlotte ISOM on March 27, 1850. Book C-3, Page 285.

BURNETT, Archibald to Mary SWEAT on July 25, 1867. Book C-5, Page 365.

BURNETT, Enoch to Parella RICKMAN on September 29, 1861. Book C-4, Page 439.

BURNETT, James R. to Malinda ROBERTS on August 9, 1879. Book C-7, Page 87.

BURNETT, Leonard to Minerva WASHINGTON on February 2, 1873. Book C-6, Page 192.

BURNETT, Oliver to Anna ROBERTS on April 19, 1877. Book C-9, Page 192.

BURNETT, William to Amanda MAGRUDER on February 22, 1877. Book C-6, Page 471.

BUTLER, Thomas to Anna MARTIN on August 30, 1835. Book C-2, Page 4.

BUTLER, Thomas to Anna GILLIAM on September 2, 1847. Book C-2, Page 168.

CARY, William G. to Sina J. CHANDLER on April 7, 1859. Book C-4, Page 279.

CHANDLER, David to Mary BURNETT on April 25, 1867. Book C-5, Page 359.

CHAVIS, Banister to Sally ROBERTS on December 1, 1842. Book C-2, 120. Married by Benjamin Johnson, JP.

CLARK, Frederick to Ellen ROBERTS on October 23, 1860. Book C-4, Page 379.

CLARK, Henry to Fanny MEANS on October 3, 1854. Book C-4, Page 22.

CLARK, Henry to Matilda CHATHAM on July 22, 1858. Book C-4, Page 234.

CLAY, Charles B. [birthdate: April 23, 1892] to Sarah MOPPINS on May 4, 1916 [colored]. Book C-17, Page 239.

CLEMENTS, Francis to Annis MARTIN on September 28, 1831. Book C-2 Page 38. Married by William W. Martin, M.G.

CONN, Emil [birthdate: October 15, 1892] to Maggie ENGLISH on September 13, 1915 [colored]. Book C-17, Page 117.

DUGGED, William to Flora Ann ROBERTS on September 27, 1865. Book C-5, Page 201.

DUNGILL, Wright to Elizabeth ROBERTS on July 31, 1851. Book C-3, Page 374.

EVANS, Pleasant to Clorinda WEAVER on December 11, 1862 by Alexander Wallace, J.P. Book C-5, Page 37.

EVANS, WILLIAM to Lulu BURNETT on May 17, 1892. Book C-8, Page 431.

FINLEY, Charles to Mary A. BONDS [birthdate: February 2, 1885] on May 24, 1917 [colored]. Book C-18, Page 132.

GUTHRIE, James to Margaret BOWMAN on December 31, 1840. Book C-2, Page 105.

HART, John O. to Sarah C. THOMPSON on April 30, 1857. Book C-4, Page 224.

HOWARD, William J. to Ellen SWEAT on January 2, 1879. Book C-7, Page 38.

IRVINE, Isaac to Fernetta A. LOCUST on December 12, 1861. Book C-4, Page 457.

JOHNSON, Peter to Lavina CLARK (no dates given). Book C-2, Page 98.

LAWSON, Charles to Lula BURKS on (no date given) [colored]. Book C-16, Page 248.

LINDLEY, Elias to Millie MOORE. License issued August 30, 1844; no minister's return. Book C-2, Page 135.

LINDLEY, Elias to Nancy DUNGILL on April 26, 1856. Book C-4, Page 110.

LOCUST, Simon to Isabella ROBERTS on June 14, 1849. Book C-3, Page 248.

LOCUST, Simon to Florence STEWART on December 12, 1885. Book C-7, Page 520.

MCGINNIS, Finley to Artilla BLACK [birthdate: September 17, 1898] on October 13, 1916 [colored]. Book C-18, Page 32.

MILLER, William E. to Lula STOCKDALE [birthdate: April 9, 1870] on December 3, 1908 [colored]. Book C-13, Page 32.

O'BANNON, Daniel W. to Hattie BURNETT on October 23, 1881. Book C-7, Page 247.

RICHARDS, Daniel to Maggie STOCKDALE [birthdate: November 8, 1885] on January 10, 1910 [colored]. Book C-13, Page 229.

ROBERTS, Elias to Unity WEAVER on October 15, 1847. Book C-3, Page 152.

ROBERTS, Ishmael to Delana REVELS. License issued on August 12, 1844, no minister's return. Book C-2, Page 134.

ROBERTS, James H. to Unity ROBERTS on March 22, 1849. Book C-3, Page 235.

ROBERTS, Wiley to Mary THOMAS. License issued on August 21, 1830, no minister's return. Book C-2, Page 29.

ROBERTS, Zachariah to Susannah EVANS on January 23, 1851. Book C-3, Page 349.

ROSS, Soloman to Julia LOCUST on February 10, 1876. Book C-6, Page 390.

SCOTT, Alfred to Martha Jane SUTHERS on January 21, 1852. Book C-3, Page 401.

SCOTT, Alvin to Jane REVELS on March 26, 1844 by Aaron Andrew, J.P. Book C-2, Page 131.

SCOTT, Alvin to Elizabeth THOMPSON on February 26, 1852. Book C-3, Page 405.

SELDEN, William H. to Laura STUTLEY [birthdate: November 14, 1888] on May 16, 1912 [colored]. Book C-15, Page 88.

SHAW, Elbert to Maggie BLACKBURN [birthdate: December 27, 1893] on [no marriage date recorded] [colored]. Book C-20, Page 80.

SNEAD, Moses to Lucinda ISOM on October 1, 1846 Book C-2, Page 157 and on October 2, 1846 Book C-3, Page 89.

SPENCER, Ernest to Christine WAYNE [birthdate: February 13, 1900] on October 25, 1917 [colored]. Book C-18, Page 195.

TALLEY, Robert [birthdate: February 7, 1891] to Bessie WHITE on September 15, 1915 [colored]. Book C-17, Page 118.

TAYLOR, Hiram to Mary E. THOMAS on December 25, 1860. Book C-4, Page 390.

THOMAS, Jordon to Candiss ROBERTS on January 11, 1838. Married by W. Trueblood, J.P. Book C-2, Page 82.

THOMAS, Joseph to Jane LEE on October 17, 1860. Book C-3, Page 334.

THOMAS, Mathew to Polly ROBERTS. Marriage license issued on December 10, 1834 -- no minister's return. Book C-2, Page 59.

THOMAS, William to Delila BURNETT on December 19, 1880. Book C-7, Page 184.

THOMAS, William L. to Anna STEWART [birthdate: July 12, 1890] on February 18, 1918 [colored]. Book C-18, Page 249.

THOMPSON, John B. to Priscilla BROWN on October 2, 1866. Book C-4, Page 134.

THOMPSON, Thomas to Sarah CHAVIS on April 11, 1859. Book C-4, Page 280.

TOLIVER, George W. to Cornelia WILSON on October 18, 1863. Book C-5, Page 75.

WALLS, John E. to Adaline THOMAS on June 24, 1871. Book C-6, Page 85.

WASHINGTON, Elias to Sabina ROBERTS on November 26, 1837. Book C-2, Page 81.

WASHINGTON, Robert to Alice ROBERTS on December 13, 1866. Book C-5, Page 320.

WATKINS, John [birthdate: December 25, 1880] to Mattie RUDD on June 1, 1914 [colored]. Book C-16, Page 173.

WHITE, Denson to Emaline NEWBY on October 7, 1858. Book C-4, Page 247.

WHITE, Thomas to Eleanor DUGGED on April 13, 1848. Book C-2, Page 176; also Book C-3, page 183.

WILSON, John to Rebecca BURNETT on February 20, 1866. Book C-5, Page 250.

Brides

BASS, Nannie to John Black.
BELL, Helen to Robert Boards.
BLACK, Artilla to Finley McGinnis.
BLACKBURN, Maggie to Elbert Shaw.
BLAINE, Ella to William Beacham.
BONDS, Mary A. to Charles Finley.
BOWMAN, Margaret to James Guthrie.
BROWN, Martha A. to Henry Bowman.
BROWN, Pearl to James R. Abel.
BROWN, Priscilla to John B. Thompson.
BURKS, Lula to Charles Lawson.
BURNETT, Allie to Oscar Bowman.
BURNETT, Delila to William Thomas.
BURNETT, Hattie to Daniel W. O'Bannon
BURNETT, Lulu to William Evans.
BURNETT, Mary to David Chandler.
BURNETT, Rebecca to John Wilson.
CHANDLER, Sina T. to William G. Cary.
CHATHAM, Matilda to Henry Clark.
CHAVIS, Sarah to Thomas Thompson.
CLARK, Lavina to Peter Johnson.

DUGGED, Eleanor to Thomas White.
DUNGILL, Nancy to Elias Lindley.
ENGLISH, Maggie to Emil Conn.
EVANS, Susannah to Zachariah Roberts.
FRYE, Gertrude to William Blackwell.
GARRETT, Alice to Arthur Blackwell.
GILLIAM, Anna to Thomas Butler.
GUTHRIE, Mary to Osmand Bond.
HILL, Penelope to Reubon Bond
HOWARD, Nannie P. to Rizzie Arnold.
ISOM, Charlotte to Aaron Burnett.
ISOM, Lucinda to Moses Snead.
JACKSON, Corvella to James Briggs.
LEE, Jane to Joseph Taylor.
LOCUST, Fernetta A. to Isaac Irvine.
LOCUST, Julia to Soloman Ross.
MAGRUDER, Amanda to William Burnett.
MARTIN, Anna to Thomas Butler.
MARTIN, Annis to Francis Clements.
MCDONALD, Martha to William T. Archey.
MEANS, Fanny to Henry Clark.

MEANS, Sarah to Frederick Bonds.
MOPPINS, Sarah to Charles B. Clay.
MOORE, Millie to Elias Lindley.
NEWBY Emaline to Denson White.
REVELS, Delana to Ishmael Roberts.
REVELS, Jane to Alvin Scott.
RICKMAN, Parella to Enoch Burnett.
ROBERTS, Alice to Robert Washington.
ROBERTS, Anna to Oliver Burnett.
ROBERTS, Candiss to Jordon Thomas.
ROBERTS, Elizabeth to Wright Dungill.
ROBERTS, Ellen to Frederick Clark.
ROBERTS, Flora Ann to William Dugged.
ROBERTS, Isabella to Simon Locust.
ROBERTS, Lucinda to Amos Baxter.
ROBERTS, Malinda to James R. Burnett.
ROBERTS, Polly to Moses Archey.
ROBERTS, Polly to Mathew Thomas.
ROBERTS, Sabina to Elias Washington.
ROBERTS, Sally to Banister Chavis.
ROBERTS, Unity to James H. Roberts.
RUDD, Mattie to John Watkins.
SHIRLEY, Sarah E. to Francis M. Able.
SHOAF, Frances A. to John Barton.
STEWARD, Anna to William L. Thomas.

STEWART, Florence to Simon Locust.
STOCKDALE, Lula to William E. Miller.
STOCKDALE, Maggie to Daniel Richards.
STUTLEY, Laura to William H. Selden.
SUTHERS, Martha Jane to Alfred Scott.
SWEAT, Ellen to William J. Howard.
SWEAT, Mary to Archibald Burnett.
THOMAS, Adaline to John E. Walls.
THOMAS, Mary to Wiley Roberts.
THOMAS, Mary A. to Monroe Bonds.
THOMAS, Mary E. to Hiram Taylor.
THOMPSON, Elizabeth to Alvin Scott.
THOMPSON, Sarah C. to John O. Hart.
TODD, Rowena to C. J. Bryant.
WASHINGTON, Minerva to Leonard
    Burnett.
WAYNE, Christine to Ernest Spencer.
WEAVER, Unity to Elias Roberts.
WEAVER, Clorinda to Pleasant Evans.
WHITE, Bessie to Robert Talley.
WHITE, Ella to Richard Brown.
WHITE, Ellen to Amos Baxter.
WILLIAMS, Lillian to Laurie Allen.
WILSON, Cornelia to George W. Toliver.

CHAPTER IX

RELIGION AND CHURCHES

African Americans and Methodism

From the beginning of its history in this country, the Methodist Church embraced people of African descent. The religious movement started in England when in 1784 the Methodist Episcopal Church separated from the Anglican Church of England. It spread rapidly in America, and the newly organized Methodist churches welcomed non-white members.

As the religious group expanded, however, some of the white members began discriminatory practices in their churches. Initially, they sought special privileges for themselves based upon wealth and social prestige, but these quickly shifted to include race.

Racial restrictions within the churches soon became intolerable to members of African ancestry.[1] In 1787 a group of them withdrew their memberships from the St. George Methodist Episcopal Church in Philadelphia, and founded the Free African Society. This religious and benevolent organization incorporated the fundamental tenets of Methodism and it functioned effectively until ideological differences between the two Black leaders caused a split in the group.

In 1794 Rev. Richard Allen organized in Philadelphia the Bethel Church of the African Methodist Episcopal Church, while Rev. Absalom Jones set up the African Protestant Episcopal Church of St. Thomas. The Episcopals, however, failed to gain popularity among Blacks outside of a few large cities because the white church system in this country persistently refused to make slavery an issue.

Interest in Methodism expanded as African Americans of other cities followed Allen's example and organized what were known as African Methodist Episcopal churches in Baltimore, Maryland; Wilmington, Delaware; Attleboro, Pennsylvania; and Salem, New Jersey.

On April 9, 1816 ministers and leaders of these independent churches met in Philadelphia and established the first national *African Methodist Episcopal (A.M.E.) Church* system, and it still endures today. The leadership, administration, and control of this organization has remained entirely with Blacks.[2]

Other African Methodist Church Systems in America

A second African Methodist denomination developed in New York City after Blacks organized in 1796 an "African chapel" called Zion. The Zionites, as they were recognized in the later years, elected not to join with Bishop Allen's group out of fear of losing their independence. In 1821 the Zionites organized their own *African Methodist Episcopal Zion Church* system. Rev. James Varick became the first bishop of the New York-based church group. This A.M.E.Z. church body still flourishes nationally today.[3]

In 1845, the Methodist Episcopal Church (white) split over the issue of slavery and southern delegates withdrew to organize the *Methodist Episcopal Church, South.* Many Blacks in the south continued as members of this church system throughout the Civil War.

In the Reconstruction Era, ex-slaves who had been former members of the M. E. Church South organized the *Colored Methodist Episcopal (C.M.E.) Church* on December 16, 1870 in Jackson, Tennessee. This third national independent religious body received the approval of the white church which turned over some of its property to the new Black independent national religious group. In May, 1954, the name was changed to *Christian Methodist Episcopal Church.*[4]

Africans in White Methodist Churches

At the same time these African Methodist denominations were functioning, a few Blacks, particularly in the North, continued to attend and hold membership in some white Methodist churches: the *Methodist Episcopal Church (North)* which joined with other bodies to form the *United Methodist Church* in 1968, the *Wesleyan Methodist Church*, the *Methodist Protestant Church*, and the *Free Methodists Church.*

Early Methodism in Indiana

Presbyterians and Quakers were well represented among the early settlers in this state, but the Methodists and Baptists were the most numerous. When the Indian wars ended and the people began to scatter, all the religious societies of the day had trouble keeping up with the demand for preachers on the frontier as new settlements formed.

Methodists were among the early settlers who crossed the Ohio River into this state from Kentucky. By 1808, the Indiana District was added to the Western Conference of the Methodist Episcopal Church, the same year that one "colored" person was reported as a church member on the Whitewater Circuit[5].

By the time Indiana achieved statehood in 1816, there were 1,877 Methodists on six circuits principally in the southwestern, southern, and southeastern-east central sectors. Orange County Methodist churches were divided between two circuits: those in the eastern part were assigned to the Blue River Circuit, and those in the western area were placed in the Patoka Circuit.[6]

Colored Members in the Paoli Methodist Church (White)

Goodspeed's Orange County history contends that the first permanent Methodist Church in Paoli was probably organized in 1820, although it is believed that for several years prior the circuit preachers held religious meetings in the old stone court house.[7]

According to the minutes of the annual Methodist Episcopal Church conferences, colored people were members of the Paoli Methodist Church as early as 1828. Table 14 is a compilation of the membership data by race in the Paoli Church as reported to the church's annual conferences for the years indicated.

TABLE 14

Colored Members of the Methodist Episcopal Church (White)
Paoli, Indiana

Year	Total in Paoli M.E. Church		Total in Paoli Church's District		Total in Indiana M.E. Conference	
	White	Colored	White	Colored	White	Colored
1826	422	0	4992	38*		
1827	600	0	4407	35		
1828	796	4	5479	48		
1829	No report available		No report available		No report available	
1830	619	7	7008	58		
1831	936	14	7052	68		
1832	538	5	4756	53		
1833	536	0	4230	53	19853	182+
1834	483	3	4419	67	23344	273
1835	526	0	4222	64	24984	229
1836	385	1	3965	62	27685	235
1837	450	0	4247	72	30750	308
1838	589	19	4720	142	34931	327
1839	472	22	5924	174	43510	442
1840	631	28	4151	57	52208	407
1841	906	1	4498	6	52692	235
1842	983	4	5699	15	62224	245
1843	560	0	4463	0	66961	257
1844	570	1	4187	4	35527	159
1845	382	0	4126	1	33528	145
1846	400	0	4522	7	32366	164
1847	370	0	4531	27	30571	174
1848	209	0	4061	38	33101	161
1849	216	0	3238	14	30056	144
1850	185	0	3348	0	31747	177
1851	170	0	2760	1	33123	145
1852	170	0	2760	1	21081	51
1853	173	0	2917	0	17637	0#

Source: <u>Minutes of the Annual Conferences of the Methodist Episcopal Church</u>. Published reports found in Indiana University Libraries, Bloomington and in the Indiana United Methodism Collection, Archives of Depauw University.

*   In 1826 Paoli M.E. Church was assigned to Indiana District, Illinois Conference; from 1827-1832 to Charleston District, Illinois Conference; 1833-1839 to Charleston District, Indiana Conference; 1840-1842 to Bloomington District; 1843-1845 to Evansville District; 1846-1849 to Bloomington District; 1850 to Vincennes District; 1851-1852 to Paoli District; 1853 to Orleans District.

+   Indiana Conference formed from Illinois Conference in 1833.

\#   No colored members reported in the Indiana Conference of the M. E. Church for many decades after 1853.

The number of colored members in the Paoli Church was always quite small, ranging from one to twenty-eight. The largest total was listed in 1840, and even then the "colored" members represented less than five percent of the total congregation.

The absence of colored members in this church after 1844, despite the fact that African Americans continued to live in the town and surrounding area, is without any plausible explanation. However, as findings in Table 14 reveal, there was a similar decline in the African American membership of other churches assigned to the same district as the Paoli Church. In fact, the Indiana Conference of the Methodist Episcopal Church reported nearly a fifty percent drop in its total colored membership in 1840, and a gradual reduction in the number of colored members until 1853 when there were none. Creating a segregated congregation of white members in the Paoli M. E. Church seemed to duplicate what was happening racially not only throughout Indiana but in other northern states.

Sudden and striking population changes were common everywhere. Swelling waves of European immigrants poured into the middle west and produced greater competition for available land and jobs. The work of the abolitionists against slavery gained little support in Indiana or the nation, as most whites believed having any African persons living in America, whether free or enslaved, threatened somehow the basic core of societal's mores and religious values. Moreover, the power struggle between economic and political factions were polarizing nationally as the Native Americans were removed forceably and territorial boundaries were expanded into westward lands. A rallying cry of "creating a white man's country" was frequently used to justify increased acts of racism and intimidation toward non-whites still living in their midst, especially the African Americans.[8] Another factor which may have contributed to the dwindling colored membership in the white churches after 1836 was the aggressive proselyting of African Methodism in Indiana.

The Lick Creek Settlement "Colored" Methodist Church

African Americans living in Orange County established their first Methodist church apart from the whites in the mid-1830s. Ishmael and Lucretia Roberts sold one acre of their farm land in South East Township on April 27, 1837 to David Dugged and Martin Scott, trustees, for the "erection of the Union Meeting House for the benefit and use of the Methodist society..."[9] All parties involved in this land transaction were African Americans.

It is difficult to determine accurately today from extant church and deed records whether the "Methodist society" mentioned in the 1837 deed referred to the white Methodist Church in Paoli, or to the African Methodist Episcopal (A.M.E.) Church movement which was expanding rapidly and establishing new churches in the Northwest Territory.

African American Pioneer Missionary

In the summer of 1836, Rev. William Paul Quinn began his missionary work in Indiana. Assigned to the Western Conference of the African Methodist Episcopal (A.M.E.) Church in Pittsburgh and later the Ohio Conference after it was organized, Quinn had been very successful in founding churches throughout Ohio before turning his proselyting efforts westward across central Indiana and into eastern Illinois. He was a courageous, solitary rider "of the cloth," and he sought out the isolated Black settlements, preaching the "word of God" and spreading the cause of African Methodism.

Diaries or records of Quinn's early travels in Indiana are missing. Clues are scarce about his routing over the woodland and prairie trails, where he stopped, how often he preached and performed religious rituals, and the size of his audiences. However, we do know that he was a very powerful orator, dedicated to his religious beliefs, and deeply identified with the plight of African Americans and the work of the abolitionists in this country.[10]

Several A. M. E. Churches in Indiana date their origins to the historical period between 1836 and 1840 when Rev. Quinn was active in the midwest. These include the pioneer ones in Randolph, Henry, Rush, Marion, Clay, Vigo, and Knox Counties in Indiana, plus at least six to eight churches founded in neighboring Illinois.

While Rev. Quinn may not have been in Orange County during his early travels, his religious influence quickly spread. Black Hoosiers were inspired by reports of his successes and they began to build their own churches apart from the whites. On the other hand some of these early colored churches may have developed initially under the auspices of the local white Methodist Church (see Table 14). In the absence of any qualified Black Methodist minister, a white preacher who lived nearby occasionally volunteered to conduct the religious services at the country "colored church" as a part of his religious missionary work.[11]

At least one man in the Lick Creek Settlement of Orange County was qualified to serve as pastor in the Black Methodist Church, but it cannot be confirmed that he actually did so. Rev. Willis R. Revels, who later became a well-known A.M.E. Church minister, teacher, physician and leader in the mid-1800s, was a resident of the Lick Creek area on or before 1840. Willis, who was born a free person in Fayetteville, North Carolina and the older brother of Hiram R. Revels, married a Susan Jones in Lawrence County, Indiana on December 22, 1836.[12] Four years later in the 1840 census, he was enumerated in Orange County with his wife and child. Presumably they once lived in the Lick Creek Settlement area. By the early 1840s, Rev. Willis Revels was playing a prominent role among the early A. M. E. Churches in southern Indiana.

Formation of the Indiana A.M.E. Church Conference

On October 2, 1840 the Indiana Conference of the A.M.E. Church system came into existence. This sixth church conference within the system of national African Methodism held its organizational meeting at the Blue River A.M.E. Church located near Carthage in Rush County, Indiana.

Bishop Morris Brown presided over the inaugural conference which was attended by twenty elders, deacons and preachers. Many of the attendees were from the Ohio A.M.E. Church Conference, and they came to Indiana for the expressed purpose to establish a new state conference.

Rev. William P. Quinn, who had been elevated to the position of elder, and Rev. Willis R. Revels, from Orange County, Indiana were identified among the conference founders.

After 1840 the A.M.E. Church movement expanded swiftly in Indiana. Five years later, the Indiana Conference had 1,777 members in thirty-nine churches divided into nine circuits and scattered in thirty-one different Indiana counties.[13] For many years thereafter the church system struggled with the persistent problem of finding qualified ministers. A solution came eventually in 1856 when the national A.M.E. Church system established Wilberforce College in central Ohio.

Early Churches in Orange County: Paoli A. M. E. Church

Actually, the first A. M. E. Church group in Orange County was founded in the town of Paoli. The minutes of the Indiana Conference listed members of the Paoli A.M.E. Church between 1842 and 1845.[14]

The 1842 annual report showed that the Paoli A.M.E. Church had 39 members and was assigned to the Salem Circuit under the direction of Rev. Major J. Wilkerson, a traveling preacher. Anchored in nearby Salem, Indiana, Wilkerson ministered to eight churches with 238 members on his circuit covering the contiguous counties of Washington, Orange, Lawrence, Floyd, Clark, Jefferson, and Jennings.

The next year, 1843, the Paoli A. M. E. Church consisted of 65 members and was still assigned to the Salem Circuit, by now in charge of Rev. Willis R. Revels. He was responsible for 437 members in eleven different churches situated in Washington, Floyd, Clark, Jennings, Lawrence, Harrison, Jefferson, Jackson, and Orange Counties.

In 1844, the Paoli A. M. E. Church remained part of the Salem Circuit but its membership had dwindled to only 13 members. Rev. James Curtis was the minister in charge of the circuit's seven churches with 156 members in Washington, Floyd, Orange, and Harrison Counties. Increasing membership enabled the Conference to create new circuits within the state, and a new Hanover Circuit in Jefferson County incorporated the A.M.E. Churches in Clark, Jennings, Jackson and Harrison Counties with a total of 123 members.

By 1845, the Paoli church continued to report thirteen members. They were pastored by Rev. James Curtis of the Salem Circuit which encompassed six churches with a total of 114 members in Washington, Harrison and Orange Counties. The A.M.E. Church in Paoli ceased functioning after 1845, and supposedly it was not replaced for many years.

The 1845 report was apparently the last one published for many years providing the name and location of individual churches assigned to circuits of the Indiana A.M.E. Church Conference. Thereafter, printed reports of the annual minutes listed statistical data on members, finances, and accomplishments either as a unit under the "circuit" headings for the smaller churches or in the name of the larger churches as these proliferated in urban communities after the 1850s.[15]

Paoli A. M. E. Church in the 1890s

The colored community in and around Paoli tried a second time to maintain an African Methodist Episcopal Church. On March 27, 1893 trustees of the church purchased the south half of lot 29 on the near west side of Paoli from Andrew J. and Annie J. Rhods for fifty dollars.[16]

A church building with seating capacity for 200 persons was erected at 309 North West Third Street between Main and Campbell Streets. A document recorded in Miscellaneous Records at the Courthouse indicated that William P. Howard was elected a trustee on December 12, 1894 with Daniel O'Bannon as Chairman and Hettie O'Bannon as secretary for the church group.[17] The next year Mrs. Hettie O'Bannon was duly elected on February 23, 1895 as a church trustee. Rev T. J. Hardison was pastor and Mrs. Lillie Evans the church's secretary.[18]

This Paoli A.M.E. Church was first mentioned in the 1896 Minutes of the Indiana A. M. E. Church Conference held in Muncie, Indiana. It reported having 37 members and was assigned to the Mitchell Circuit within the Evansville District. Rev. E. E. Gregory was in charge of the circuit which included also the A. M. E. churches in Bedford and Mitchell.[19]

The next year when the Indiana Conference met in Terre Haute Rev. Gregory reported for the same three churches on the Mitchell Circuit. Instead of membership totals this annual report contained the names of members who paid "dollar money" to help defray the 1897 conference expenses.

While the listing did not specify the churches on the Mitchell Circuit to which each person belonged, the following Paoli members were identified:

> James Phelps, Vermilia Taylor, Sarah Coates, Amanda Finley, Hettie O'Bannon, Harry O'Bannon, Martha Garner, Jenetta Irving, Fannie Allen, Henrietta Lewis, Fannie Churchill, Mollie Mabray, Oscar Bonds, Bertha Thomas, William Thomas, Fred Burnett, Annie Bonds, Ellen Allen and Ellen Rain.

The Indiana Conference of the A.M.E. Church met in Marion, Indiana on August 30, 1898. Minutes disclosed that the Bedford and Paoli churches were combined into one circuit in charge of Rev. Henry Norman. The Mitchell A. M. E. Church was assigned to Rev. H. Hubbard Brewer.

There was no listing of the Paoli Church in the 1899 minutes although the Mitchell and Bedford Circuit report included the A. M. E. Church in Seymour; all were in charge of Rev. Henry C. Norman.

It is unknown how long the Paoli Church functioned or when the church property was sold. A short article entitled, "African (Colored) Church, Paoli, Ind." appeared in the booklet, *History of Churches of Orange County* published in 1940 by the *Paoli Republican* newspaper. It reported that the structure was still standing but no longer used for church purposes. Mary Lindley, who lived nearby, recalled that her mother was often invited to preach or to direct "the colored congregation." It mentioned also that Hettie O'Bannon was once a minister in the church. Oscar Bowman was the only surviving member (in 1940), and others who were once identified with the church included persons from the Thomas, Bowman, O'Bannon, Burnett, Phillips and Howard families.[20]

A. M. E. Church in the Lick Creek Settlement

The first documentation of an A. M. E. Church in the rural Lick Creek Settlement east of Paoli is a land deed dated December 14, 1843. Thomas Roberts, and his wife, Matilda, sold one acre of their 120 acres to five church trustees for five dollars. The deed stated explicitly that the trustees, Elias Roberts, Mathew Thomas, Thomas Roberts, Isaac Scott and Samuel Chandler, were to erect or cause to be erected "a house as place of worship for the use of the members of the African Methodist Episcopal Church in the United States of America..."[21]

The Lick Creek Settlement A. M. E. Church was not located on the same land where six years earlier the colored Methodist Union Meeting House had been established. Land transaction entries show clearly that while both churches were in the same vicinity, each was positioned on adjoining properties owned by different members of the Roberts family: Ishmael Roberts for the 1837 church, and Thomas Roberts for the 1843 A. M. E. Church.[22]

Nothing in the literature explains why the trustees of the second church decided to erect a new church building rather than to combine forces and use the existing Union Meeting (Methodist) House. It is possible that both churches functioned concurrently for a period of time before the first church was disbanded.

The Lick Creek A.M.E. Church thrived for almost twenty years. In 1844 the church was reported in the fifth annual conference of the Indiana A. M. E. Church to have 34 members, or almost three times as many as were listed for the A. M. E. Church in Paoli, less than ten miles away. Both of these churches were assigned to the Salem Circuit (Washington County) in charge of Rev. James Curtis.

By 1845, the last year for which the beginning church conference reports are available, the Lick Creek Church reported still having 34 members, and the Paoli Church had only 13 members. Rev. Curtis continued for the second year his assignment to the Salem Circuit. In his charge were also four additional churches with 66 members in Washington and Harrison counties.

A brief document dated June 10, 1851 and pertaining to the election of church trustees in the Lick Creek Settlement was filed at the court house for record in *Deed Book 14*, page 183. An official election was called to fill vacancies created by recent resignations. The three new trustees for the Lick Creek A. M. E. Church were: Amos Baxter, Solomon Newby and Henry Scott. The recorded notice was signed by Rev. John Morgan, Presiding Elder, and Amos Baxter, secretary.

Neither the Lick Creek A. M. E. Church nor the Salem Circuit appeared in annual conference minutes for the years 1845-1867 (scattered issues still available today). Proceedings of the 1854 conference held in Chicago presented the church's statistics in a changed format. No longer were listings given for the individual churches which comprised the circuits in the conference. All reports identified only the Circuits by name, e.g., "Salem Circuit," and the names of larger churches in the cities. Why the church conference changed its system for reporting annual church statistics was not explained in the minutes.

The Indiana A.M.E. Church leaders may have decided to discontinue releasing information about the location of their small, isolated, primarily rural congregations to the general public in order to protect their members against racial harrassment or being kidnapped as runaway slaves. Strife dominated national politics as sectional differences increased over the issues of settlement in Kansas and Nebraska Territories, slave versus free market labor, and the enforcement of the 1850 Federal Fugitive Slave Law in northern states.

However, in 1854 minutes, the Salem A.M.E. Church Circuit in Indiana, to which both Orange County churches had been assigned in previous years, reported a total of 194 members. Rev. Austin Woodfork was in charge of the circuit and his salary was $170.00 for the year's labors. Rev. Richard Bridges was assigned to take over the Salem Circuit for the next year. For the record, in 1854 there were 3,493 members in the Indiana A. M. E. Church Conference.[23]

When the Indiana Conference met in Indianapolis on August 15, 1862, Rev. Levi W. Bass was in charge of the Salem Circuit which consisted of thirty-seven members and nine probationers. For next year Rev. James Bass was assigned as the new pastor to the Salem Circuit. In the same 1862 minutes, the "Lick Creek Circuit" was identified as a separate unit having twenty-two members and one probationer in charge of Rev. Levi W. Bass on the Salem Circuit. No minister assignment was made to the Lick Creek Circuit for the coming year, 1863.[24]

Additional listings for the Lick Creek A. M. E. Church or the Salem Circuit were not found in the available church conference minutes after 1862.

The church property in the Lick Creek Settlement was sold for five dollars on March 8, 1869 by Bishop William P. Quinn of the A. M. E. Church to Eli Roberts of Orange County. The one acre tract was located in Section 27, Township 1 North, Range 1 East.[25] This sale probably resulted after the church was closed for several years due to the small number of members left in the settlement after the Civil War. Between 1860 and 1870 the number of African Americans residing in South East Township dropped from 74 to 16!

French Lick A. M. E. Church

A group of local citizens met in a private home in 1902 to organize an A.M.E. Church in French Lick. Mrs. Maggie Morgan, William Payne and Mrs. Ike Lloyd were among those in attendance. The church society continued to meet in different homes until a building was completed.[26]

On August 10, 1904 they purchased Lot 12 in the H. E. Wells addition, French Lick, from James A. Wells and Will W. Cave, executors for the estate of Hiram E. Wells for $175. William Payne, George Scott, and Maggie Morgan were listed as the A.M.E. Church trustees.[27]

Further details about the church's membership, officers, ministers assigned and the early history remain obscure. However, a deed dated September 25, 1928 indicates that the trustees, Isaac Lloyd, Louis Shockency, Margaret Morgan, Carrie Martin, Carrie Pittman, Alice McKenney, Mollie Payne and Robert Holden purchased Lot 9 in the same addition as the A. M. E. Church for $3000 from the Lost River Investment Company, West Baden, Indiana. The document was signed by Perry McCart, President, and Winifred Dailey, Secretary.[28]

On July 6, 1951, trustees of the French Lick A. M. E. Church sold lots 9 and 12 in French Lick to the "Trustees of the Indiana Annual Conference of A. M. E. Church" for $1.00. Local trustees were Mattie W. Smith, Gerald S. Smith, John W. Frazier, Jerry A. Lewis and Solomon C. Pitman.[29]

Rev. H. E. Edmonds, Paoli, was listed as pastor of the French Lick A. M. E. Church when Stout's supplement to the *History of Orange County* (1884) was reprinted in 1960. Rev. Robert H. Bennett was assigned to this church between 1960-1977 when it was a part of the Mitchell Circuit. "Brother Bob" Bennett, as he was known locally, may have been the last A. M. E. minister in the French Lick church. For many years after retirement, Rev. Bennett and his wife, Cora, lived on Unionville Road south of Paoli (see Chapter XII).

Dwindling membership eventually forced this church to close its doors. The land and building were sold to Oral and Velma Marie Carnes, French Lick, for $1.00 on December 7, 1977. The following trustees of the Indiana Annual Conference of the A. M. E. Church formalized the legal transfer: Harold D. Gray, Marion County; Juanita Alexander, Marion County; Jessie Jacobs, Marion County; Gwendolyn E. Gibson, Lake County; Dorothy C. Murphy, Tippecanoe County; and Richard Claude Watkins, Grant County.[30] The church structure was demolished a few years later.

First Baptist Church in West Baden

It seems remarkable that the number of African Americans living in the Springs Valley area was ever sufficient to support two different churches: a Methodist denomination in French Lick and a group of Baptists in West Baden.

On February 6, 1909, the deacons and trustees of the First Baptist Church (colored) purchased from the West Baden Springs Company Lot 2 in the West Baden Springs Company addition for one dollar. Lee W. Sinclair, president, signed for the selling company and the following persons represented the church: James Palmer, Wright Potter, John L. Thomas, Robert J. Holden and William M. Scott.[31]

Peter H. Clark and his wife, Emma Clark, sold Lot 1 which adjoins the church property on October 26, 1920 to the First Baptist Church for $850.00. This is believed to be the land on which the parsonage was constructed.[32]

Only meager details are known about the church's history, its members and officers, and its program over the years of religious, social and civic activities. This church, like the A.M.E. Church in French Lick, faced the same survival difficulties as its membership dwindled during the economic decline of the resort and mineral water industries. Rev. W. A. Davis of Louisville, Kentucky was listed in 1960 as pastor of the West Baden First Baptist Church. The vacant church structure stands today north of the Kimble Piano Company plant grounds at the corner of Sinclair and Elm Streets. Mrs. Artie Smith is said to be its last surviving member.

NOTES

1. Wade Crawford Barclay, "The Church and Interracial Relations," in *Early American Methodism: 1769-1844* (New York: The Board of Missions and Church Extension of The Methodist Church, 1950), v. 1, 52-60.

2. Carter G. Woodson, *The History of the Negro Church* (Washington, D.C.: The Associated Publishers, 1921), 71-78. Daniel A. Payne, *History of the African Methodist Episcopal Church* (Nashville: A.M.E. Sunday School Union, 1891; repr., New York: Arno Press, 1969), 4-6.

3. William J. Walls, *The African Methodist Episcopal Zion Church: Reality of the Black Church* (Charlotte, N.C.: A.M.E.Z. Publishing House, 1974).

4. Othal Hawthorne Lakey, *The History of the CME Church* (Memphis: Publishing House, 1985), pp. 23-46.

5. *Minutes of the Annual Conferences of the Methodist Episcopal Church (1773-1828)*, v. I, 159.

6. William W. Sweet, "Early Methodist Churches in Indiana," *Indiana Magazine of History*, 10 (1914), 359-368.

7. *History of Lawrence, Orange and Washington Counties, Indiana* (Chicago: Goodspeed Bros. & Co., 1884), Chap. 8, "Religious History of the County," 530-31.

8. Leon F. Litwack, *North of Slavery: The Negro in the Free States 1790-1860* (Chicago: University of Chicago Press, 1961), Chapter 8, "The Crisis of the 1850's," 247-279. Ronald G. Walters, *The Antislavery Appeal: American Abolitionism After 1830* (New York: W. W. Norton & Co., 1978), "Religion: Evangelical Protestantism and the Reform Impulse," 37-53. Eric Foner, *Free Soil Free Labor, Free Men: The Ideology of the Republican Party before the Civil War* (New York: Oxford University Press, 1970), especially the overview in chapter 1 on "Free Labor: The Republicans and Northern Society," 11-39.

9. *Deed Book F*, Orange County, Indiana, 140. The Roberts farm and this church land were located in the west half of the north west quarter, Section 27, Township 1 North, Range 1 East. Elias Roberts and Benjamin Roberts witnessed this deed.

10. Religious historians do not agree about Quinn's origins or even that he was an African American. Some biographers report that he was born in Calcutta, India on April 10, 1788. Quinn, a brown-skinned man with long black straight hair, converted to African Methodism after arriving in America around 1808. For many years he pastored A.M.E. churches in New Jersey and Pennsylvania before the 1830s when he was assigned to the Western or Ohio A. M. E. Church Conference as a circuit preacher.

In 1844 Rev. Quinn became the fourth Bishop in the Church. He adopted Richmond, Indiana as his home and he died there on February 3, 1873 after serving the longest term as Bishop in the history of the A.M.E. Church. Quinn's body was buried in the Earlham Cemetery at Richmond.

A number of educational institutions and churches throughout the country were named in his honor. Bishop Richard R. Wright Jr., *The Bishops of The African Methodist Episcopal Church* (Nashville, TN., The A.M.E. Sunday School Union, 1963), 283-286.

11. A similar situation was found in the history of African Americans in Morgan County, Indiana. Reed's Chapel was established in the hills south of Martinville in the 1840s and it continued to be used by members of the Methodist faith over the next forty-fifty years. There is no record that the church body ever became a part of African Methodism. Whites in the region also attended services in this predominately "colored" church which at one time pastored by white ministers assigned to the Bloomington, Indiana Methodist Episcopal Church (white). See Coy D. Robbins, *African Heritage in Morgan County, Indiana,* (Bloomington, Ind.: Indiana African American Historical and Genealogical Society, 1991), 29-33.

12. *Marriage Records,* Lawrence County, IN., 34. Couple obtained the license on December 5, 1836, two weeks prior to their marriage by Samuel G. Hoskins, Justice of the Peace. There is the possibility that Willis was related to Delena Revels, the woman who married Ishmael Roberts in Orange County, Indiana on August 12, 1844. Ishmael Roberts and his wife, Lucretia, were owners of the land where the first Methodist Church was built in the Lick Creek Settlement. Apparently, Lucretia Roberts died before 1844. Rev. Hiram R. Revels, Willis' younger brother, also came to Indiana, became an A.M.E. minister, and after the Civil War, he was the first person of African ancestry to serve as a Senator in the United States Congress.

13. By 1845 the Indiana Conference of the A.M.E. Church included congregations in three other states: Kentucky, Illinois and Missouri.

14. Minutes of the Indiana Annual Conference, African Methodist Episcopal Church published in the *African Methodist Episcopal Church Magazine,* George Hogarth, editor, for the years 1840-1845. We find only limited information about history of this first A. M. E. Church publication which was established in 1840 under the editorship of Rev. Hogarth, New York City. From the Coy D. Robbins' personal collection of early A. M. E. Church records.

15. In the 1860 U. S. Census Thomas Strother and his wife, Fanny, were enumerated in Paoli Township. He was listed as a farmer owning both real and personal estates with the additional occupation of "Minister, African Methodist." This could mean that Rev. Strother was an A.M.E. minister of either the Paoli or the Lick Creek Settlement A.M.E. Church -- or both. Of course, there is always the possibility that he had no church assignment at the time of this census.

16. *Deed Book 43,* Orange County, IN., 168-169. The indenture does not list names of the trustees. This deed makes no reference to standing structures on the premise at the time of land transfer, so it is assumed that the A.M.E. Church constructed its own building.

17. *Miscellaneous Record No. 2,* 305 recorded on 14 December 1894 by Lloyd Kimmel, Recorder of Orange County.

18. Document recorded in *Miscellaneous Record No. 2,* 338 on 25 March 1895, Recorder's Office, Orange County.

19. Information gleaned from Indiana A.M.E. Church Conference minutes for the years indicated found in the Bishop Arnett Papers and Collection, Archives, Rembert E. Stokes Learning Center, Wilberforce University, Ohio. Serials are incomplete or missing for early years, especially Vol. 34. This collection covers 1848-1912.

20. *History of Churches of Orange County,* 26-27.

21. *Deed Book J-10,* 225-228, Orange County Recorder's Office, Paoli, Ind. Henry Holmes, local justice of peace, and Samuel Chandler witnessed the signatures, and Josiah Hazlewood recorded the document on January 9, 1845.

22. *Deed Book F,* page 140 for the one acre lot deeded to the Union Meeting House Trustees on April 28, 1837; *Deed Book J-10,* page 225 for the one acre lot deeded to the African Methodist Episcopal Church Trustees on December 14, 1843. A different conclusion resulted after finding the record in *Deed Book 25,* page 547 where William Paul Quinn, Bishop of the African Methodist Episcopal Church, deeded the one acre church lot to Eli Roberts on December 14, 1863. Eli was the son of Elias Roberts, and grandson of Ishmael Roberts. In 1887 Eli Roberts died while holding title to 80 acres which his heirs deeded in 1887 and 1888 to the Studebaker Brothers Manufacturing Company, South Bend, Indiana.

23. *Journal of Proceedings of the Fifteenth Annual Conference of the African Methodist Episcopal Church, for the District of Indiana, held at Indianapolis, September 6, 1854,* (Indianapolis: Printed by Rawson Vaile, 1854), 8-9, 11, 13, 91. Copy found in the Indiana State Library.

24. Arnett Collection, Wilberforce University Archives, Vol. 35, 1-29.

25. *Deed Record Book 25,* 547-548.

26. *French Lick Centennial 1857-1957, Historical Souvenir Program,* 15.

27. *Deed Book 55,* 375, Orange County's Recorder Office.

28. *Deed Record 78,* 430. It was recorded on January 10, 1929 by William C. Hancock, Orange County Recorder.

29. *Deed Record 96,* 319-320. Recorded on July 14, 1951 by Dorothy L. Cable, Orange County Recorder.

30. *Deed Record 129,* 790-793, Grant M. Rutherford, Orange County Recorder. In the Supplement to Orange County History (Goodspeed's) reprinted by Stout in 1965, Rev. H. E. Edmonds, of Paoli, was listed as pastor of the French Lick A. M. E. Church, p. 317.

31. *Deed Record 61,* 186-187.

32. *Deed Record Book 73,* 117. Interestly enough, names of the church trustees were not mentioned in this land transaction.

MAP: Cemeteries and Burying Grounds

	Bethel Cemetery	Green Hill Cemetery	
	Orangeville Township	Orleans Township	

K of P
Cemetery

Newberry
Friends Church

Lick Creek
Friends Church

French Lick
Township

Paoli
Township

Lick Creek Settlement
Cemetery

South East Township

(Map by author)

CHAPTER X

CEMETERIES

Burials in the Lick Creek Settlement Cemetery

This graveyard is known locally as the "Little Africa Cemetery,"--an epithet which came into usage many years after the original settlers were no longer in the environs.

It is located on Hoosier National Forest property about one and one-half miles south of Chambersburg in Section 27, Township 1 North, Range 1 East of South East Township. Today, it can be reached via highway 150 east of Paoli to Grease Gravy Road which is about a mile west of Chambersburg. Grease Gravy Road travels south, soon becoming a graveled byway terminating at the wooden gate entrance to the Forest Service property. Walking approximately two miles on a meandering road is necessary to reach the isolated cemetery situated northeast of the entrance gate.[1]

A deed for the actual cemetery property has not been located. Its proximity to the site of the Lick Creek A. M. E. Church suggests that it once belonged to the church trustees. Yet, deed transactions for the purchase (1843) and the sale (1869) of the church property contained no mention of a cemetery. Land transaction records indicate that the cemetery ground was privately owned at different times by members of the Roberts and Thomas families who used it as a private burying ground.[2]

Little has been done to maintain this cemetery since the work of the members of Boy Scout Troop 85 under the leadership of Scoutmaster Harold Smith.[3] In 1970 they cleared the overgrowth and erected rows of wooden white crosses on unmarked graves, copied inscriptions from standing markers, constructed a rectangular monument of concrete and field stones in which were imbedded two bronze government plaques for the two war veterans interned here, and surrounded the cemetery with a low, split wood railing fence.

Harry Clements, Paoli attorney and member of the Scouting Committee, assisted the boys in checking historical records in the courthouse. While local newspaper articles publicizing this Boy Scouts' project were based upon their understanding of African heritage in the state and county at that time, some printed facts were inaccurate and apparently based upon local folklore.[4]

The stone memorial created for the cemetery entrance reads: "A. M. E. Union Meeting House Cemetery, Est. 1830 Restored 1970 By B. S. A. Troop 85." The name concocted for this historic cemetery was not entirely correct. As described in the preceding chapter there were actually *two* different church buildings in the Lick Creek Settlement, and current research failed to indicate that they ever united into a single religious organization. Only one church survived. The African Methodist Episcopal (A.M.E.) Church functioned in the vicinity of this cemetery for sixteen years between 1843 and 1869.

The bronze U. S. Veterans Administration plaque obtained for Simon Locust and incorporated in the stone memorial contained some informational errors about this Civil War soldier said to be the last person buried here. Traditionally, including the word " Tennessee" in a veteran's gravestone inscription indicates either the soldier's birthplace or his state of residence when entering military service (see second item in "Gravestone Information").

In either case, the implications are incorrect for Simon Locust. He was a native Hoosier and born in Orange County, Indiana. Furthermore, he was *drafted* from Orange County for one year's military service on September 23, 1864. Military and pension records clearly show that Locust was mustered out of the U. S. Army at Nashville, Tennessee when his term of service expired.

Locust never served with "Confederate States Army" as engraved on this plaque. He was in the *Union Army* with the rank of private in Company E, 13th Infantry Regiment, United States Colored Troops (USCT), and not the "Colo Inf" as was inscribed.[5]

To the left side of the stone monument the Boy Scouts constructed a large wooden billboard painted dark brown on which the following message was imprinted in bold yellow paint[6]:

AFRICAN METHODIST EPISCOPAL
UNION MEETINGHOUSE CEMETERY

FREE MEN OF COLOR WHO CAME TO INDIANA EARLY IN THE 1800'S TO FIND FREEDOM SETTLED IN THIS AREA WHAT IS NOW KNOWN AS LITTLE AFRICA THE FORMER SLAVES WERE GIVEN THE OPPORTUNITY TO TOIL AND EARN THEIR OWN LIVING, AND THEIR CHILDREN WOULD HAVE THE RIGHTS AND PRIVILEGES OF ALL MEN IN THIS NEW COUNTRY. THEY TOOK THEIR PLACE IN THE STATE AND NATION AS SOLDIERS, FARMERS, AND MOST OF ALL - - - - FREE MEN.

Gravestone Information

The list printed below was compiled from three different surveys of burials in this cemetery: (1) one taken in November, 1962 by members of the Lost River Chapter (Paoli), Daughters of American Revolution (DAR); (2) one executed by members of Boy Scout Troop 85 in the summer of 1970, and (3) two done by Coy D. Robbins on September 22, 1979 and July 16, 1990.[7]

1. Bond, Frances M.
        Daughter of M[onroe] & M[ary] Bond
        Born: September 22, 1864
        Died: November 29, 1867
2. Locust, Simon (Plaque embedded in entrance Memorial)
        Tennessee Pvt Co E 13 Regt Colo Inf
        Confederate States Army
        1824-1891
3. Morton, Albert
        Son of I & P.A. Irvin

Born: Apr 17, 1864
Died: July 27, 1876

4. Roberts, Alice
   Wife of Nelson Roberts
   Born July 17, 1824
   Died Sept 19, 1858

5. Roberts, Ishmael (Plaque embedded in entrance Memorial)[8]
   North Carolina
   Pvt Shepards Co 10 NC Regt
   Revolutionary War

6. Roberts, James
   Son of Ann Roberts
   Born: Oct 3, 1853
   Died: Jan 16, 1877

7. Roberts, Mary E.
   Wife of Eli Roberts
   Born: Nov 1, 1812
   Died: May 2, 1867
   "May her soul rest in peace"
           -- E. T. Salyards
   Orleans [stone craver]

8. Thomas, Frances L.
   Daughter of Mathew and Mary Thomas
   Born: September 30, 1857
   Died: October 30, 1858

9. Thomas, Joseph N.
   Son of M&M Thomas
   Born: Sept 26, 1835
   Died: May 3, 1866

10. Thomas, Mary
    Wife of Mathew Thomas
    Born: Apr 2, 1817
    Died: June 30, 1867

11. Thomas, Mathew
    Born Oct 8, 1808
    Died Dec 10, 1870
    Aged 62 yrs 2 M 2 ds

12. Thomas, Samuel A.
    Son of Mathew and Mary Thomas
    Born: May 29, 1853
    Died: August 5, 1856

13. Thomas, Sarah D.
    [daughter of M and M Thomas]

14. Thompson, Homer
    Son of Thomas M. and Sarah Thompson
    Died: February 7, 1879, aged 3 years, 7 months, 28 days.

Summary of Lick Creek Cemetery

Although the above list is fragmentary, it helps to provide some history of burial practices in the cemetery. These gravestone inscriptions are striking for their completeness of details to include both the birth and death dates.

Recorded burials began around 1856 and continued until 1891. All but three of the fourteen internments took place after the Civil War. The three burials in 1867 were the largest number done in any single year. Seven burials were for members of the Mathew Thomas family, and four additional ones were Robertses. The fact no gravestones or record of other family groups interned in this cemetery seems to confirm the idea that it was privately owned. Unfortunately, the ravishes of time, vandalism, and irregular maintenance have caused some destruction of gravestones in this pioneer African American cemetery in southern Indiana.

The K of P Cemetery

This second "colored" cemetery in Orange County was opened by the Proserpine Lodge No. 27, (Colored) Knights of Pythias, French Lick, Orange County, Indiana in 1913. It is located on State Road 56, two miles southwest of French Lick, west of the Country Club and adjacent to Mount Lebanon (white) Cemetery in French Lick Township (Section 17, Township 1 North, Range 2 West).

In the central area of the cemetery near its eastern entrance stands a 12-15 foot obelisk with the following words inscribed on the base:

Dedicated A. D. 1923 to the Memory of Those
Who Rest Here

Proserpine Lodge No. 27
Knights of Pythias

To date no written history or record of burials in this cemetery has been located. It is still used for internments today. Jean and Coy D. Robbins surveyed all gravestones during 1992, and copied the following data from the stone markers:

1.   Allen, Laurie E.
2.   Austin, Thomas E. 1890-1959
3.   Austin, Martha B. 1897-19--
4.   Babbage, Henry Lee died June 2, 1921 Age 51 yrs 7 mo.
5.   Babbage, John A. [govt marker] Pvt U S Army World War I, May 23, 1893-Jan 16, 1980.
6.   Babbage, Marie SEBREE 1895-1958
7.   Banks, Helen Jan 4, 1906-June 9, 1952
8.   Barrett, Birdie Aug 13, 1965
9.   Barrett, Charlie Feb 18, 1975
10. Beacham, Ella 1879-1927
11. Belton, Bertha 1889-1941
12. Belton, William S. 1888-1941
13. Bohannon, Pauline Nov 16, 1898-Mar 12, 1990 Beloved Mother
14. Brannon, Roland T. Sept 24, 1976 [funeral marker]
15. Brown, Gus Departed June 9, 1937

16.   Brown, Irene Departed Nov 23, 1938
17.   Brown, Louis June 15, 1886-1917
18.   Buckholder, Irene
19.   Buckholder, Collie Wm.
20.   Burnett, Alvin V. 1893-1923
21.   Burnett, Odis Jr. 1897-1914
22.   Burnett, Odis M. 1872-1923
23.   Campbell, Hattie B. Apr 12, 1906-Mar 18, 1984
24.   Carroll, Margaret A. Sept 30, 1890-Apr 17, 1962
25.   Carter, Azalea June 1, 1846-Mar 3, 1922
26.   Carter, Ivanhoe [govt marker] Indiana Pvt 152 Depot Brigade WWI Aug 10, 1896-Feb 16, 1952
27.   Cartwright, Charles 1905-1989
28.   Conn, Mary E. Dec 14, 1876-Nov 18, 1917
29.   Dorsey, James Died Feb 19, 1943
30.   Dorsey, Susan Dec 13, 1927 Age 70 yrs
31.   Drye, Eugene [govt marker] Indiana Pvt 809 Pioneer Inf December 8, 1936
32.   Gardner, Alexander V. [govt marker] Indiana Pvt Student Army Tng Corps World War I January 3, 1890-May 22, 1948
33.   Garrett, Lula Bell Clarksville, Tenn. Aug 12, 1892-Dec 12, 1972
34.   Hanley, Baby Jan 8, 1916
35.   Hayes, Mary June 14, 1877-Sept 13, 1934 At Rest
36.   Henderson, Gertrude P. 1887-1947 Sister
37.   Hicks, Herbert 1903-1981
38.   Hill, Anna Lee 1880-1954 Mother
39.   Holden, Carry S. June 27, 1883-Sept 7, 1962
40.   Holden, Robert J. Apr 1, 1885-July 26, 1968
41.   Hooker, Edward 1891-1960
42.   Hooker, Sallie 1898-1969
43.   Hurley, Willa C. June 6, 1867-Nov 7, 1957
44.   Jackson, Sanford Died Nov 26, 1939
45.   Johnson, Delos R. 1902-1968
46.   Kennedy, Willis
47.   Killebrew, Leroy 1885-1957
48.   King, Thomas A. [govt marker] ST1 U S Navy Oct 6, 1904-May 1, 1975
49.   Latham, James Thomas [govt marker] Illinois Sgt 365 Inf 92 Div June 3, 1936 Born Apr 11, 1893
50.   Lawrence, Hallie B. Aug 22, 1882-Feb 2, 1927
51.   Lewis, Mattie V. 1885-1948
52.   Lloyd, Ida Feb 13, 1882-July 8, 1961
53.   Lloyd, Isaac W. Feb 6, 1881-Sept 14, 1960
54.   Lynn, Harrison [govt marker] Kentucky Pvt 317 SN TN 92 Div World War I Sept 7, 1894 Sept 7, 1966
55.   Lynn, Henietta 1900-1987
56.   McFarland, Lelia C. 1879-1965
57.   McGowan, Hulga 1856-Aug 2, 1923 Mother
58.   Martin, Purvis July 19, 1879-April 27, 1939
59.   Mason, Gwen B. Jan 6, 1927-Nov 25, 1990

60. Morgan, Maggie Sept 12, 1857-May 12, 1933 Mother
61. Morrison, Bernice Hanley Nov 15, 1964
62. Morton, Celeste 1886-1940
63. Morton, Infant son of Charles & Celeste Morton May 8, 1924
64. Overton, Edward H. [govt marker]   Tennessee Wagoner Btry A 351 FID Arty
    March 7, 1891-Jan 28, 1965
65. Overton, Ollie wife of Edward H. Overton
66. Payne, William Oct 1, 1867-May 7, 1925
67. Perry, Josephine L. 1888-1970
68. Perry, Oscar 1900-1968
69. Pitman, Carrie
70. Pitman, Elsie
71. Pitman, Nathan
72. Pitman, Ray [govt marker] Indiana Pvt Stu Army Tng Corps World War I Oct 21,
    1897-Sept 8, 1854
73. Pitman, Solomon
74. Pollard
75. Porter, Roxie Ann 92 1872-1964
76. Potter, Rosa Wright Aug 9, 1941-Dec 4, 1928
77. Randall, Thelma Payne 1904-1937 At Rest
78. Rawlings, Erline From Ruby and Lu
79. Rawlings, Holmes [govt marker] Ohio Pvt 92 QM Co 72 Inf Div World War II Sept
    24, 1904-Oct 7, 1965
80. Rice, Hugh "Cap" 1877-1956
81. Robinson, A. Delores 1909-
82. Robinson, James A. 1906-1959
83. Rogers, Edward H. 1883-1958
84. Rogers, Rosetta M. 1894-1961
85. Rudd, Robert W. July 4, 1872-Sep 23, 1936
86. Sebree, Birdie Sept 18, 1891-Mar 16, 1965
87. Sebree, Dudley Dec 31, 1864-Feb 5, 1936 Father
88. Sebree, Edward T. Apr 18, 1887-Apr 30, 1921
89. Sebree, Hannah L. Feb 18, 1867-Oct 15, 1930
90. Sebree, James [Dr] Oct 25, 1885-Apr 16, 1908
91. Sebree, William W. Sep 2, 1899-May 3, 1926
92. Simmons, Mary A wife of Samuel Moore Dec 30, 1876-May 22, 1919
93. Sims, Joe Will Departed this life Nov 2, 1967
94. Smalls, Charles Oct 10, 1857-Aug 9, 1934 Father
95. Smith, Artie "Smitty" 1912-
96. Smith, Doris "Shorty Jo" 1916-
97. Steward, Alice J. Mar 16, 1874-June 1, 1959
98. Stockdale, Pearl B. Feb 5, 1880-Aug 8, 1928
99. Stockman, Susie July 3, 1866-Apr 16, 1943
100. Thomas, Daniel 1851-1926
101. Thomas, Florence wife of J. L. Thomas Jan 1, 1881-Sept 1, 1923
102. Thomas, John May 3, 1872-Feb 14, 1964
103. Thomas, John L. son of John & Florence Thomas June 27, 1906-Feb 1, 1921
104. Thomas, Mary E. [wife of Daniel T.] 1851-1917

105. Waddy, George W. 1872-1942
106. Waddy, Nannie B. 1877-19[60]
107. Webb, Donald C. [govt marker] Indiana Cpl 1077 Base Unit AAF World War II Dec 3, 1901-Sep 19, 1962
108. Wigginton, Maj. Y. C. Apr 11, 1870-Dec 6, 1923
109. Wilkins, Harry E. Jan 25, 1870-Sep 24, 1922
110. Wilson, Ben 1883-1954
111. Wilson, Lucille Feb 9, 1959 At Rest
112. Wing, Lillian G. 1887-1970
113. Yellow, Thelma B. LYNN Nov 16, 1900-Nov 4, 1976

Newberry (Quaker) Cemetery

This burying ground is located in Section 34, Township 2 North, Range 1 West two miles west of Paoli on state road 56. In 1826 the Newberry Friends Monthly Meeting was established from the Lick Creek Friends Church east of the county seat.

Cemetery Records compiled by the Lost River Chapter, Daughters of American Revolution (DAR) in Orange County (1947) show that one section of this burying ground contained the graves of colored people.[9] They reported the following graves with markers:

1. BOWMAN, Henry, January 6, 1835-October 31, 1903.
2. BOWMAN, Martha, July 6, 1838-August 18, 1881.
3. BOWMAN, James A., son of H & MA Bowman, September 9, 1863-November 12, 1864.
4. BOWMAN, Richard Edgar, son of H & M Bowman, November 11, 1857-March 12, 1875.
5. BURNETT, Amos, [son of Thomas & Winey] died December 23, 1871, aged 23y/9m/19d.
6. BURNETT, Charles, son of Lewis & Mary, died August 23, 1863 at age 3 years.
7. BURNETT, Jonathan, July 18, 1857-May 5, 1897.
8. BURNETT, Louis, October 16, 1837-January 31, 1910.
9. BURNETT, Mary A., daughter of Enoch & Parlee.
10. BURNETT, Viletta, daughter of Enoch & Parlee, 1873-1876.
11. BURNETT, Thomas, died February 19, 1883, aged 77y/11m/4d.
12. BURNETT, Winey Ann, wife of Thomas, October 16, 1815-January 24, 1908.
13. HOWARD, William J., 1847-1913.
14. HOWARD, Margarieth, 1858-1916.
15. RICKMAN, Parlee [daughter of J. A. Rickman]

The DAR reported the following burials were in *unmarked* graves:

1. BURNETT, Arch, died 1900.
2. BURNETT, Mary, his wife, died 1893.
3. HOWARD, Caroline (daughter of Nancy Sweat; wife of William Howard), died 1890.
4. SWEAT, Nancy, died 1893.
5. THOMAS, Susan, died 1897.

Roberts Graves

This abandoned burying ground is located in Stampers Creek Township Section 14, Township 1 North, Range 1 East. The county's DAR Records stated that the Roberts families were among the early settlers in the township. Marion Buchanan reported to the DAR that some members of the family were buried in a small group of unmarked graves. James Roberts owned land in this section in 1835, and his son, John Roberts, was the first person buried in the Pleasant Grove Cemetery.

The summary continues, "One report is to the effect that some of the burials here were colored people. As Stampers Creek Township, and indeed, much of Orange County, was settled largely by people from the South, this is quite possible, and may account for numbers of unmarked graves in numerous little family graveyards over the country. Colored retainers, faithful and devoted, accompanied many of the settlers from the South, and according to custom, were given burial in a section of family burying grounds."[10]

Bethel Cemetery (Orangeville Township)

Located in Section 31, Township 3 North, Range 1 West one and one-half miles north of Orangeville, this cemetery dates to 1821 and the north part of the old section was said to have been used as an Indian burying ground. The present nearby church structure dates to 1871, and the Independent Order of Odd Fellows (IOOF) addition to the cemetery was opened in 1892. There are many unmarked graves.[11] The following African American couple is buried there:

Bond, Reuben, d. Aug 1 1834 age 36 years
Bond, Penelope, d. Nov 1885, age about 80 years

Green Hill Cemetery (Orleans Township)

This cemetery is one of three adjoining cemeteries on the western edge of the town of Orleans and located in Section 30, Township 3 North, Range 1 East. Green Hill, or Old Town Cemetery, was laid off when the town was founded in 1815. There are a number of unmarked graves and many inscriptions are too worn to decipher. The Independent Order of Odd Fellows (IOOF) Cemetery is opposite on the north side of Jefferson Street, and the Fairview Cemetery opened in 1910 lies west of the IOOF addition.

African Americans known to be buried in Green Hill are all members of one family:

1. Todd, Amanda J, died July 28, 1866, age 23y, 6m, 5d.
2. Todd, Fannie, died Nov 19, 1877, age 16 y, 10m, 18d.
3. Todd, Green, died Dec 5, 1879, age 27y, 9m, 2d.
4. Todd, Green A., colored, Private, 9th U. S. Cavalry, Indiana. Died May 13, 1915.
5. Todd, Mary A, died Oct 9, 1878, age 21y, 3d.
6. Todd, Melvina, Dec 5, 1825-Dec 16, 1896.
7. Todd, Morris B, died Oct 25, 1864, age 23 y, 2m, 18d.
8. Todd, Pearson, died Aug 12, 1866, age 56y, 4m, 2d.
9. Todd, Quinn, died Sept 23, 1865.

Burials in Other Cemeteries

It is likely that African Americans are buried in other cemeteries located in Paoli Township. Around the turn of this century and in recent years some internments were reported to be made in the "Old Town" and "Community" Cemeteries in the town of Paoli. During this research oral reports were received of the burials of "colored people" in other cemeteries near Chamberburg, the Stampers Creek area, and French Lick, but no attempt was made to locate any confirming documents.

Death records are kept by the County Department of Public Health in the Courthouse Annex building. In addition to the "Indexes to the Death Records" compiled by the Works Progress Administration (W.P.A.) in the 1940s, they have the original "Register of Funerals 1897-1904" kept by the Maris Funeral Home in Paoli.

NOTES

1. Visitors unfamiliar with the area are advised to seek help to locate this cemetery. Contact the Ranger, Hoosier National Forest Office, 210 SW Court Street, Paoli, IN 47454, telephone 812/723-5368. Hopefully the travel route will be improved for self-guided tours to this historic site.

2. Current forestry maps provide an inaccurate location of the Lick Creek (Little Africa) Cemetery in the Hoosier National Forest area. Rather than being located near the north center of Section 27, it is actually situated one quarter section farther north and only a very short distance from the boundary line between Sections 27 and 22. Once there was a roadway southward from Chambersburg into the settlement. This direct route passed near the properties of Elias Roberts and Mathew Thomas, and connected with other roads leading to the church and cemetery lands as well as the entire settlement region. Based on local legends and maps in the Lick Creek Settlement Collection, Hoosier National Forest.

According to land records presently available for research, this cemetery was near but not did adjoin the property which Thomas and Matilda Roberts sold from their 120 acres farm to the trustees of the A. M. E. Church in 1843. On March 10, 1851 the Thomas Robertes sold their acreage in the settlement, and the land on which the cemetery was situated went to Elias Roberts. When Elias Roberts died in 1866, his estate was divided among the heirs which included Mathew Thomas. Prior to dying intestate in 1870, Mathew Thomas acquired a total of 322 acres which eventually was sold by his heirs. Thus, at different periods of time, this private cemetery actually belonged to the Roberts and Thomas families.

3. Detailed reports of these activities appeared in the January 3, 1971 issue, *Sunday Herald-Times*, Bloomington, Indiana, TARGET, Sec.4, p. 33, under the general heading, "Little Africa Cemetery." Articles written by Wanda G. Williams, staff writer, included: "Page in History Is Uncovered; Little Africa Cemetery Found," "Negroes Insecure in Early Indiana," and "Negro Count Was Taken." Coverage included photographs of the monument stone containing the bronze plaques for Ishmael Roberts and Simon Locust; an overview picture of cemetery showing rows of white crosses and the split railing fence; an interior cemetery picture of local boy scouts studying gravestones; and, close-up views of a white cross and broken marker for baby daughter, Frances Bond, who died in 1864, and the large, well preserved marker for Albert Morton, 12-year old son of I & P. A. Irvin.

4. "Scouts Unearth History Chapter at County's Dense Little Africa," *The Paoli News*, Thursday, December 31, 1970. Contains a lengthy article and photograph of Boy Scouts at work. Troop members identified with project were: Jon Newlin, Gerald Scott, George Jones, David Newlin, Danny Newlin, Ronnie Runyon, Jerry Meahan, Calvin Parrott, Steve Franz, Norman Jones and Tom Clements. Eagles Duane Smith and Mark McCoy served as assistant Scout leaders and did much of the record searching. Scout fathers assisting were Roe McCoy, Howard King, Norman Jones, Leslie Cox, George Condra, and Harry Clements. Bob Patton contributed the masonry work to construct the monument. According to this newspaper article, the Paoli Troop 85 was committed through an arrangement with the U. S. Forest Service to clean the cemetery annually.

5. Information on this bronze plaque should be corrected. Harry Clements and the Boy Scouts received this grave marker without cost in 1970 from the U. S. Veterans Service.

6. Inclusion of the word "Union" in the name of the church on the sign at the cemetery entrance actually created a religious denomination which did not exist. The Boy Scouts, lacking familiarity with the history of African Methodism made some incorrect assumptions after discovering deeds for two different "colored" churches in the Hoosier National Forest area. Concluding both churches were the same, they combined the name of "Union Meeting House" found in the 1837 deed with "African Methodist Episcopal Church" referred to in the 1843 deed, ending up with the designation, "African Methodist Episcopal Union Meetinghouse." See Chapter IX on Religion and Churches.

7. Based upon the 1970 report of legible tombstone markings published in article, "Negro Count Was Taken," January 3, 1971, *Sunday Herald-Times*, Bloomington, IN., p. 33. Coy D. Robbins last visited this cemetery on July 16, 1990. Only a few stones were readable. Many half and broken gravestones were scattered among the weeds and small shrubs.

8. Heinegg's Research completed in 1992 on the Roberts family in North Carolina indicates that Ishmael Roberts, the Revolutionary War soldier, died and was buried in Chatham County, N. C. North Carolina land records and copy of Ishmael Roberts' will show that he purchased and sold several hundred acres of land in Robeson County, N.C. between 1787 and 1825. Final sales to his sons, Richard, James and Aaron Roberts, were signed on 2th and 12th February 1825, prior to his death. One son, Aaron Roberts, married Jary Teary [Terry] in Robeson County, N. C. on October 10, 1816. In the 1840 U. S. Census, an Aaron Roberts was listed as

head of household containing five "free colored" persons in Washington Township, Owen County, Indiana. Correspondence dated October 8, 1992 between Coy D. Robbins and Paul Heinegg, researcher and writer of the book, *Free African Americans in North Carolina* (privately printed by author, 1992).

9. Typewritten cemetery manuscripts in the Paoli Public Library and the collections of Mrs. Wilma Davis, Orange County Historian. Newberry Cemetery listings on pages 67-68.

10. DAR Cemetery Records for Orange County, Indiana, p. 267.

11. Lost River Chapter, DAR, *Cemetery Records of Orange County, Indiana* (Paoli: Private printing, 1947), 117.

CHAPTER XI

EDUCATION

Early Schools in Indiana

The racial majority in Indiana acted no differently when setting up their educational system than they did when establishing other religious, health and human service organizations: it was intended for whites only. For reasons never explained, some exceptions to the racially exclusive classroom did take place in Indiana pioneer schools.

How commonplace were these interracial school experiences? Under what circumstances did these occur and how long did they continue? Few early school records which might provide answers to these questions have survived. On the other hand, educational traditions were recorded, and oftentimes information about integrated classes was hidden in local and county histories.

Perhaps genealogists and historians will survey extant historical documents for possible references to the education of African American children before the Civil War.

The Developing School System

Early schools in Indiana were wholly inadequate, in spite of the lofty objective declared in its first Constitution of 1816 "to provide by law for a general system of education, ascending in gradation from township schools to a State University, wherein tuition be gratis and equally open to all."[1]

School laws were soon passed, but implementation was extremely slow. Money was scarce, a lack of qualified teachers, and most Hoosiers lived in the scattered, isolated regions where land had been the easiest to obtain. Furthermore, expensive public improvements were sorely needed everywhere: building roads, clearing the land, and expanding the waterways to deliver farm products to markets. Many pioneers felt these needs were more urgent than the luxury of providing free education to children at the expense of taxpayers.

The first school laws made no mention of color, and it is possible that a few African American children attended the early township schools. By 1837, nevertheless, a law was passed which restricted the organization of the tax supported school system to "the white inhabitants of each congressional township."[2]

Private and church elementary schools existed in the territory prior to statehood, and afterwards the number increased rapidly. Quakers, Presbyterians, and Catholics played an important role. What they contributed to the education of pioneer children can be found in county histories. The enrollment of colored children in these schools varied, depending upon such factors as racial attitudes among whites residents, individual teachers, and the ability of African American families to pay the tuition and transport their students to the school.

Public schools in Indiana remained exclusively for white children until after the Civil War. The number of tax supported schools on the township or district level increased gradually in the 1830s and 1840s. At first they differed little from other schools. In some cases, existing private and church schools were subsidized by tax monies. Academies or seminaries were developed at the same time to meet the educational needs between the "common school" and college. Beginning in 1850 there was a movement to abolish county seminaries and to replace them with public high schools.[3]

None of the public schools were free. All charged tuition to pay part of the costs. It was not until after the Civil War that Indiana developed a school system comparable to those of the more advanced states.

Reference to integrated classes in pioneer schools may be discovered in traditional county histories in the section on "Schools" or "Education." For example, one such account was located in the 1884 Goodspeed *History of Washington County, Indiana* under the heading, "An Old Method of Correction." A man recalled how as a young teacher he handled a classroom discipline problem involving "a very bad, white boy named Dan Richardson, and a peaceable, quiet, well disposed colored (italics added) boy named Dempsey Nixon."[4]

Colored School Children in Orange County

In the 1850 U. S. Population Census report for Orange County, Indiana, six African American children--one boy and five girls--were reported as attending school. This information came out of an academic study on the history of the early education of Negro children in Indiana, and the author, Herbert Lynn Heller, discovered some astounding details about the extent to which African Americans were trying without the benefit of public schools to educate their children.[5]

Orange County was not unique for having non-white children attending school in 1850 as Black children in Martin and Washington Counties also received some type of formal education in a school setting (table 15).

TABLE 15:

African American Children Identified in the 1850 Census
as Attending School in Orange and Adjoining Counties

County	Total Black Population	School Age* Children	Black Children in School		
			Total	Boys	Girls
Crawford	1	0	0	0	0
Dubois	21	8	0	0	0
Lawrence	94	34	+	+	+
Martin	96	41	12	9	3
ORANGE	251	85	6	1	5
Washington	252	102	11	9	2

Continued on next page

Table 15--*Continued*

County	Total Black Population	School Age* Children	Black Children in School		
			Total	Boys	Girls
Total in Indiana	11,262	4,505	1,026	526	500

Source: Heller, "Negro Education in Indiana from 1816 to 1869." Extracted from data in Tables 1-6, Appendix on pages 275-292.

*between ages 5-21 years.   +no report given.

A. M. E. Church Day and Sabbath Schools

Some children attending school in 1850 may have enrolled in the private subscription schools sponsored by individuals or religious groups, such as the Quakers.[6]

On the other hand, Black children did attend schools established in their own communities. As early as 1845, the annual minutes of the Indiana Conference of the A. M. E. Church highlighted reports on established day and sabbath schools in its churches.

Ministers at the 1845 conference, for example, described the following schools on their circuits:

(1) Indianapolis [Marion County], Day and Sabbath Schools.
(2) Blue River [Carthage, Rush County], Day and Sabbath Schools.
(3) Flat Rock [Henry County], Day School.
(4) Cambridge City [Wayne County], Day School.
(5) Richmond [Wayne County], Day School.
(6) Cabin Creek [Randolph County], Day School.
(7) Salem [Washington County], Day School.
(8) Newport [Fountain City, Wayne County], Sabbath School.
(9) Lafayette [Tippecanoe County], Sabbath Schools.
(10) Terre Haute [Vigo County], Sabbath Schools.[7]

In the historical context of the period, the term "day school" referred to educational classes conducted on week days in the church building, while "sabbath school" referred to the traditional religious training in Sunday School. In actuality, however, it was probably impossible to make these distinctions between the types of educational focus pursued in the two settings at that time. The need for formal education was so great and the resources were so limited that the church's teaching programs varied to accommodate the demands encountered locally.

In the above list of schools within the church system, the Day School reported for the "Salem Circuit" probably included from one-to-three A.M.E. Churches in Washington, Jackson and Orange Counties. Further details about the Day School are lacking: its location, residence of its pupils, teaching staff, costs to church and supporting families, etc.

What can be realized from these data is that as early as 1845 some African Americans in Indiana provided within their own churches the education denied to their children in the tax-supported public school system. Even more astonishing is the discovery that this single African Methodist church system became so widely dispersed over the state just five years after it was organized. Stop for a moment and consider that each of the ten listings in 1845 represented only the names of "church circuits." Each circuit was composed of several different congregations located in the general region of the principal church. Here is indisputable evidence of a thriving religious network among the free people of color throughout Indiana almost one hundred and fifty years ago.

Separate Public Schools: 1869-1954

Pressures mounted after the Civil War ended for Black children to attend the public schools. Thousands of newcomers, many of whom were former slaves, flocked into the state with a desire for an education second only to the vital need for food and shelter. Congregations of Black churches everywhere strained their limited resources to meet the increased demands for education, and the additional schools which developed mainly in urban areas were still insufficient to fill the gap.

Meanwhile, the Indiana legislature delayed any effort to use public funds for the educational needs of non-whites. White leaders did not advocate that colored children be admitted to the existing schools in the state, but rather they sought separate schools as a concession to public opinion which opposed the mingling of the races. Many Hoosiers feared that providing public schools for Black children would only serve as an inducement for Indiana to be overrun eventually by Blacks. Opposition was often summarized with the comment, "Our government was established by white men, for white men and women, and children, and their posterity."[8]

By 1869, Indiana and Illinois were the only two northern states which still had not provided for the public education of Black children. Finally, at the special legislative session in which the 15th Amendment to the Federal Constitution was ratified, Indiana enacted a law requiring school trustees to organize separate schools for Black children where there was a large enough group to justify such a school.[9]

In September, 1869 the first public schools for colored children were opened in Indianapolis, Evansville, Terre Haute, Vincennes, Connersville, Shelbyville, and in some rural areas, such as Lost Creek Township in Vigo County. By 1875, two thirds of the almost seven thousand children enrolled in Indiana's colored schools lived in nine counties. Where their numbers were small, some children had been admitted to white schools.[10]

The state school law as amended in 1877 allowed school authorities to still maintain separate schools, but where separate schools did not exist officials could allow colored children to attend the public schools with white children. The amendment also gave school authorities the choice of admitting colored pupils to white schools under certain circumstances, and it opened the way for Blacks to be admitted to public high schools. After passage of the 1877 law, local authorities held the option of keeping segregated or non-segregated schools.

Actually, the first African American graduate from an Indiana high school took place one year before the 1877 law was adopted. In 1872, Mary Rann enrolled at the Indianapolis High School, later Shortridge High School, through special arrangements completed between members of the

Indianapolis colored community and the Superintendent of City Schools. She graduated four years later.

Slowly a small number of Blacks were reported as high school graduates in other parts of the state. Since the local school administrators retained the final word about the teaching staffs, facilities, and school expenditures as well as using racially separated schools, the quality of education varied greatly for non-white students in Indiana public schools.

The school patterns established before 1900 continued unchanged for the most part until the 1950s. In some areas separate schools prevailed on all educational levels, and although the preponderance of segregated schools were in the southern counties, they existed elsewhere--in the state's capitol, Indianapolis, and in the industrial communities of Terre Haute, Anderson, Kokomo, South Bend, Fort Wayne, and the Calumet region. In towns with a small population of Black school-age children, separate schools were often maintained on the elementary level, but racially mixed classes were taught in junior high and high schools.[11]

Our nation was finally forced to face the inadequacies of its segregated educational system after the 1954 U. S. Supreme Court decision in the case of BROWN V. THE BOARD OF EDUCATION. Scarcely any sector of the nation was unaffected by this pivotal legal decision. Almost fifty years after the ruling that segregated schools in the United States were unconstitutional, many communities still find it difficult to comply with the "law of the land."

Today, information about how these educational issues were ultimately resolved by local school systems is meager or non-existent. Furthermore, until recently, historians have paid little attention to this subject and how the Black children were educated in Indiana's mixed schools. The only written literature of any note which has survived comes from a few preserved contemporary newspaper accounts. For example, contents of the two documents printed below shed some light on the manner in which the Paoli schools handled racial issues after 1869.

Integration of Paoli Schools

The following handbill was distributed in response to efforts by the Paoli School Board to integrate classes in September, 1888:[12]

IMPORTANT   NOTICE

The undersigned citizens and Tax payers in the town of Paoli, respectfully ask the School Board of said town to reconsider their action in regard to mixing the colored pupils with the white pupils in our Public or High Schools. We respectfully submit that in our judgement it will have a very injurious effect on the reputation of our School, especially outside of our immediate neighborhood, and suggest that a shorter term with the pupils separated would be much more satisfactory and result in more good to both white and colored.

To the end that a fair expression of the sentiments of the community may be heard and the best interests of all concerned may be protected we request that the School Trustees and teachers meet with the citizens of Paoli at the Court room this evening Sept. 20, 1888, at 7 o'clock.

Ben Stinson	*Thos. Hunt*	*J. L. Megenity*
G. W. Thomas	*Jas. M. Andrew*	*L. S. Bowles*

Paoli, September 20, 1888.

Several days later an editorial on the subject appeared in the *Paoli Republican*, September 26, 1888. Written by A. W. Bruner and R. F. Clark, co-editors, it summarized the efforts to integrate the local schools:[13]

MIXED SCHOOLS

During the last few days a few of the citizens of Paoli have been troubled in mind over the question of mixed schools on Paoli. There has been no trouble in the school. True, Mr. Warren resigned after he found that two or three colored children were going to attend school in his grade. But the school went right on. Mr. H. F. Patton, whose splendid qualifications all will acknowledge, was employed in Mr. Warren's place. True, some of the white children withdrew from the school when it was known that five or six colored children were going to attend. But it is also true that they have since returned to school. The School Trustees did not expect trouble. In other localities mixed schools cause no trouble. Colored students attend the State Normal at Terre Haute [now Indiana State University, Terre Haute, IN. Editor]. The faculty did not resign. The students from Orange County did not return home. In the past, the terms of the free schools for the white children have been too short. The colored children have had incompetent teachers, short terms, and poor accommodations. Taxes in Paoli are too high. The free school term is too short. There are not enough colored children to form a colored school. Separate schools mean high taxes, or shorter terms. In this matter the School Trustees should continue to do what they are now doing, what is right and best for all concerned.

First Black High School Graduate

The name of Arthur "Army" Howard became renowned in the Paoli community, not because he was the first African American to graduate from the local school, but for his athletic skills on the school's basketball and track teams. He was an honor student and graduated with the class of 1917.[14]

Born on August 17, 1897, Arthur was the youngest of five children. His father, William J. Howard, was a native of Kentucky who migrated to Paoli in the 1870s, and his mother, Helen Sweat Howard was born in Orange County.

After his spectacular athletic and academic careers in high school, Arthur worked for years as a bellboy at the West Baden and French Lick hotels. When he died in 1963 without any surviving family, he was still remembered warmly by his former high school classmates.

Several photographs of Howard during his high school days have survived. He is in the formal picture of the 1917 basketball team which hangs on the entrance corridor wall across from the principal's office in the Paoli High School today. Another one was with his graduating class, and it was reprinted in the local newspaper with the announcement in 1987 that there would be no seventieth class reunion as only one of the four surviving members still lived in Paoli.

Schools in French Lick

The influx of African American families in the early 1900s to the flourishing mineral waters and hotel industries in the Springs Valley area of French Lick Township soon made it necessary for the public school system to come up with a plan to educate the colored children eligible to attend school.

It probably was due to the larger number of non-white pupils involved that French Lick, only nine years after the town was incorporated, established in 1911 the only racially segregated school building to ever exist in Orange County.[15]

The School Board purchased what was known as the old Christian Church building on West Wells Street and converted it into an elementary school for colored children. The first teacher was William H. Circey and it was called the Dunbar School, named after Paul Lawrence Dunbar (1872-1906), the famous African American poet from Dayton, Ohio.

Classes were held continuously in this school building until the end of the school year 1936-37. Miss Ivanetta Hughes, a 1930 graduate of the French Lick High School, was the last teacher in the colored school. The enrollment was reportedly never more than 15 or 16 students, and it dropped to 6 or 7 during the last few years of the school's existence.

The French Lick High School was commissioned in the spring of 1909, although a Normal School prepared to teach high school subjects had been operating in the community as early as 1901-02. Two boys were in the first graduating class of 1908-09, and the first basketball team under the Indiana State High School Athletic Association was organized in 1915.[16]

It is unknown when the first colored student attended this high school where the graduating classes each year between 1909-1920 contained from two to thirteen members. Scattered issues of the "Plutonian" high school year book in the local library contained pictures of African American students as early as 1914. No figures on their enrollment or early graduates have been located.

In the 1930 year book at the end of the graduating class photographs, one page contained the pictures and commentary about the three non-white seniors: (1) *Alyce Holden*, who was active in the orchestra and commercial clubs, (2) *Ivanetta Hughes*, a member of the commercial club (she later became a teacher in the colored school), and (3) *Frances Saulsberry*, who was in the Dunbar Literary Society; the Commercial, Science and Girl Reserve Clubs; the state-wide Bible Contest; and the Basketball team. These may have been the first Black graduates of the high school.

Winslow Pace, an African American member of the 1936 graduating class, returned for its 50th class reunion on July 4, 1986.[17] In the next year's annual, Raymond Ross, Harold Smith,

Edgar Clapp, Mary Smith and Arnold Wallace--all African Americans--were pictured among the high school students in 1937.

NOTES

1. Kettleborough, Charles (ed.), *Constitution Making in Indiana: a Source Book of Constitutional Documents with Historical Introduction and Critical Notes* (3 vols., Indianapolis, 1916-1930); Vols. I, II, XVII, Indiana Historical *Collections*; 112-114. Art. IX, Sec. 2.

2. *Laws of Indiana*, 1836-37 (general), 15; ibid., 1840-41 (general), 82.

3. John D. Barnhart and Donald F. Carmony, *Indiana: From Frontier to Industrial Commonwealth* (2 vols. New York, 1954; reprint, Indiana Historical Bureau, 1979), I:255-275; II: 105-128; Richard C. Boone, *A History of Education in Indiana* (New York: D. Appleton & Co., 1892; reprint, Indiana Historical Bureau, 1941), 30-112; Emma Lou Thornbrough, *The Negro in Indiana* (Indianapolis: Indiana Historical Bureau, 1957), 160-162.

4. *History of Lawrence, Orange and Washington Counties, Indiana* (Chicago: Goodspeed Bros. & Co., Publishers; Stout reprint, 1965), 834-5. The school, probably a private subscription school, was unidentified in the account and neither was the incident dated.

5. Herbert Lynn Heller, "Negro Education in Indiana from 1816 to 1869" (Ph.D., diss., Indiana University, 1951), 18-38.

6. Historical marker placed at the Society of Friends Church (Quakers) near Chambersburg indicates that the "Lick Creek Seminary" functioned near this site from 1831-1878.

7. A.M.E. Church minutes for years indicated in author's personal collection. Other churches outside of Indiana but within the Indiana Conference's jurisdiction and reporting day schools in 1845 included: (1) Shawneetown [Illinois], (2) Louisville [Kentucky], and (3) Mississippi [churches in the state of].

8. Quoted by Thornbrough, *The Negro in Indiana*, 321.

9. "An Act to render taxation for common-school purposes uniform, and to provide for the education of the colored children of the State," passed May 13, 1869. Boone, *History of Education in Indiana*, 239-240.

10. Thornbrough, *The Negro in Indiana*, 325. Counties with separate schools and their colored enrollments for 1875 were: Marion, 1,196; Vanderburgh, 537; Clark, 427; Vigo, 389; Floyd, 309; Spencer, 347; Wayne, 279; Jefferson, 278; and Gibson, 245. Chapter contains some interesting historical details about the legal definition of "colored children," the employment of teachers, inadequate funding, substandard facilities, etc.

11. Emma L. Thornbrough, *Since Emancipation: A Short History of Indiana Negroes, 1863-1963* (Indianapolis: Indiana Division American Negro Emancipation Centennial Authority, 1963), 53-69.

12. Arthur L. Dillard, compiler, *History of the Orange County Courthouse* (Paoli, Ind.: By the author; undated), 113.

13. Ibid., 114.

14. Obituary printed in the *Paoli Republican*, Tuesday December 10, 1963; census, marriage and Newberry Cemetery records.

15. "Historical Souvenir Program," *French Lick Centennial 1857-1957*, 23. Only known source of written history about the Dunbar School. For years the school was next door to the French Lick A. M. E. Church building which was demolished in the early 1980s. Today the former school building houses a commercial plumbing company.

16. *Plutonian* 1930 yearbook contains a history of the French Lick High School, including the number of graduates from 1909-1929. Much of the school identity is tied to the local mineral springs industry and "Pluto" water is still available for purchase today. West Baden and French Lick High Schools were consolidated in 1957. Early athletic teams were called the "Red Devils," after the Pluto Company's trademark symbol. Now, they are called the "Hawkeyes." Perhaps the best known graduate of this school in recent years has been Larry Bird, who graduated from Indiana State University in Terre Haute and gained national fame as a professional basketball player.

17. *Springs Valley Herald*, July 9, 1986, 1.

CHAPTER XII

MISCELLANEOUS DOCUMENTS

The legal records summarized below may be of special interest to our readers. These documents with both genealogical and historical significance were located during the course of research for this book. However, due to the singular nature of their contents, it was difficult to incorporate them into other chapters. Names are printed in CAPITALS of all parties believed to be African Americans in the documents discussed below.

Indentured Poor Black Children

One system used by governmental officials in the early nineteenth century to care for destitute and orphaned children involved legally placing them to live with responsible adults in the community. In return for providing the daily necessities, such as shelter, food, and clothing, the indentured child had to pay for the care by working at assigned tasks for a specified period or until the child reached the age of majority.

From the time Orange County was organized in 1816, the care of poor persons or paupers, as they were then called, was assumed at public expense. "Overseers of the Poor" were appointed on the township level and their duties were to look after the needs of the poor and to report what they spent to the County Board for settlement.[1]

Three indentures found among the old deed records of Orange County pertained to African American children who had been legally placed and bound by the Overseers of the Poor in South East Township. The race or color of parties involved in these documents was not specified although in other Indiana counties similar indentures clearly indicated that the child or parents were "colored."[2] Racial confirmation of the three children identified in the Orange County indentures came from other sources, such as census and family history data.

There were many similarities of the legal language used in documents to bind out children who were destitute and those who were apprenticed for training in a specialized trade. Two features of the indenture document distinguished its basic purpose. In cases of orphaned or indigent children, the name of a person with the title, "Overseers of the Poor," was always a party of the legal action; and, secondly, the term "poor" was usually included in the descriptive label of the child being indentured.

The exploitation and abuse of indentured or bound out children in America's history has been well documented. Meager records located about them in Orange County, however, failed to explain the final outcome of the individual child placements.

Not only was it surprising to learn that free children of African ancestry were indentured in this county before the Civil War, but equally so was that they were actually placed legally with

African American families.

ANDREW SCOTT

On October 1, 1840, Kinsey Veach and Jefferson Moore, Overseers of the Poor in South East Township, placed and bound ANDREW SCOTT, "a poor boy aged ten years eleven months and seventeen days" as an apprentice to MARTIN SCOTT.[3]

The indenture located in Deed Book G, pages 449-450 stated that Andrew was to receive training in the art, trade and occupation of farming until he reached the age of twenty-one years. At the expiration of his term of service, MARTIN SCOTT assented to furnish the boy "one suit of good linsey jeans cloth, fur hat, good shoes, horse saddle and bridle worth forty dollars."

HENRY WEAVER

Two months later on December 17, 1840, the same Overseers Kinsey Veach and Jefferson Moore signed another indenture found in Deed Book H, pages 26-27. It placed and bound a poor boy, HENRY WEAVER, to MARTIN SCOTT for training in farming--"after the best way and manner that he can." Henry was only one year and six months old and his term of service was for nineteen years and six months. At the end of the apprenticeship, MARTIN SCOTT agreed to provide the child "a suit of new Jeans cloths."[4]

CATHARINE WEAVER

The third indenture of a poor child was recorded in Deed Book K, pages 621-622. On January 31, 1846, Jesse Barnett and William Holoday, Overseers of the Poor in South East Township, placed CATHARINE WEAVER, a poor girl about two years old, with HENRY SCOTT. For the term of fifteen years and six months, HENRY SCOTT, a mulatto wagon maker in the Lick Creek Settlement, promised to train Catharine in the occupation of "house wifery." There were no provisions for the girl to receive any material benefits at the completion of her apprenticeship.[5]

Apprenticeship Records

Indentures were found for eleven children of color who were apprenticed in Orange County between the years 1821 and 1868. Apprenticing children to learn a trade or occupation from an adult with established skills was a long standing practice which became legalized in the western European culture long before the discovery of America.

Usually pre-adolescent and adolescent boys were apprenticed. Society generally placed little value on the training of girls beyond the skills to become a housewife. Apprenticeship terms varied, but as depicted from the collection found in Orange County, the child served until reaching adulthood: 21 years for males and 18 years for females.

In return for the training, lodging, food, and necessary clothing, the apprentice worked under the supervision of the craftsman without salary or money. The craftsman, however, might profit greatly from the labor of apprentices. In actual day-by-day practice, this legal system of apprenticeship resulted in much abuse and misuse of children. Eventually, in the twentieth century, child labor restrictions and compulsory school attendance laws in this country helped to bring some corrective changes in the legalized apprenticing of children.

As noted earlier in this chapter, difficulties are encountered in attempts to distinguish accurately between those children who were apprenticed for specialized training from those who were indentured because they were poor, orphaned, and dependent children. For this study, all indenture documents were classified as "apprenticeship"--unless at least one party to the agreement was identified as "overseers of the poor."

It should be noted that the majority of children in these indentures were apprenticed to African Americans.

WILLIAM B. THOMAS - 1821

LUCY THOMAS indentured her son, WILLIAM B. THOMAS, to Thomas F. Chapman in 1821, only five years after Indiana achieved statehood. This chronicle in handscript is recorded on page 363 in Deed Book A. Representing one of the oldest legal documents found in Orange County pertaining to African Americans to date, an edited version reads:

THIS INDENTURE, made this fourteenth day of September in the year of our Lord one thousand eight hundred amd twenty one betwixt Thomas F Chapman of the one part and Lucy Thomas, mother of William B Thomas an infant under the age of fourteen years of the other part,

Witnesseth that the said Lucy Thomas, mother of said William B. for the consideration here unto mentioned, doth covenant promise and agree to and with the said Thomas F Chapman, his executors and administrators, by these presents or manner following;

that the said William B Thomas, infant son of the said Lucy, shall and will for and during the term and time of fourteen years and six months when the said William B shall arive to full age of twenty one years to begin and be accounted from the date of these presents, serve oblige and continue with the said Thomas F Chapman his covenants servant and diligently and faithfully according to the best and utmost of his power exercise and employ himself in and do and perform all such service and business as the said Thomas F shall from time to time order direct and appoint to and for the most profit and advantage to the said Thomas that he can, that he will be just and faithful and readily obey all his lawful commands, and in all things as a good and honest servent will demean and behave himself towards his said master and all his,

And in consideration of the premise and of several matters and things by the said William B infant son of said Lucy to be performed as aforesaid, the said Thomas F doth covenant promise and agree to and with the said Lucy mother aforesaid that the said Thomas F shall and will find and provide unto and for said William B at his dwelling house, meat, drink, washing, lodging, clothing and all other necessaries fit and convenient for such servent during the term aforesaid

and when the said William B shall arive at the full age of twenty one and the aforesaid term of service shall have expired, he, the said Thomas F will make and execute to the said William B a good and sufficient deed in fee simple of a half quarter section of land not worse than second rate, will also furnish at the same time a colt worth thirty dollars, also a good plain saddle and bridle also a decent freedom suit of clothes also during the time aforesaid shall give him the said William a good common school education.

In witness whereof the said Thomas F Chapman and Lucy Thomas above named have hereunto set our hands and seals the day and year aforesaid.

	her
In presence of Witnesses }	*Lucy X Thomas (SEAL)*
J W Pichard }	*mark*
Thomas Tindal }	*Thomas F Chapman (SEAL)*
Bryant Thomas }	

Paoli September 14th 1821

Whereas Lucy Thomas did by articles of indenture bearing date September 14th 1821 bind to me her son William B Thomas aged six years and six months to serve until he shall have arived at the full age of twenty one years, I do agree with the said Lucy that if I should finally move with my family to reside in any other state (prior to the expiration of the said William B time of service) not to move this William B but to leave him in the state of Indiana and to allow him full compensation for his services from the date above written to the time of such removal.

T F Chapman

Attest: Z Lindley

Recorded November 13th AD 1821 J[ohn] McVey, ROC [Recorder Orange County][6]

Thomas F. Chapman, the other party in this legal transaction, was a white businessman and an early resident family of Paoli. In 1822, he owned a dry-goods store with two partners, and later served as Orange County Agent.[7]

Nothing further was found in Orange County about William B. Thomas or his mother, Lucy Thomas, after she apprenticed the second son, Mathew Thomas (see next document). Both boys were probably related to Jordon Thomas, the child who was apprenticed in 1822, but no confirming documentation has been located.

MATHEW THOMAS - 1821

Less than one month later on October 6, 1821, LUCY THOMAS indentured her thirteen year old son, MATHEW, to Zachariah Lindley for a term of eight years. This document was recorded in Deed Book A, page 365, and its language and general content are similar to the previous one. When Mathew was 21 years old and completed his term of service, Lindley agreed to provide him with: (1) eighty acres of land "to be as good as second rate," (2) a colt worth twenty dollars, (3) a "freedom" suit, and (4) six months schooling.

MATHEW THOMAS (1808-1870) finished his service, received the land as promised, and eventually became a large landowner in the Lick Creek Settlement. His family history is included in Chapter XV under, "Mathew and Mary Thomas."

Much has been recorded about Zachariah Lindley. A Quaker and early white settler from North Carolina, he purchased government land in Paoli Township and was elected Sheriff in 1816 and 1822. He served in other appointed and elected county offices including those of Collector, Treasurer, leader of a band of regulars and Colonel in the 13th Regiment, Indiana Militia.[8]

JORDON THOMAS - 1822

On December 5, 1822, BRYANT THOMAS apprenticed a child named JORDON THOMAS to Lewis Byram. The document was recorded in Deed Book B, page 2. In the usual language of such indentures, it affirmed that the boy, over six years old, was bound to Lewis Byrum for a term of fifteen years, five months and thirteen days to learn "the art and mystery of farming." Upon completion of his apprenticeship, Jordon was to receive a deed for forty acres of land. Lewis Byram (white) was listed during the 1819 election as a voter in Northwest Township.[9]

The relationship between BRYANT THOMAS and JORDON THOMAS was never specified. Nor is it known whether either one or both of these Thomases were related to Lucy Thomas, the woman who indentured her two sons one year earlier. However, BRYANT THOMAS did witness the apprenticeship papers which Lucy Thomas signed the previous year for her son, William B. Thomas. In the 1820 census Bryant Thomas headed a household of four persons: two adults (male and female), plus two girls under age 14 years old.

Jordon Thomas obtained forty acres of land and completed his apprenticeship upon reaching his twenty-first birthday. He married CANDISS ROBERTS on January 11, 1838 and they had at least nine children before he died in 1853. (Further details about Jordon Thomas in Chapter XV).

OSBORN BOND - 1845

This apprenticeship document was found in Deed Book J-10, pages 517-518. Leonard Green, legal guardian of OSBORN BOND, age 14 years, bound over the boy for apprenticeship training in the "art of farming," to John G. Clendenin. The term of service was to expire on May 15, 1851 when Osborn would be twenty one years old. At the completion of this service, Clendenin agreed to give the boy fifty dollars which was "to be paid by the said Leonard Green."

Marriage records in Orange County reveal that OSBORN (OSMAND) BOND and MARY GUTHRIE married on August 4, 1853. By the 1860 census, Osborn and Mary Bond, mulattoes, lived on a farm in French Lick Township with their three small daughters, Mary, Lucinda and Margaret.

In 1840 Leonard Green (white), who was Osborn's legal guardian in 1845, served on the committee of three appointed to superintend the county's poor farm. John G. Clendenin (white) was an early settler who operated dry goods stores in Paoli. He was a Presbyterian, active in local politics and served as an Indiana State Representative from 1822-1827.[10]

JOHN GILLIAM - 1847

John is one of the two boys who were apprenticed to MOSES SNEED, an African American shoemaker who maintained his business in the town of Paoli. This indenture is located in Deed Book 12, pages 39-40 and states that HANNAH BUTLER placed her son, JOHN GILLIAM, with MOSES SNEED on November 11, 1847.[11] Sneed agreed to teach the boy "the art, trade and occupation of a shoe and boot maker."

Apprenticeship term was of four years. Sneed agreed to provide the boy three months common school education in addition to the customary food, lodging, washing and clothing; and at the completion of service, he promised to give John a set of bench tools "sufficient for a journeyman."[12]

WILLIAM R. ROBERTS - 1850

On May 6, 1850 ELIAS ROBERTS apprenticed his minor son, WILLIAM R. ROBERTS, to MOSES SNEED to learn "the mystery of a boot and shoemaker" until August 10, 1852. Located in the Apprentice Record Book 1, page 13-14, this indenture specified the usual conditions except there were no provision for William to receive anything upon the completion of service.

In the 1850 census William was enumerated as an 18 year old mulatto shoemaker living with the Moses Sneed family in the town of Paoli.

SARAH ELIZABETH EVANS - 1852

BRAZILLA EVANS apprenticed her one year old daughter, SARAH ELIZABETH EVANS, to ANDERSON SMITH on August 11, 1852 for training as a housekeeper. The term of apprenticeship was for seventeen years or until the child reached the age of eighteen years. At the expiration of her term of service, Smith agreed to give Sarah "two new suits of wearing apparel worth at least ten dollars." This document was found in Apprentice Record Book 1, pages 35-37.

Nothing further is known about Brazilla Evans, the mother, although several young adults with the Evans surname were enumerated in the 1850 census. On the other hand, ANDERSON SMITH, mulatto, was a farmer and landowner in Lick Creek Settlement in South East Township. The 1850 census revealed that the Smiths' household had ten children. They were not listed in later censuses.[13]

LYDIA AND MERIDAN DAVIS - 1863

On September 4, 1863, ELIZABETH DAVIS indentured her daughter, LYDIA, and her infant son, MERIDAN, to CHURCHILL ISOM. Recorded in Apprentice Record Book 1, page 96, this document failed to indicate any specific training for Lydia, who was aged three years, five months and eighteen days. However, Meridan, aged one year, eleven months and twenty two days was to be taught farming. Term of service was until Lydia reached age eighteen years, and her brother had to serve until he was twenty one years old. No provision made for either child to receive any additional benefits when the term expired.

No information found about the mother, Elizabeth Davis. Both children, however, were enumerated in the 1870 census as living with Churchill Isom, a 33-year old African American farmer in Orangeville Township. Lydia, age 10 years, and Marion (Meridan), age 8 years, carried the Isom surname. There was also a 6 years old, James Isom, in the family unit which did not contain any adult female.[14]

ALLIE E. ROBERTS - 1866

Found in Apprentice Record Book 1, page 98, this indenture was dated February 14, 1862 and involved SARAH ROBERTS, who apprenticed her daughter, ALLIE E. ROBERTS, to ISAAC IRVIN.

No special training was designated for the one year old apprentice, Allie. However, when her term of service expired on January 18, 1883, Isaac Irvin agreed to give Allie "good freedom cloth[es] and one bed and bedding."

In 1870, four years after this indenture was formalized, Isaac Irvin was listed as a mulatto farmer in Stampers Creek Township. With his 37-year old wife, Jenetta, they had seven children which included a five-year old Allie Isom, who appears to be the same child apprenticed to them in 1866. No additional record was found for the child or family in Orange County.[15]

FELIX POLK - 1868

ABIGAIL POLK apprenticed her eleven year old son, FELIX POLK, to AARON BURNETT for training in the "art, trade and mystery of farming" until February 11, 1878. This indenture was recorded in Apprentice Record Book 1, page 105. At the completion of service, Burnett agreed to provide Felix a suit of "freedom" clothes and one good horse saddle and bridle and one hundred dollars in money.

Two years later, Felix Polk was not listed with the Aaron Burnett household when the 1870 census was enumerated. Aaron, a 50-year old farm laborer, lived in Orleans Township with his wife, Mary, and their six children ranging in ages from 8 to 28 years.[16]

Summary of Poor and Apprenticed Children

A content analysis of the fourteen indentures located in Orange County for African American children who were bound out between 1821 and 1868 as poor or apprenticed children revealed some interesting conclusions:

1. <u>Sex of child placed</u>: 10 boys and 4 girls.
2. <u>Ages, at time of placement</u>: ranged from a one month old girl to one boy who was 18-years old. A more detailed breakdown reveals that over one-half of the children were under the age of seven years when bound out.
3. <u>Term of service</u>: ranged from two children who served 5 years or less to a total of nine children who had to serve between 11-15 years.
4. <u>Race of adult to whom child was indentured or apprenticed</u>: ten children went to Black families, and only four to white families. It appears that at least two children were placed with relatives having the same surname.

Insufficient records prevented a determination of what happened to most of these fourteen children after the indentures were formalized. However, it is known that at least two of them, Mathew Thomas and Jordon Thomas, remained in Orange County where they died during adulthood.

The Will of Reuben Bond - 1834

Reuben Bond, a free man of color and resident of Orange County, prepared his final will and testament on June 25, 1834. Recorded on page 76, Will Book #1 (1816-1852), the document revoked an earlier will made in South Carolina on an unspecified date.

He bequeathed all of his real and personal estate to his wife, Penelope Bond, and their four children: Martha Jane Bond, John Bond, Nancy An[n] Ellyn Bond, and Mary Ann Henrietta Bond. Following in the legal custom of the male-dominated society at that time, Bond restricted his wife's benefits from his estate only as long as she remained his widow. Should she ever married, the will declared that the remaining portion of the estate was to be divided among his children. Ezer Cleveland, a white man, was appointed executor of the will which was probated in open court on August 24, 1834. Cleveland was a native of New York and a landowner in Orangeville Township, Orange County, since 1816.[17]

Reuben Bond married Penelope Hill in Orange County, Indiana on June 7, 1832. Cemetery records indicate that he died in Orangeville Township on August 1, 1834. He was thirty-six years old at the time of his death and only married to Penelope for about two years. These data suggest the possibility that some of the children listed in his will were from a previous marriage.

No probate and land documents about the final disposition of the Bond real estate in Orangeville Township were located. In the 1840 census, Penelope Bond was listed as a "colored" female, age range 36-55 years, and heading a family household of five persons.

Ten years later in the 1850 census, she was enumerated in North West Township, Black color, age 40 years, born in North Carolina, and owning real estate valued at $300. In the household were three children: John M. Bond, age 19 years, born in North Carolina, and a farmer by occupation; 13-year old Mary Bond was born in Indiana; and 10 year old Monroe Bond also born in Indiana. One 17-year old daughter also named Mary Bond was away from home and listed with the Elias Lindley (white) family, presumably working as a domestic. This Mary was born in Indiana and the age would place her birth in 1833, shortly before her father's death.[18]

In 1860, Penelope Bond was still living in Orangeville Township. She was 55 years old, Black, a farmer by occupation, and owning real and personal estate valued at $750. She was also blind. In the same household were listed four children: John Bond, age 22 years and a farmer; Mary Bond, age 20 years; Martha Bond, age 26 years; and a Nancy Guthrie, age 12 years.[19]

Marriage Records disclosed that a Monroe Bond married Mary A. Thomas on October 29, 1863. In the 1870 census, Monroe and Mary A. Bond family lived in Paoli Township with two children: Penelope, age 5 years, and William, age 2 years. Monroe Bond, age 31 years, was a laborer.[20]

In 1880, Mary A. Bond, age 40 years, was listed as married and head of the family with no mention of her husband's, Monroe Bond, whereabouts. There were five children ranging in ages from five years to 15 years. Also in the household was Mary's 33 year old brother, William Thomas.[21]

Will of Benjamin Roberts - 1853

When Benjamin Roberts made out his final will on May 16, 1853, he owned 80 acres of land which he purchased in two 40-acre parcels from the United States of America (patent) on September 29, 1832 and May 15, 1834. The land was located in Section 28, Township 1 north, Range 1 East in

Lick Creek Settlement. He bequeathed the land and personal estate to his wife, Sarah. To his daughter, Irena Adams, and his son, Ishmael Roberts, he gave each one dollar.

In his certificate of freedom obtained in Chatham County, North Carolina on November 24, 1824 and recorded in Orange County, Indiana on January 7, 1833, Benjamin Roberts and his family were identified as free people of color and long time residents of Chatham County. His wife was Sally, and their three children were Serena Roberts, Ishmael Roberts and Archibald Roberts.

In the 1850 census, Benjamin Roberts was enumerated in Paoli Township as a 70-year old farmer having real estate valued at $200. In the household was his wife, Sally, aged 47 years, and a boy, Benjamin Roberts, aged 13 years, who was probably a relative.[22]

It is assumed that the daughter, Irena Adams, mentioned in the will was the same child identified earlier as "Serena." On May 24, 1854, Benjamin's son, Ishmael Roberts and his wife, Delena Roberts, both residents of Hamilton County, Indiana, sold the 40 acres (patent) in Orange County which Ishmael had acquired from the government on March 28, 1836.[23]

In his will which was recorded on pages 17-18 in Will Book #2 (August 1852-July 1892), Benjamin Roberts appointed Henry Holmes, a white citizen, as executor of the will. In 1839 Holmes was one of the six Justices of the Peace serving in Orange County, and in January, 1853 he was elected as an Orange County Director of the newly organized "The Washington and Orange District Agricultural Society."[24]

The Benjamin Roberts' will was probated in court on September 19, 1853. The executor, Henry Holmes, made his final report to the court on November 17, 1854 and showing a balance of $67.67 to be paid to the widow.[25]

Sarah Roberts, Benjamin's widow, received title to 80 acres of land on September 19, 1853. She sold the land six years later to Granville P. Peyton on October 31, 1859 and recorded in Deed Book 19, page 306.

NOTES

1. Section on "The County Paupers," *History of Lawrence, Orange and Washington Counties, Indiana,* 425-26. The county's poor farm was first purchased in 1836.

2. Coy D. Robbins, "Indentured Colored Children," *African Heritage in Morgan County, Indiana* (1991), 41-42, for an account of three indentures issued in 1832-42.

3. The name of Andrew Scott does not appear in the 1850 or in subsequent censuses for Orange County, Indiana.

4. In the 1850 U. S. Census, Henry Weaver is listed with the Martin Scott family in South East Township as an eight year old mulatto boy (Appendix B).

5. In the 1850 U. S. Census, Henry Scott, a 50-year old mulatto, held real estate valued at $100. The family unit consisted of his 45-year old wife, Lucy, and two teen-aged children: Jane and Martin. Catharine Weaver, the child apprenticed to Henry Scott in 1846, was not listed in this household.

6. Some minor editing done to facilitate the reading of this old indenture. Commas and paragraghs added to the original which is in handscript and consists primarily of a long, single paragraph. Author believes this final provision was added at the mother's request to prevent Chapman from taking her son, William Thomas, during the term of his indenture to a state where slavery was legal, e.g., nearby Kentucky.

7. *History of Lawrence, Orange and Washington Counties, Indiana,* 391, 415, 473, 474, 476, 548.

8. Ibid., 377, 378, 382, 384, 406, 412, 413, 414, 415, 436, 439, 440, 446, 449, 450, 473, 508. Of interest is the section, "The Public Services of Zachariah Lindley" and especially the account on page 450 about his treatment of a negro suspect when Lindley served as sheriff.

9. Ibid., 388.

10. Ibid., <u>Leonard Green</u>, 426, 436, 482; <u>John G. Clendenin</u>, 379, 415, 424, 436, 438, 441, 473, 474, 532, 549.

11. It is possible that John's mother is the same Hannah Gillium listed in the Guardianship Records for nearby Washington County, Indiana. On January 25, 1858, an America Anderson, Black, was appointed guardian of the person and estate of Jacob Gillium "minor heir of Hannah Gillium deceased." Jacob was 13 years old and the estate consisted of $25.00 cash. June Voyles, *Guardianships 1820-1859 Washington County, Indiana*, (Salem: Washington County Historical Society, 1989), 132.

12. The Moses Sneed family was listed in the 1850 U. S. Census (Town of Paoli, Dwelling 344, Family 345) with John H. Gilliam identified as 14 years old, mulatto and born in North Carolona. No other Gilliam listings found in Orange County (Appendix B).

13. 1850 U. S. Census, Orange Co., Ind.: Anderson-Lymma Smith, South East Twp., Dwelling 204, Family 204 (Appendix B).

14. 1870 U. S. Census, Orangeville Township, Orange County, Indiana: Churchill Isom, Dwelling 25, Family 25 (Appendix B).

15. 1870 U. S. Census for Orange County, Indiana: Stampers Creek Twp., Dwelling 136, Family 135 (Appendix B).

16. 1870 U. S. Census, Orange County, Indiana: Aaron-Mary Burnett, Orleans Twp., Dwelling 129, Family 130 (Appendix B).

17. Biographical sketch of Matthew Cleveland, son of Ezer and Martha (Watkins) Cleveland, *History of Lawrence, Orange and Washington Counties, Indiana*, 625-626.

18. 1850 U. S. Census for North West Twp., Orange County, Indiana: Penelope Bond, Dwelling 1204, Family 1208 (Appendix B).

19. 1860 U. S. Census, Orangeville Twp., Orange County, Indiana: Penelope Bond, Dwelling 1055, Family 1055 (Appendix B).

20. 1870 U. S. Census, Paoli Twp., Orange County, Ind,: Monroe Bond, Dwelling 102, Family 102 (Apppendix B).

21. 1880 U. S. Census, Paoli Township, Orange County, Ind.: Mary A. Bond, Dwelling 178, Family 185, (Appendix B). Section on "Mathew and Mary Thomas Family" in Chapter XV for details about Mary Thomas Bond and her brother, William Thomas.

22. 1850 U. S. Census for Paoli Twp., Orange County, Ind.: Benjamin Roberts, Dwelling 584, Family 585 (Appendix B).

23. Entries 88 and 89, "Landowners in Lick Creek Settlement Area," (Appendix C).

24. Henry Holmes entries in *History of Lawrence, Orange and Washington Counties, Indiana*, 432, 436.

25. *Probate Order Book 5*, Orange County, Indiana, 408.

CHAPTER XIII

SPRINGS VALLEY RESORTS

The Developing Industries

At the end of last century, the flourishing sanitarium and resort industry lured a new wave of African Americans into Orange County. The mineral water health craze swept the state of Indiana in the late 1880s. Scores of springs and wells in Henry, Montgomery, Morgan, Warren and other counties were exploited commercially as the American public learned that mineral water with its taste and smell of rotten eggs had curative effects for health ailments.[1]

The best known of the early springs in the middle west were located in French Lick Township where large numbers of African Americans were imported for employment in the spas and hotels. Each spring and fall wealthy celebrites descended upon the little towns of French Lick and West Baden "to take the cure." Patrons usually spent three weeks for the required treatment of drinking and bathing in the waters at their favorite sanitarium. Hotels were lavish enclaves offering every service guests needed for a lengthy stay. Staffs stood by readily available to pamper the clientele.

The French Lick Resort

Centuries before the fancy resorts came into existence, these salty mineral springs in what became the west central region of Orange County, Indiana were well-known to the buffalo and Native Americans. The first Euro-Americans in this region were probably the French adventurers who came into the valley from the Vincennes settlement fifty miles to the west on the Wabash River. Early traders and settlers attempted to manufacture salt from the waters until forced to abandon the land by the Native Americans.[2]

Once Indiana achieved statehood in 1816, the new government declared most springs in this region as "saline lands." Sixteen years later the State of Indiana sold 1500 acres which included all the large springs to William A. Bowles. Prior to 1840, Bowles, a physician, established the first health resort hotel in the French Lick area, a ramshackle, three story frame building. It was an immediate success. Bowles helped to charter the town of French Lick in 1857.

By 1860 the French Lick House and the nearby West Baden Inn were well established and considered among the more prosperous mineral springs resorts of Indiana.[3]

The local resort industry received an immediate boost when the Louisville, New Albany and Chicago Railroad, known as "The Monon," opened its direct route to the springs area in April, 1887. Now guests arrived by train from as far as Chicago and Louisville, coming as early as March each year for therapeutic baths and mineral waters.

The French Lick hotel was nearly destroyed by fire in 1897. Four years later its ruins were purchased by a syndicate headed by the then mayor of Indianapolis, Thomas J. Taggart. Under his management the French Lick Springs Resort was built and soon rocketed to international prominence.

New wings were rebuilt to the old hotel and the Monon Railroad was persuaded to lay a special spur and run daily trains between Chicago and its front entrance. Golf courses were installed, baths were modernized and expanded. "Pluto Water" was bottled for national distribution. After Taggart was named Democratic National Chairman in 1904, the elite of politics and society suddenly "discovered" French Lick Springs.[4]

Each May after the Kentucky Derby was run in Louisville, fashionable and wealthy classes from the eastern half of the United States gathered at their favorite resort in the Indiana hills to take "the cure," to play, to conduct business, and to gamble. Outside the hotels gambling flourished for years in nearby casinos in flagrant violation of state law. The last casinos were closed in 1949.

Taggart, the hotelman, became a powerful politician in the National Democratic Party. It was at the French Lick Hotel in 1931 that Franklin D. Roosevelt garnered support at a Democratic governor's conference for his party's presidential nomination.

Thomas J. Taggart died in 1929. His son, Thomas D. Taggart, carried on. With the depression, however, the popular Springs Valley resorts declined. There was a momentary revival during World War II, but in 1946 young Tom Taggart sold out to a New York syndicate. The Sheraton Corporation bought the property in 1954 and restored the famed spa to its former grandeur. Since 1979 the hotel has been purchased and sold several times as business continued to decline.

West Baden Springs Hotel

Down the road south of French Lick, John A. Lane constructed the Mile Lick Inn in the early 1850s. Lane, a salesman of patent medicines, had leased the French Lick House while its owner, Dr. Bowles served in the Mexican War. The name of the town, Mile Lick, was soon changed to the West Baden after the famous mineral springs and spa town of Weisbaden, Germany. Lane also changed the name of his facility to West Baden Inn, and still later it became the West Baden Springs hotel.[5]

In the early twentieth century this hotel was transformed into a sophisticated resort establishment. Lee W. Sinclair, a Salem, Indiana textile manufacturer and banker, bought controlling interest in the West Baden Springs hotel in 1888. One year earlier the Monon Railroad extended its service to Springs Valley with direct connections between Chicago and Louisville.

Sinclair recognized the business potential of the area and proceeded over the next ten years to change it into a first-class resort with many of the present day attractions and amenties. He built an opera house in 1893, and a casino in 1895. By then the hotel had 500 guest rooms, each with electric lights and steam heat. A Sports Complex on the grounds featured a covered two-decker bicycle and pony track with a full size baseball diamond within the track oval.

Most of the old frame buildings at the West Baden Springs Hotel were destroyed in the disastrous fire on June 14, 1901. Flames were visible to operators in the fire tower eighty miles away at Louisville, Kentucky. Ten days before this fire, Thomas J. Taggart had purchased the rival French

Lick Springs Hotel.

Sinclair rebuilt in less than a year. His new fire-proof hotel was in the Moorish style of architecture and highlighted the world's largest unsupported glass dome. This self-proclaimed "Eighth wonder of the world" held six tiers of rooms looking down upon a huge circular atrium or Pompeian Court. Sinclair named his new resort the "Carlsbad of America" and it was first opened for guests in September, 1902. The resort's success peaked during the Sinclair years.[6]

Lee Sinclair died in 1916 and shortly after his daughter sold the grand 708-room resort to Charles E. Ballard, owner of the Hagenback Wallace Circus. Under his leadership the West Baden Springs Hotel achieved national stature as a flamboyant gambling casino. During World War I it served as a army hospital, and flourished again as a hotel in the twenties.

After the "great depression" of the thirties turned the entire Springs Valley resort community into a ghost town, Ballard eventually closed his hotel. Later he donated it to the Jesuit Order of Priests who converted it into the West Baden Springs University. The Catholics left the hotel in 1964.

Local efforts to turn it into an opera and arts center failed, and it was privately purchased and became a branch college of Northwood Institute of Michigan, a business and technical school with an emphasis on hotel and restaurant management. Once again, the grand old hotel was abandoned in 1983. Although it has been named a national historic landmark, the fate of the old West Baden Springs Hotel today is in the hands of a California bankruptcy court.

African Americans in the Valley

As early as 1850, a small number of African Americans lived in French Lick Township. They may have been employed in the resorts although this cannot be documented from the limited historical information found thus far.

The first African American directly connected with the hotel industry in Springs Valley was Eli Roberts. In the 1860 census, Roberts, a 27 year old native born African American Hoosier, was listed with a white family headed by William A. Bowles. His employer, the "father" of the area's mineral springs health industry, owned the prosperous French Lick Inn.[7]

In 1870, Peter Jewitt and his wife, Clara, were enumerated as hotel cooks and other members of their household were classified as "hotel laborers." Additionally, Lizzie Dyol, was identified as a laborer in the household of Ephraim Tucker, a hotel keeper.

By the 1880, only Abbie Polk was listed as a cook with John A. Lane, proprietor of the West Baden Springs Hotel.

When the health resorts in Orange County expanded at the turn of this century, a large number of the workers from outside the local area were employed. Labor recruiters turned readily to Louisville, Kentucky, a large urban community only eighty miles to the south east with daily railroad transportation into Springs Valley.

In view of the out-of-state recruitment of African American workers for the Orange County

MAP: Springs Valley in French Lick Township

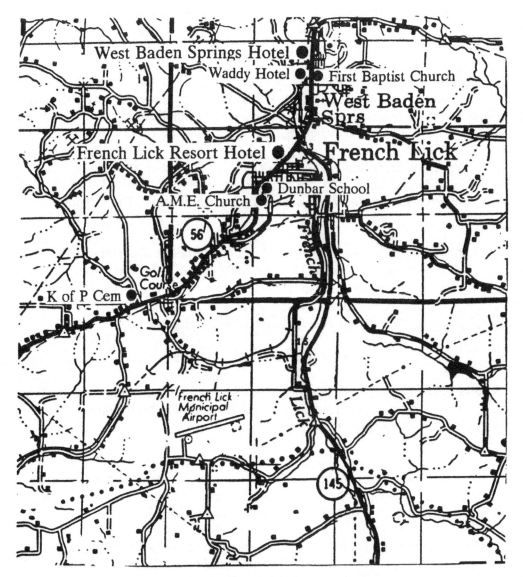

(Adaptation of map courtesy Forest Service, U. S. Dept. of Agriculture)

Site locations on map:

West Baden Springs Hotel (1850-1983)
Waddy Hotel (1913-1951)
First Baptist Church (1909-1960s)
French Lick Resort Hotel (1840-)
Dunbar Colored School, French Lick (1911-1937)
French Lick A.M.E. Church (1902-1977)
Knights of Pythias (K of P) Cemetery (1913-)

industries, it seemed doubtful that many native-born Hoosiers were ever employed. Tabulated data on the frequency of birthplaces reported by the residents in the 1900 and 1910 censuses substantiated that only a small number were born in Indiana, and that the vast majority came from Kentucky (see Table 16).

TABLE 16: Birthplaces of African Americans in French Lick Township
as Reported in the 1900 and 1910 U. S. Censuses

State	1900	1910
Alabama	1	2
Arkansas	0	2
Colorado	0	1
Connecticut	0	1
CANADA	1	1
Florida	0	1
Georgia	4	4
Illinois	0	3
Indiana	10	39
Kansas	0	1
Kentucky	80	204
Louisiana	1	2
Maryland	2	1
Michigan	2	0
Missouri	1	1
Mississippi	2	2
New York	1	0
North Carolina	0	1
Ohio	1	2
Pennsylvania	0	1
Tennessee	12	36
Unknown	1	0
Virginia	4	3
WEST INDIES	1	1
West Virginia	0	1

The total number of persons born in either Tennessee or Indiana was relatively small in contrast with the high number of Kentucky birthplaces reported in both censuses. The listed birthplaces were diversed, covered a wide range of American states plus two foreign lands, and suggested that some African Americans traveled extensively after the Civil War.

Characteristics of the People

Data were collected to provide some information about the numbers and general characteristics of African Americans who migrated into the French Lick and West Baden Springs community (see Table 17).[8]

TABLE 17: Characteristics of African American Population
in French Lick Township, 1900 and 1910

Characteristic	1900	Total	1910	Total
Sex:	----	124	----	325
Male	97	----	201	----
Female	27	----	124	----
Marital Status:	----	124	----	325
Married	73	----	153	----
Single	49	----	145	----
Divorced-Widowed	2	----	25	----
Family Groups*	----	20	----	67
Children:	----	10	----	43
Up to 5 years	6	----	19	----
6-18 years	4	----	24	----
Boarders+	----	4	----	116

Source: U. S. Population Census Reports for years indicated.
*Tabulation based on units so classified in each census.
+Numbers do not include those persons enumerated as residing
the in hotel facilities as "servants."

Several characteristics were noteworthy. First, the large majority enumerated in both censuses were males (1900: 78%; 1910: 61%) and almost half of the total population was married (1900: 48%; 1910: 47%). While by 1910 the number of females and family groups increased significantly, still many married males working in the hotels and resorts were without their families.

The second finding relates to the number of school age children in these families. Certainly the four children enumerated in 1900 was not large enough to justify any separate educational facility, but the twenty-four children reported ten years later was a sizeable increase, one which undoubtedly led to the establishment of the French Lick Colored School in 1911 (see Chapter XI).

Another revealment from these data involves the large number of "boarders" in the 1910 census. Over one-third of the total population was listed living with other African American families or in boarding houses. By the way, this figure does not include those individuals who were counted in the hotels where it is presumed they lived in facilities provided by the owners. The housing available for African Americans in these small, very racially segregated communities must have been extremely limited.

Occupations

Employment of African Americans in white hotels has traditionally been restricted to service occupations such as "waiters, porters, bell-boys and maids"--some of the most difficult and underpaid jobs in the business. While the resorts in Springs Valley tended to use persons of African ancestry in conventional job assignments, it was enlightening to discover the full range of occupations they reported in both the 1900 and 1910 censuses (table 18).

TABLE 18: Occupations of African Americans in French Lick Township

	1900	1910
Barber	0	1
Barber, own shop	0	1
Bathman	4	16
Bathwoman	0	6
Bell-boy (man)	12	21
Carpetman	1	0
Chamber maid	1	0
Clerk, hotel	0	1
Coffee man	0	1
Cook	2	6
Domestic	0	2
Dressmaker	0	1
Driver, livery stable	0	1
Elevator boy	1	3
Fireman, power house	0	2
Hairdresser	0	3
Harness maker	0	1
Hat man, hotel	0	1
Houseman	1	2
Housekeeper, hotel	0	1
Kitchen man	1	0
Kitchen assistant	0	2
Landlady, boarding house	0	2
Landlady, hotel	0	1
Office man	1	0
Manager, hotel	0	1
Minister	0	1
Musician	2	1
Nurse	0	3
Porter	5	10
Proprietor, pool room	0	1
Proprietor, news stand	0	1
Proprietor, own saloon	0	1
Restaurant owner	0	1
Seamstress	0	2
Servant, hotel	1	0
Shoe black	1	1
Shoe black, own business	0	1
Shoe maker, own store	0	1

Continued on next page

Table 18-*Continued*

	1900	1910
Solicitor, insurance	0	1
Tailor.	0	2
Tailor shop worker	0	2
Tailor shop owner	0	2
Ticket agent, bathhouse	0	1
Water dipper, Pluto Springs	0	1
Waiter	52	101
Waitress	0	1
Total	85	211
Total African American		
Population in Township	124	325

Source: U. S. Population Censuses, Orange County, Indiana, 1900 & 1910

The vast majority, or sixty-one percent of the individuals reporting occupations in 1900, were employed as waiters. Ten years later, however, the percentage dropped to less than fifty although the total number of waiters doubled over the decade.

The 1910 census findings included a number of different occupations not previously reported by African Americans ten years earlier, such as barber, bathwoman, hotel clerk, coffee man, dressmaker, livery stable driver, power house fireman, hairdresser, harness maker, hotel hat man, hotel housekeeper, kitchen assistants, landlady (boarding house and hotel), hotel manager, nurses, proprietor (pool room, news stand, own saloon), restaurant owner, seamstresses, shoe maker, insurance company solicitor, tailors, bathhouse ticket agent, water dipper, and waitress.

Also by 1910, a small number of African Americans reported having their own businesses: barber shop (Jefferson Williams), saloon (William Poper[?]), restaurant (Erbin Slye), shoe maker (Thomas Thurman), and tailor shops (Robert Holden and William O. Martin).   These entrepreneurships suggest that by this time in history there may have been a cadre of permanent Black residents who remained in the Valley throughout the year after the summer tourist season ended.

One minister, Rev. Lee Mason, was also listed in the 1910 census. Both the Bethel A. M. E. Church in French Lick and the First Baptist Church in West Baden existed by this date, so this 40-year old unmarried "man of the cloth" born in Kentucky could have been assigned to either one of these congregations (see Chapter IX).

Three African Americans, two females and one male, were employed as nurses in 1910, perhaps in the health spas: 53-year widow Maggie Morgan, who organized the French Lick A. M. E. Church in 1902; 23-year old Louisa Burnett, a Kentucky native; and, Will Bee, a 40-year old married man from Kentucky.

There was also one "insurance company solicitor" in the 1910 census: Erwin Smith, a 35-year native of Maryland, who may have been representing one or more of several national African American insurance companies which flourished in this period of time.

Yarmouth Wigginton, a 40-year old widower and native of Kentucky, gave his occupation in 1910 as "water dipper, Pluto Springs." He was employed in the Pluto Springs bottling plant built by the Taggarts near the French Lick hotel to satisfy their customers. The emblem of Pluto became the trademark for the bottled springs water which was sold internationally, and Yarmouth Wigginton dressed in a flaming red devil costume and dispensed Pluto Water to visitors in the area.[9]

Fraternal Organizations

In addition to establishing their own businesses, churches and having a "colored" public school for their children to attend, African Americans living in Springs Valley established their own fraternal organizations very early in this century.

Fraternal organizations captured the interests of African Americans in the late ninteenth and early twentieth centuries. To name only a few from a long list, these included the Masonic Bodies, the Grand United Order of Odd Fellows, the Improved Benevolent and Protective Order of Elks, the United Order of True Reformers, the Grand United Order of Galilean Fisherman, the Nation Order of Mosaic Templars of America, the Knights and Daughters of Tabor, and the Knights of Pythias. Indiana was no exception, and Blacks here established and held in high esteem their fraternal organizations and benevolent societies which were dedicated to social and cultural uplift, economic advancement, and mutual relief.

The Colored Knights of Pythias

The K of Ps, a non-sectarian and non-political fraternity with its mottoes of Friendship, Charity and Benevolence, was patterned after the Order instituted by Justus H. Rathbone in Washington, D. C. on February 19, 1864.[10] After the Civil War, the white K of Ps refused to accept the applications from several Black men although there was nothing in its charter and organizing documents to suggest any racial restrictions on members.

Finally the fraternal degrees were unwittingly conferred on a group of Blacks led by Dr. George A. Place of Macon, Miss., Dr. Thomas W. Stringer, Vicksburg, Miss., and Mr. A. E. Lightfoot, Lauderdale, Miss.

Dr. Stringer, who is regarded as the founder of the "colored" Order, organized the first lodge at Vicksburg on March 26, 1880. The female department, known as the Order of Calanthe, was authorized and the first Subordinate Court of Calanthe instituted at Whitehall, Louisiana on May 14, 1883. The Military Department, known as the Uniform Rank, Knights of Pythias, was authorized in May, 1883. There was also a Military Cadet Department for boys, and a Juvenile Department for girls and boys attached to the Calanthe Order.

A phenomenal growth of the fraternal organization resulted nationally. By 1917, there were a total of 3,113 lodges consisting of 118,210 members. About 80,000 women were in the Calanthe Order and 25,000 members of the Military Department. There were 28 Grand Lodges or State Organizations of men, and 25 Grand Courts or State Organizations of women. The Military

Department modeled after the U. S. Army held encampments of 5,000 Sir Knights every two years. Pythian Temples existed in many states and the Supreme Order owned and operated the Pythian Sanitarium and Bath House at Hot Springs, Ark.[11]

It was somewhat startling to learn that residents of Springs Valley once maintained branches of this fraternal organization. Two lodges of the <u>Knights of Pythias of North America, South America, Europe, Asia, Africa and Australia</u> were chartered in French Lick, Indiana. The first one was on May 2, 1906 and was granted to "Pluto Company No. 5" under the authority of J. H. Green, Supreme Chancellor, Robert S. Jackson, Major General Commanding, and Stuart D. Fowler, Adjutant General.

A second charter was given one year later on May 1, 1907 to "Proserpine Lodge No. 27". From the scanty amount of extant lodge records located, it was not possible to ascertain if these lodges functioned simultaneously in the community, or if later they consolidated into a single fraternal entity.

The K of P lodge left to the local community one lasting monument of its existence: the privately owned "colored" cemetery located about two and one-half miles west of downtown French Lick (see Chapter X on Cemeteries).

The Rochelle Court No. 14, French Lick, Indiana of the Order of Calanthe (Women's Department) of the Knights of Pythias was chartered on June 20, 1907. "Brother" Yarmouth Wigginton's name was listed as representative of the men's organization, and the following persons named as chartered members: Maggie Morgan, Mollie Payne, Pearl Stockdale, Eva Carter, Carrie Pittsman, Carrie Freeds, Madie Thurman, Alice Hughes, Hannah Laws, Ida Floyd, Nannie Procter, Ida Webster, and Susie Rice.

No written historical account of any local lodge has been found, nor one for either the Indiana Grand Lodge or the Supreme Lodge. In the French Lick community, however, there is a carefully preserved cache of K of P pictures, uniforms, handbooks on rituals, handwritten minutes and account books for the Rochelle Court No. 14--in addition to their original charters. Noticeably absent are any lists of officers, members or historical narratives of their establishments, achievements and dissolutions.[12]

One lodge document is worth noting for its genealogical contents. In a 18 by 20 inches black wooden frame which probably hung on the wall of the lodge's meeting room, its reads:

K of P Proserpine Lodge No. 27
In Memory of Our Deceased BROTHERS

Whereas, as It Has Pleased the Almighty God To Call from Labor to Rest by Death, Our Esteemed Brothers & Co-laborers, Who Have for Years Occupied a Prominent Rank on Our Midst

Sleep on Souls in Death; until God bid thee Rise. And May a Band of Angels meet thee in the Sky.

| *Name* | *Month Date Year* |

1. Henry Williams
2. Edward Kennedy   *March 10, 1906*
3. Eddie Lillard
4. John Cornish   *June 18, 1907*
5. Albert Collins
6. Geo[rge] Cepher
7. Johnnie Chanault   *July 10, 1909*
8. Thomas Cole   *Dec 8, 1910*
9. Joseph Williams   *Sept 25, 1911*
10. Joseph Taylor   *Sept 3, 1912*
11. Robert L. Clark   *Oct 13, 1912*
12. Thomas Smith   *May 15, 1912*
13. Charlie Morgan   *Jan 1, 1914*
14. George Williams   *Feb 9, 1914*
15. Gus Hocker   *June 6, 1916*
16. Wm. O. Martin   *Oct --, 1916*
17. Henry Shores   *Feb 5, 1918*
18. John Humphries   *May 15, 1918*
19. Chas. Phillips   *Jan 3, 1920*
20. Arthur Thomas   *July 5, 1920*
21. Burrell Echols   *Aug 20, 1920*
22. John Moore   *Feb 8, 1921*
23. Ben Dennis   *Apr 28, 1921*
24. Henry Lee Babbage   *June 2, 1921*
25. Henry H. Hilliard   *Sept 16, 1921*
26. Charles Allen   *Feb 21, 1922*
27. Harry E. Wilkins   *Feb 24, 1922*
28. Ed L. Hurley   *June 1, 1923*
29. Odis Burnette   *Sept 1, 1923*
30. Y. C. Wigginton   *Dec 6, 1923*
31. Joseph C. Rice   *July 7, 1924*
32. Thomas Taylor   *July 10, 1924*
33. Wm. Davis   *Oct 31, 1924*
34. Willie Sebree   *May 3, 1925*
35. Wm. Payne   *May 7, 1925*
36. Daniel Thomas   *Jan 24, 1926*
37. Turn Morgan   *June 19, 1926*
38. George Hart   *Jan 22, 1927*
39. William Hill   *June 13, 1927*
40. H. Frank McCarroll   *Oct 20, 1927*
41. Enos Reed   *June 6, 1928*
42. William L. Hayden   *July 23, 1928*
43. Horace Robinson   *Apr 28, 1929*
44. John Loving   *Feb 18, 1930*
45. James W. Cook   *May 21, 1930*
46. Louis Shockney   *May 30, 1931*
47. Sam Hocker   *Oct 10, 1931*

Colored Masonic Lodge

Freemasonry among African Americans date to 1784 when Prince Hall, a minister and recognized leader of his people, applied to the Grand Lodge of England and received a charter to organize the African Lodge No. 459 in Boston, Massachusetts. Other lodges soon followed in Philadelphia and Providence, Rhode Island. Gradually, African Masonry spread over the land and three Grand Lodges came into existence by 1815.

The first African Masonic lodge in Indiana was organized at Indianapolis in 1848, followed by a second one in the same city, and one each in Madison and Terre Haute. These earliest lodges were under the jurisdiction of the Ohio Grand Lodge until 1856 when the Grand Lodge of Indiana was organized. Lodges soon followed in other parts of the state, but many became defunct after the Civil War when the African American population shifted from the rural areas. Thereafter, lodges with expanding memberships thrived primarily in Indiana's urban communities.

The Lost River Lodge No. 50 in French Lick, Indiana was chartered on August 21, 1919 by the Grand Lodge of Free and Accepted Masons of Indiana and Its Jurisdiction. Officers of the Lost River Masonic Lodge No. 50 in 1920 were Robert J. Holden, Thomas M. Hawley, Yarmouth Wigginton, Solomon C. Pittman, Charles I. Barnett, Clarence P. Stockdale, Meadie G. Wing, Jerome A. Lewis, John A. Babbage and Maunsell M. King. Additional members included Odis Burnett, Isaac Loyd, William Payne Sr., William Payne Jr., John L. Thomas and A. W. Tutt.[13]

The Waddy Hotel

Between 1913 and 1951, the Waddy Hotel on Sinclair Street in West Baden Springs catered primarily to African Americans from the midwest who came to Springs Valley for mineral water baths, treatments, gambling and relaxation.

The hotel consisted of the lobby, dining room, bath house, about 36 bedrooms, a beauty shop, laundry, and kitchen. It was a white frame, two-story oblonged building with three hallways and a railed veranda on two sides. In time the building was covered with brick siding. A train entrance on the west side made it possible for guests to quickly enter the facility. Originally built and operated by a white man named Fisher, it was sold to George and Nannie Waddy in 1913.

In 1900 George W. Waddy (1872-1942), a native of Tennessee, worked as a waiter in John C. Howard (white) Hotel in Springs Valley. Within the next decade, he had married, was working as a "bathman" and headed a household consisting of his wife, Nannie B. (1877-1960), his 13-year old brother, Nicko Waddy, and four boarders. With over ten years of experiences in the industry, Waddy provided services for those Americans racially excluded by Indiana's public accommodation laws from other spas and resort hotels.[14]

The Waddy Hotel operated throughout the peak period of the resort industry in the region. During the 1920s African American celebrities came in from Indianapolis, Chicago and Louisville for the waters and fun. After World War II a number of boxers came to this retreat to train, including the famous Joe Louis. Mrs. Nannie Waddy continued the business a short time after her husband's death before selling it in the fall of 1942 to Artie "Smitty" Smith during his first visit to the hotel.

A native of Brinkley, Arkansas, Smith grew up in Chicago where his family moved when he was five or six years old. It was happenstance he learned about this Indiana resort from an uncle in Chicago who had been making annual treks to French Lick.

Over the next nine years, Smitty operated the hotel, redecorated and enlarged its facilities, and increased the resort's regular clientele to include well known prize fighters, such as Ezzard Charles, Sugar Ray Robinson and Bob Montgomery in addition to Joe Louis.

In 1949, Smitty became interested in one of his guests, Dorothy "Shorty Jo" Brandt of Columbus, Indiana. She was a native Hoosier making her first visit to the resort hotel. They were married on July 3, 1950 in Chicago by one of Smitty's uncles who was a minister in a large south-side Baptist Church. After their marriage, Mrs. Smith became involved with the hotel's daily operation which included a staff of four-five persons.

Normally their business picked up the week before the Kentucky Derby in May and continued steadily until Labor Day. Hotel rates in the 1940s were three dollars and fifty cents a day which included two meals (breakfast and evening dinner) served family style in the hotel's dining room. Bath and massage services cost an additional one dollar and fifty cents, or both for two dollars. Winter months in the hotel were quiet, and waiters working at the white hotels often stayed at the Waddys during their slow business months.

A major catastrophe for the Smiths happened in 1951 when fire destroyed the Waddy Hotel. Eventually they recovered from their financial and personal losses, and rebuilt their present home on the site of the former hotel. Mrs. Smith designed and supervised the construction of the rustic style house with its large natural stone fireplace. Today, this retired couple forms the core of the community's twenty-five to thirty permanent African American residents. Smitty continues to enjoy the outdoors and hunting which attracted him initially to the region, and his wife still finds living here compatible with her love of animals and especially riding horses.[15]

Miss Birdie Sebree

In October, 1964, Birdie Sebree was honored with a siver tea at the French Lick American Legion Club for the more than a half-century of devoted service to the public. She worked as a chiropodist and practical nurse in the office of Dr. H. L. Miller for forty-two years. Over 250 persons of both races attended the tea which was planned by her white friends. Out-of-town visitors came from Mitchell, Crawfordsville, Jasper and Shoals, Indiana and Chicago, Louisville, and St. Louis.

A native of Louisville, Miss Sebree was quite young when her family moved to West Baden. At age 15 years she started employment as a hairdresser in the local famous resort hotel, and later served as a bath attendant at the Homestead Hotel while working with Dr. Miller.

The daughter of Dudley and Hannah Sebree, she was the second oldest of five children. She was also the great-granddaughter of John Hart, who was owned by Governor Isaac Shelby and said to be one of the first slaves brought directly into Kentucky from Africa. While unable to obtain a higher education herself, Miss Sebree helped to pay the college expenses for a brother who became a school teacher and artist.

Sick at the time of her silver tea, she died at the DuBois County Memorial Hospital on March 16, 1965 and was buried in the K of P Cemetery, French Lick, Indiana. Since 1908, she was a member of the First Baptist Church in West Baden and once served as Sunday School superintendent. She was the last of her family, survived only by a brother-in-law, John Babb, of Louisville.[16]

NOTES

1. W. D. Thornbury, "The Mineral Waters and Health Resorts of Indiana: A Study in Historical Geography," *Indiana Academy of Science Proceedings*, L (1940), 154-164. Invalids and visitors came to mineral springs in large numbers. The peak of popularity of health resorts came between 1890 and 1910 when at least thirty hotels and sanitoriums operated in Indiana springs. The automobile was probably the major factor in their decline after 1910.

2. Goodspeed, *History of Lawrence, Orange and Washington Counties, Indiana*, 390-395.

3. Robert M. Taylor, Jr., "Soaking, Sluicing, and Stewing in Hoosier Mineral Waters," *Traces*, 4, (Winter 1992), 4-9. First major geological survey of the nation's mineral springs was conducted by Albert C. Peale in 1883-84 for the Department of Interior. Indiana ranked second among the eleven states in the North Central Region in the number of spring sites (101) and the number of individual springs (151). Nationally, there were over eight thousand entries in these two categories. Other well established Hoosier resort communities outside Orange County included Trinity Springs in Martin County, several around Martinsville in Morgan County, and Mudlavia in Warren County.

4. *French Lick Centennial Historical Souvenir Program: 1857-1957*, 7-11.

5. Gregory S. Gatsos, *History of the West Baden Springs Hotel*, (Paoli, Ind., private printing, 1985), 6-23.

6. Jeanette Vanausdall, "'A Miracle of Rare Devices: Images of the West Baden Springs Hotel," *Traces*, Winter 1992; 10-19.

7. 1860 U. S. Census (Appendix B) for Eli Roberts. Others enumerated in French Lick Township in 1860 included: Nina Baxter, along with the Two Evans brothers in her home, the Osborne Bond family, and the Aaron Burnett family. All male adults except Burnett, a farmer, were laborers and could have also worked in the nearby hotels in Springs Valley.

8. Numerical count completed from a composite report for census years as listed in Appendix B. All definitions used as provided in actual censuses. The total number of family groups was obtained by counting each new "Family #" given in the census for these individuals. Many families had independent living arrangements, but others, especially couples without children, were indentified as "boarders" in other families. Total number of "Boarders" determined from actual count of persons so classified in the census. Individuals reported as living in the hotel facilities are not included in this total since the census enumerator identified them simply as "Servants."

9. *French Lick Centennial Historical Souvenir Program: 1857-1957*, 19.

10. Frank Bowers, *A History of the Order of Knights of Pythias in Indiana, with the Story of Damen and Pythias* (Indianapolis: Carlon & Hollenbeck, printers, 1885), 21-25.

11. Clement Richardson, ed., *The National Cyclopedia of the Colored Race*, (Montgomery, AL: National Publishing Co., 1919), s.v. "The Knights of Pythias of North America, South America, Europe, Asia, Africa an Australia" by John J. Jones, Supreme Vice-Chancellor; I, 585-587. Executive officers of departments were: Smith L. Green, New Orleans, La., Supreme Chancellor of Lodge Department; Joseph L. Jones, Cincinnati, Oh., Supreme Worthy Counsellor of the Order of Calanthe; R. R. Jackson, Chicago, Ill., Major General of the Uniform Rank; J. L. V. Washington, Louisville, Ky., Royal Potentate of the Dramatic Order of Knights of Omar.

12. We are deeply indebted to Lin Wagner, present owner, who permitted us to survey this collection which she plans to turn over eventually to a local historical museum.

13. Minutes of the *64th Annual Communication of the Grand Lodge of the Free and Accepted Masons of the State of Indiana held at Noblesville, Indiana August 18, 19, and 20, 1920* (Seymour, Ind.: Graessle-Mercer Co., printer, 1920), 112-113. By this time there were 50 subordinate lodges in the state with a total of 3,318 members. Daniel W. Caine, Seymour, Indiana was the Most Worshipful Grand Master.

14. The Waddys were buried in the K of P Cemetery west of French Lick. Mrs. Nannie Waddy's obituary appeared in the *Paoli News*, Thursday, December 15, 1960.

15. Personal interviews with Mr. and Mrs. Artie Smith during 1991 visits to their home.

16. Newspaper article, "Silver Tea Planned Sunday Honors Miss Birdie Sebree," *Paoli News*, October 22, 1964 and the death notice published in the same newspaper on March 18, 1965. The Sebree family plot in the K of P cemetery contains a gravestone listing her birthdate as Sept 18, 1891 and her deathdate on March 16, 1965. Other stones identify the following: Father, Dudley Sebree (December 31, 1864-February 5, 1936); Mother, Hannah L. Sebree (February 18, 1867-October 15, 1930); [Dr.] James Sebree (Oct 25, 1885-Apr 16, 1908); Edward T. Sebree (Apr 18, 1887-Apr 30, 1921); William W. Sebree (Sept 2, 1899-May 3, 1926).

CHAPTER XIV

MORE TOWN DWELLERS

In the previous chapter the development of the African American community in Springs Valley from the turn of this century was chronicled. At the same time other persons of African ancestry lived in the towns of Paoli and Orleans. This chapter will describe briefly some families whose members remained in Orange County for several decades.

The Stage Coach Driver in Paoli

The name of Oscar Bowman (1861-1943) became legendary in Orange County as the "colored" stage coach driver. For more than twenty-five years he drove the route between Paoli and New Albany, Indiana without ever missing a scheduled run.

The business was owned and operated by the Rhodes Brothers, William and Beverly, who maintained a livery on East Main Street. After they obtained the U. S. Mail contract in the 1890s, Bowman was one of six drivers whose responsibility was to see that the mail and passengers reached their designations without delay. They used a two-horse team pulling a western style stage coach with two seats and a luggage rack on top. Mail bags were placed in the space called a "booth" beneath the driver's feet and another big booth in back was used to store luggage.[1]

The Rhodes Brothers inherited the business from their father, Andrew J., who returned from the Civil War and opened a furniture store at Paoli. Andrew was commissioned as the Paoli Postmaster in 1872, and after nine years in the post office he returned to general merchandising and feed business. His livery was opened in 1877, and in time the businesses were turned over to his sons.[2]

Bowman was no stranger to horses or to the town's people when he became one of the stage coach drivers in the 1880s. When only 17 years old and still living with his parents on a small farm on the outskirts of town, Oscar and his father worked as teamsters in Paoli. He was born in Orange County. His parents, Henry Bowman (1835-1903) and Martha A. Brown (1838-1881) were married in Paoli on February 22, 1856. They had at least eight children including: Richard Edgar Bowman (1857-1875), Beatrice, Oscar, Francis (Frank), Gertrude, Mary Elena, Ardie and Susan.[3]

Oscar married Allie Burnett in Paoli on November 10, 1885.[4] She was also a native Orange Countian and the daughter of Enoch and Parlee Rickman Burnett. The Oscar Bowmans parented at least seven children: Earl (1886), Olia (1888), Hershel (1892), Irene (1894), Jess (1897), Mable (1899), Elsie (1903), and Lawrence (1906).[5] For years the family lived in a frame house on North Gospel Street where the Paoli Town Office now stands.

In 1910 Oscar Bowman was still driving for the stage lines but his days in this employment were numbered. Eventually the mail was delivered by truck to Hardinsburg where it was picked up by the stage from Paoli. Oscar Bowman, the last stage coach driver, drove that short run until it was finally replaced by motor delivery.

Oscar died on November 17, 1943 at the home of his daughter in Spencer, Indiana.[6] He was buried in Newberry Cemetery near the graves of his wife and parents. One of his sons, Jess E. Bowman, became a building contractor in Springfield, Illinois where he died and was buried in 1960. Relatives from Paoli, Hardinburg and Marengo, Indiana attended the funeral.[7]

Paoli's Honor Student and Basketball Star

In 1917 Arthur Howard was the first African American to graduate from Paoli High School. One has to look carefully to make sure the neatly dressed, shy appearing young man kneeling in the front row of the class picture taken in front of the school building is racially any different than his seventeen classmates.

"Army," as he was nicknamed, was an honor student as well as a star athlete in track and basketball. The same year of his graduation, he posed in his playing uniform with the coach, Emory O. Muncie, and members of his high school's basketball team: Ralph Lingle, Dallas Fleming, Earl Whitmore and Dwight Morris. This photograph is featured today in the wall collection of annual basketball team pictures on display in the high school building.

Arthur, the son of William J. Howard and Helen Sweat Howard, was born in Paoli on August 17, 1897. The youngest of five children, he had three sisters, Mary, Nancy and Josephine, plus an older brother, Elmer. During the 1920s Arthur moved with his family to Springs Valley where he worked for years as a bell boy in the West Baden and French Lick hotels.

He died on December 7, 1963 at the Keller Nursing Home in Mitchell, Indiana where he had been a patient for three months. The 66-year old Arthur never married, and he was the last surviving member of his family with no living relatives. His former high school classmates and friends completed the funeral arrangements and started a fund to erect a marker at his grave in Mount Lebanon Cemetery, French Lick, Indiana.[8]

1970 Woman of the Year in Paoli

Lillian Norris, an African American native of Lawrence County, Indiana, was honored in 1970 as the community's "Woman of the Year" by the Paoli Business and Professional Women group. Over half of her lifetime was spent in Paoli where she became quite active in community affairs.[9]

Born in nearby Mitchell, Indiana on August 28, 1912, Mrs. Norris was the daughter of Lenwood and Stella Ganaway Kendall. Her first husband, Willie Cooper, died in Mitchell, leaving her with two children: John Cooper (born October 18, 1932) and Madge Cooper (November 11, 1941). She moved to Paoli after marrying her second husband, William Ernest Norris, on November 24, 1943 at her parents' home in Mitchell.

William "Bill" Norris was born on April 16, 1916 in Boone County, Kentucky, and he moved to Paoli with his family in 1937 when his father took over operation of the Lingle farm south of town. One of his brothers, Stanley Norris, attended the Paoli High School and was president of his senior class.   Mr. Norris once operated his own paint and body shop in Paoli.   Following a stint of employment at the Lehigh Plant in Bedford, he ended up working for many years at the Paoli Chair Company before retiring in 1983.

The Norrises had three children in their marriage: William Ernest Norris, Jr. (August 13, 1944), Mildred Norris (October 7, 1946) and, Ronnie Norris (December 27, 1948).

Mrs. Lillian Norris maintained a private catering service while working as a practical nurse in addition to keeping up with her home and family duties.   She was an elder of the Paoli Presbyterian Church and served as president of the church Women's Association.   She was also chaplain of the local Veterans of Foreign Wars (VFW) Auxiliary and was active for many years in mental health work.   At the time of her death, Lillian was vice-president of the Orange County Mental Health Association and on the Board of directors of Southern Hills Mental Health Clinic in New Albany.   She became a Gold Volunteer in the county's mental health association, and for many years she served the annual Christmas dinner for mental hospital and nursing home patients.   She was also an active member in the homemakers organization of the Orange County Extension Office.

During a visit with relatives in Indianapolis, Mrs. Norris became ill and died unexpectedly at the Community Hospital on July 23, 1978.

Several years later William E. Norris Sr. married Cornelia May Cox of LaGrange, Indiana. They continue to reside in Paoli and maintain close family ties with his children and grandchildren. John Cooper lives with his wife and four children in North Vernon, Indiana. Madge Cooper is divorced from her husband, Wilber Thornton, and lives with her four children in Bedford. William Norris Jr., a graduate of Oakland City College, owns a Chrysler-Plymouth dealership in Utica, N. Y. Mildred Norris, divorced from her husband, Edgar Bolin, lives with her two children in French Lick. Rev. Ronnie Norris, also a graduate of Oakland City College, lives with his wife and two sons in Evansville, Indiana where he is pastor of the Alexander A. M. E. Church.

Rev. and Mrs. Robert H. Bennett

Anticipating his retirement from pastoral duties in the African Methodist Episcopal (A.M.E.) Church, the Bennetts purchased in 1962 a country home with eighty acres on Unionville Road about four miles south of Paoli.   After retirement in the 1970s, both felt comfortable living in the area where they had relatives in addition to the many friends and acquaintances developed during A.M.E. Church assignments in French Lick and Mitchell, Indiana.[10]   Rev. Bennett retained memberships in the Orange County Ministerial Society and the Paoli Kiwanis Club.

He lived in the community when the Paoli Boys Scouts embarked on their special campaign in 1970 to clean up the "Little Africa Cemetery" and he visited the project once in the Hoosier National Forest.

Although born in South Carolina, Rev. Bennett grew up in Indianapolis and graduated from Crispus Attucks High School. As a young boy he worked after school in the Indianapolis City Market where racial discrimination and bigotry confronted him constantly as he learned to speak French, German and Greek languages fluently from his employers in the fruit and vegetable business. He managed to augment his foreign language skills with travels and military service in Europe during World War I.

In 1921 he married Elsie Turner and they lived in Indianapolis where he worked for many years as a landscape designer. His wife died in 1940, and four years later he married for a second time to his present wife, Cleo Crouch. Employed by the *Indianapolis Times* newspaper for more than eighteen years, Mr. Bennett received his call to preach while still at the newspaper. Over the course of several years he took religious courses at Payne Theological Seminary and Wilberforce College in Ohio before his ordination as a minister in the African Methodist Episcopal (A.M.E.) Church.

His first ministerial appointment was to a small A.M.E. Church in Indianapolis, but the assignment, however, permitted him to continue working at the newspaper job on weekdays. Eventually he received an appontment to the two churches on the Bedford-French Lick Circuit where he remained until retirement. After her huband's death in 1985, Mrs. Bennett moved to Indianapolis where she resides in a nursing home.

The following notice was published in the *Paoli Times*, Thursday, October 17, 1985:

Robert H. Bennett

Local services are being held at 11 a.m. Thursday at Paoli Central Baptist Church for Rev. Robert H. Bennett, 85, Paoli R1, who died at 3 p.m. at Dunn Memorial Hospital in Bedford. Rev. Coy Camp is officiating.

A second service will take place at 11 a.m. Friday at Allen Chapel A. M. E. Church in Indianapolis, where Rev. Bennett was a member. Visitation there will be at the church from 10 a.m. until the time of service. Rev. Leonard Williams will officiate at rites. Burial will be at Crown Hill Cemetery in Indianapolis.

He was born Oct. 27, 1899 in Indianapolis to Robert H. and Elizabeth Martin Bennett Sr. He married Elsie Turner in 1921, and she died in 1940. In 1944 he married Cleo Crouch, who survives.

Also surviving is a son, Richard H. Bennett of Indianapolis; two daughters, Mrs. E. A. Simons of Detroit, Mich., and Mrs. Mary Katherine Newbold of Indianapolis; a brother, Theodore Bennett of Los Angeles, Calif., a sister, Ella Quishenberry of Los Angeles; four grand-children and eight great-grandchildren.

He was an active member of Paoli Kiwanis Club and an army veteran of World War I.

Town of Orleans

Census data and public records confirm that a small number of African Americans once lived in the town of Orleans and Orleans Township.

As early as 1840, "Pierce Todd," a single colored male in the age range 24-36, was enumerated in the census. Ten years later, Pearson and Melvina Todd owned a farm in Orleans Township where they lived with their five children: Morris B., Amanda J., William P. Q., Hiram H., and John E. All of these children were native-born Hoosiers although their parents migrated from Hardin County, Kentucky.

In the 1860 census, Pearson and Melvina Todd held real estate in Orleans Township valued at $300 and had seven children in the home, ranging from four month old daughter, Fanny, to the twenty year old son Morris. By 1880, Melvina, a 53-year old widow, kept house in Orleans for a family of five: William and his young wife, Bell, and their baby son, Augustus; Harris F. C., 18 years old, and a 15 year old son, George W. Todd. In 1900, there were 16 inhabitants in Orleans including two Todd households: (1) Fred H. and Anna Todd with three daughters, and (2) George Todd, a single, 29 year old man. Additional families were the Burnetts, Finleys, and Pierces. Ten years later, the Frederick Todd and Charity Burnett families made up the total African American community in Orleans.

Some details about these families are chronicled in the 1989 publication by Mary Edith Johnson Yancey, *Rocked in the Cradle of the Deep*.[11] A resident of Harrisburg, Pennsylvania, the author was born in Bloomington, Indiana on October 20, 1920, the second daughter and child of George Anderson Johnson and Edith Todd Johnson.

Her mother, Edith Todd Johnson (1889-1975), was the youngest daughter of Fred Harris Todd and Anna Burnett Todd (1866-1917) and grew up in Orleans, Indiana. Her two older sisters were Hallie Burnett Todd Evans (1884-1920), and Rowena Todd Bryant (1886-1928).[12]

Her great-grandfather was Pearson Todd, who died on April 12, 1866 at the age of 56 years and was buried in the Green Hill Cemetery in Orleans (see Chapter X on Cemeteries). Copy of a Certificate of Freedom in the family's possession identified Pearson's mother, Amanda Todd, as a resident of Hardin County, Kentucky for thirty-seven years who was preparing to move to the state of Indiana when the document was completed. Unfortunately the date of this legal instrument was not published.[13]

Aaron Burnett and Charity (Charlotte) Isom were married in Orange County, Indiana on March 27, 1850. He was the son of Louis and Polly Burnett, who reportedly arrived in the county around 1811.[14] Aaron and Charity Burnett had three daughters, Delilah Susan, who married William Thomas on December 18, 1880; Jane, who married and soon left Lace Allen of nearby Mitchell; and Anna, who married Fred Todd.

Yancey wrote a warm, personal story of family events and oral traditions which she recalled from her early childhood. She dedicated the book to her progeny who might never hear the stories told orally by ancestors as she did. References to important family documents are scattered throughout the book, and the absence of genealogical charts create some problems for readers to sort out family lines of the more than six generations covered in this book.

Her father was George A. Johnson, a native of Kentucky who attended the Banneker "Colored" School in Bloomington and graduated from Indiana University in 1915. Later he became principal of Dunbar High School, Fort Smith, Arkansas and of the Howard High School in Wilmington, Delaware.

Mrs. Yancey graduated from Indiana University in 1941, and when her daughter, Judith, graduated from the same school in 1965, the family had three living generations of I. U. graduates. Several family members have pursued careers in the educational and professional fields.

NOTES

1. Newspaper articles, "19th Century Album," *Paoli Republican*, February 13, 1968; "Stage coach traveled to & fro" *The Republican*, April 30, 1991.

2. *History of Lawrence, Orange and Washington Counties, Indiana*, 597.

3. *Marriage Records*, Orange Co., Ind., Book C-4, 161. Information about children gleaned from 1870 and 1880 census data about the family (Appendix B).

4. *Marriage Records*, Orange Co., Ind., Book C-7, 513.

5. Details about children based on data found about this family in the 1900 and 1910 censuses (Appendix B). In the 1910 census, Oscar was identified as "Sidney Bowman" but the pertinent information matches previously recorded data about the family.

6. Death notice in *The Paoli Republican*, Thursday Nov. 18, 1943. Family burials in Newberry Cemetery given in Chapter 9.

7. Article "Former Countian Dies in Illinois," *Paoli News*, Thursday, April 14, 1960.

8. Article, "Army Howard Expires at 66; Rites Monday," *The Paoli Republican*, December 10, 1963.

9. Family information provided by Mr. William E. Norris in interviews at his home in Paoli on January 7, 1992 and March 23, 1992; newpaper obituary for Mrs. Lillian Norris, *Paoli Republican*, Tuesday, July 25, 1985.

10. Death notice, Robert H. Bennett, *Paoli News*, Thursday October 17, 1985.

11. Mary E. Yancey, *Rocked in the Cradle of the Deep*, (privately printed by author: 1844 Forester Street, Harrisburg, P.A. 17103). After this chapter was written, word received that Mrs. Mary Edith Johnson Yancey died on January 22, 1993.

12. Ibid., 162-167.

13. Ibid., 258. Reportedly these "Free Papers" were found between the pages of McGuffey's Fourth Electic Reader belonging to Eva Lena Todd when she attended the Orleans Elementary school in 1866. Yancey identified the children of Pearson and Melvina Todd as George, Fred, Fannie, Green and Bishop who served in the Civil War and was buried in Petersburg, Va.

14. Ibid., 160-167.

CHAPTER XV

FAMILY HISTORIES

Isaac and Jamima Kelly Scott Family

Isaac Scott, was born near Fayetteville in Cumberland County, North Carolina on November 27, 1801, the son of Zachariah and Mary Scott. He and his parents were free-born and never in slavery. Physically, Isaac was of "a rather light complexion" and stood five feet ten inches tall.[1]

In the Orange County's "Register of Negro and Mulattoes," Isaac was described simply as being "about half white." His racial heritage, like that of other Scotts listed in this legal book was probably a mixture of African and European (Scotch-Irish) strains, intermingled with some Native American ancestors.[2]

Jamima Kelly was his first wife and mother of their twelve children (see Chart I). Six years younger than her husband, she was also free born and from Cumberland County, N. C. where they were married on November 6, 1828.[3] In the Orange County's "Register of Negroes and Mulattoes," Jamima was described as a "light mulatto, high cheek bones, 5 ft 4 1/2 inches high."

Their first child, Alfred Scott, was born on October 5, 1828 near Raleigh in the St. Mathews District of Wake County, North Carolina.[4] Three other children were born in Wake County: William T., 1831; Joseph K., 1833; and Elizabeth in 1835.[5]

Presumably, Isaac was a farmer during the seven years they lived in Wake County. On February 7, 1835, he obtained a certificate of freedom--the legal document which all free Blacks were required to carry when traveling beyond their immediate environs. Language used in Isaac's paper gave the purpose as "to move west or to some other county."

Orange County, Indiana

The Scotts left Raleigh, North Carolina in 1835 and arrived in Indiana later the same year. Isaac Scott acquired his first 40 acres of land in what was to become the Lick Creek Settlement by September 16, 1835. The fact that he was financially able to purchase land within eight months after leaving North Carolina suggests that the family carried some assets with them. One month earlier, a Martin Scott, perhaps a relative of Isaac, purchased 40 acres in the same vicinity.[6]

Over the next twenty years, the Isaac Scott family accumulated a total of 400 acres in the "colored settlement," plus a lot in the town of Chambersburg. They continued the pattern of having mostly sons and Isaac played a responsible role in the local community. For example, in December, 1843, he served as one of the five trustees who founded the first African Methodist Episcopal Church in the Lick Creek Settlement.

By 1850, their farm home was a bit crowded. Alfred, the eldest son, was 22 years old and still living with his parents. Nine other children shared the household: William, 18; Joseph, 16; Elizabeth, 14; Zachariah, 13; Sanders, 10; Needham, 8; Littlejohn, 6; Daniel, 4; and Doctor Franklin, 3.[7]

They lived in the midst of other families who were former North Carolina residents. Nearby were three families with the Scott surname: (1) Henry and Lucy Scott, a 50-year old wagon maker and two children, Jane 19, and Martin, 18; (2) Martin, a 63-year old farmer, and his wife, Mary, with their son, Alvin, his three small children, and another grandchild, Henry Weaver; and (3) Joseph, a 35-year old farmer with his wife, Fanny, and three small children.[8]

Shortly before his 23rd birthday, Alfred M. Scott married Martha Jane Suthers in Paoli, Indiana on January 19, 1852.[9] Little is known about the bride except that she was born in Virginia around 1835. In local public documents the spelling of her surname varies as "Suthers", "Southers", "Sudders" and "Southard".

After the marriage, Alfred and Martha J. Scott established a household in Orange County as evidenced by their separate listing in "Register of Negroes and Mulattoes" on September 17, 1853-- fully three months before his father got around to making registrations for the other family members.[10]

Isaac and Jamima's first grandchild, Jane E. Scott, was born during the first year of her parents' marriage. The next year, young Alfred Scott settled his family in nearby Washington County (see Chart II).

By 1855, when Isaac Scott held title to 400 acres of land, he started gradually to dispose of his real estate. First to go was the large 160 acres tract purchased four years earlier and sold on October 13, 1855. Then he marketed the town lot in Chambersburg on March 24, 1856. Three years later on March 4, 1859, they disposed of an 60-acre sector. The final 180 acres were sold on September 29, 1862.

Kent County, Ontario, Canada

Details remain obscure regarding the date and circumstances which led to the Scott family's leaving Orange County. Their departure was denoted by the absence of any listing for them in the federal population censuses after 1850.

The family ended up in the Buxton Settlement near Chatham, Canada. Several references to the Isaac Scott family were located in the genealogical collections, Raleigh Township Centennial Museum at North Buxton, Ontario.

Apparently, all members except Alfred, lived in Kent County during the 1860s. A marriage record reveals that Isaac Scott remarried a second time to Christina Beddoes Graves, age 56, on March 13, 1865.[11] Seemingly his first wife, Jamima, died in Canada prior to this date.

A number of African Americans from Indiana moved to this area of Canada starting in the 1850s. Other families from Orange County, in addition to the Isaac-Jamima Scott family, were the Chavises, Herman and Martha Linch, Solomon and Margaret Newby, and the Chandlers.[12]

CHART I

Descendants of Isaac Scott, Orange County, Indiana

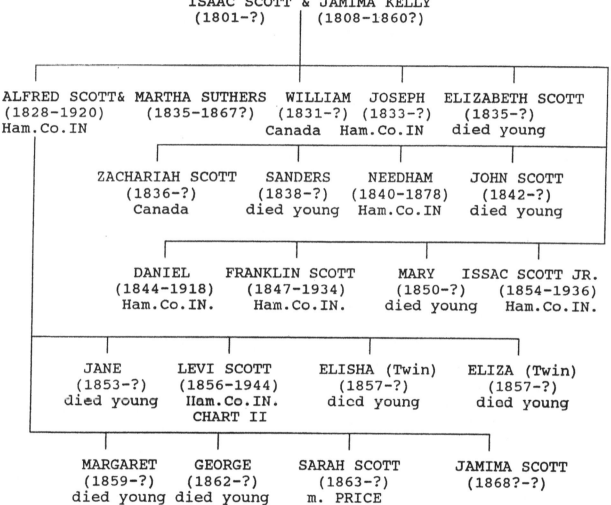

Coy D. Robbins/1992

CHART II

Descendants of Levi Scott, Hamilton County, Indiana

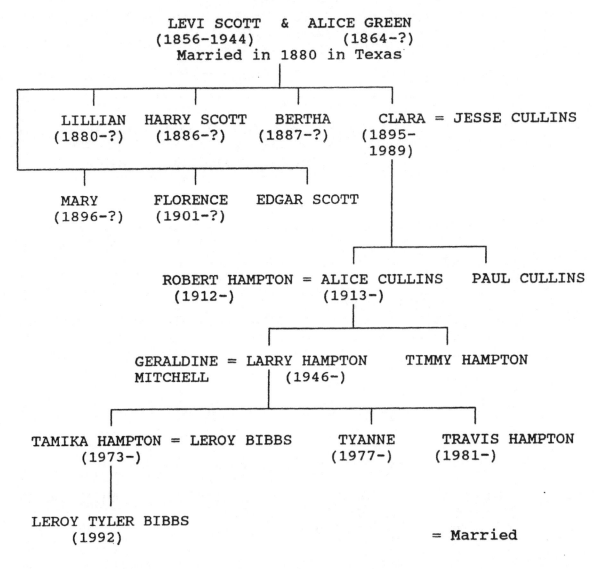

LEVI SCOTT & ALICE GREEN
(1856-1944)   (1864-?)
Married in 1880 in Texas

LILLIAN   HARRY SCOTT   BERTHA   CLARA = JESSE CULLINS
(1880-?)   (1886-?)   (1887-?)   (1895-
                                          1989)

MARY   FLORENCE   EDGAR SCOTT
(1896-?)   (1901-?)

ROBERT HAMPTON = ALICE CULLINS   PAUL CULLINS
(1912-)   (1913-)

GERALDINE = LARRY HAMPTON   TIMMY HAMPTON
MITCHELL   (1946-)

TAMIKA HAMPTON = LEROY BIBBS   TYANNE   TRAVIS HAMPTON
(1973-)   (1977-)   (1981-)

LEROY TYLER BIBBS
(1992)   = Married

Coy D. Robbins/1992

Two sons of Isaac and Jamima married and remained forever in Canada. William Thomas Scott married Margaret L. Robbins ca. 1852 in North Buxton, and they had four children. Zachariah L. Scott married Mary Ann Robbins, Margaret's sister, in the 1860s, and they also had four children.

Descendants of William and Zachariah Scott are well known today in the North Buxton community, those who stayed there and those who eventually settled in the United States.

A third son, Joseph K. Scott, was married in London, Middlesex County, Ontario between 1865-1871. Nothing further is known about this marriage or any possible offspring. Joseph migrated later to Hamilton County, Indiana and married Samira Hammonds on January 28, 1894. He died there in 1916.

The Alfred Scott Family

In Washington County, Indiana

Alfred remained in Indiana after his parents and siblings went to Canada. Over the next ten years he supported the family by working as a farm laborer near Salem in Washington Township. During this period, Alfred and Martha J. Scott had the following children:

Jane E. Scott, around 1853.
Levi William Scott, December 17, 1855.
Elisha Eli Scott (twin), October 28, 1857.
Mary Eliza Scott (twin), October 28, 1857.
Margaret A. Scott, January 22, 1859.
George Scott, February 29, 1862.
Sarah Scott, around 1863.[13]

The Civil War Years

The sequence of events in this family's life between 1860 and 1867 is blurry. Before 1863 when Alfred enlisted in the military service during the Civil War, they had moved from Washington County to Hamilton County located in central Indiana north of Indianapolis.

Alfred enrolled into the Union Army at Noblesville, Indiana on December 31, 1863. Two days later he was in Indianapolis and a private in Company C, 28th Regiment, United States Colored Troops, commanded by Captain Redenaugh.

Medical records revealed that Alfred, now 35 years old, was treated for the measles. Later, while stationed at City Point, Virginia, he suffered from severe diarrhea due to the "bad water" and improper diet available to the soldiers.

He was discharged from service with his company at Corpus Christie, Texas on November 3, 1865, and he returned to Indianapolis soon afterwards.[14]

In Howard County, Indiana

Sometime between 1865 and 1868, Alfred Scott moved his family to a farm located near Kokomo in Center Township of Howard County, Indiana--about 40 miles north of Noblesville. Their eighth child, Jamima, was born in 1868, and Martha died soon after childbirth. She was 33 years old at the time of her death.

A widower left with the care of four children including an infant daughter, Alfred entered a second marriage to a Hannah Scott. The marriage lasted only a short time and ended in divorce.[15]

In 1870, while still living on a farm in Howard County, Alfred married for the third time to an Eliza J. Todd, who had a ten-year old son. The family unit now comprised of five children: (1) Margaret Scott, 11 years; (2) Levi William Scott, age 8; Sarah Scott, 7 years; Jemimah Scott, 2 years; and James Todd, 9 years old.[16]

Return to Hamilton County

By 1880, Alfred Scott had moved his family back to Hamilton County, Indiana near Noblesville. Here he farmed for the remainder of his lifetime.[17]

His third wife, Eliza J. Todd Scott, died in Noblesville, Indiana on February 22, 1891. Six months later, Alfred Scott married a widow, Fannie Lucas, on August 23, 1891. Mrs. Lucas brought two young children into this marriage: Andrew and Sallie Lucas.[18]

After his step-daughter, Sallie Lucas, married Arthur Bush on July 8, 1903, Alfred and Fannie Scott, in time, moved in with the young Bushes. Descendants of the Bush family still reside in Noblesville today.

From May 20, 1912 until his death, Alfred Scott received a small monthly pension for his Civil War disability. He died on February 5, 1920 at the age of 92 years and was buried in Crownland Cemetery in Noblesville.[19]

Children of Alfred M. Scott

Public documents indicate there were eight children fathered by Alfred M. Scott, and likely only three of them survived into adulthood.[20] Little is known about the adult children except his son, Levi Scott, who resided in Noblesville, Indiana for many years.

Born on December 17, 1855 in Washington County, Indiana, Levi William Scott was about 13 years old when his mother died. During his growing up years on farms in Howard and Hamilton Counties, Indiana, he had two step-mothers. In 1872 when only seventeen years old, Levi enlisted in the regular army of the United States. Over the next five years in the military, he fought the Indians in Texas and other western states.

When discharged from the army in 1877, he went to Texas and married a Mary Alice Green. They moved to Noblesville, Indiana two years later and raised a family of seven children. For many years Levi worked in the local industries of National Carbon Company, the Strawboard owned by the Ball Brothers Company of Muncie, and the Noblesville School Board.

Levi Scott died in Noblesville on Wednesday, November 1, 1944, after an illness which extended over three to four years. His widow survived with the following children: Edgar and Harry Scott, Mrs. Clara Scott Cullins Allen, and Mrs. Florence Scott Forrest of Noblesville; Mrs. Bertha Scott Wilkins and Mrs. Mary Scott Wilkins, both of Muskegon, Michigan; and, one sister, Mrs. Sarah Scott Price of Union City, Indiana. There were five grandchildren and one great-grandchild. One descendant, Paul Cullins, was in the military service and stationed in New Guinea at the time of his grandfather's death.[21]

Isaac and Jamima Scott's Other Children

Genealogical research located personal data for at least twelve children. In addition to (1) Alfred, who ended up in Noblesville, Indiana, there were (2) William, who became a Canadian citizen in North Buxton; (3) Joseph, who also went to Canada but settled finally in Noblesville, Indiana; and (4) Zachariah, who also married and remained in Canada.

No record was found for the following children after they left Orange County, and presumably they died before reaching adulthood: (5) Elizabeth, (6) Sanders, (7) John "Littlejohn," and (8) Mary A. Scott.

Besides Alfred and Joseph, at least three other Scotts eventually settled in Noblesville. (9) Needham L. Scott (born: ca. 1840) married Emiline Gilmore in Noblesville on September 10, 1867. He died there on June 27, 1878. (10) Daniel J. Scott (born: ca. 1844, Orange County, Indiana) died in Noblesville on April 21, 1918 and was buried at Crownland Cemetery.[22]

(11) Isaac "Bud" Scott Jr., the youngest child, was born in Orange County, Indiana in 1854 and was quite young when the parents migrated to Canada. In the 1871 Canadian Population Census, he was 19 years old and living in London, (Middlesex County) Ontario with his older brothers, Joseph and Franklin. He came to Noblesville around 1880 and married Belle Roberts on June 1, 1882. They had no children, and were long-time members of the local A. M. E. Church. Isaac Scott Jr. died on March 15, 1936 and was buried at Crownland Cemetery.[23]

(12) Franklin Doctor Scott led a life nearly as colorful as that of his older brother, Alfred. Born in Orange County, Indiana on February 4, 1847, "Doc" was a young boy when the family left Indiana for Canada.

Nothing more is known about him until April 1, 1864 when he enlisted as a private in Company K, 102nd Michigan Volunteers Colored Infantry, United States Colored Troops, Union Army at Pontiac, Michigan. Franklin was 17 years old.

He was discharged at Charleston, South Carolina on September 1, 1865. Apparently, he returned directly to Canada where in 1871 he was living with his older brother, Joseph, and younger brother, Isaac "Bud" in London, Ontario.

In 1872, Franklin married Sarah Ann Coursey, Raleigh Township, Kent County and they had three daughters: (1) Elizabeth Ann Scott, (2) Mattie Scott, and (3) Lulu M. P. Scott. This marriage was dissolved in Canada on June 17, 1890.

Before this divorce was finalized, however, Franklin had married his second wife, Kessiah Hoard, in Noblesville on December 27, 1887. Couple later divorced. His third marriage to Bertha

Lulu Graham in Noblesville on June 16, 1895 lasted only five months before their divorce was granted on November 16, 1895.

His fourth and final marriage was to Louie Daisy Sweat (1881-1972) on May 19, 1901 at Noblesville. They had two sons: Wilbur O. Scott (1907-1987) and William E. Scott (1912-).

Franklin died on April 25, 1934 and was buried at Crownland Cemetery, Noblesville.[24]

Thus, the Isaac-Jamima Scott family which was once a part of the Lick Creek Settlement in Orange County, Indiana continues today through their many descendants living in North Buxton and Chatham, Canada; Noblesville and Hamilton County, Indiana; Indianapolis; Pontiac, Michigan; Cleveland, Ohio and scattered portions of the United States.

The Roberts Family

The ancestry of the Roberts family as "free people of color" goes back for more than two hundred years in this country (Appendix D). In 1790, when the first United States Population Census was enumerated, 639 free Black families lived in the state of North Carolina. Robertses headed seven of these families which all together contained a total of 39 members.[25]

The exodus of free people of color out of North Carolina starting in the mid-1820s was a direct response to the increased number of oppressive acts against them by the white society. The Robertses joined their friends and neighbors and migrated westward in search of a haven in the newly opened states of the Northwest Territory.

They did not, however, leave North Carolina at the same time, nor is there any indication in their preserved family records that they ever accompanied the Quakers to Indiana. The Roberts migrations extended into the 1840s as more and more of them in the "tarheel" state disposed of their land properties and joined their relatives in Indiana.

In 1830, Indiana had 14 different free Black Roberts families living in five counties (Monroe, Orange, Owen, Rush and Union). North Carolina, for the same year, had 15 free Black families with the Roberts surname living in six counties (Beaufort, Chatham, Cumberland, Northampton, Pasquotank and Robeson). In the entire United States, there were 174 free Blacks with the Roberts surname heading households.[26]

By 1840, free Blacks with the Roberts surname resided in nine Indiana counties, with the largest concentrations in the rural settlements of Rush, Orange, Vigo and Hamilton Counties (see Table 19).

Finding so many different free Black families with the Roberts surname reported in the early U. S. Population Censuses presents the genealogist with a formidable task of sorting out the individual family connections. This challenge becomes more arduous for those researchers working with data recorded prior to the 1850 U. S. Census which was first one to provide the first names for all persons living in the same household.

Other research complications resulted when attempting to assign individuals to specific family groups. The Roberts descendents often used the naming pattern to repeat a favorite given name for several generations. Brothers, cousins and nephews frequently had the same Christian name.

Table 19

1840 Indiana: Roberts in Free Black Families

County	Number
Clarke	1
Fayette	4
Hamilton	24
Orange	30
Owen	5
Randolph	6
Rush	51
Union	8
Vigo	26
Total	155

Roberts in Rush County, Indiana

Around the mid-1820s Robertses from the Northampton-Halifax County area in North Carolina moved westward and were among the early settlers in Ripley Township of Rush County, Indiana. The families of Elijah Roberts, Anthony Roberts, James Roberts, and Willis Roberts joined with members of the Cary, Gilmore, Lassiter, Scott and Williams families to form what eventually became known as the Beech Settlement in Rush County.[27]

The incoming families soon discovered that the most desireable farm lands had already been sold or was too expensive for them to purchase. As soon as it was practical, they dispersed to other parts of the state seeking better possibilities for land purchases and settling their families.[28]

Roberts in Orange County, Indiana

The Lick Creek Settlement in Orange County appears to be the second community where the Robertses from North Carolina gathered in the Hoosier state. By the time they arrived in Orange County in the late 1820s, however, African Americans had been living in the region for more than ten years.

The 1830 U. S. Census showed that five of the twenty-one Black families in the county carried the Roberts surname: Benjamin, Elias, Ishmael, Kinchen, and Richard. The two Roberts families headed by Kinchen and Richard tarried for about three years in Orange County before moving westward to Vigo County, Indiana where they became early pioneers of the Lost Creek Settlement.

All of these Robertses in Orange County came from North Carolina. While they were probably closely related by blood to the Rush County families, their ancestral heritage needs further research to document the actual family connections.[29]

Benjamin Roberts (1780-1853) obtained a certificate of freedom in Chatham County, N. C. on November 24, 1824. The document identified his wife, Sally, and three children, Serena, Ishmael and Archibald in the family group "about to remove to the State of Indiana." He acquired 80 acres in the Lick Creek Settlement which went to his wife and two children upon his death.

Elias Roberts (1793-1866) may have come to Indiana directly from Northampton County, N. C. His wife, Nancy, and several children survived his death in 1866 at which time he held title to 304 acres in the Lick Creek Settlement.

Ishmael Roberts, the Revolutionary War veteran,[30] lived in Chatham Co., N. C. and headed a household of ten members when the 1790 census was enumerated. By 1830 he was living in Orange County, Ind. heading a family of eight persons. Ishmael acquired 80 acres in the Lick Creek Settlement, and the patent deed was recorded on March 28, 1836. The following year, 1837, he and his wife, Lucretia, deeded one acre of this land for building the first church in the settlement. They sold the remaining 79 acres in 1846 to Solomon Newby. It is believed that he died and was buried in Lost Creek Settlement Cemetery shortly after this sale was completed. His widow, Lucretia, age 65 years, had her name entered in the county's Negro Register on September 3, 1853.

An Ishmael Roberts Jr. purchased 40 acres of land in the settlement in 1836 and he is thought to be the son of Ishmael and Lucretia Roberts. Young Ishmael Roberts obtained a license in Orange County on August 12, 1844 to marry Delana Revels. When they sold their Orange County property in 1854, Ishmael and Delana Roberts were listed as residents of Hamilton County, Indiana.

Thomas Roberts, obtained a certificate of freedom in Chatham Co., N. C. on September 2, 1836 which stated that he was a son of Ishmael and Cusa (Lucinda) Roberts. The document indicated that Thomas had been bound to a Lindley in North Carolina and served until reaching the age of 21 years. In 1841, Thomas Roberts and his wife, Matilda, purchased a town lot in Chambersburg and 120 acres in the Lick Creek Settlement. Two years later in 1843, they sold one acre of their farm to the trustees of the A. M. E. Church.

By May, 1851 the couple had disposed of all their land holdings and were absent in any subsequent public records found in the county. Additional details about the Ishmael-Lucretia Roberts family ties remain a mystery.

Wiley Roberts obtained a certificate of freedom in Fayetteville, Cumberland County, N. C. on March 21, 1829 at which time he was 21-22 years old, free-born, and single. In Orange County, Indiana on August 21, 1830, Wiley married Mary Thomas. Ten years later, Wiley, who never acquired any real estate, headed a household of seven children. Wiley and his family were listed in the 1850 and 1860 censuses, and their later whereabouts are unknown.

Zachariah Roberts was 47 years old, married, and with six children when he secured a certificate of freedom in Chatham Co., N. C. on December 3, 1847. Three years later when the 1850 census was taken he was living in Orange County, Indiana with his wife, Amy, and six children. He was not listed in the 1860 census, but his son, Zachariah Jr., age 25 years, was enumerated with his wife, Katherine, and four children, ranging in ages from five months to five years. The son's real estate holdings were valued at $4000.

Other Roberts families migrated into or were developed in the Lick Creek Settlement before the end of the 19th century. For example, the families of Ettel and Dicey Roberts, James and Unity Roberts, John and Nancy Roberts, Nelson and Alice Roberts, and William and Sally Roberts -- all were identified for the first time in the 1850 U. S. Census.

Roberts in Vigo County, Indiana

By 1830 there were seventeen African American families composed of 99 individuals living in Vigo County. The largest groups were the Jethro Bass, Joseph Patterson, Bryant Thomas, (who had resided in Orange County, Indiana in 1820), Mathew Stewart, Joseph Wilson and Thomas Wilson families.[31]

Around 1832, the Kinchen and Richard Roberts families moved from Orange County to the Lost Creek Settlement area in Vigo County. There they joined the Andersons, Archers, Chavises, Roberts, Stewarts and Trevans families who had traveled by caravan from North Carolina in the early 1830s.

Kinchen Roberts (1777-1870) is believed to have been a son of James and Ann Roberts of Northampton Co., N. C., and a brother to Jonathan, Elias, Charles, James Jr., Richard, Elijah, Claxson, John James, William and Marthaline Roberts.[32] The family history reported by Dr. Carl G. Roberts indentifies Kinchen's wife as Liza Copeland and lists the following children: Anthony Roberts, Richard Roberts, Elijah Roberts, John P. Roberts, and James Roberts.

Between 1832 and 1835 Kinchen Roberts, along with other Black pioneers, purchased land in Lost Creek Township from the U. S. Government. With Nancy Stewart Roberts, who was probably his second wife, Kinchen sold an acre of their farm land in 1838 for the erection of the first schoolhouse for colored children in the settlement. The same school building served as a church until the Lost Creek A. M. E. Church was constructed across the road in 1840.[33]

Both Kinchen and Nancy were buried in the Roberts Cemetery which served the residents of Lost Creek, Otter Creek and Nevin Townships.

Roberts in Hamilton County, Indiana

The Roberts Settlement in Hamilton County, Indiana was founded in 1835 by several former North Carolinian families from the Beech Settlement in Rush County, Indiana who obtained patent deeds for land in Jackson Township of Hamilton County.

Early pioneers in what became known in time as Roberts Settlement were John Roads (also Rhodes), Micajah Walden (also Waldron), Bryant Walden, Hansel Roberts, Elias Roberts, Jonathan Roberts Jr., Stephen Roberts, Elijah Roberts, James Roberts, Denison White, Guilford Brooks, and Harry Winburn.[34] A Wesleyan Methodist Church with adjoining cemetery was established around 1841. Though greatly diminished in its Black population, the community thrives today around the church called "Roberts Chapel."

Solomon and Margaret Newby Family

In the British Methodist Episcopal Church Cemetery, North Buxton, Ontario, Canada stands a gravestone with the following inscription:"Jas Nuby, Co I, 3 U.S.C. Inf--James Harling Nuby, 1842-1928--NATIVE OF INDIANA, U. S. A." The deceased, an African American, was born in Orange County.

The North Carolina Beginning

James was the third child of Solomon and Margaret Newby, who lived in the Lick Creek Settlement from 1840 to 1862. Both Solomon and Margaret came originally from North Carolina. According to the certificate of freedom which Solomon obtained on September 5, 1840 in Orange County, North Carolina, both were free born as were their parents--they were never in slavery.

Solomon, born circa 1800 probably in Orange County, obtained a bond to marry Margaret Benton [Barton?] in Chatham County, North Carolina on May 25, 1830.[35] When the 1830 U. S. Census was enumerated, Solomon Newby and his bride were then living in the Second Regiment, Randolph County, North Carolina.[36]

Two daughters, Lucinda (1834) and Emaline (1838), were also born in North Carolina before the family migrated in 1840 to Orange County, Indiana. Four additional children were native Hoosiers: James Newby, born in 1843, George J. in 1847, Moses W. in 1849, and Charity Jane in 1856.[37]

Orange County, Indiana

On December 1, 1846, Solomon Newby purchased 79 acres located in the Lick Creek Settlement from Ishmael and Lucretia Roberts for $195.[38] Meanwhile the family took an active role in the community affairs and the African Methodist Episcopal Church, where Solomon Newby was elected to the Board of Trustees in 1851. The parents and five children were registered in the county's "Register of Negroes and Mulattoes" on September 1, 1853. Their 20-year old daughter, Emaline, married Denison White in Orange County on October 8, 1858.[39]

No explanation has been found for why the Newbys and others migrated to Canada in 1862. Solomon sold his 79-acre farm to Jesse Thompson on September 17, 1862 for $100--nearly one-half the price he paid for the land sixteen years earlier. He was one of the seven Black farmers who suddenly disposed of their real estate in the settlement during the month of September, 1862. Several of these families ended up in Canada with the Newbys.[40]

North Buxton, Kent County, Ontario, Canada

Soloman and Margaret Newby acquired a home and farmland at the edge of North Buxton, not far from the British Methodist Episcopal Church, Township School No. 13, and one of the two cemeteries in the village.[41]

Meanwhile, their eldest son, James Harling Newby, responded to the Civil War raging in his native land. Only twenty years old, he traveled to Philadelphia, Pennsylvania and enlisted on July 21, 1863 for three years in the Union Army. A private in Company I, Third Regiment Infantry, United States Colored Troops, James was mustered out of service at Jacksonville, Florida on October 31, 1865.[42]

Afterwards he remained in Florida for eighteen months before returning home to North Buxton. In 1871, he was still single and residing with his parents, a fifteen year old sister, Charity Ann, and Eliza Jane Rann (Newby)--the 18-year old native Canadian who would one day become his bride.[43]

James and Eliza were married in nearby South Buxton on March 6, 1873 by Rev. Frank Lacy. Her parents were William Henry and Melaney Rann and she was born on July 9, 1850. This couple continued to live with James' parents where the following children were born:

(1) Charles Newby (1872-1953)
(2) Mariah Ellen Newby (1873-1966)
(3) William Alfred Newby (1875-1966)
(4) Margaret Melanie Newby (1876-1955)
(5) Mary Rachel Newby (1879-?)
(6) James Andrew Newby (1881-1971)

James Newby Sr. died on June 22, 1928 and Eliza Jane died on February 22, 1932, leaving a host of descendants now scattered over many sectors of Canada and the United States. Both are buried in the family's plot at the British Methodist Episcopal Church cemetery near the graves of Solomon and Margaret Newby.[44]

On display in the Raleigh Township Centennial Museum in North Buxton is an attractive, hand-crafted, rectangular hinged box which Solomon Newby constructed to hold the original copy of his certificate of freedom. A family legend declares that for years after arriving in Canada, Solomon kept the valuable paper buried in an underground backyard cache, fearing that the paper might be stolen or destroyed. When the threat of slavery subsided finally, he constructed the wooden storage box. On special occasions when family members gathered, he would display his historical document to the grandchildren.

The Thomas Family

Census data and apprenticeship records verify that members of the Thomas family were among the early migrants into Orange County, Indiana. They were free people of color and where they originated in North Carolina and exactly when they arrived in Indiana can only be conjectured from the limited details located about their pioneer history.

The following genealogical facts can be authenticated about the early Thomas families. (1) *Bryant Thomas*, his probable wife and two young daughters, were the only free colored persons with the Thomas surname enumerated in Orange County, Indiana when the 1820 Federal Census was completed. (2) *Bryant Thomas* was witness to the signing of apprenticeship papers of William B. Thomas in Orange County on September 14, 1821. (3) *Bryant Thomas* apprenticed a child named, *Jordon Thomas*, about seven years old, to Lewis Byram in Orange County on December 5, 1822. (4) No additional record was located of *Bryant Thomas* in Orange County, however in the 1830 census, he headed a household of four members counted in Vigo County, Indiana. (5) *Lucy Thomas*, a widow, apprenticed two sons in Orange County, Indiana: *William B. Thomas*, six and one-half years old, on September 14, 1821, and *Mathew Thomas*, age thirteen years, on October 6, 1821.

The names of *Lucy Thomas* and *William B. Thomas* did not show up in other documents found in Orange County. Presumably, both died after the indentures were initiated. There are many significant unknowns: the name of Lucy's husband and where he died, if she were also the mother of *Jordon Thomas*, where the family lived before coming to Indiana, and the time and place of her death.

Two of the three Thomas boys, Mathew and Jordon, who were apprenticed in 1821-1822, completed their indentures and remained living in Orange County throughout their adult lives.

Mathew and Mary Thomas Family

At the completion of his apprenticeship training, Mathew Thomas (1808-1870) acquired 80 acres from Zachariah and Margaret Lindley on May 21, 1831 (Appendix B, #159).

Two years later, he secured a certificate of freedom to prove his free status in Indiana.[45] The document, created to save him "from the molestation of those who might probably apprehend him as a slave," was signed on October 19, 1833 by twelve white male Orange County residents: Abraham Carson, A. W. Wilson, Ephriam Doan, W. D. Lynch, Thomas Coffin, D. Dayhuff, I. H. Pierce, Josiah Hazlewood, John H. Campbell, Philip Cook, St Wells, John Dixon.

An additional declaration was attached to the certificate by Zachariah Lindley, who stated that Mathew had been bound to him by his mother, who was a widow, and he served the term "faithfully and honestly." Others who also signed this declaration were: John G. Clendenin, Samuel Chambers, James Clark, H. Braxton, and Daniel Dayhuff. Mathew waited for twenty years before having his "free papers" recorded at the courthouse on August 28, 1853--one day after his name was enrolled in the county's Negro Register.

On December 10, 1834 Mathew Thomas married Mary "Polly" Roberts (1817-1867).[46] She was seventeen years old and several years younger than her husband. Mathew remained a farmer and steadily increased his land holdings throughout his marriage. No doubt, in addition to being an industrious worker, he received considerable help with the farming chores from his wife and maturing children. At the time of his death on December 10, 1870, Mathew, a widower, held title to 322 acres in the Lick Creek Settlement area.

The Children of Mathew Thomas

Mathew and Mary Thomas had thirteen children, but so far names have been identified for only eleven of them.[47]

(1) *Joseph N. Thomas*, born September 26, 1835 and died May 3, 1866. On October 17, 1860, he married Jane Lee in Orange County. No record found of any children in this marriage.

(2) *Mary A. Thomas*, born ca. 1839. She married Monroe Bond, son of Penelope Bond, on October 29, 1863. They had five children: Penelope Bond (1865), William Bond (1868), Austin Bond (1870), Annie Bond (1873), and Alonzo Bond (1875).

(3) *Sarah D. Thomas*, born ca. 1841. She died sometime between 1850 - 1860 and was buried in the Lick Creek Settlement Cemetery.

(4) *Jeremiah Thomas*, born ca. 1844. He left the family between 1860-1870. When his

CHART III

Descendants of Mathew and Mary Thomas

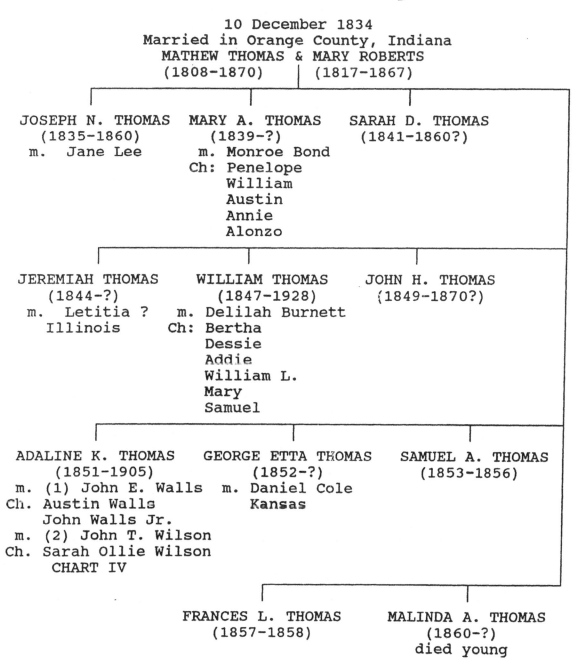

10 December 1834
Married in Orange County, Indiana
MATHEW THOMAS & MARY ROBERTS
(1808-1870)   (1817-1867)

JOSEPH N. THOMAS   MARY A. THOMAS   SARAH D. THOMAS
   (1835-1860)   (1839-?)   (1841-1860?)
 m.   Jane Lee   m. Monroe Bond
                        Ch: Penelope
                            William
                            Austin
                            Annie
                            Alonzo

JEREMIAH THOMAS   WILLIAM THOMAS   JOHN H. THOMAS
   (1844-?)   (1847-1928)   (1849-1870?)
 m. Letitia ?   m. Delilah Burnett
    Illinois   Ch: Bertha
                          Dessie
                          Addie
                          William L.
                          Mary
                          Samuel

ADALINE K. THOMAS   GEORGE ETTA THOMAS   SAMUEL A. THOMAS
   (1851-1905)   (1852-?)   (1853-1856)
 m. (1) John E. Walls m. Daniel Cole
Ch. Austin Walls   Kansas
    John Walls Jr.
 m. (2) John T. Wilson
Ch. Sarah Ollie Wilson
    CHART IV

            FRANCES L. THOMAS   MALINDA A. THOMAS
               (1857-1858)   (1860-?)
                                       died young

Coy D. Robbins/1992

CHART IV

Descendants of Adaline K. Thomas
Owen County, Indiana

Married in Orange County, Indiana
24 June 1871
ADALINE K. THOMAS & (1)JOHN E. WALLS
(divorced)

```
           ┌──────────────┴──────────────┐
    AUSTIN WALLS              JOHN WALLS JR.
    Mitchell, Ind.           New Albany, Ind.
```

Second marrage:

ADALINE K. THOMAS & (2)JOHN T. WILSON
(1851-1905) | (1840-1907)

SARAH OLLIE WILSON
(ca. 1878-?)
married
Rev. PRESTON EAGLESON, Bloomington. IN

Children:

1. WILSON FASHON EAGLESON (1898-1921) - West Virginia

2. JOHN NEWLIN EAGLESON (1907-died in infancy)

3. BUENA MAE ELIZABETH EAGLESON (1908-)
married
Albert Bridgewaters, Bloomington, Indiana

Coy D. Robbins/1992

father's estate was settled in the 1880's, Jeremiah and his wife, Letitia, were listed as residents of Coles County, Illinois.

(5) *William Thomas*, born April 4, 1847, and grew to adulthood on the farm where he was born. He married the first time to Delilah Burnett, daughter of Aaron and Charlotte Burnett, on December 19, 1880. They had six children: Bertha Thomas (1881-1909), Dessie Thomas (1884-), Addie Thomas (1886-), William Leslie (1889-), Mary Ellen (1891-) and Samuel Ernest, who died in infancy. Delila died on April 15, 1897 and was buried at Newberry Friends Church cemetery west of Paoli. The following year William married a second time on October 16, 1898 to Mrs. Susan Terrell of Mitchell, Indiana.

For 46 years before his death William Thomas lived on and managed the Amos Stout farm south of Paoli. He died on June 17, 1928, survived by his wife, three daughters, Mrs. Dessie Stevenson, Mrs. Mary Finney, and Miss Addie Thomas, a son, and four grandchildren.[48]

(6) *John H. Thomas*, born ca, 1849 and died between 1860 - 1870.

(7) *Adaline K. Thomas*, (1851-1905) married John E. Walls, Paoli, on June 24, 1871. They had two sons before the Walls were divorced. Adaline married a second time to John T. Wilson (1840-1907), who was a barber in Spencer (Owen County), Indiana. Wilson, originally from Vigo County, had four children from his previous marriage. Adaline had one child in her second marriage. This daughter, Sarah Ollie Wilson, who was born in Spencer on June 10, 1878, later married Preston Emmanuel Eagleson of Bloomington (Monroe County), Indiana.[49]

The Eagleson family also came from Orange County, Indiana. Preston E. (1878-1911) and his brother, William H. (1880-1951), were the sons of Halston (1851-1921) and Elizabeth Baxter Eagleson and born in Chambersburg. Following the death of their mother, Elizabeth, the family moved to Mitchell, Indiana. Halston later married Eliza Loggins, who became the mother of Walter (1887-1928), Katie Mae (1889-1935), Halston Jr., and Oran Wendell Eagleston. In 1889 the family moved to Bloomington, Indiana where Halston owned and operated a barber shop until his death in 1921. Several members of this family are buried in Rose Hill Cemetery, Bloomington, Indiana.[50]

Five of the six Eagleson children attended Indiana University, and several achieved great success in the educational and professional fields. Preston Emmanuel Eagleston graduated in 1896, and ten years later received a M. A. degree in Philosophy -- the first graduate degree awarded by Indiana University to a person of African descent. An A.M.E. minister, Preston taught in St. Louis, Missouri schools, and the "colored" elementary school in Spencer, Indiana before his death on August 11, 1911.

Halston Vashon Eagleson Jr. received a Ph.D. in Physics in 1939, became the first African American at Indiana University to be elected to Sigma Xi, the scientific honorary fraternity, and taught at Morehouse and Clark colleges in Atlanta, Georgia before becoming a professor of Physics at Howard University, Washington, D.C. (1947-71).

Oran Wendell Eagleston was granted a doctoral degree in Psychology in 1935, was also elected to Sigma Xi, and retired as Dean of Instruction and Professor of Psychology at Spellman College, Atlanta, Georgia. Both Halston V. Jr. and Oran W. were awarded honorary science degrees from Indiana University in 1985.

Preston Emmanuel and Sarah Wilson Eagleson (1878-1939) had three children: Wilson Fashon Eagleson (1898-1921); John Newlin Eagleson (1907), who died in infancy, and Buena Mae Elizabeth Eagleson, who was born in Bloomington on June 4, 1908.

Their youngest child, Elizabeth Eagleson, remained in the community of her birth. She graduated from the Banneker "colored" School and Bloomington High School before receiving a B.A. degree in Psychology at Indiana University. She married Albert Louis Bridgwaters and they parented nine children: Albert Louis Jr., David Preston, John Newlin, Oliver Fashon, Thomas Wilson, Richard Lee, Elizabeth Ann, Mary Judith, and Vivian Marie. Now a widow, Mrs. Elizabeth Bridgwaters was elected for two terms on the Bloomington School Board of Education, serving as president in 1972-73, and pursued an active career in religious, political, educational, civil rights, and community organizations. Today she is an ordained minister in the A. M. E. church and has many descendants including great-grandchildren living in Indiana, Massachusetts, Texas, and California.[51]

(8) *George Etta Thomas*, born ca. 1853. During the land transactions after her father's death, George Etta Thomas Wade was mentioned initially in 1870. However, by 1880-1885 transactions, she and her husband, Daniel Cole, were residents of Barber County, Kansas.

(9) *Samuel A. Thomas* (1853-1856), died in early childhood.

(10) *Frances L. Thomas* (1857-1858), died in infancy.

(11) *Malinda A. Thomas* (1860), died in early childhood.

Jordon and Candiss Thomas Family

Although no documents exist to confirm the family connection, Jordon and Mathew Thomas were probably brothers: both were born in North Carolina, both were apprenticed in Orange County at nearly the same time, and both remained living in the county throughout their lifetimes.

Around the time his apprenticeship with Lewis Byram expired, Jordon Thomas acquired forty acres of land on February 1, 1836. On January 11, 1838, he married Candiss Roberts, who was the daughter of Elias and Nancy Roberts. Born in Chatham County, North Carolina ca. 1819, Candiss and her parents were free born and never in slavery.[52] She was probably related also to Mary "Polly" Roberts, who married Mathew Thomas.

Jordon purchased a total of 150 acres of land in the Lick Creek Settlement, but ended up holding title to only 70 acres when he died in 1853. He and Candiss had several children: Samira, Nancy, Mary Ellen, Benjamin, Elias W., William A., Helen M., and Jordon T.

After Jordon's death, Mathew Thomas was appointed as guardian of the minor children and handled the disposition of the estate. The seventy-acre farm was sold on February 16, 1854 to Jordon Thomas' father-in-law, Elias Roberts.[53]

Mrs. Candiss Roberts Thomas, widow, and her children were enumerated in the 1860 census for Orange County. She was 43 years old and living in the Lick Creek Settlement with the following children: Nancy, age 21 years; Mary E., 18 years; Benjamin F., 17 years; Elias W., 16 years; William A., 13 years; Helen M., 11 years; Sarah E., 9 years; and Jordan T., 7 years old. On Christmas Day 1860, her daughter, Mary Ellen Thomas, married Hiram Taylor in Orange County.

When the estate of her father, Elias Roberts, was probated in 1867, Candiss Thomas was listed as a resident of Parke County, Indiana. Several years later when her mother's estate in Orange County was divided in 1876, Candiss Thomas was living in Boone County, Indiana.[54]

NOTES

1. Information regarding the names of his parents comes from the marriage application to his second wife in Kent County, Ontario, Canada. Other details from Isaac Scott's certificate of freedom abstracted in Chapter 3.

2. For more information on subject, see John Hope Franklin, *The Free Negro in North Carolina, 1790-1860*, especially Chap. 2 and section on "Miscegenation," 35-39; Marvin L. Michael Kay and Lorin Lee Cary, "A Demographic Analysis of Colonial North Carolina with Special Emphasis upon the Slave and Black Populations" in *Black Americans in North Carolina and the South*, edited by Jeffrey J. Crow and Flora J. Hadley (Chapel Hill: University of North Carolina Press, 1984), 110-117 on the subject of mulattoes; Duane Meyer, *The Highland Scots of North Carolina, 1732-1776* (Chapel Hill: University of North Carolina Press, 1987 printing), 102-130.

3. Marriage Bond for Isaac Scott and Mimy [Jamima] Kelly, Cumberland County, N. C. issued on November 6, 1828, 500 pounds current money signed by Isaac Scott and Abraham Scott. Clerk's Office, Courthouse, Fayetteville.

4. Three different birthdates were found for Alfred Scott. The 1828 date was reported by his father when securing the certificate of freedom in Wake County on February 7, 1835. We chose to use this date, although Alfred provided two additional birthdates, Oct. 5, 1830 and Oct 5, 1832, in his correspondence during later years with the U. S. Bureau of Pension (Civil War).

In the 1830 U. S. Census for North Carolina, Isaac Scott was enumerated in St. Mathews District, Wake Co. He was between ages 24-36 years with 3 persons in household. Carter G. Woodson, *Free Negro Heads of Families in the United States in 1830* (Washington, D. C., The Association for the Study of Negro Life and History, Inc., 1925), 122.

5. Elizabeth Scott's birthdate as recorded on the certificate of freedom appears was "1831." However, she is listed in the 1850 census as the fourth child with her age given as 14 years old. In the "Negro Register" she was registered on August 3, 1854 and reported to be 20 years old. These data confirm that she was born in 1835, before the family set out for Indiana.

6. Martin Scott had a patent deed on 40 acres recorded on August 24, 1835 (Appendix C). Dates of first land purchase in the Lick Creek Settlement by other Scotts were: (1) Alvin Scott, 1841; (2) Calvin Scott, 1838; and (3) Joseph Scott, 1842.

7. 1850 (7th) U. S. Census, South East Twp., Orange Co., Ind., dwelling #194, family #194. Isaac Scott's real estate valued at $500. Early records in Orange County, Indiana identified the tenth child as "Doctor Franklin." However, public records created for him as an adult used the given name of "Franklin" or "Frank." Among the family members and friends in Noblesville, he was called informally, "Doc." His gravestone in Crownland Cemetery, Noblesville, IN reads "Franklin D. Scott" -- and we elected to follow the same practice for all references to him outside of the official documents. Reportedly there was a southern naming practice in the nineteenth century for parents to use "Doctor" as the first name of their seventh living son. According to the legend, the seventh son was suppose to have enhancing powers and medicinal skills -- hence the name-title of "doctor."

8. 1850 U. S. Census data for Orange County, Indiana. A Martin Scott obtained a bond to marry Mary Briesland on January 5, 1804 in Cumberland County, N. C. with Thomas Fox listed as the bondsman and Robinson Mumford, witness (Marriage Records, Courthouse, Fayetteville, N. C.).

9. *Marriage Records*, Book C-3, Orange County, Ind., 401.

10. "Register of Negroes and Mulattoes": Alfred Scott, registration #102, Martha J. Scott, #103 (Chapter 6).

11. Marriage records, Kent County Court House, Chatham, Ontario, Canada. Much of the genealogical data on the Scotts and other families in the Buxton and Chatham communities in Canada was contributed by Arlie C. Robbins, genealogist and writer, North Buxton, during correspondence with Coy D. Robbins from 1984 until her death in 1985.

12. Data in the Canadian Population Censuses for 1861 and 1871 contains many listings of African Canadians who indicated their birthplaces were in Indiana during the antebellum era. Kent County, located across the river from Detroit, Michigan, was reputedly the terminal for the so-called "underground railroad." Fred Landon, "The Negro Migration to Canada After the Passing of the Fugitive Slave Act," *The Journal of Negro History*, V (1920), 22-36; Autobiography, *The Life of Josiah Henson: Formerly A Slave*, (Boston: Arthur D. Phelps, 1849; reprint 1984, Uncle Tom's Cabin Museum, Dresden, Ontario, Canada); Daniel G. Hill, *The Freedom Seekers: Blacks in Early Canada*, Agincourt, Canada: The Book Society, 1981); Arlie C. Robbins, *Legacy to Buxton*, (Chatham: Ideal Printing, 1983); Dorothy Shadd Shreve, *The AfriCanadian Church: A Stabilizer* (Jordan Station, Ontario: Paideia Press, 1983); Gwendolyn and John W. Robinson, *Seek the Truth: A Story of Chatham"s Black Community* (Privately printed, 1989).

13. Census data for Washington County, Indiana and materials found in Alfred's Civil War pension records.

14. Civil War Pension Records for Alfred Scott, National Archives, Washington, D. C. Information about his military and disability histories were taken from his "Declaration for Invalid Army Pension." Marital and family details were provided by the pensioner in correspondence dated Sept. 28, 1897 and Jan. 2, 1915.

15. "Declaration for Widow's Pension" in Alfred Scott Civil War pension records completed by Fannie Scott on February 9, 1920.

16. 1870 U. S. Census, Howard County, Center Township, page 13, Dwelling 99, Family 98, enumerated August 14, 1870. In this listing all the children but William Levi were identified as "white." We assume that the other children of Alfred and Martha J. Scott not included in this listing died in early childhood. We found no evidence that Alfred Scott ever lived in either one of the two African American Settlements in Howard County. Both were located in Erwin Township in the northwest region near the Cass County line.

They were situated in the valley of Little Deer Creek. The "Upper Settlement" or "Rush Settlement" was in the eastern part of the township. An African Methodist Episcopal Church was established here after the Civil War, and the Hardimans was one of its leading families.

The "Lower Settlement" or "Bassett Settlement" was located several miles west. One of its leading citizens, Richard Bassett, settled here in the 1840's, and was a successful farmer and pastor of the Baptist Church which dominated this settlement. Rev. Bassett, a Republican, was elected to the Indiana Legislature in 1892.

Membership in both settlements decreased rapidly toward the end of the 19th century as the residents migrated into the urban communities of Kokomo, Peru and Logansport.

17. 1880 (10th) U. S. Census, Noblesville Twp., Hamilton Co., dwelling #6, family #6: Alfred-Eliza Scott family, James Todd, 11 years old, step-son, and Jemima Scott, 12 years old.

18. Hamilton County Marriage Records, Book C-2, p. 14. Household composition comes from 1900 (12th) U. S. Population Census, Hamilton County, Indiana, Noblesville Township: Dwelling #187, Family #188.

19. Death date comes from records in his pension file. Alfred and two of his wives are buried in the same section in Crownland: Alfred, Sec. 9, lot 4, grave 12; Eliza Todd Scott, Sec 9, lot 4, grave 7: Hannah (Fannie) Scott, Sec. 9. lot 4, grave 13.

20. Alfred Scott, in his letter dated September 22, 1897 to the Bureau of Pensions, Dept. of Interior, Washington, D. C., and responding on the printed form to a query about the names of his living children, wrote, "Yes, three by 1st wife and none by last wife. Names: Levi, Sarah J., Jamima."

21. Obituary, *Noblesville Daily Ledger*, Wednesday, November 1, 1944, 3. Levi's last surviving child and a great-great grandaughter of Isaac and Jamima Scott, Clara Scott Allen, died at Riverview Hospital, Noblesville on July 17, 1989 at the age of 94 years. She was survived by a daughter, Alice Cullins Hampton, and a son, Paul Cullins; three grandchildren; five great-grandchildren; and one great-great grandson.

22. Vital statistics for both Needham and Daniel Scott found in the Hamilton County Marriage and Death Records, and the Crownland Cemetery records in Noblesville.

23. Newspaper article, "Isaac Scott Dead at Age 82," *Noblesville Daily Ledger*, Monday, March 16, 1936, 1.

24. Marital data comes from correspondence found in his Civil War pension records. Additional notes taken from a copy of the obituary read at his funeral (copy in author's collection). His son, Wilbur O. Scott Sr., died on May 12, 1987 in Riverview Hospital, Noblesville. A lifetime Hamilton County resident, Wilbur was 82 years old. Survivors were three sons, Edward A. Scott, Wilbur Scott Jr., and Marvin D. Scott, all of Noblesville; three daughters, Betty Lou Scott and JoAnn Scott Perdue, both of Noblesville and Shirley Scott Thomas of Wright Patterson AFB, Dayton, Ohio; a brother, William E. Scott of Noblesville; 13 grandchildren; and 3 great-grandchildren. His wife, Lorene Tompkins Scott, died in 1971. "Obituary," *Noblesville Daily Ledger*, May 13, 1987.

25. Debra L. Newman, comp., *List of Free Black Heads of Families in the First Census of the United States--1790*, (Washington, D.C., National Archives Record Service, 1973), 26-32.

Paul Heinegg, *Free African Americans of North Carolina* (Saudi Arabia: By the author, c/o ARAMCO Box 7030, Udhailiyah 31311, 1992), 270 reported public records in Northampton County, Virginia dated 20 December 1715 which indicated that Elizabeth Roberts, born perhaps 1690, "a negro" came into court to bind her children, John and William Roberts, to a Thomas Preson.
Other documents summarized by Heinegg show definitely that several free people of color with the Roberts surname owned many acres of land in Virginia and North Carolina before the Revolutionary War.

Joseph Jenkins Roberts was born in 1809, the son of free African Americans living in Norfolk, Va. He grew up in Petersburg, Va., and migrated to Africa when only 20 years old. After conducting a successful merchantile business, Roberts became the first President of Liberia in 1849. Luther P. Jackson, "Free Negroes of Petersburg, Virginia," *Journal of Negro History*, XII (1927), 378.

26. Carter G. Woodson, *Free Negro Heads of Families in the United States in 1830*, 225-6. A David Roberts, a free Black heading a family of six members in Hertford County, North Carolina in 1830, also owned two slaves. Carter G. Woodson, *Free Negro Owners of Slaves in the United States in 1830*, (Washington, D.C., Association for the Study of Negro Life and History, 1924), 25.

27. Genealogical history of these Robertses has been incorporated into the writings about Roberts Settlement in Hamilton County, Indiana (Notes:34).

In Northampton County, N.C., they lived in the vicinity of Rich Square, a town about seven miles southeast of Jackson, the county seat. Quakers were the dominant settlers in the region; Samuel Glenn Baugham, *The Town of Rich Square: A History 1717-1983*, (Jackson, NC: privately printed, 1983). George Moses Horton, originally from Rich Square Township, is beleved to be the first Black professional writer with the publication of his book of poems, *The Hope of Liberty*, in 1827. His last book, *Naked Genius*, (1865) was sponsored by Union soldiers.

The Meherrin Indians were the predominant tribe in Northampton County, and were in the area as early as 1675. The Saponi Indians also lived here. In 1775 colonial records show 28 Indians still in the county. "Many mulattoes in the Winton area of Hereford County and the Woodland area of Northampton are of Meherrin Blood." *Footprints in Northampton: 1741-1776-1976*, (Northampton County Bicentennial Committee, 1976), 6.

Not all Roberts families left North Carolina in the 1830 exodus. Three brothers, sons of Watkins and Maretha Roberts, were outstanding Black citizens in Northampton County in the 1800's. In 1883 Watkins Roberts Jr. became one of the first commissioners of Rich Square when it was incorporated. Exum E. Roberts owned a store in Rich Square and was elected Registrar of Deeds in Northampton County in 1886. Winifred Roberts was appointed the first Black postmaster of Rich Square in 1886. Roberts Street in Rich Square, N.C. is named for these three brothers. *Footprints in Northampton*, pp. 120-121.

28. Carl Glennis Roberts, M.D., "Explanatory Notes" to The Roberts Settlement Core Collection, Indiana State Library, especially section entitled, "Exodus From North Carolina," 2-10.

This collection contains a record from a family bible printed in 1816 and owned by Willis Roberts Sr., who bequeathed it to his son, Elias, who passed it to his son, Rev. Dolphin P. Roberts, who bequeathed it to his daughter, Helen. It contains birth data in North Carolina from the years 1803-1819, and deaths for 1820-1832.

For a summarized history of free people of color in Michigan, including some Roberts, see Roma Jones Stewart, "The Migration of a Free People: Cass County's Black Settlers from North Carolina," *Michigan History*, 71-1 (Jan-Feb 1987), 34-39.

29. Documentation for references in this section will be found in other chapters of this book.

30. National Archives military and pension records for Ishmael Roberts contain no personal data. They confirm that this name appeared on the original Revolutionary War paymaster rolls as a private in Captain Shepards company, 10th North Carolina Regiment from June 3, 1777 to June 1778 (vol. 6, page 8). (Photocopy in author's personal collection). Recent research findings suggest that the "Ishmael Roberts," who fought in the Revolutionary War died in Chatham Co., N. C. and never migrated to Indiana. However, his son, Aaron Roberts, did migrate to Owen County, Indiana where he was enumerated in the 1840 U. S. Census. See Paul Heinegg, *Free African Americans of North Carolina* (1992).

31. Other 1830 families in Vigo County besides those given in the text were: Charles Batty, Isaac Beatty, Dotson Bass, Adam Riley, Merritt Smith, Joseph Artis, Benjamin Bushnell, Price Cozzens, Mark Florence and Andrew Lewis. Names taken from Carter G. Woodson, *Free Negro Heads of Families in 1830*.

32. Genealogical charts and notes in the Carl G. Roberts Collection, Library of Congress.

33. There are several written accounts on the history of the Lost Creek Settlement including: John D. Lyda, "History of Terre Haute, Indiana," *The Indiana Negro History Society Bulletin*, (mimeographed) January, 1944 entire issue; John D. Lyda, *The Negro in the History of Indiana*, (Coatesville, Ind. Hathaway Printery, 1953), pp. 13-31; and Beulah Ross Edwards, "History of Lost Creek Township" in *Our Community Roots*, published privately by the Lost Creek Community Club, 1979.

34. The Robertses in Rush and Hamilton Counties managed to preserve much of their history through the efforts of one of their descendants, Dr. Carl G. Roberts, a Chicago physician. In 1944, he turned over a considerable wealth of family historical documents to the Library of Congress, Washington, D. C. Microfilm copies of the collection are now located under the heading, "Roberts Settlement" in the Manuscript Section, Indiana State Library and in genealogy collections of the Noblesville-Southeastern Public Library.

Included in this collection are genealogical charts covering the known Roberts and their progeny up to the 1940's. As far as we have been able to determine, these charts fail to account for the many Roberts relatives who lived primarily in the Lick Creek (Orange County) and Lost Creek (Vigo County) Settlements.

At least two academic studies based upon this collection exist: Edgar C. Conkling, "Roberts Settlement--A Mixed-Blood Agricultural Community in Indiana" (M.A. diss., University of Chicago, 1957). Stephen Vincent, "The Robertses and Roberts Settlement: Emergence of a Black Rural Community" (B. A. Honors Thesis, History Dept., Indiana University, Bloomington, 1981).

The Indiana Historical Society Library has additional materials in folders under "Beech Settlement of Rush County" and "Roberts Settlement of Hamilton County." Additional collections in Archives Box M-325 listed as "Elijah Roberts Papers 1832-1914" donated in 1979 by Milton Baltimore Jr.

Most recent academic literature is by Stephen A. Vincent, "African-Americans in the Rural Midwest: The Origins and Evolution of Beech and Roberts Settlements, ca., 1760-1900" (Ph. D. diss., Brown University, 1991). Genealogists will find most helpful data in his chapters on "Southern Origins, ca. 1760-1830" and "Migration to the Frontier."

35. Marriage Bond in handscript from Chatham County in the North Carolina State Archives. Solomon Newby and Larkin Nicholson were bonded for the sum of 500 pounds. Witness was Wm. Albright. Dated 25 May 1830.

36. Woodson, *Free Negro Heads of Families in the United States in 1830*, 121.

37. The Newbys were unable to read and write, and varying ages and birthdates were provided in public documents for all family members. Birthdates used by this author are only close approximations. In the 1860 U. S. Census for Orange County, Indiana, Charity Jane is listed as "Clarissa L" but the census, marital, and death records located in Canada clearly indicate that she was named "Charity" rather than "Clarissa."

38. *Deed Book K*, Orange County, Indiana, p. 266-7.

39. *Marriage Records*, Book C-4, Orange County, IN., 247. Nothing further is known about Denison and Emaline Newby White and whether they later migrated to Canada.

40. The sellers were: (1) Jarmon Rickman, Joseph Scott and Jonathan Thompson on September 10, 1862; (2) Harmon Lynch on September 13, 1862; (3) Alvin Scott on September 16, 1862; (4) Solomon Newby on September 17, 1862; and, (5) Isaac Scott on September 29, 1862. Total acreage in the Lick Creek Settlement sold in this one month: 559 acres!

41. In the 1871 Canadian Population Census, Kent County, Raleigh Township, the Newby family was enumerated as follows:
Newby, Soloman, 63 years old, Birthplace: US. Religion: BME.
   " , Margaret, 50 years old, US, BME.
   " , [Charity] Jane, 15 years old, US, BME.
   " , James, 25 years old, US, BME.
   " , Eliza, 18 years old, Can, BME [Believed to be Eliza Jane Rann, who married James Newby in 1873.]

"BME" stands for the British Methodist Episcopal Church, an African Canadian Church which began in the 1820s as a part of the African Methodist Episcopal (A.M.E.) movement in the United States. The Canadian Conference severed ties with the American church in 1856 when the British Methodist Episcopal Church was founded in Chatham, Canada. Some Canadian congregations continued to be affiliated with the A.M.E. Church. See Dorothy S. Shreve, *The AfriCanadian Church*, 78-84.

42. Military and pension records for James Nuby, National Archives, Washington, D. C. These records have much historical significance for the Canadians since the pension correspondence contains several documents written by once prominent leaders in the North

Buxton community. It is believed that James Newby continued to use the "Nuby" spelling of his surname after the Civil War spelling error was made in his military records so that he could avoid any identification difficulties when cashing his monthly U. S. pension checks while living in Canada.

43. 1871 Canadian Population Census, Raleigh Township, Kent County, Ontario. Microfilm records available at Raleigh Township Centennial Museum, North Buxton.

44. Family particulars came from the Newby (Nuby) genealogical charts prepared by Arlie Robbins and on file in the RTC Museum, North Buxton. When attending the North Buxton Annual Homecoming and Labour Day Celebration in 1984, this author talked at length about the Solomon-Margaret Newby family history with their three granddaughters: Muriel G. Newby, Watsonville, California; Geraldine Newby Salters, Allegan, Michigan; and Sulena Newby Motley, Detroit, Michigan.

45. *Deed Record Book 15*, Orange Co., Ind., 471.

46. Marriage license was issued on this date for Mathew Thomas and Polly Roberts, but there was no record of the minister's return.

47. Obituary for William Thomas, who died in 1928, reported that he was seventh of thirteen children, all of whom preceded him in death.

48. William Thomas obituary, *The Paoli News*, June 27, 1928.

49. Marriage records, Orange County, Indiana; land transactions and estate records for her father, Mathew Thomas, 1870-1888. Also, 1880 U. S. Census, Owen County, Washington Township, Town of Spencer (page 17, dwelling 164). Gravestone, Wilson (colored) Cemetery, two miles west of Spencer. John M. Walls (1852-1891), Adaline's first husband, is also buried in this cemetery.

50. Frances V. H. Gilliam, *A Time to Speak: A Brief History of the Afro-Americans of Bloomington, Indiana 1865-1965* (Bloomington, IN., Pinus Strobus Press, 1985), pp. 43-46. Death Records, Monroe County, IN.; Rose Hill Cemetery Records, Blloomington, IN.; death notice of Preston V. Eagleson, in Bloomington *Daily Telephone*, August 11, 1911, p. 1.

51. Ibid., pp. 97-99. Also personal interviews conducted by author with Mrs. Elizabeth Bridgwaters in Bloomington between October, 1991 and February, 1992.

52. Elias Roberts certificate of freedom, Orange County *Deed Record Book D*, 432-433. *Marriage Records*, Orange County, IN., Book C-2, 82.

53. Orange County, Indiana Probate Court transaction on January 17, 1854, Probate Order Book 5 (Feb 1853-Apr 1856), p. 215, p. 226, p. 250. The 70 acres of land were appraised and sold to Elias Roberts for $280 on Feb 21, 1854. Case was closed on May 13, 1854 when the widow, Candiss Thomas, was granted possession of property, p. 304.

54. Land Records for Elias and Nancy Roberts (Appendix C-103). Candiss Roberts Thomas acquired land in the Lick Creek Settlement from her father in 1859 after her husband, Jordon Thomas, died in 1853 (Appendix C-150).

APPENDIX A
NEWSPAPER NOTICE
FROM ORANGE COUNTY

Original newspaper clipping was found among the pages of the <u>Register of Negroes and Mulattoes</u>, for Washington County, Indiana in the historical collections of the Stevens Memorial Museum, Salem, Indiana. It probably came from <u>The American Eagle</u>, a six-column folio newspaper which was Democratic in politics and published irregularly in Paoli by D. O. Comingore between 1848 and 1874. Orange County's <u>Negro Register</u> contained entries dated between June 24, 1853 and June 10, 1861.

TO FREE
NEGROES AND MULATTOES

NOTICE is hereby given, that all free negroes and mulattoes, residing within the bounds of Orange County, who were inhabitants of the State of Indiana prior to the 1st day of November, 1851, and are entitled to reside therein, are required to come forward and have their names registered in the office of the Clerk of the Circuit Court of said county, with as little delay as possible, agreeably to an act passed by the Legislature of the State of Indiana, approved June 11th 1852; the provisions of said act are as follows:

Section 1. Be it enacted by the General Assembly of the State of "Indiana, That it shall not be lawful for any negro or mulatto to come into, settle in, or become an inhabitant of the State.

Sec. 2. The clerk of the several circuit courts in this State shall (give) notice, by publication in the newspaper in their respective counties having the greatest circulation, and if no newspaper be published therein, then by printed hand-bills posted up in three of the most public places in each township of each county, requiring all negroes and mulattoes who were inhabitants of the State prior to the first day of November, A. D. 1851; and entitled to reside therein, to appear before him for registry.

Sec. 3. It shall be the duty of each clerk of the said circuit courts to provide a suitable book, to be called the register of negroes and mulattoes, on which he shall record the name, age, description, place of birth and residence of each and every negro mulatto who may present himself or herself before him for the purpose of being registered, and also, the names of the witnesses by whom the right to such negro or mulatto to reside in the State of Indiana shall have been proven.

Sec. 4. The clerk of the said circuit court, when any negro or mulatto shall come before him for the purpose of being registered, shall have the power to cause to come before him such witnesses as may be necessary to prove the right of inhabitation of such negro or mulatto, by process of subpeona, and shall proceed to hear and determine the right of such negro or mulatto.

Sec. 5. When the right of any such negro or mulatto shall have been proven to the satisfaction of such clerk, he shall register the said negro or mulatto in his register of negroes and mulattoes, and shall also issue to such negro or mulatto a certificate, under the seal of the said court, and attested by such clerk, setting forth the facts contained in the register; which certificate shall be conclusive evidence of the facts therein stated in all prosecution against the employers of negroes and mulattoes, unless it is shown that said employer had notice that the same was obtained by fraud or other undue means, or was not genuine, and the same shall be prima facie evidence only in all other cases, and shall be issued to such negro or mulatto without charge.

Sec. 6. All contracts made with negroes or mulattoes who shall have come into the State of Indiana subsequent to the first day of November, A. D. 1851, are hereby null and void.

Sec. 7. Any person who shall employ a negro or mulatto who shall have come into the State of Indiana subsequent to the thirty-first day of October, in the year one thousand eight hundred and fifty-one, or shall hereafter come into the said State, or who encourage such negro or mulatto to remain in the State shall be fined in any sum not less than ten dollars nor more than five hundred dollars.

Sec. 8. This act shall apply only to contracts made with negroes and mulattoes subsequent to the passage of this act.

Sec. 9. Any negro or mulatto who shall come into or settle in this State contrary to, and in violation of the provisions of the constitution, and of the first section of this act, shall be fined in any sum not less than ten, nor more than five hundred dollars.

April, 25-3t.   A. M. BLACK, Clerk.

APPENDIX B
BLACK POPULATION IN ORANGE
COUNTY, INDIANA
1820-1910

1820 (4th) U. S. Census:

(Name of Head of Household, Sex, Age Range, and Number of Persons in Family)

BROADY, Jonathan, M, 26-44, 10.
BURNETT, Lewis, M, 26-44, 8.
CANON, Judah, M, 26-44, 2.
CONSTANT, Darcus, F, 45+, 2.
CUMMINS, Hazel, F, 14-25, 3.
DUGGED, David, M, 26-44, 4.
GOINGS, Charles, M, 26-44, 8.
GOINGS, Claiborne, M, 45+, 4.
GOINGS, Simeon, M, 45+, 11.
POTRIDGE, Richard, M, 45+, 8.
THOMAS, Bryant, M, 26-44, 4.

Total: 63 (males, 27; females, 36)

1830 (5th) U. S. Census:

(Name of Head of Household, Sex, Age Range, and Number of Persons in Family)

ANDERSON, Jordon, M, 24-36, 7.
ARCHEY, Moses, M, 36-55, 4.
CLARK, Thomas, M, 24-36, 6.
CLEMENS, Francis, M, 36-55, 1.
CLENDENIN, Peter, M, 55-100, 2.
COLLINS, Squash, M, 36-55, 3.
DUGGED, David, M, 36-55, 8.
GOING, Charles, M, 24-36, 9.
GOING, James, M, 55-100, 2.
HUSBAND, Alexander, M, 10-24, 1.
LINDLEY, Peter, M, 24-36, 7.
LOCUST, Moses, M, 36-55, 4.
ORCHARD, Grinage, M, 55-100, 3.
ROBERTS, Benjamin, M, 36-55, 5.
ROBERTS, Elias, M, 36-55, 7.
ROBERTS, Ishmael, M, 36-55, 8.
ROBERTS, Kinchen, M, 55-100, 7.
ROBERTS, Richard, M, 24-36, 4.
SHUMATE, William, M, 36-55, 9.
TRAVAN, Henry, M, 24-36, 6.
WHITE, Solomon, M, 36-55, 9.

Total: 112 (males, 58; females, 54)

1840 (6th) U. S. Census:

(Name of Head of Household, Sex, Age Range, and Number of Persons in Family)

ADAMS, John, M, 24-36, 5.
BOND, Penelope, F, 36-55, 5.
CLARK, Levi, M, 55-100, 5.
CLEMENTS, Francis, M, 55-100, 8.
CHRISTY, Samuel, M, 36-55, 3.
DUGGETT, David, M, 36-55, 11.
JASPER, Alexander, 36-55, 6.
JEFFERS, Birkel, M, 24-36, 5.
LINCH, Harmon, M, 24-36, 5.
LOCUST, Moses, M, 55-100, 5.
REVELS, Willis, M, 24-36, 3.
ROBERTS, Benjamin, M, 55-100, 6.
ROBERTS, Elias, M, 36-55, 8.
ROBERTS, Ishmael, M, 36-55, 5.
ROBERTS, Thomas, M, 24-36, 4.
ROBERTS, Wiley, M, 24-36, 7.
SCOTT, Henry, M, 24-36, 4.
SCOTT, Isaac, M, 36-55, 9.
SCOTT, Martin, M, 55-100, 4.
SMITH, Anderson, M, 24-36, 8.
THOMAS, Mathew, M, 24-36, 4.
TODD, Pierce, M, 24-36, 1.
WASHINGTON, Elias, M, 24-36, 3.

Total: 124 (males, 67; females, 57)

1850 (7th) U. S. Census
(Listing arranged in alphabetical order)

ANTHONY, Dudley (Orleans Twp, Dwelling 92, Family 91): 25 years old. Male. Black. Laborer. Birthplace: Ky. (Listed with Henry Lingle [white] family)

ARCHER, William F. (See Roberts, Nelson family)

BARTON, Washington (Southeast Twp, Dwelling 200, Family 200): 53 years old. Male. Mulatto. Farmer. Bpl: N. C.
    ---, Eunice. 30 years old. Female. Mulatto. Bpl: NC.
    ---, Henton A. 13 years old. Female. Mulatto. Bpl: NC.
    ---, Rebecca. 12 years old. Female. Mulatto. Bpl: NC.
    ---, William. 10 years old. Male. Mulatto. Bpl: NC.
    ---, Mary. 8 years old. Female. Mulatto. Bpl: NC.
    ---, John. 6 years old. Male. Mulatto. Bpl: NC.
    ---, Priscilla. 4 years old. Female. Mulatto. Bpl: NC.
    ---, Rosanah. 1 year old. Female. Mulatto. Bpl: NC.

BOND, Mary (French Lick Twp, Dwelling 987, Family 990): 17 years old. Female. Mulatto. Bpl: IN. (Listed with Elias Lindley [white] family]

BOND, Penelope (North West Twp, Dwelling 1204, Family 1208): 40 years old. Female. Black. Real estate value: $300. Birthplace: NC.
    ---, John M. 19 years old. Male. Black. Farmer. Bpl: NC.
    ---, Mary. 13 years old. Female. Black. Bpl: Ind.
    ---, Monroe. 10 years old. Male. Black. Bpl: Ind.

BURNETT, Aaron (Paoli Twp, Dwelling 692, Family 695): 30 years old. Male. Mulatto. Laborer. Bpl: NC.
    ---, Charlotte. 25 years old. Female. Mulatto. Bpl: VA.

BURNETT, Oliver (Paoli Twp, Dwelling 323, Family 324): 28 years old. Male. Black. Laborer. Bpl: NC. (Listed with Samuel Lindley [white] family)

BURNETT, Thomas (Town of Paoli, Dwelling 758, Family 759): 40 years old. Male. Black. Birthplace: NC.
    ---, Winny. 35 years old. Female. Black. Bpl: Ind.
    ---, Enoch. 14 years old. Male. Black. Bpl: Ind.
    ---, Lewis. 12 years old. Male. Black. Bpl: Ind.
    ---, Mary E. 11 years old. Female. Black. Bpl: Ind.
    ---, Rebecca. 9 years old. Female. Black. Bpl: Ind.
    ---, Archibald. 7 years old. Male. Black. Bpl: Ind.
    ---, William. 5 years old. Male. Black. Bpl: Ind.
    ---, Amos. 3 years old. Male. Black. Bpl: Ind.
    ---, George. 1 year old. Male. Black. Bpl: Ind.

BUTLER, Thomas (Paoli Twp, Dwelling 656, Family 657): 86 years old. Male. Black. Real estate value: $100. Birthplace: MD.
    ROBERTS, Wiley. 45 years old. Male. Mulatto. Bpl: NC.
    ---, Elizabeth J. 17 years old. Female. Mulatto. Bpl: NC.
    ---, Alexander. 15 years old. Male. Mulatto. Bpl: Ind.
    ---, Jonathan P. 10 years old. Male. Mulatto. Bpl: Ind.
    ---, Ellen. 7 years old. Female. Mulatto. Bpl: Ind.
    ---, Bryant. 5 years old. Male. Mulatto. Bpl: Ind.
    ---, Mary C. 3 years old. Female. Mulatto. Bpl: Ind.
    ---, Harriet. 1 year old. Female. Mulatto. Bpl: Ind.

CHANDLER, Samuel (Paoli Twp, Dwelling 588, Family 589): 56 years old. Male. Mulatto. Laborer. Bpl: NC.
    ---, Martha. 46 years old. Female. Mulatto. Bpl. Ind.
    ---, Nancy. 27 years old. Female. Mulatto. Bpl. Ind.
    ---, David. 10 years old. Male. Mulatto. Bpl. Ind.
    ---, Sinah J. 9 years old. Female. Mulatto. Bpl. Ind.
    ---, Martha (Jr). 5 years old. Female. Mulatto. Bpl. Ind.
    ---, Josey A. 3 years old. Female. Mulatto. Bpl. Ind.
    ---, Clorenda. 2 years old. Female. Mulatto. Bpl. Ind.

CHAVIS, Banister (Southeast Twp, Dwelling 201, Family 201): 27 years old. Male. Mulatto. Farmer. Real estate value: $350. Birthplace: NC.
    ---, Sally. 27 years old. Female. Mulatto. Bpl: NC.
    ---, Henry. 7 years old. Male. Mulatto. Bpl: Ind.
    ---, Nancy. 5 years old. Female. Mulatto. Bpl: Ind.
    ---, Rachel. 3 years old. Female. Mulatto. Bpl: Ind.

---, Riley. 1 year old. Male. Mulatto. Bpl: Ind.

EVANS, Susan. 25 years old. Female. Mulatto. Bpl: NC.

CLEMENTS, Francis (Paoli Twp, Dwelling 665, Family 666): 62 years old. Male. Black. Farmer. Bpl: VA.

---, Anna. 50 years old. Female. Black. Bpl: VA.

---, Martha A. 18 years old. Female. Black. Bpl: Ind.

---, Sarah J. 17 years old. Female. Black. Bpl: Ind.

---, William H. 14 years old. Male. Black. Bpl: Ind.

---, Polly A. 12 years old. Female. Black. Bpl: Ind.

---, Mary E. 10 years old. Female. Black. Bpl: Ind.

---, Maria L. 8 years old. Female. Black. Bpl: Ind.

DUGGED, David (Paoli Twp, Dwelling 581, Family 582): 60 years old. Male. Black. Farmer. Birthplace: Md.

---, Savory. 48 years old. Female. Mulatto. Bpl: N.C.

---, Mary E. 17 years old. Female. Mulatto. Bpl: Ind.

---, Charles. 15 years old. Male. Mulatto. Bpl: Ind.

---, William. 13 years old. Male. Mulatto. Bpl: Ind.

---, Samuel. 8 years old. Male. Mulatto. Bpl: Ind.

DUGGED, John R. (Paoli Twp, Dwelling 568, Family 569): 33 years old. Male. Saddler. Real estate value: $50. Birthplace: Ind.

---, Josey A. 23 years old. Female. Mulatto. Bpl: S.C.

---, Argus E. 4 years old. Male. Mulatto. Bpl: Ind.

---, Joanna F. 2 years old. Female. Mulatto. Bpl: Ind.

---, Alonzo E. 1/12 year old. Male. Mulatto. Bpl: Ind.

GILLIAM, Nancy F. 18 years old. Female. Mulatto. Bpl: S.C.

---, Martha E. 12 years old. Female. Mulatto. Bpl: S.C.

GILLIAM, Curtis (French Lick Twp, Dwelling 986, Family 990): 20 years old. Male. Black. Laborer. Bpl: N.C. (Listed with Sarah Henley [white] family)

GUTHRIE, James. (Southeast Twp, Dwelling 236, Family 236): 53 years old. Male. Black. Farmer. Real estate value: $80. Birthplace: N.C.

---, Peggy. 38 years old. Female. Mulatto. Bpl: N.C.

---, Harry. 17 years old. Male. Mulatto. Farmer. Bpl: N.C.

---, Mary. 16 years old. Female. Mulatto. Bpl: N.C.

---, Camelia A. 14 years old. Female. Mulatto. Bpl: N.C.

---, Wesley. 12 years old. Male. Mulatto. Bpl: N.C.

---, John. 10 years old. Male. Mulatto. Bpl: Ind.

---, Thornton E. 8 years old. Male. Mulatto. Bpl: Ind.

---, William. 7 years old. Male. Mulatto. Bpl: Ind.

---, Elbridge. 5 years old. Male. Mulatto. Bpl: Ind.

---, Nancy E. 2 years old. Female. Mulatto. Bpl: Ind.

HAMMONS, Littleton (Paoli Twp, Dwelling 607, Family 608): 22 years old. Male. Mulatto. Laborer. Birthplace: N.C.

---, Mary J. 24 years old. Female. Black. Bpl: Ind.

---, Willis. 1 year old. Male. Mulatto. Bpl: Ind.

HATAWAY, Alfred (French Lick Twp, Dwelling 949, Family 953): 22 years old. Male. Mulatto. Laborer. Bpl: Ind. (Listed with Joel Lindley [white] family)

HATAWAY, John (Paoli Twp, Dwelling 689, Family 690): 28 years old. Male. Mulatto. Laborer. Bpl: Ind. (Listed with Jonathan Lindley [white] family)

HAWKINS, Jeremiah (Town of Paoli, Dwelling 758, Family 759): 60 years old. Male. Black. Farmer. Real estate value: $500. Birthplace: Va.

---, Eunice. 60 years old. Female. Black. Bpl: Va.

CLARK, Lize. 50 years old. Female. Black. Bpl: N.C.

---, Henry. 16 years old. Male. Black. Laborer. Bpl: Ind.

---, Frederick. 14 years old. Male. Black. Bpl: Ind.

---, Armstrong. 6 years old. Male. Black. Bpl: Ind.

HUSBANDS, Alexander (Paoli Twp, Dwelling 659, Family 660): 47 years old. Male. Black. Peddler. Bpl: N.C. (Listed with Edward McVey [white] family)

JOHNSON, Peter (North West Twp, Dwelling 1209, Family 1213): 46 years old. Male. Black. Farmer. Bpl: Va.

---, Melvina. 30 years old. Female. Black. Bpl: N.C.

---, Andrew. 10 years old. Male. Black. Bpl: Ind.

---, Catharine. 8 years old. Female. Black. Bpl: Ind.

---, Sarah E. 6 years old. Female. Black. Bpl: Ind.

---, William H. 4 years old. Male. Black. Bpl: Ind.

---, John H. 2 years old. Male. Black. Bpl: Ind.

LINDLEY, Elias (French Lick Twp, Dwelling 986, Family 990): 26 years old. Male. Black. Laborer. Bpl: Ind. (Listed with Sarah Henley [white] family)

LOCUST, Moses (Stamper Creek Twp, Dwelling 17, Family 17): 67 years old. Male. Black. Farmer. Real estate value: $700. Birthplace: NC.

---, Feraby. 61 years old. Female. Black. Bpl: NC.

---, Stephan A. 26 years old. Male. Black. Farming. Bpl: Ind. [idiotic]

---, Fernotty Ann. 19 years old. Female. Black. Bpl: Ind.

LOCUST, Simon (Stamper Creek Twp, Dwelling 18, Family 18): 24 years old. Male. Black. Farming. Bpl: Ind.

---, Isabella. 27 years old. Female. Mulatto. Bpl: NC.

ROBERTS, Flora Ann. 5 years old. Female. Mulatto. Bpl: NC.

LOCUST, John W. 8/12 year old. Male. Black. Bpl: Ind.

DUNGEON, Joseph J. 19 years old. Male. Mulatto. Farmer. Bpl: NC.

LYNCH, Harmon (Southeast Twp, Dwelling 233, Family 233): 35 years old. Male. Black. Farmer. Real estate value: $200. Birthplace: NC.

---, Martha. 39 years old. Female. Black. Bpl: NC.

---, Millie M. 15 years old. Female. Black. Bpl: NC.

HUSBANDS, Alsa. 24 years old. Female. Black. Bpl: NC.

---, Malora. 21 years old. Female. Black. Bpl: NC.

MEANS, Fanny (Town of Paoli, Dwelling 736, Family 737): 14 years old. Female. Black. Bpl: Ind. (Listed with Patrick Dougherty [white] family)

MEANS, Nancy (Town of Paoli, Dwelling 776, Family 778): 50 years old. Female. Black. Bpl: NC.

---, Maria, 6 years old. Female. Black. Bpl: Ind.

MILLIS, Brazilla (Paoli Twp, Dwelling 321, Family 321): 21 years old. Male. Black. Laborer. Bpl: NC.

NEWBY, Solomon (Southeast Twp, Dwelling 199, Family 199): 49 years old. Male. Black. Real estate value: $200. Birthplace: NC.

---, Margaret. 30 years old. Female. Mulatto. Bpl: NC.

---, Lucinda. 16 years old. Female. Black. Bpl: NC.

---, Emaline. 11 years old. Female. Black. Bpl: NC.

---, James. 7 years old. Male. Black. Bpl: Ind.

---, George C. 3/12 year old. Male. Black. Bpl: Ind.

ROBERTS, Benjamin (Paoli Twp, Dwelling 584, Family 585): 70 years old. Male. Black. Farmer. Real estate value: $200. Birthplace: NC.

---, Sarah. 47 years old. Female. Black. Bpl: NC.

---, Benjamin (Jr.). 13 years old. Male. Black. Bpl: NC.

ROBERTS, Elias (Paoli Twp, Dwelling 579, Family 580): 57 years old. Male. Black. Farmer. Real estate value: $1000. Birthplace: NC.

---, Nancy. 50 years old. Female. Mulatto. Bpl: NC.

---, Lucinda. 25 years old. Female. Mulatto. Bpl: Ind.

---, Zachariah. 17 years old. Male. Mulatto. Bpl: Ind.

---, John. 13 years old. Male. Mulatto. Bpl: Ind.

---, Angeline. 13 years old. Female. Mulatto. Bpl: Ind.

---, Eliza. 3 years old. Female. Mulatto. Bpl: Ind.

ROBERTS, Ettel (Southeast Twp, Dwelling 202, Family 202): 77 years old. Male. Black. Farmer. Bpl: NC.

---, Dicy. 70 years old. Female. Black. Bpl: NC.

---, Amy. 33 years old. Female. Black. Bpl: NC.

---, Sarah A. 4 years old. Female. Mulatto. Bpl: NC.

---, Archie. 2 years old. Male. Mulatto. Bpl: NC.

---, Alice. 8/12 year old. Female. Mulatto. Bpl: Ind.

ROBERTS, James (Southeast Twp, Dwelling 206, Family 206): 22 years old. Male. Black. Farmer. Bpl: NC.

---, Unity. 23 years old. Female. Mulatto. Bpl: NC.

---, Lucretia. 3 years old. Female. Mulatto. Bpl: Ind.

ROBERTS, John (Paoli Twp, Dwelling 596, Family 597): 35 years old. Male. Black. Laborer. Bpl: NC.

---, Nancy. 24 years old. Female. Mulatto. Bpl: NC.

---, Eliza J. 1 year old. Female. Mulatto. Bpl: Ind.

ROBERTS, Nelson (Paoli Twp, Dwelling 609, Family 610): 35 years old. Male. Black. Farmer. Bpl: NC.

---, Alice. 26 years old. Female. Mulatto. Bpl: NC.

---, William. 15 years old. Male. Mulatto. Bpl: NC.

---, Hugh. 2 years old. Male. Mulatto. Bpl: NC.

ARCHER, William F. 34 years old. Male. Black. Bpl: NC.

ROBERTS, William (Southeast Twp, Dwelling 203, Family 203): 27 years old. Male. Black. Farmer. Bpl: NC.
    ---, Sally. 27 years old. Female. Black. Bpl: NC.
    ---, Eliza. 8 years old. Female. Black. Bpl: NC.
    ---, Elias. 5 years old. Male. Black. Bpl: NC.
    ---, Frances. 2 years old. Female. Black. Bpl: NC.
ROBERTS, Zachariah (Southeast Twp, Dwelling 198, Family 198): 49 years old. Male. Black. Farmer. Real estate value: $200. Birthplace. NC.
    ---, Amy. 40 years old. Female. Mulatto. Bpl: NC.
    ---, Zachariah (Jr.). 20 years old. Male. Black. Farmer. Bpl: NC.
    ---, Jane. 17 years old. Female. Black. Bpl: NC.
    ---, Martha. 13 years old. Female. Black. Bpl: NC.
    ---, Gilliam. 11 years old. Female. Black. Bpl: NC.
    ---, Emaline H. 10 years old. Female. Black. Bpl: NC.
    ---, John A. 6 years old. Male. Black. Bpl: NC.
SCOTT, Alfred (Paoli Twp, Dwelling 598, Family 599): 20 years old. Male. Black. Laborer. Bpl: NC. (Listed with Henry Henley [white] family)
SCOTT, Henry (Southeast Twp, Dwelling 196, Family 196): 50 years old. Male. Mulatto. Wagon maker. Real estate value: $100. Birthplace: NC.
    ---, Lucy. 45 years old. Female. Mulatto. Bpl: NC.
    ---, Jane. 19 years old. Female. Mulatto. Bpl: NC.
    ---, Martin. 18 years old. Male. Mulatto. Farmer. Bpl: NC.
SCOTT, Isaac (Southeast Twp, Dwelling 194, Family 194): 48 years old. Male. Black. Farmer. Real estate value: $500. Birthplace: NC.
    ---, Jamima. 42 years old. Female. Mulatto. Bpl: NC.
    ---, Alford M. 20 years old. Male. Mulatto. Farmer. Bpl: NC.
    ---, William T. 18 years old. Male. Mulatto. Farmer. Bpl: NC.
    ---, Joseph K. 16 years old. Male. Mulatto. Farmer. Bpl: NC.
    ---, Elizabeth. 14 years old. Female. Mulatto. Bpl: NC.
    ---, Zachariah S. 13 years old. Male. Mulatto. Bpl: Ind.
    ---, Sanders F. 10 years old. Male. Mulatto. Bpl: Ind.
    ---, Needham L. 8 years old. Male. Mulatto. Bpl: Ind.
    ---, Littlejohn. 6 years old. Male. Mulatto. Bpl: Ind.
    ---, Daniel Q. 4 years old. Male. Mulatto. Bpl: Ind.
    ---, Doctor F. 3 years old. Male. Mulatto. Bpl: Ind.
SCOTT, Joseph (Southeast Twp, Dwelling 237, Family 237): 35 years old. Male. Mulatto. Farmer. Real estate value: $150. Birthplace: NC.
    ---, Fanny. 25 years old. Female. Mulatto. Bpl: NC.
    ---, Nancy. 5 years old. Female. Mulatto. Bpl: Ind.
    ---, Hiram. 3 years old. Male. Mulatto. Bpl: Ind.
    ---, William. 2 years old. Male. Mulatto. Bpl: Ind.
SCOTT, Martin (Southeast Twp, Dwelling 197, Family 197): 63 years old. Male. Mulatto. Farmer. Real estate value: $350. Birthplace: NC.
    ---, Mary. 69 years old. Female. Mulatto. Bpl: NC.
    ---, Alvin. 36 years old. Male. Mulatto. Farmer. Real estate value: $300. Birthplace: Bpl: NC.
    ---, Sarah A. 5 years old. Female. Mulatto. Bpl: Ind.
    ---, Berry. 4 years old. Male. Mulatto. Bpl: Ind.
    ---, Reed. 2 years old. Male. Mulatto. Bpl: Ind.
    WEAVER, Henry. 8 years old. Male. Mulatto. Bpl: Ind.
SMITH, Anderson (Southeast Twp, Dwelling 204, Family 204): 53 years old. Male. Mulatto. Farmer. Real estate value: $400. Birthplace: NC.
    ---, Lymma. 45 years old. Female. Mulatto. Bpl: VA.
    ---, Alford M. 20 years old. Male. Mulatto. Farmer. Bpl: NC.
    ---, Allen H. 28 years old. Male. Mulatto. Bpl: NC.
            [Idiot]
    ---, Nancy A. 17 years old. Female. Mulatto. Bpl: NC.
    ---, Martha J. 15 years old. Female. Mulatto. Bpl: Ind.
    ---, Edward J. 13 years old. Male. Mulatto. Bpl: Ind.
    ---, Lymma (Jr). 11 years old. Female. Mulatto. Bpl: Ind.
    ---, Ileana. 9 years old. Female. Mulatto. Bpl: Ind.

---, Anderson (Jr). 6 years old. Male. Mulatto. Bpl: Ind.

---, Clarinda. 4 years old. Female. Mulatto. Bpl: Ind.

---, Delphina. 2 years old. Female. Mulatto. Bpl: Ind.

SNEAD, Moses (Town of Paoli, Dwelling 344, Family 345): 28 years old. Male. Black. Shoemaker. Bpl: Ky.

    ---, Lucinda. 24 years old. Female. Mulatto. Bpl: VA.

    ISOM, John W. 8 years old. Male. Mulatto. Bpl: Ind.

    SNEAD, George W. 3/12 years old. Male. Mulatto. Bpl: Ind.

    ROBERTS, William B. 18 years old. Male. Mulatto. Shoemaker. Bpl: Ind.

    GILLIAM, John H. 14 years old. Male. Mulatto. Bpl: NC.

    ---, Martha. 12 years old. Female. Mulatto. Bpl: SC.

THOMAS, Jordon F. (Southeast Twp, Dwelling 195, Family 195): 32 years old. Male. Black. Farmer. Real estate value: $100. Birthplace: NC.

    ---, Candy. 31 years old. Female. Mulatto. Bpl: NC.

    ---, Jamima. 11 years old. Female. Mulatto. Bpl: Ind.

    ---, Nancy. 10 years old. Female. Mulatto. Bpl: Ind.

    ---, Mary E. 9 years old. Female. Mulatto. Bpl: Ind.

    ---, Benjamin. 8 years old. Male. Mulatto. Bpl: Ind.

    ---, Elias W. 6 years old. Male. Mulatto. Bpl: Ind.

    ---, William A. 3 years old. Male. Mulatto. Bpl: Ind.

    ---, Helen M. 1 year old. Female. Mulatto. Bpl: Ind.

THOMAS, Matthew (Paoli Twp, Dwelling 580, Family 581): 41 years old. Male. Black. Farmer. Real estate value: $500. Birthplace: NC.

    ---, Mary. 33 years old. Female. Mulatto. Bpl: NC.

    ---, Joseph. 15 years old. Male. Mulatto. Bpl: Ind.

    ---, Mary A. 11 years old. Female. Mulatto. Bpl: Ind.

    ---, Sarah A. 9 years old. Female. Mulatto. Bpl: Ind.

    ---, Jeremiah. 6 years old. Male. Mulatto. Bpl: Ind.

    ---, William. 4 years old. Male. Mulatto. Bpl: Ind.

    ---, John H. 1 year old. Male. Multto. Bpl: Ind.

THOMPSON, John (Southeast Twp, Dwelling 235, Family 235): 50 years old. Male. Black. Farmer. Real estate value: $150. Birthplace: NC.

    ---, Mary. 33 years old. Female. Black. Bpl: NC.

    ---, Elizabeth. 16 years old. Female. Black. Bpl: NC.

    ---, Martha. 15 years old. Female. Black. Bpl: NC.

    ---, Mary (Jr). 13 years old. Female. Black. Bpl: NC.

    ---, Thomas. 10 years old. Male. Black. Bpl: NC.

    ---, Sally. 9 years old. Female. Black. Bpl: NC.

    ---, John (Jr). 7 years old. Male. Black. Bpl: NC.

TODD, Pearson (Orleans Twp, Dwelling 134, Family 134): 40 years old. Male. Black. Farmer. Real estate value: $210. Birthplace: KY.

    ---, Melvina. 30 years old. Female. Black. Bpl: KY.

    ---, Morris B. 9 years old. Male. Black. Bpl: Ind.

    ---, Amanda J. 7 years old. Female. Black. Bpl: Ind.

    ---, William P. Q. 5 years old. Male. Black. Bpl: Ind.

    ---, Hiram H. 2 years old. Male. Black. Bpl: Ind.

    ---, John E. 4/12 year old. Male. Black. Bpl: Ind.

WEAVER, Nancy (Town of Paoli, Dwelling 737, Family 738): 30 years old. Female. Mulatto. Birthplace: NC. (Listed with Benjamin Polson [white] family.

1860 (8th) U. S. Census
(Listing Arranged in Alphabetical Order)

BAXTER, Amos (Paoli Twp. Dwelling 815, Family 815): 49 years old. Male. Mulatto. Farmer. Real Estate: $200. Personal estate: $100. Birthplace: KY.

    ---, Ellen. 35 years old. Female. Mulatto. Bpl: Ind.

    ---, Sabra E. 7 years old. Female. Mulatto. Bpl: Ind.

    ---, Keziah H. 5 years old. Female. Mulatto. Bpl: Ind.

---, William E. 4 years old. Male. Mulatto. Bpl: Ind.

---, Richmond L. 2 years old. Male. Mulatto. Bpl: Ind.

---, Eliza A. 3/12 year old. Female. Mulatto. Bpl: Ind.

BAXTER, Nathaniel (Northwest Twp, Dwelling 1418, Family 1418): 26 years old. Male. Black. Farmer. Personal estate: $325. Birthplace: KY. (Listed with James Fausett [white] family)

BAXTER, Nina (French Lick Twp, Dwelling 1338, Family 1338): 34 years old. Female. Mulatto. Birthplace: KY.

EVANS, Pleasant. 21 years old. Male. Mulatto. Laborer. Bpl: Ind.

---, Samuel. 23 years old. Male. Mulatto. Laborer. Bpl: Ind.

BAXTER, Priscilla (Paoli Twp, Dwelling 935, Family 935): 13 years old. Female. Black. Bpl: Ind. (Listed with Patricia Walden [white] family)

BOND, Osborne (French Lick Twp, Dwelling 1194, Family 1194): 26 years old. Male. Mulatto. Laborer. Personal estate value: $250. Birthplace: SC.

---, Mary. 24 years old. Female. Mulatto. Bpl: NC.

---, Mary (Jr) Female. Mulatto. Bpl: Ind.

---, Lucinda. 4 years old. Female. Mulatto. Bpl: Ind.

---, Margaret J. 2 years old. Female. Mulatto. Bpl: Ind.

BOND, Penelope (Orangeville Twp, Dwelling 1055, Family 1055): 55 years old. Female. Black. Farmer. Real Estate: $600. Personal estate: $150. Birthplace: NC. [Blind]

---, John. 22 years old. Male. Mulatto. Farmer. Bpl: Ind.

---, Mary. 20 years old. Female. Mulatto. Bpl: Ind.

---, Martha. 26 years old. Female. Mulatto. Bpl: Ind.

GUTHRIE, Nancy. 12 years old. Female. Black. Bpl: Ind.

BOWMAN, Henry (Paoli Twp, Dwelling 732, Family 732): 30 years old. Male. Mulatto. Laborer. Bpl: NC.

---, Martha. 25 years old. Female. Mulatto. Servant. Bpl: Unknown.

---, Edgar. 4 years old. Male. Mulatto. Bpl: Ind.

---, Unnamed. 1 year old. Female. Mulatto. Bpl: Ind.

HALLOWELL, Mary. 22 years old. Female. White. Bpl: Ind.

BROWN, Richard M. (Paoli Twp, Dwelling 640, Family 640): 19 years old. Male. Mulatto. Bpl: TN. (Listed with Josiah Trueblood [white] family)

BURNETT, Aaron (Paoli Twp, Dwelling 843, family 843): 44 years old. Male. Mulatto. Farmer. Personal estate: $500. Bpl: Ind.

---, Charlotte. 34 years old. Female. Mulatto. Bpl: VA.

---, Delila. 6 years old. Female. Mulatto. Bpl: Ind.

---, Nancy J. 3 years old. Female. Mulatto. Bpl: Ind.

CONSTANT, Thomas. 70 years old. Male. Mulatto. Farmer. Bpl: NC.

BURNETT, Enoch (French Lick Twp. Dwelling 1334, Family 1334): 27 years old. Male. Mulatto. Bpl: Ind. (Listed with Jesse Osborne [white] family)

BURNETT, Lewis (Paoli Twp, Dwelling 932, Family 932): 22 years old. Male. Mulatto. Farmer. Bpl: Ind.

---, Mary. 20 years old. Female. Mulatto. Bpl: Ind.

---, Rebecca. 20 years old. Female. Mulatto. Bpl: Ind.

---, Archibald. 16 years old. Male. Mulatto. Bpl: Ind.

---, William. 14 years old. Male. Mulatto. Bpl: Ind.

---, Amos. 12 years old. Male. Mulatto. Bpl: Ind.

---, George. 10 years old. Male. Mulatto. Bpl: Ind.

---, Leonard. 8 years old. Male. Mulatto. Bpl: Ind.

---, Edward. 6 years old. Male. Mulatto. Bpl: Ind.

---, Frederick. 4 years old. Male. Mulatto. Bpl: Ind.

---, Jonathan. 2 years old. Male. Mulatto. Bpl: Ind.

---, Charles. 1 year old. Male. Mulatoo. Bpl: Ind.

BURNETT, Oliver (Orangeville Twp, Dwelling 1040, Family 1040): 37 years old. Male. Mulatto. Farmer. Real estate: $480. Personal estate: $290. Bpl: Ind.

---, Jane. 36 years old. Female. Mulatto. Bpl: Va.

---, Mary E. 13 years old. Female. Mulatto. Bpl: Ind.

---, James R. 10 years old. Male. Mulatto. Bpl: Ind.

---, Elwood. 8 years old. Male. Mulatto. Bpl: Ind.

CARLISLE, Jeremiah (North West Twp, Dwelling 1448, Family 1448): 40 years old. Male. Black. Laborer. Personal estate: $100. Birthplace: NC.

---, Elizabeth. 27 years old. Female. Black. Bpl: KY.

---, William. 9 years old. Male. Black. Bpl: Ind.

---, Martha. 6 years old. Female. Black. Bpl: Ind.

---, Edmond. 4 years old. Male. Black. Bpl: Ind.

---, Nathaniel. 2 years old. Male. Black. Bpl: Ind.

CHANDLER, Samuel (Paoli Twp, Dwelling 840, Family 840): 66 years old. Male. Mulatto. Laborer. Bpl: NC.

    ---, Martha. 57 years old. Female. Mulatto. Washerwoman. Bpl: NC.

    ---, Nancy. 37 years old. Female. Mulatto. Washerwoman. Bpl: Ind.

    ---, Martha (Jr). 17 years old. Female. Mulatto. Washerwoman. Bpl: Ind.

    ---, Joycy A. 14 years old. Female. Mulatto. Bpl: Ind.

    ---, Clorinda. 14 years old. Female. Mulatto. Bpl: Ind.

    ---, Mary A. 8 years old. Female. Mulatto. Bpl: Ind.

    ---, Samuel A. 4 years old. Mulatto. Bpl: Ind.

    ---, Mariah M. A. 2/12 year old. Female. Mulatto. Bpl: Ind.

CLARK, Frederick (Paoli Twp, Dwelling 640, Family 640): 24 years old. Male. Mulatto. Bpl: TN. (Listed with Josiah Trueblood [white] family)

CLARK, Henry (Paoli Twp, Dwelling 726, Family 726): 28 years old. Male. Mulatto. Farmer. Bpl: Ind.

    SHIRLEY, John. 10 years old. Male. Black. Bpl: Ind.

    ---, Sarah E. 16 years old. Female. Black. Bpl: Ind.

    CLARK, Mitilda. 24 years old. Female. Mulatto. Bpl: Ind.

    SHIRLEY, William W. 8 years old. Male. White. Bpl: Ind.

    ---, John M. 1 year old. Male. White. Bpl: Ind.

CLEMENTS, Francis (Paoli Twp, Dwelling 809, Family 809): 76 years old. Male. Black. Farmer. Personal estate: $100. Birthplace: VA.

    ---, Nancy J. 40 years old. Female. Black. Bpl: VA.

    ---, Martha A. 24 years old. Female. Black. Bpl: IN.

    ---, Sarah J. 22 years old. Female. Black. Bpl: IN.

    ---, William. 20 years old. Male. Black. Bpl: IN.

    ---, Elizabeth. 18 years old. Female. Black. Bpl: IN.

    ---, Sarah. 70 years old. Female. White. Seamstress. Bpl: Unknown.

CLEMENTS, William (Stamper Creek Twp, Dwelling 47, Family 47): 26 years old. Male. Black. Farm laborer. Personal estate: $40. Bpl: IN. (Listed with Joseph Hall [white] family)

DUGGED, David (Paoli Twp, Dwelling 814, Family 814): 69 years old. Male. Mulatto. Birthplace: NC.

    ---, Sabra. 63 years old. Female. Mulatto. Bpl: NC.

    ---, Charles. 25 years old. Male. Mulatto. Farmer. Bpl: IN.

    ---, Samuel A. 19 years old. Male. Mulatto,. Farmer. Bpl: IN.

    ---, William H. 14 years old. Male. Mulatto. Bpl: IN.

    ---, Thomas. 12 years old. Male. Mulatto. Bpl: IN.

    ---, Sarah A. 10 years old. Female. Mulatto. Bpl: IN.

DUNGEON, William (Paoli Twp, Dwelling 801, Family 801): 21 years old. Male. Black. Bpl: IN. (Listed with William Stout [white] family)

GUTHRIE, John (Paoli Twp, Dwelling 830, Family 830): 55 years old. Male. Black. Farmer. Real estate: $500, Personal estate: $100. Bpl: NC.

    ---, Peggy. 55 years old. Female. Black. Bpl: NC.

    ---, Camelia. 22 years old. Female. Black. Domestic. Bpl: NC.

    ---, Wesley. 21 years old. Male. Black. Laborer. Bpl: IN.

    ---, John. 18 years old. Male. Black. Laborer. Bpl: IN.

    ---, Thornton. 16 years old. Male. Black. Laborer. Bpl: IN.

    ---, Elbridge. 14 years old. Male. Black. Bpl: IN.

    ---, Nancy. 13 years old. Female. Black. Bpl: IN.

    ---, Josephine. 9 years old. Female. Black. Bpl: IN.

GURHRIE, Wesley (Paoli Twp, Dwelling 699, Family 699): 21 years old. Male. Black. Laborer. Bpl: NC. (Listed with J. S. Merritt [white] family)

HAWKINS, Jeremiah (Paoli Twp, Dwelling 724, Family 725): 60 years old. Male. Mulatto. Farmer. Real estate: $200. Personal estate: $300. Bpl: VA.

    CLARK, Lency. 50 years old. Female. Black. Washerwoman. Bpl: NC.

IRVINE, Isaac (Paoli Twp, Dwelling 841, Family 841): 26 years old. Male. Mulatto. Laborer. Bpl: KY.

    BUTLER, Thomas. 26 years old. Male. Black. Farmer. Bpl: IN.

    GUTHRIE, Anzy. 7 years old. Female. Black. Bpl: IN.

LINDLEY, Elias (Orangeville Twp, Dwelling 1090, Family 1090): 38 years old. Male. Mulatto. Farmer. Real estate: $800. Personal estate: $700. Bpl: IN.

    EVANS, Jane. 20 years old. Female. Mulatto. Bpl: Unknown.

---, Mary. 15 years old. Female. Mulatto. Bpl: Unknown.

LINDLEY, Martha E. 4 years old. Female. Mulatto. Bpl: IN.

LOCUST, Moses (Stamper Creek Twp, Dwelling 28, Family 28): 76 years old. Male. Black. Farmer. Real estate: $700. Personal estate: $140. Bpl: NC.

---, Pheribe. 72 years old. Female. Mulatto. Bpl: NC.

---, Phenetta. 30 years old. Female. Black. Bpl: NC.

LOCUST, Simon (Stamper Creek Twp, Dwelling 27, Family 27): 33 years old. Male. Black. Bpl: Ind.

--, Isabella. 34 years old. Female. Mulatto. Bpl: NC.

ROBERTS, Flora A. 13 years old. Female. Mulatto. Bpl: NC.

LOCUST, John W. 10 years old. Male. Black. Bpl: IN.

---, Moses. 7 years old. Male. Black. Bpl: IN.

---, Dillon B. 5 years old. Male. Black. Bpl: IN.

---, Julia E. 4 years old. Female. Black. Bpl: IN.

---, Cassius M. 2/12 year old. Male. Black. Bpl: IN.

LYNCH, Harmon (Southeast Twp, Dwelling 244, Family 244): 51 years old. Male. Black. Farmer. Real estate: $400. Personal estate: $125. Bpl: NC.

---, Martha. 49 years old. Female. Black. Bpl: NC.

---, Milly. 24 years old. Female. Black. Bpl: NC.

---, Mathew E. 9 years old. Male. Black. Bpl: IN.

---, Iolitha J. 4 years old. Female. Black. Bpl: IN.

HAYWOOD, William. 3 years old. Male. Black. Bpl: IN.

LYNCH, Todd. 1 year old. Male. Black. Bpl: IN.

NEWBY, Lucinda (Paoli Twp, Dwelling 950, Family 950): 25 years old. Female. Black. Washerwoman. Bpl: NC. (Listed with Samuel Hobson [white] family)

NEWBY, Solomon (Southeast Twp, Dwelling 227, Family 227): 55 years old. Male. Black. Farmer. Real estate: $300. Personal estate: $200. Bpl: NC.

---, Margaret. 45 years old. Female. Black. Bpl: NC.

---, Lucinda. 29 years old. Female. Black. Bpl: NC.

---, James. 16 years old. Male. Black. Bpl: IN.

---, George C. 10 years old. Male. Black. Bpl: IN.

---, Clarisa L. 4 years old. Female. Black. Bpl: IN.

RICKMAN, James A. (Southeast Twp, Dwelling 240, Family 240): 38 years old. Male. Mulatto. Farmer. Real estate: $400. Personal estate: $200. Bpl: TN.

---, Elizabeth. 25 years old. Female. White. Bpl: NC.

---, Parlee. 16 years old. Female. Mulatto. Bpl: TN.

---, Joseph. 14 years old. Male. Mulatto. Bpl: TN.

---, James A. 5 years old. Male. Mulatto. Bpl: IN.

---, Jemima. 2 years old. Female. Mulatto. Bpl: IN.

ROBERTS, Ann (Stamper Creek Twp, Dwelling 121, Family 121): 32 years old. Female. Black. Washerwoman. Personal estate: $50. Bpl: NC.

---, S. C. 14 years old. Female. Mulatto. Bpl: NC.

---, Archibald. 12 years old. Male. Black. Bpl: IN.

---, Allis. 10 years old. Female. Black. Bpl: IN.

---, James. 8 years old. Male. Black. Bpl: IN.

---, Martha. 6 years old. Female. Black. Bpl: IN.

---, Simpson. 4 years old. Female. Black. Bpl: IN.

---, R. E. 3 years old. Male. Black. Bpl: IN.

---, R. F. 2 years old. Male. Black. Bpl: IN.

---, M. E. 5/12 years old. Female. Mulatto. Bpl: IN.

ROBERTS, Eli (French Lick Twp, Dwelling 1162, Family 1162): 27 years old. Male. Black. Bpl: IN. (Listed with William A. Bowles [white] family)

ROBERTS, Elias (Paoli Twp, Dwelling 811, Family 811): 68 years old. Male. White. Farmer. Real estate: $1600. Personal estate: $400. Bpl: NC.

---, Nancy. 63 years old. Female. White. Bpl: NC.

CHAMBERS, Nancy. 15 years old. Female. Mulatto. Bpl: IN.

ROBERTS, Eliza J. 14 years old. Female. Mulatto. Bpl: IN.

CHAMBERS, Henry. 16 years old. Male. Mulatto. Farmer. Bpl: IN.

ROBERTS, Wiley (Stamper Creek Twp, Dwelling 120, Family 120): 56 years old. Male. Black. Farmer. Personal estate: $250. Bpl: NC.

---, Mary. 47 years old. Female. Black. Bpl: IN.

---, J. P. 20 years old. Male. Black. Bpl: IN.

---, Eleanor. 18 years old. Female. Black. Bpl: IN.

---, E. J. 26 years old. Female. Black. Bpl: IN.

---, Bryant. 15 years old. Male. Black. Bpl: IN.

---, M. C. 14 years old. Female. Black. Bpl: IN.

---, F. W. 7 years old. Male. Black. Bpl: IN.

ROBERTS, Zachariah (Southeast Twp, Dwelling 232, Family 232): 25 years old. Male. Black. Farmer. Real estate: $4000. Personal estate: $1200. Bpl: IN.

---, Katharine. 24 years old. Female. Black. Bpl: VA.

---, Sarah H. 5 years old. Female. Mulatto. Bpl: IN.

---, Angeline D. 3 years old. Female. Mulatto. Bpl: IN.

---, Nancy H. 1 year old. Female. Mulatto. Bpl: IN.

---, Morris W. 5/12 year old. Male. Mulatto. Bpl: IN.

SCOTT, Alvin (Southeast Twp, Dwelling 241, Family 241): 50 years old. Male. Mulatto. Farmer. Real estate: $350. Personal estate: $150. Bpl: NC.

---, Elizabeth. 26 years old. Female. Black. Bpl: NC.

---, Sarah A. 15 years old. Female. Black. Bpl: IN.

---, Berry. 13 years old. Male. Mulatto. Bpl: IN.

---, Reed. 12 years old. Male. Mulatto. Bpl: IN.

---, Rachel. 8 years old. Female. Mulatto. Bpl: IN.

---, Mary. 6 years old. Female. Mulatto. Bpl: IN.

---, Martha. 5 years old. Female. Mulatto. Bpl: IN.

---, Budd. 5 years old. Male. Mulatto. Bpl: IN.

SCOTT, Joseph (Southeast Twp, Dwelling 243, Family 243): 30 years old. Male. Mulatto. Farmer. Real estate: $400. Personal estate: $100. Bpl: NC.

---, Fanny. 30 years old. Female. Mulatto. Bpl: NC.

---, Nancy. 15 years old. Female. Mulatto. Bpl: NC.

---, Hiram. 14 years old. Male. Mulatto. Bpl: IN.

---, William. 12 years old. Male. Mulatto. Bpl: IN.

---, Willis. 9 years old. Male. Mulatto. Bpl: IN.

---, Joseph (Jr). 7 years old. Male. Mulatto. Bpl: IN.

---, Augustus. 6 years old. Male. Mulatto. Bpl: IN.

---, Martha. 3 years old. Female. Mulatto. Bpl: IN.

---, Ephriam. 1 year old. Male. Mulatto. Bpl: IN.

SCOTT, Joseph (Paoli Twp, Dwelling 731, Family 731): 30 years old. Male. Mulatto. Laborer. Bpl: NC. (Listed with James Lindley [white] family)

SCOTT, Mary (Southeast Twp, Dwelling 242, Family 242): 90 years old. Female. Mulatto. Personal estate: $20. Bpl: NC.

SHIRLEY, Lavine (Paoli Twp, Dwelling 722, Family 722): 36 years old. Female. Black. Washerwoman. Personal estate: $200. Bpl: NC.

---, William H. 14 years old. Male. Black. Bpl: IN.

HARDIN, William. 33 years old. Male. Mulaltto. Bpl: TN.

SMITH, David I. (Southeast Twp, Dwelling 213, Family 213): 49 years old. Male. Black. Farmer. Real estate: $200. Personal estate: $300. Bpl: VA.

---, Jane 30 years old. Female. Black. Bpl: IN.

---, Elizabeth. 5 years old. Female. Black. Bpl: IN.

---, William H. 3 years old. Male. Black. Bpl: IN.

---, Mary A. 1 year old. Female. Black. Bpl: IN.

STROTHER, Thomas (Paoli Twp, Dwelling 813, Family 813): ___ years old. Male. Black. Minister, African Methodist [Church]. Farmer. Real Estate: $200 Personal estate: $200. Birthplace: VA.

---, Fanny. 29 years old. Female. Mulatto. Bpl: PA.

TAYLOR, Elizabeth (Orleans Twp, Dwelling 31, Family 31): 40 years old. Female. White. Servant. Bpl: Ohio.

---, Hiram. 23 years old. Male. Mulatto. Laborer. Bpl: KY.

THOMAS, Candess (Southeast Twp, Dwelling 228, Family 228): 43 years old. Female. Black. Birthplace: IN.

---, Nancy. 21 years old. Female. Black. Bpl: IN.

---, Mary E. 18 years old. Female. Black. Bpl: IN.

---, Benj. F. 17 years old. Male. Black. Bpl: IN.

---, Elias W. 16 years old. Male. Black. Bpl: IN.

---, William A. 13 years old. Male. Black. Bpl: IN.

---, Helen M. 11 years old. Female. Black. Bpl: IN.

---, Sarah E. 9 years old. Female. Black. Bpl: IN.

---, Jordan T. 7 years old. Male. Black. Bpl: IN.

THOMAS, Mathew (Paoli Twp, Dwelling 812, Family 812): 52 years old. Male. Black. Farmer. Real estate: $1000. Personal estate: $600. Birthplace: NC.

---, Macy. 15 years old. Male. Mulatto. Farmer. Bpl: IN.

---, Mary A. 22 years old. Female. Mulatto. Bpl: IN.

---, Jeremiah. 15 years old. Male. Mulatto. Bpl: IN.

---, William. 13 years old. Male. Mulatto. Bpl: IN.

---, John H. 11 years old. Male. Mulatto. Bpl: IN.

---, Adaline. 9 years old. Female. Mulatto. Bpl: IN.

---, George A. 7 years old. Male. Mulatto. Bpl: IN.

---, Malinda A. 2/12 year old. Female. Mulatto. Bpl: IN.

THOMPSON, Fanny (North West Twp, Dwelling 1373, Family 1373): Female. White. Personal estate: $150. Birthplace: NC.

---, John. 14 years old. Male. White. Bpl: NC.

---, Betsy. 3 years old. Female. Mulatto. Bpl: NC.

---, Mary. 10 years old. Female. Mulatto. Bpl: NC.

---, Joseph. 7 years old. Male. Mulatto. Bpl: NC.

---, Nancy. 8 years old. Female. Mulatto. Bpl: NC.

---, Susan. 3 years old. Female. Mulatto. Bpl: NC.

THOMPSON, John (Southeast Twp, Dwelling 215, Family 215): 58 years old. Male. Black. Farmer. Real estate: $300, personal estate: $200. Bpl: NC.

---, Priscilla. 60 years old. Female. Black. Bpl: VA.

HART, Mary. 21 years old. Female. Black. Bpl: NC.

---, Francis. 2 years old. Male. Black. Bpl: IN.

THOMPSON, John M. 11 years old. Male. Black. Bpl: NC.

THOMPSON, John M. (II) (Paoli Twp, Dwelling 798, Family 798): 16 years old. Male. Black. Laborer. Bpl: IN. (Listed with David Thompson [white] family)

THOMPSON, Thomas (Southeast Twp, Dwelling 226, Family 226): 29 years old. Male. Black. Farmer. Real estate: $300. Personal estate: $300. Bpl: NC.

---, Sarah. 35 years old. Female. Black. Bpl: NC.

CHAVIS, Henry. 17 years old. Male. Black. Bpl: IN.

---, Rachel. 12 years old. Female. Mulatto. Bpl: IN.

---, Riley. 11 years old. Male. Mulatto. Bpl: IN.

---, Thomas B. 9 years old. Male. Mulatto. Bpl: IN.

---, John. 6 years old. Male. Mulatto. Bpl: IN.

---, Elvina. 5 years old. Female. Mulatto. Bpl: IN.

THOMPSON, Noah. 1 year old. Male. Mulatto. Bpl: IN.

TODD, Pierson (Orleans Twp, Dwelling 32, Family 32): 50 years old. Male. Black. Farmer. Real estate: $300. Personal estate: $200. Birthplace: KY.

---, Malvina. 39 years old. Female. Black. Bpl: KY.

---, Morris B. 20 years old. Male. Black. Bpl: IN.

---, Amanda J. 17 years old. Female. Black. Bpl: IN.

---, William P. 15 years old. Male. Black. Bpl: IN.

---, Hiram H. 11 years old. Male. Black. Bpl: IN.

---, Augustus E. 9 years old. Male. Black. Bpl: IN.

---, Mary A. 3 years old. Female. Black. Bpl: IN.

---, Fanny. 4/12 year old. Female. Black. Bpl: IN.

TURNER, Martha (Greenfield Twp, Dwelling 542, Family 542): 45 years old. Female. Black. Birthplace: VA.

---, Reecy E. 12 years old. Female. Black. Bpl: IN.

---, Mary J. 8 years old. Female. Black. Bpl: IN.

---, Nancy C. 6 years old. Female. Black. Bpl: IN.

(Listed with Rachel McDonald [white] family)

WEAVER, Henry (Paoli Twp, Dwelling 799, Family 799): 21 years old. Male. Mulatto. Laborer. Personal estate: $100. Birthplace: IN. (Listed with Hiram Lindley [white] family)

WEBB, Colatims (Orleans Twp, Dwelling 100, Family 100): 24 years old. Male. Black. Barber. Bpl: IN.

GUTHRIE, Wesley. 18 years old. Male. Black. Laborer. Birthplace: IN.

WOODS, Jefferson (Paoli Twp, Dwelling 963, Family 963): 30 years old. Male. Mulatto. Laborer. Birthplace: IN.

---, Jane. 25 years old. Female. Mulatto. Bpl: IN.
---, William. 5 years old. Male. Mulatto. Bpl: IN.
(Listed with William Clark [white] family)
WRIGHT, Edmond (North East Twp, Dwelling 585, Family 585): 70 years old. Male. Black. Servant. Birthplace: NC. (Listed with William O. Bryant [white] family).

1870 (9th) U. S. Census
(Listing Arranged in Alphabetical Order)

BOND, Monroe (Paoli Twp, Dwelling 102, Family 102): 30 years old. Male. Black. Laborer. Birthplace: IN.
---, Mary A. 31 years old. Female. Black. Bpl: IN.
---, Penelope. 5 years old. Female. Black. Bpl: IN.
---, William. 2 years old. Male. Black. Bpl: IN.
BOWMAN, Henry (Town of Paoli, Dwelling 14, Family 14): 35 years old. Male. Mulatto. Laborer. Birthplace: NC.
---, Martha. 30 years old. Female. Mulatto. Bpl: TN.
---, Edgar. 13 years old. Male. Mulatto. Bpl: IN.
---, Beatrice. 11 years old. Female. Mulatto. Bpl: IN.
---, Oscar. 9 years old. Male. Mulatto. Bpl: IN.
---, Francis. 7 years old. Male. Mulatto. Bpl: IN.
---, Gertrude. 5 years old. Female. Mulatto. Bpl: IN.
---, Mary. 5/12 year old. Female. Mulatto. Bpl: IN.
BURNETT, Aaron (Orleans Twp, Dwelling 129, Family 130): 50 years old. Male. Black. Farm laborer. Personal estate: $600. Bpl: NC.
---, Mary. 48 years old. Female. Black. Bpl: NC.
---, James C. 20 years old. Male. Black. Laborer. Bpl: IN.
---, Caroline. 28 years old. Female. Black. Bpl: IN.
---, Susan. 16 years old. Female. Black. Bpl: IN.
---, Charles. 14 years old. Male. Black. Bpl: IN.
---, Samuel. 12 years old. Male. Black. Bpl: IN.
---, Cora. 8 years old. Female. Black. Bpl: IN.
BURNETT, Archie (Town of Paoli, Dwelling 91, Family 95): 25 years old. Male. Mulatto. Teamster. Personal estate: $100. Bpl: IN.
---, Mary. 19 years old. Female. Mulatto. Bpl: IN.
SWEAT, Nancy. 45 years old. Female. Mulatto. Bpl: IN.
---, Helen. 12 years old. Female. Mulatto. Bpl: IN.
BURNETT, Enoch (Town of Paoli, Dwelling 62, Family 62): 37 years old. Male. Mulatto. Works in mill. Real estate: $300. Personal estate: $100. Birthplace: IN.
---, Parella. 30 years old. Female. Mulatto. Bpl: TN.
---, Hattie. 5 years old. Female. Mulatto. Bpl: IN.
---, Alice. 3 years old. Female. Mulatto. Bpl: IN.
---, Edward. 1/12 year old. Male. Mulatto. Bpl: IN.
BURNETT, George (Orleans Twp, Dwelling 106, Family 106): 20 years old. Male. Mulatto. Laborer. Birthplace: IN.
BURNETT, Lewis (Town of Paoli, Dwelling 70, Family 74): 30 years old. Male. Mulatto. Teamster. Personal estate: $100. Birthplace: IN.
BURNETT, Oliver (Orangeville Twp, Dwelling 24, Family 24): 50 years old. Male. Black. Farmer. Real estate: $1200. Personal estate: $400. Bpl: IN.
---, Jane. 47 years old. Female. Mulatto. Bpl: VA.
---, Mary E. 22 years old. Female. Mulatto. Bpl: IN.
---, James R. 20 years old. Male. Mulatto. Bpl: IN.
---, Elwood. 19 years old. Male. Mulatto. Bpl: IN.
BURNETT, Thomas (Paoli Twp, Dwelling 53, Family 53): 65 years old. Male. Black. Farmer. Real estate: $2000. Personal estate: $700. Birthplace: NC.
---, Muncie Ann. 50 years old. Female. Black. Bpl: IN.
---, Amos. 22 years old. Male. Black. Farmer. Bpl: IN.
---, George. 23 years old. Male. Black. Farmer. Bpl: IN.
---, Leonard. 18 years old. Male. Black. Bpl: IN.
---, Edward. 16 years old. Male. Black. Bpl: IN.
---, Frederick. 14 years old. Male. Black. Bpl: IN.
---, Jonathan. 12 years old. Male. Black. Bpl: IN.

---, Austin. 8 years old. Male. Black. Bpl: IN.

BURNETT, William (Town of Paoli, Dwelling 120, Family 124): 24 years old. Male. Mulatto. Hostler. Personal estate: $100. Birthplace: IN.

CLEMENTS, Frank (Paoli Twp, Dwelling 120, Family 120): 86 years old. Male. Black. Laborer. Birthplace: KY.

    ---, Annie. 60 years old. Female. Black. Bpl: KY.

    ---, Sarah J. 35 years old. Female. Black. Bpl: KY.

    ---, Elizabeth. 28 years old. Female. Black. Bpl: KY.

    ---, Maria. 26 years old. Female. Black. Bpl: KY.

    ---, Homer. 11 years old. Male. Black. Bpl: KY.

    ---, Agnes R. 5 years old. Female. Black. Bpl: KY.

    ---, Charles M. 4 years old. Male. Black. Bpl: KY.

COLE, George (Paoli Twp, Dwelling 192, Family 192): 40 years. Male. Black. Farm laborer. Birthplace: Ky. (Listed with Josiah Trueblood [white] family)

COLLEM, James (Orangeville Twp, Dwelling 71, Family 72): 19 years old. Male. Black. Farm laborer. Personal estate: $100. Birthplace: TN. (Listed with Alfred Brown [white] family)

CONSTINI, Martha (Orangeville Twp, Dwelling 148, Family 150): ___ years old. Female. Black. Keeping house. Birthplace: NC.

    ---, Malinda J. 16 years old. Female. Black. Bpl: IN.

    ---, Marietta. 12 years old. Female. Black. Bpl: IN.

    ---, Frances. 9 years old. Female. Black. Bpl: IN.

    ---, Elizabeth. 6 years old. Female. Black. Bpl: IN.

    ---, Lucinda. 3 years old. Female. Black. Bpl: IN.

    ---, Mary. 1 year old. Female. Black. Bpl: IN.

FOREE, Polly Ann (Jackson Twp, Dwelling 19, Family 19): 6 years old. Female. Black. Domestic labor. Bpl: KY. (Listed with John Roberts [white] family)

HAMMOND, Littleton (Paoli Twp, Dwelling 101, Family 101): 42 years old. Male. Black. Laborer. Personal estate: $150. Birthplace: NC.

    ---, Samira. 32 years old. Female. Black. Bpl: IN.

    ---, Josephine. 11 years old. Female. Black. Bpl: IN.

    ---, Emma. 9 years old. Female. Black. Bpl: IN.

    ---, Nancy. 7 years old. Female. Black. Bpl: IN.

    ---, Henry. 5 years old. Male. Black. Bpl: IN.

    ---, Ettie. 3 years old. Female. Black. Bpl: IN.

    ---, Elijah. 1 year old. Male. Black. Bpl: IN.

HAMMOND, Willis (Paoli Twp, Dwelling 60, Family 60): 21 years old. Male. Black. Farm laborer. Bpl: IN. (Listed with Hiram Lindley [white] family)

IRVIN, Isaac (Stamper Creek Twp, Dwelling 136, Family 135): 40 years old. Male. Mulatto. Farmer. Real estate: $1400. Personal estate: $500. Birthplace: KY.

    ---, Jenetta. 37 years old. Female. Mulatto. Bpl: IN.

    ---, George S. 7 years old. Male. Mulatto. Bpl: IN.

    ---, Albert M. 6 years old. Male. Mulatto. Bpl: IN.

    ---, Allie. 5 years old. Female. Mulatto. Bpl: IN.

    ---, Minnie G. 5 years old. Female. Mulatto. Bpl: IN.

    ---, Carrie L. S. 3 years old. Female. Mulatto. Bpl: IN.

    ---, Arzella W. 2 years old. Female. Mulatto. Bpl: IN.

    ---, William J. 8/12 year old. Male. Mulatto. Bpl: IN.

ISOM, Churchill (Orangeville Twp, Dwelling 25, Family 25): 33 years old. Male. Black. Farmer. Personal estate: $250. Birthplace: IN.

    ---, Lida. 10 years old. Female. Mulatto. Bpl: IN.

    ---, Marion. 8 years old. Male. Mulatto. Bpl: IN.

    ---, James. 6 years old. Male. Mulatto. Bpl: IN.

JEWETT, Peter (French Lick Twp, Dwelling 275, Family 275): 42 years old. Male. Mulatto. Hotel cook. Bpl: MD.

    FINLEY, Preston. 46 years old. Male. Mulatto. Hotel Cook. Bpl: KY.

    ---, Clara. 25 years old. Female. Mulatto. Hotel Cook. Bpl: IN.

    ---, Dilly. 12 years old. Female. Mulatto. Hotel laborer. Bpl: IN.

    ---, Alexander. 21 years old. Male. Mulaltto. Hotel laborer. Bpl: IN.

    DAVIS, Jerry. 36 years old. Male. Mulatto. Hotel laborer. Bpl: KY.

    DYOL, Lizzie. 43 years old. Female. Mulatto. Hotel laborer. Bpl: AL.

    ---, Edward. 9 years old. Male. Mulatto. Bpl: KY.

        (Listed with Ephriam Tucker, Hotel Keeper [white])

LEWIS, Alexander (Town of Paoli, Dwelling 111, Family 114): 43 years old. Male. Mulatto. Laborer. Bpl: VA.
   ---, Nancy J. 27 years old. Female. Mulatto. Bpl: KY.
   ---, Mary. 10 years old. Female. Mulatto. Bpl: KY.
   ---, Charles. 8 years old. Male. Mulatto. Bpl: KY.
LOCUST, Simon (Stamper Creek Twp, Dwelling 36, Family 35): 44 years old. Male. Mulatto. Farmer. Real estate: $1900.
   Personal estate: $600. Bpl: IN.
   ---, Isabella. 45 years old. Female. Mulatto. Bpl: IN.
   ---, William F. 20 years old. Male. Mulatto. Farm laborer. Bpl: IN.
   ---, Moses. 17 years old. Male. Mulatto. Farm laborer. Bpl: IN.
   ---, Dillon. 15 years old. Male. Mulatto. Farm laborer. Bpl: IN.
   ---, Cassius. 8 years old. Male. Mulatto. Farm laborer. pl: IN.
   ---, Julia. 8 years old. Female. Mulatto. Bpl: IN.
   ---, Robert. 6 years old. Male. Mulatto. Bpl: IN.
PARKER, Sarah (Town of Paoli, Dwelling 67, Family 70): 40 years old. Female. Black. Domestic. Bpl: KY. (Listed with Joseph Cox
   [white] family)
REED, John (Orleans Twp, Dwelling 128, Family 129): 30 years old. Male. Black. Laborer. Personal estate: $100. Birthplace: KY.
   ---, Mary. 28 years old. Female. Black. Bpl: KY.
   ---, James. 1 year old. Male. Black. Bpl: IN.
ROBERTS, Eli (Paoli Twp, Dwelling 103, Family 103): 38 years old. Male. Black. Farmer. Real estate: $500. Birthplace: IN.
   ---, Amanda A. 8 years old. Female. Black. Bpl: IN.
   ---, Charles H. 7 years old. Male. Black. Bpl: IN.
   ---, Nancy. 70 years old. Female. Black. Real estate: $600. Personal estate: $500. Birthplace: NC.
ROBERTS, James (Paoli Twp, Dwelling 111, Family 111): ___ years old. Male. Black. Laborer. Birthplace. IN.
ROBERTS, Nancy (Paoli Twp, Dwelling 238, Family 239): 70 years old. Female. Black. Real estate: $1000. Personal estate: $300.
   Birthplace: NC.
   ---, Eliza J. 22 years old. Female. Mulatto. Bpl: IN.
   ---, Frances. 8 years old. Female. Mulatto. Bpl: IN.
   ---, Charles. 6 years old. Male. Mulatto. Bpl: IN.
   ROBBINS, Eli. 37 years old. Male. Mulatto. Teamster. Bpl: IN.
THOMAS, Mathew (Paoli Twp, Dwelling 119, Family 119): 58 years old. Male. Black. Farmer. Real estate $1500. Personal estate:
   $600. Birthplace: KY.
   ---, Adaline. 18 years old. Female. Black. Bpl: IN.
   ---, George Esther. 16 years old. Female. Black. Bpl: IN.
THOMPSON, Elizabeth (Northwest Twp, Dwelling 25, Family 25): 36 years old. Female. Black. Keeping house. Personal estate: $100.
   Birthplace: NC.
   ---, Joseph. 17 years old. Male. Black. Laborer. Bpl: NC.
   ---, Emaline. 10 years old. Female. Black. Bpl: IN.
   ---, Sarah M. 5 years old. Female. Black. Bpl: IN,
THOMPSON, Thomas (Southeast Twp, Dwelling 262, Family 262): 36 years old. Male. Black. Farmer. Real estate: $1000. Personal
   estate: $375. Bpl: NC.
   ---, Sarah. 40 years old. Female. Black. Bpl: NC.
   ---, John. 16 years old. Male. Black. Bpl: IN.
   ---, Nathaniel. 11 years old. Male. Black. Bpl: IN.
   ---, Thomas. 8 years old. Male. Black. Bpl: IN.
   ---, Clary. 7 years old. Female. Black. Bpl: IN.
   ---, Elvina. 13 years old. Female. Black. Bpl: IN.
   ---, Mary. 5 years old. Female. Black. Bpl: IN.
TODD, Green (Orleans Twp, Dwelling 127, Family 129): 22 years old. Male. Black. Laborer. Personal estate: $100. Birthplace: IN.
   ---, Belle. 20 years old. Female. Black. Bpl: IN.
   CARPENTER, Frank. 21 years old. Male. Black. Barber. Personal estate: $100. Birthplace: IN.
WALLS, John E.(Town of Paoli, Dwelling 12, Family 12): 37 years old. Male. Black. Barber. Personal estate: $100. Birthplace: PA.
WILSON, John (Town of Paoli, Dwelling 109, Family 112): 28 years old. Male. Mulatto. Laborer. Real estate: $150. Personal estate:
   $150. Bpl: IN.
   ---, Rebecca. 29 years old. Female. Mulatto. Bpl: IN.
   ---, Mary E. 3 years old. Female. Mulatto. Bpl: IN.
   ---, Alice. 1 year old. Female. Mulatto. Bpl: IN.
   ---, Emma. 3/12 year old. Female. Mulatto. Bpl: IN.

1880 (10th) U. S. Census

Stampers Creek Township

LOCUS, William B. (Dwelling 4, Family 4): Mulatto. Male. 26 years old. Farmer. Birthplace: IN. Father's Bpl: IN. Mother's Bpl: NC.

    ---, Mary F. Mulatto. Female. 23 years old. Wife. Keeping house. Birthplace: IL. Father's Bpl: ---. Mother's Bpl: ---.

    ---, William B. [Jr.] Mulatto. Male. 1 year old. Birthplace: IN. Father's Bpl: IN. Mother's Bpl: IL.

    RUSSEY(?), Mary J. Mulatto. Female. 2 years old. Single. Birthplace: IN. Father's Bpl: IN. Mother's Bpl: IL.

LOCUS, Simon. (Dwelling 5, Family 5): Black. Male. 56 years old. Married. Farmer. Birthplace: IN. Father's Bpl: NC. Mother's Bpl: NC.

    ---, Isabel. Mulatto. Female. 58 years old. Wife. Married. Keeping house. Birthplace: NC. Father's Bpl: NC. Mother's Bpl: NC.

    ---, Cashus M. Black. Male. 20 years old. Son. Single. Assist in farm. Birthplace: IN. Father's Bpl: IN. Mother's Bpl: NC.

    ---, Robert B. Mulatto. Male. 18 years old. Son. Assist in farm. Birthplace: IN. Father's Bpl: IN. Mother's Bpl: IN.

    ROBERTS, John. Black. Male. 10 years old. Servant. Single. Assist in farm. Birthplace: IN. Father's Bpl: IN. Mother's Bpl: NC.

MAYS, William. (Dwelling 6; Family 6): Black. Male. 46 years old. Farmer. Married. Birthplace: KY. Father's Bpl: KY. Mother's Bpl: KY.

    ---, Jane(?). Black. Female. 30 years old. Wife. Keeping house. Married. Birthplace: KY. Father's Bpl: KY. Mother's Bpl: KY.

    ---, Maggie. Black. Female. 3 years old. Daughter. Birthplace: IN. Father's Bpl: KY. Mother's Bpl: KY.

    ---, William. Mulatto. Male. 1 year old. Son. Birthplace: IN. Father's Bpl: KY. Mother's Bpl: KY.

O'BANNON, Joseph. (Dwelling 7; Family 7): Black. Male. 23 years old. Married. Laborer. Birthplace: KY. Father's Bpl: KY. Mother's Bpl: KY.

    ---, Josie. Mulatto. Female. 20 years old. Wife. Married. Keeping house. Birthplace: KY. Father's Bpl: KY. Mother's Bpl: KY.

    ---, Palina. Black. Female. 18 years old. Sister. Single. Assist in keep house. Birthplace: KY. Father's Bpl: KY. Mother's Bpl: KY.

    ---, William T. Black. Male. 8/12 years old. Dec. Son. Birthplace: IN. Father's Bpl: KY. Mother's Bpl: KY.

    STOVEALL, Lucinda. Black. Female. 50 years old. Mo-in-law. Widow. Assist in home. Birthplace: KY. Father's Bpl: KY. Mother's Bpl: KY.

    DUPROPHET, Gino. Black. Male. 75 years old. Laborer. Birthplace: KY. Father's Bpl: KY. Mother's Bpl: KY.

    ---, Phebe. Black. Female. 16 years old. Servant. Birthplace: KY. Father's Bpl: KY. Mother's Bpl: KY.

    COX, Andrew. Black. Male. 36 years old. Servant. Single. Birthplace: IN. Father's Bpl: VA. Mother's Bpl: VA.

McCLENDON, Lewis. (Dwelling 2; Family 2): Mulatto. Male. 63 years old. Married. Farmer. Birthplace: MD. Father's Bpl: VA. Mother's Bpl: VA.

    ---, Levie A. Mulatto. Female. 33 years old. Wife. Keeping house. Birthplace: KY. Father's Bpl: KY. Mother's Bpl: KY.

    ---, Samuel. Mulatto. Black. 17 years old. Son. Assist in Farm. Single. Birthplace: IN. Father's Bpl: MD. Mother's Bpl: KY.

    , Mark. Mulatto. Male. 10 years old. Single. Assists in farm. Birthplace: IN. Father's Bpl: MD. Mother's Bpl: KY.

    ---, Katie. Mulatto. Female. 8 years old. Single. Birthplace: IN. Father's Bpl: MD. Mother's Bpl: KY.

    ---, Andrew. Mulatto. Male. 5 years old. Son. Single. Birthplace: IN. Father's Bipl: MD. Mother's Bpl: KY.

    ---, Abie. Mulatto. Female. 4 years old. Daughter. Single. Birthplace: IN. Father's Bpl: MD. Mother's Bpl: KY.

    ---, Morton. Mulatto. Male. 3 years old. Son. Single. Birthplace: IN. Father's Bpl: MD. Mother's Bpl: KY.

    ---, Robert L. Mulatto. Male. 1 year old. Son. Single. Birthplace: IN. Father's Bpl: MD. Mother's Bpl: KY.

South East Township

THOMPSON, Thomas. (Dwelling 11; Family 11): Black. Male. 42 years old. Married. Farmer. Birthplace: NC. Father's Bpl: NC. Mother's Bpl: NC.

    ---, Sarah. Black. Female. 49 years old. Wife. Married. Housekeeper. Birthplace: NC. Father's Bpl: NC. Mother's Bpl: NC.

    ---, Clara. Black. Female. 16 years old. Daughter. Single. Assist H. Keeper. Consumption. Birthplace: IN. Father's Bpl: NC. Mother's Bpl: NC.

    ---, Mary. Black. Female. 14 years old. Daughter. Single. Assist H. Keeper. Birthplace: IN. Father's Bpl: NC. Mother's

Bpl: NC.

CHAVIS, Robert. Black. Male. 14 years old. Single. Farm hand. Birthplace: IN. Father's Bpl: NC. Mother's Bpl: NC.

French Lick Township

POLK, Abbie (Dwelling 187; Family 187): Black. Female. 45 years old. Cook. Widow. Birthplace: KY. Father's Bpl: KY. Mother's Bpl: KY. (Listed with John A. Lane, white, Proprietor West Baden Springs).

North West Township

NOTT, Robert B. (Dwelling 150, Family 150): White. Married. Laborer. Birthplace: IN. Father's Bpl: NC. Mother's Bpl: NC.
   ---, Emily J. Mulatto. Female. 20 years old. Wife. Keeping house. Married. Birthplace: IN. Father's Bpl: NC. Mother's Bpl: NC.
   ---, Joseph M. Mulatto. Male. 3 years old. Son. Single. Birthplace: IN. Father's Bpl: IN. Mother's Bpl: IN.
   THOMPSON, Elizabeth. Mulatto. Female. 46 years old. Mo-in-law. Single. Keeping house. Birthplace: NC. Father's Bpl: NC. Mother's Bpl: NC.
   ---, Sarah M. Mulatto. Female. 15 years old. Sis-in-law. Helping at home. Birthplace: IN. Father's Bpl: IN. Mother's Bpl: NC.
MOFFITT, Samuel J. White. Male. 39 years old. Married. Works on farm. Birthplace: IN. Father's Bpl: KY. Mother's Bpl: TN.
   ---, Mary F. Mulatto. Female. 31 years old. Wife. Married. Keeping house. Birthplace: NC. Father's Bpl: NC. Mother's Bpl: NC.
   ---, Thomas A. Mulatto. Male. 11 years old. Son. Single. Birthplace: IN. Father's Bpl: IN. Mother's Bpl: IN.
   ---, Susan. Mulatto. Female. 9 years old. Daughter. Single. Birthplace: IN. Father's Bpl: IN. Mother's Bpl: NC.
   ---, Joseph F. Mulatto. Male. 8 years old. Son. Single. Birthplace: IN. Father's Bpl: IN. Mother's Bpl: NC.
   ---, Oscar C. Mulatto. Male. 6 years old. Son. Single. Birthplace: IN. Father's Bpl: IN. Mother's Bpl: NC.
   ---, Elizabeth A. Mulatto. Female. 4 years old. Daughter. Single. Birthplace: IN. Father's Bpl: IN. Father's Bpl: IN. Mother's Bpl: NC.
   ---, Sarah J. Mulatto. Female. 3 years old. Daughter. Single. Birthplace: IN. Father's Bpl: IN. Mother's Bpl: NC.
THOMPSON, Joseph (Dwelling 169, Family 170): Mulatto. Male. 27 years old. Married. Laborer. Birthplace: NC. Father's Bpl: NC. Mother's Bpl: NC.
   ---, Mary. White. Female. 25 years old. Wife. Married. Keeping house. Birthplace: IN. Father's Bpl: NC. Mother's Bpl: NC.
   ---, Emily J. Mulatto. Female. 1 year old. Single. Birthplace: IN. Father's Bpl: NC. Mother's Bpl: IN.
   ---, William A. Mulatto. Male. 8/12 year old (Oct.). Son. Single. Birthplace: IN. Father's Bpl: NC. Mother's Bpl: IN.
   MACINEY, Rachel T. White. Female. 13 years old. Niece. Single. Helping at home. Birthplace: IN. Father's Bpl: NC. Mother's Bpl: NC.

Orangeville Township

BURNETT, Elwood. (Dwelling 130, Family 130): Black. Male. 26 years old. Boarding. Single. Woodchopper. Birthplace: IN. Father's Bpl: NC. Mother's Bpl: VA. (with John L. Collins, white family)
TODD, William. (Dwelling 130, Family 130): Black. Male. 27 years old. Boarding. Single. Teamster. Birthplace: IN. Father's Bpl: ---. Mother's Bpl: ---. (with John L. Collins, white family)
BURNETT, Mary E. (Dwelling 132, Family 132): Mulatto. Female. 33 years old. Head. Single. Keeping house. Birthplace: IN. Father's Bpl: NC. Mother's Bpl: VA.
BURNETT, Riley J. Black. Male. 35 years old. Head. Married. Farmer. Birthplace: IN. Father's Bpl: NC. Mother's Bpl: VA.
   ---, Malinda J. Black. Female. 25 years old. Wife. Married. Keeping house. Birthplace: IN. Father's Bpl: IN. Mother's Bpl: IN.
   ---, Milton A. Black. Male. 7 years old. Son. Single. Birthplace: IN. Father's Bpl: IN. Mother's Bpl: IN.
   ---, Eli A. Black. Male. 6 years old. Son. Single. Birthplace: IN. Father's Bpl: IN. Mother's Bpl: IN.

Orleans Town - Orleans Township

TODD, Melvina (Dwelling 44, Family 53): Mulatto. Female. 53 years old. Widow. Keeping house. Birthplace: IN. Father's Bpl: KY. Mother's Bpl: KY.
   ---, Willis G. Mulatto. Male. 26 years old. Son. Single. Laborer. Birthplace: IN. Father's Bpl: KY. Mother's Bpl: IN.
   ---, Harris F. C. Mulatto. Male. 18 years old. Son. Single. Laborer. Birthplace: IN. Father's Bpl: KY. Mother's Bpl: IN.
   ---, George W. Mulatto. Male. 15 years old. Son. Single. Laborer. Birthplace: IN. Father's Bpl: KY. Mother's Bpl: IN.
   ---, Bell. Mulatto. Female. 25 years old. Dau-in-law. Birthplace: IN. Father's Bpl: IN. Mother's Bpl: IN.

---, Augustus. Mulatto. Male. 4/12 [Jan.] years old. Grdson. Birthplace: IN. Father's Bpl: IN. Mother's Bpl: IN.
BURNETT, Aaron. Mulatto. Male. 64 years old. Married. Farmer. Birthplace: IN. Father's Bpl: NC. Mother's Bpl: NC.
   ---, Charity. Mulatto. Female. 53 years old. Wife. Keeping house. Birthplace: VA. Father's Bpl: VA. Mother's Bpl: VA.
   ---, Jane. Mulatto. Female. 23 years old. Daughter. Single. Birthplace: IN. Father's Bpl: IN. Mother's Bpl: VA.
   ---, Amanda. Mulatto. Female. 13 years old. Daughter. Single. Birthplace: IN. Father's Bpl: IN. Mother's Bpl: VA.
   ---, James L. Mulatto. Male. 8 years old. Son. Single. Birthplace: IN. Father's Bpl: IN. Mother's Bpl: VA.
   HARRIS, George W. Mulatto. Male. 13 years old. Servant. Laborer. Birthplace: IN. Father's Bpl: KY. Mother's Bpl: IN.

Paoli Township

CHANDLER, William (Dwelling 15, Family 16): Black. Male. 44 years old. Married. Laborer. Birthplace: IN. Father's Bpl: NC. Mother's Bpl: IN.
   ---, Mary. Black. Female. 41 years old. Married. Keeping house. Birthplace: IN. Father's Bpl: KY. Mother's Bpl: IN.
   ---, Sarah. Black. Female. 11 years old. Single. At home. Attend sch. Birthplace: IN. Father's Bpl: IN. Mother's Bpl: IN.
   ---, Thomas. Black. Female. 8 years old. Single. Birthplace: IN. Father's Bpl: IN. Mother's Bpl: IN.
   ---, John. Black. Male. 5 years old. Single. Birthplace: IN. Father's Bpl: IN. Mother's Bpl: IN.
   ---, Nellie. Black. Female. 3 years old. Single. Birthplace: IN. Father's Bpl: IN. Mother's Bpl: IN.
BURNETT, Lewis (Dwelling 69, Family 70): Black. Male. 44 years old. Employee. Single. Farm laborer. Birthplace: IN. Father's Bpl: KY. Mother's Bpl: IN. (with Thomas Farlow, white, family)
BURNETT, William. (Dwelling 69, Family 71): Black. Male. 34 years old. Married. Farmer. Birthplace: IN. Father's Bpl: KY. Mother's Bpl: IN.
   ---, Amanda. Black. Female. 21 years old. Wife. Married. Keeping house. Birthplace: IN. Father's Bpl: KY. Mother's Bpl: KY.
   ---, Alonzo Black. Male. 2 years old. Son. Birthplace: IN. Father's Bpl: IN. Mother's Bpl: IN.
BURNETT, Thomas. (Dwelling 70, Family 72): Black. Male. 76 years old. Married. Farmer. Birthplace: KY. Father's Bpl: KY. Mother's Bpl: KY.
   ---, Winnie A. Black. Female. 68 years old. Wife. Keeping house. Birthplace: IN. Father's Bpl: MD. Mother's Bpl: MD.
   ---, Jonathan L. Black. Male. 23 years old. Son. Single. Farm Laborer. Birthplace: IN. Father's Bpl: KY. Mother's Bpl: IN.
   ---, Austin O. Black. Male. -- years old. Son. Single. Farm Laborer. Birthplace: IN. Father's Bpl: KY. Mother's Bpl: IN.
   ---, Frederick. Black. Male. 14 years old. Son. Single. Farm Laborer. Birthplace: IN. Father's Bpl: KY. Mother's Bpl: IN.
BOND, Mary H. (Dwelling 178, Family 185): Black. Female. 40 years old. Married. Keeping house. Birthplace: IN. Father's Bpl: IN. Mother's Bpl: IN.
   ---, Penelope. Black. Female. 15 years old. Daughter. Single. Birthplace: IN. Father's Bpl: IN. Mother's Bpl: IN.
   ---, William. Black. Male. 12 years old. Son. Single. IN. Father's Bpl: IN. Mother's Bpl: IN.
   ---, Austin. Black. Male. 10 years old. Son. Single. Birthplace: IN. Father's Bpl: IN. Mother's Bpl: IN.
   ---, Annie. Black. Female. 7 years old. Daughter. Birthplace: IN. Father's Bpl: IN. Mother's Bpl: IN.
   ---, Alonzo. Black. Male. 5 years old. Son. Birthplace: IN. Father's Bpl: IN. Mother's Bpl: IN.
   THOMAS, William. Black. Male. 33 years old. Brother. Single. Farmer. Birthplace: IN. Father's Bpl: IN. Mother's Bpl: IN.
WEATHERS, Theo(?). (Dwelling 179, Family 186): Black. Male. 23 years old. Employee. Single. Farm Laborer. Birthplace: IN. Father's Bpl: IN. Mother's Bpl: IN. (Listed w/Thomas Lindley, white family).
CLEMENTS, Annis. (Dwelling 241, Family 249): Black. Female. 100 years old. Widow. Keeping house. Birthplace: VA. Father's Bpl: VA. Mother's Bpl: VA.
   ---, Marta. Black. Female. 42 years old. Daughter. Keeping house. Single. Birthplace: IN. Father's Bpl: VA. Mother's Bpl: VA.
   ---, Sarah J. Black. Female. 42 years old. Daughter. Single. At home. Birthplace: IN. Father's Bpl: VA. Mother's Bpl: VA.
   ---, Maria. Black. Female. 40 years old. Daughter. Single. At home. Birthplace: IN. Father's Bpl: VA. Mother's Bpl: VA.
   ---, Homer. Black. Male. 22 years old. Gr-son. Farm Laborer. Birthplace: IN. Father's Bpl: IN. Mother's Bpl: IN.
   ---, Frances. Black. Female. 18 years old. Gr-Dau. Single. At home. Birthplace: IN. Father's Bpl: IN. Mother's Bpl: IN.
   ---, Milton. Black. Male. 14 years old. Gr-son. Single. Birthplace: IN. Father's Bpl: IN. Mother's Bpl: IN.
DUPROPHET, Daniel (Dwelling 252, Family 260): Black. Male. 65 years old. Domestic Laborer. Birthplace: KY. Father's Bpl: KY. Mother's Bpl: KY. (with Eli Lindley, white family)
BOWMAN, Henry (Dwelling 282, Family 290): Black. Male. 46 years old. Married. Teamster. Birthplace: NC. Father's Bpl: NC.

Mother's Bpl: NC.

---, Martha. Black. Female. 40 years old. Wife. Keeping house. Birthplace: TN. Father's Bpl: TN. Mother's Bpl: TN.

---, Oscar. Black. Male. 17 years old. Son. Single. Teamster. Birthplace: IN. Father's Bpl: NC. Mother's Bpl: TN.

---, Frank. Black. Male. 13 years old. Son. Single. Birthplace: IN. Father's Bpl: NC. Mother's Bpl: TN.

---, Gertrude. Black. Female. 11 years old. Daughter. Single. Birthplace: IN. Father's Bpl: NC. Mother's Bpl: TN.

---, Elina. Black. Female. 9 years old. Daughter. Single. Birthplace: IN. Father's pl: NC. Mother's Bpl: TN.

---, Ardie. Black. Female. 7 years old. Daughter. Single. Birthplace: IN. Father's Bpl: NC. Mother's Bpl: TN.

---, Susie. Black. Female. 5 years old. Daughter. Single. Birthplace: IN. Father's Bpl: NC. Mother's Bpl: TN.

BURNETT, Enoch (Dwelling 344, Family 354): Black. Male. 45 years old. Married. Engineer in mill. Birthplace: IN. Father's Bpl: NC. Mother's Bpl: IN.

---, Parlee. Black. Female. 36 years old. Wife. Keeping house. Birthplace: IN. Father's Bpl: IN. Mother's Bpl: IN.

---, Nettie. Black. Female. 14 years old. Daughter. Birthplace: IN. Father's Bpl: IN. Mother's Bpl: IN.

---, Alice. Black. Female. 11 years old. Daughter. Single. Birthplace: IN. Father's Bpl: IN. Mother's Bpl: IN.

---, Edward. Black. Male. 9 years old. Birthplace: IN. Father's Bpl: IN. Mother's Bpl: IN.

---, Lula. Black. Female. 8 years old. Birthplace: IN. Father's Bpl: IN. Mother's Bpl: IN.

YOUNG, Ellen (Dwelling 383, Family 394): Black. Female. 40 years old. Domestic. Widow. Cook. Birthplace: KY. Father's Bpl: KY. Mother's Bpl: KY.

LYON, Mary. Black. Female. 7 years old. Domestic. Birthplace: IN. Father's Bpl: KY. Mother's Bpl: KY.

BURNETT, George. Black. Male. 30 years old. Hired hand. Single. Farm Laborer. Birthplace: IN. Father's Bpl: KY. Mother's Bpl: MD.

(All of these listed with Thomas Braxton, white family)

BURNETT, Arch. (Dwelling 391, Family 402): Black. Male. 36 years old. Married. Teamster. Birthplace: IN. Father's Bpl: KY. Mother's Bpl: IN.

---, Mary. Black. Female. 23 years old. Wife. Keeping house. Birthplace: IN. Father's Bpl: IN. Mother's Bpl: IN.

---, Emma. Black. Female. 8 years old. Birthplace: IN. Father's Bpl: IN. Mother's Bpl: IN.

---, James. Black. Male. 6 years old. Birthplace: IN. Father's Bpl: IN. Mother's Bpl: IN.

---, Stella. Black. Female. 2 years old. Birthplace: IN. Father's Bpl: IN. Mother's Bpl: IN.

---, Thomas. Black. Male. 1 year old. Birthplace: IN. Father's Bpl: IN. Mother's Bpl: IN.

CHANDLER, Nancy (Dwelling 392, Family 403): Black. Female. 60 years old. Widow. Keeping house. Birthplace: IN. Father's Bpl: IN. Mother's Bpl: IN.

CHANNING, Daniel. Black. Male. 26 years old. Boarder. Single. Horse trainer. Father's Bpl: KY. Father's Bpl: KY. Mother's Bpl: KY.

MITCHELL, Arthur. Black. Male. 22 years old. Boarder. Single. Stable boy. Birthplace: IN. Father's Bpl: IN. Mother's Bpl: IN.

SOUTHERS, Samuel. Black. Male. 22 years old. Boarder. Single. Stable boy. Father's Bpl: MI. Father's Bpl: VA. Mother's Bpl: VA.

BOWMAN, Frank (Dwelling 403, Family 414): Black. Male. 15 years old. Employee. Single. Day Laborer. Birthplace: IN. Father's Bpl: IN. Mother's Bpl: IN. (listed with Arthur Simpson, white family)

HILL. Thomas H. (Dwelling 415, Family 426): Black. Male. 25 years old. Married. Farm Laborer. Birthplace: KY. Father's Bpl: KY. Mother's Bpl: KY.

---, Eliza. Black. Female. 20 years old. Wife. Keeping house. Birthplace: KY. Father's Bpl: KY. Mother's Bpl: KY.

EVANS, Samuel. Black. Male. 48 years old. Married. Farm Laborer. Birthplace: IN. Father's Bpl: SC. Mother's Bpl: SC.

---, Nancy. Black. Female. 37 years old. Wife. Keeping house. Birthplace: IN. Father's Bpl: IN. Mother's Bpl: SC.

---, Dora C. Black. Female. 5 years old. Daughter. Birthplace: IN. Father's Bpl: IN. Mother's Bpl: IN.

---, John N. Black. Male. 3 years old. Son. Birthplace: IN.Father's Bpl: IN. Mother's Bpl: IN.

HOWARD, William (Dwelling 437, Family 448): Black. Male. 29 years old. Married. Farmer. Birthplace: IN. Father's Bpl: IN. Mother's Bpl: IN.

---, Helen. Black. Female. 25 years old. Wife. Keeping house. Birthplace: NC. Father's Bpl: NC. Mother's Bpl: NC.

1900 (12th) U. S. CENSUS

French Lick Township

FARMER, Henry (Dwelling 95, Family 95): Head. Black. Male. Birthdate: Jan 1871. 29 years old. Married. 9 years. Birthplace: KY. Father's Bpl: KY. Mother's Bpl: KY. Occupation: waiter.

---, Mattie. Wife. Black. Female. Birthdate: Aug 1871. 28 years old. Married 9 years. 4 children, 3 living. Birthplace: KY. Father's Bpl: KY. Mother's Bpl: KY.

---, Cecil. Son. Black. Male. Birthdate: June 1892. 7 years old. Single. Birthplace: IN. Father's Bpl: KY. Mother's Bpl: KY.

---, Jeannie. Daughter. Birthdate: Jan 1895. 5 years old. Single. Birthplace: IN. Father's Bpl: KY. Mother's Bpl: KY.

---, Jacque. Daughter. Birthdate: Dec 1899. 5/12 year old. Single. Birthplace: IN. Father's Bpl: KY. Mother's Bpl: KY.

GRANT, Edward (Dwelling 96, Family 96): Head. Black. Male. Birthdate: Apr 1865. 35 years old. Married 6 years. Birthplace: KY. Father's Bpl: KY. Mother's Bpl: KY. Occupation: Bathman.

---, Anna. Black. Female. Birthdate: Mar 1871. 29 years old. Married 6 years. 0 children. Birthplace: KY. Father's Bpl: KY. Mother's Bpl: KY.

PITMAN, Soloman. Boarder. Black. Male. Birthdate: Unk. 23 years old. Married 3 years. Birthplace: KY. Father's Bpl: KY. Mother's Bpl: KY. Bellman.

---, Carrie. Boarder. Black. Female. Birthdate: May 1876. 24 years old. Married 3 years. 1 child living. Birthplace: KY. Father's Bpl: KY. Mother's Bpl: KY.

FAULKNER, Burt (Dwelling 399, Family 399): Head. Black. Male. Birthdate: Jan 1853. 47 years old. Married 22 years. Birthplace: IN. Father's Bpl: VA. Mother's Bpl: VA. Hotel porter.

---, Molly. Wife. Black. Female. Birthdate: Mar 1864. 36 years old. Married 22 years. 2 children. Birthplace: NY. Father's Bpl: NY. Mother's Bpl: NY. Hotel lady.

DRAIN, Mamie (Dwelling 400, Family 400): Black. Female. Birthdate: July 1879. 20 years old. Widow. Birthplace: KY. Father's Bpl: KY. Mother's Bpl: KY.

KING, Eugene (Dwelling 426, Family 426): Head. Birthdate: Mar 1874. 26 years old. Birthplace: KY. Father's Bpl: KY. Mother's Bpl: KY. Hotel waiter.

---, Susie. Wife. Black. Female. Birthdate: Oct 1876. 23 years old. 1 child living. Birthplace: KY. Father's Bpl: KY. Mother's Bpl: KY.

---, Willie E. Son. Black. Male. Birthdate: Nov 1899. 2 years old. Birthplace: KY. Father's Bpl: KY. Mother's Bpl: KY.

MCDOWELL, William (Dwelling 430, Family 432): Head. Black. Male. Birthdate: June 1854. 45 years old. Married 2 years. Birthplace: KY. Father's Bpl: KY. Mother's Bpl: KY.

---, Addie. Wife. Black. Female. Birthdate: June 1868. 32 years old. Married 2 years. Birthplace: TN. Father's Bpl: KY. Mother's Bpl: KY.

TEMPLE, Robert (Dwelling 430, Family 433): Head. Black. Male. Birthdate: Feb 1867. 33 years old. Married 0 years. Birthplace: KY. Father's Bpl: KY. Mother's Bpl: KY. Waiter.

---, Katie. Wife. Black. Female. Birthdate: May 1874. 26 years old. Married 0 years. Birthplace: MS. Father's Bpl: MS. Mother's Bpl: MS.

RICE, Charles P. (Dwelling 442, Family 445): Head. Black. Male. Birthdate: July 1871. 28 years old. Married 4 years. Birthplace: TN. Father's Bpl: OH. Mother's Bpl: VA. Hotel waiter.

---, Susie. Wife. Black. Female. Birthdate: July 1871. 28 years old. Married 4 years. 0 children. Birthplace: KY. Father's Bpl: VA. Mother's Bpl: KY.

GUTHRIE, Lawson (Dwelling 450, Family 453): Head. Black. Male. Birthdate: Sept 1857. 42 years old. Married 12 years. Birthplace: MO. Father's Bpl: MD. Mother's Bpl: MO. Hotel waiter.

---, Anna. Wife. Black. Female. Birthdate: Mar 1860. 40 years old. 0 children. Birthplace: KY. Father's Bpl: KY. Mother's Bpl: KY.

SHUCK, Henry (Dwelling 452, Family 455): Head. Black. Male. Birthdate: Oct 1868. 31 years old. Married 4 years. Birthplace: KY. Father's Bpl: KY. Mother's Bpl: KY. Hotel waiter.

---, Ida. Wife. Black. Female. Birthdate: Dec 1876. 23 years old. Married 4 years. 0 children. Birthplace: KY. Father's Bpl: KY. Mother's Bpl: KY.

BURNETT, Adis (Dwelling 453, Family 456): Head. Black. Male. Birthdate: June 1872. 27 years old. Married 8 years. Birthplace: KY. Father's Bpl: KY. Mother's Bpl: KY. Hotel waiter.

---, Lolah. Wife. Black. Female. Birthdate: Dec 1874. 26 years old. Married 8 years. 2 children. Birthplace: KY. Father's Bpl: KY. Mother's Bpl: KY.

---, Alain. Son. Black. Male. Birthdate: Sept 1893. 6 years old. Single. Birthplace: KY. Father's Bpl: KY. Mother's Bpl: KY.

---, Adis. Son. Black. Male. Birthdate: Mar 1897. Single. Birthplace: IN. Father's Bpl: KY. Mother's Bpl: KY.

HUGHES, George C. (Dwelling 454, Family 457): Head. Black. Male. Birthdate: July 1875. 24 years old. Married 5 years. Birthplace: KY. Father's Bpl: Canada. Mother's Bpl: KY. Hotel waiter.

---, Alice. Wife. Black. Female. Birthdate: Oct 1874. 24 years old. Married 5 years. Father's Bpl: KY. Father's Bpl: KY. Mother's Bpl: KY.

HOCKER, Gus. Bro-in-law. Black. Male. Birthdate: Oct 1874. 25 years old. Single. Birthplace: KY. Father's Bpl: KY. Mother's Bpl: KY. Hotel waiter.

MASON, William M. (Dwelling 455, Family 458): Head. Black. Male. Birthdate: May 1874. 26 years old. Married 7 years. Birthplace: KY. Father's Bpl: KY. Mother's Bpl: KY.

---, Anna. Wife. Black. Female. Birthdate: Mar 1874. 26 years old. Married 7 years. 1 child. Birthplace: KY. Father's Bpl: KY. Mother's Bpl: KY.

MASON, Emma (Dwelling 456, Family 459): Sister. Black. Female. Birthdate: ---, 1879. 22 years old. Single. Birthplace: KY. Father's Bpl: KY. Mother's Bpl: KY.

All the following listed with Lee St. Clair, white hotel proprietor (Dwelling 592, Family 595):

BEVEL, Charles. Servant. Black. Male. Birthdate: Sept 1870. 29 years old. Married. Birthplace: KY. Father's Bpl: KY. Mother's Bpl: KY. Club room porter.

THOMAS, John. Servant. Black. Male. Birthdate: Feb 1882. 18 years old. Single. Birthplace: KY. Father's Bpl: KY. Mother's Bpl: KY.

HENDALL, Martin. Servant. Black. Male. Birthdate: Mar 1860. 40 years old. Married 12 years. Birthplace: KY. Father's Bpl: KY. Mother's Bpl: KY. Hotel carpetman.

OVERSTREET, Robert. Servant. Black. Male. Birthdate: Feb 1850. 50 years old. Married 6 years. Birthplace: KY. Father's Bpl: KY. Mother's Bpl: KY. Bathman.

FAULKNER, Henry C. Servant. Black. Male. Birthdate: May 1851. 49 years old. Married 9 years. Birthplace: KY. Father's Bpl: KY. Mother's Bpl: VA. Hotel porter.

HARDING, Charles. Servant. Black. Male. Birthdate: June 1882. 18 years old. Single. Birthplace: TN. Father's Bpl: KY. Mother's Bpl: KY. Elevator boy.

SIMMS, James. Servant. Black. Male. Birthdate: June 1875. 25 years old. Single. Birthplace: MS. Father's Bpl: MS. Mother's Bpl: MS. Hotel porter.

CORNISH, Eliza. Servant. Black. Female. Birthdate: June 1840. 60 years old. Married 39 years. 1 child. Birthplace: KY. Father's Bpl: VA. Mother's Bpl: KY. Chamber maid.

VINABLE, Howard. Servant. Black. Male. Birthdate: May 1849. 51 years old. Married 25 years. Birthplace: VA. Father's Bpl: VA. Mother's Bpl: VA. Houseman.

JENNINGS, John. Servant. Black. Male. Birthdate: Oct 1862. 35 years old. Single. Birthplace: KY. Father's Bpl: KY. Mother's Bpl: KY. Hotel waiter.

RABBIE, Meyery(?). Servant. Black. Male. Birthdate: Jan 1868. 32 years old. Single. Birthplace: KY. Father's Bpl: KY. Mother's Bpl: KY. Kitchen man.

BATTLES, Linsay C. Servant. Black. Male. Birthdate: Nov 1859. 40 years old. Married 15 years. Birthplace: GA. Father's Bpl: GA. Mother's Bpl: GA. Hotel waiter.

MILLER, John W. Servant. Black. Male. Birthdate: Nov 1874. 25 years old. Single. Birthplace: OH. Father's Bpl: KY. Mother's Bpl: KY. Hotel waiter.

SIMMONS, William. Servant. Black. Male. Birthdate: Mar 1858. 42 years old. Married 15 years. Birthplace: KY. Father's Bpl: KY. Mother's Bpl: KY. Hotel waiter.

CORNISH, John. Servant. Black. Male. Birthdate: Sept 1868. 32 years old. Married 7 years. Birthplace: MD. Father's Bpl: MD. Mother's Bpl: KY. Hotel waiter.

BAKER, Harry. Servant. Black. Male. Birthdate: Oct 1862. 37 years old. Married 9 years. Birthplace: TN. Father's Bpl: MS. Mother's Bpl: TN. Hotel waiter.

MOOREHEAD, Hezikiah. Servant. Black. Male. Birthdate: Mar 1875. 25 years old. Married 0 years. Birthplace: KY. Father's Bpl: KY. Mother's Bpl: KY. Waiter.

WILLIAMS, Henry. Servant. Black. Male. Birthdate: Mar 1873. 27 years old. Single. Birthplace: KY. Father's Bpl: TX. Mother's Bpl: KY. Waiter.

MOOREHEAD, Pussy. Servant. Black. Male. Birthdate: Mar 1866. 34 years old. Married 5 years. Birthplace: KY. Father's Bpl: KY. Mother's Bpl: KY. Waiter.

PAYTON, Charles. Servant. Black. Male. Birthdate: Dec 1870. 29 years old. Married 2 years. Birthplace: KY. Father's Bpl: KY. Mother's Bpl: KY. Hotel waiter.

THOMAS, Daniel. Servant. Black. Male. Birthdate: Dec 1870. 29 years old. Married 2 years. Birthplace: KY. Father's Bpl: KY. Mother's Bpl: TN. Hotel waiter.

HOLLAND, Claude. Servant. Black. Male. Birthdate: Feb 1881. 19 years old. Single. Birthplace: KY. Father's Bpl: KY. Mother's Bpl: KY. Waiter.

RICE, Joseph. Servant. Black. Male. Birthdate: Nov 1875. 24 years old. Married 0 years. Birthplace: TN. Father's Bpl: VA. Mother's Bpl: VA. Waiter.

GUTHRIE, Charles. Servant. Black. Male. Birthdate: Mar 1851. 49 years old. Married 4 years. Birthplace: VA. Father's Bpl: VA. Mother's Bpl: VA.

TISVEL, Joshua. Servant. Black. Male. Birthdate: Jun 1874. 26 years old. Married 0 years. Birthplace: KY. Father's Bpl: KY. Mother's Bpl: KY. Waiter.

GRISON, Henry. Servant. Black. Male. Birthdate: Dec 1864. 34 years old. Single. Birthplace: KY. Father's Bpl: KY. Mother's Bpl: KY. Waiter.

CASWELL, Witham. Servant. Black. Male. Birthdate: May 1876. 34 years old. Single. Birthplace: KY. Father's Bpl:

KY. Mother's Bpl: KY. Waiter.

CARNIS, Alfred. Servant. Black. Male. Birthdate: Feb 1834. 66 years old. Married 7 years. Birthplace: MD. Father's Bpl: MD. Mother's Bpl: MD. Office man.

---, Mamie. Servant. Black. Female. Birthdate: Dec 1860. 39 years old. Married 7 years. Birthplace: KY. Father's Bpl: KY. Mother's Bpl: KY. Servant.

GUTHRIE, Charles (Dwelling 593, Family 596): Head. Black. Male. Birthdate: Mar 1851. 49 years old. Married 4 years. Birthplace: VA. Father's Bpl: VA. Mother's Bpl: VA. Hotel waiter.

---, Susie. Wife. Black. Female. Birthdate: May 1861. 39 years old. Married 4 years. Birthplace: KY. Father's Bpl: KY. Mother's Bpl: KY.

GRIFFIN, Emma. Servant. Black. Female. Birthdate: Feb 1865. 35 years old. Single. Birthplace: KY. Father's Bpl: KY. Mother's Bpl: KY. Servant.

PAYNE, Charles. Head. Black. Male. Birthdate: Sept 1875. 24 years old. Married 0 years. Birthplace: KY. Father's Bpl: KY. Mother's Bpl: KY. Waiter.

---, Ulyses(?). Wife. Black. Female. Birthdate: Oct 1876. 23 years old. Married 0 years. Birthplace: KY. Father's Bpl: KY. Mother's Bpl: KY.

All the following listed with John C. Howard, white hotel proprietor, (Dwelling 599, Family 602):

KIZER(?), Emmet. Servant. Black. Male. Birthdate: Aug 1864. 35 years old. Single. Birthplace: KY. Father's Bpl: KY. Mother's Bpl: KY. Bathroom man.

ADAMS, Omah(?). Servant. Black. Male. Birthdate: Mar 1876. 24 years old. Single. Birthplace: GA. Father's Bpl: GA. Mother's Bpl: GA. Bathroom man.

JOHN, William O. Servant. Black. Male. Birthdate: Jun 1878. 22 years old. Single. Birthplace: KY. Father's Bpl: KY. Mother's Bpl: KY. Bathroom man.

WIGGINTON, Yarmouth. Servant. Black. Male. Birthdate: Apr 1870. 30 years old. Single. Birthplace: KY. Father's Bpl: KY. Mother's Bpl: KY. Private waiter.

MORTON, Charles. Servant. Black. Male. Birthdate: Dec 1873. 26 years old. Single. Birthplace: KY. Father's Bpl: KY. Mother's Bpl: KY. Bell boy.

RAMSEY, Thomas. Servant. Black. Male. Birthdate: Aug 1869. 30 years old. Single. Birthplace: Canada. Father's Bpl: Canada. Mother's Bpl: VA. Musician.

ROBINSON, Frank. Servant. Black. Male. Birthdate: Oct 1879. 20 years old. Single. Birthplace: KY. Father's Bpl: KY. Mother's Bpl: KY. Hotel bell boy.

MORGAN, Charles A. Servant. Black. Male. Birthdate: Mar 1872. 28 years old. Single. Birthplace: KY. Father's Bpl: KY. Mother's Bpl: KY. Hotel bell boy.

GRAVES, Carrolton. Servant. Black. Male. Birthdate: Feb 1879. 21 years old. Single. Birthplace: KY. Father's Bpl: KY. Mother's Bpl: KY. Bell boy.

HILL, George. Servant. Black. Laborer. Birthdate: Mar 1873. 21 years old. Single. Birthplace: VA. Father's Bpl: UNK. Mother's Bpl: UNK. Bell boy.

MORTON, James B. Servant. Black. Laborer. Birthdate: Aug 1868. 31 years old. Single. Birthplace: KY. Father's Bpl: KY. Mother's Bpl: KY. Shoe Black.

SCOTT, William. Servant. Black. Male. Birthdate: May 1871. 29 years old. Single. Birthplace: KY. Father's Bpl: KY. Mother's Bpl: KY. Bell boy.

EVANS, George. Servant. Black. Male. Birthdate: July1875. 24 years old. Single. Birthplace: KY. Father's Bpl: KY. Mother's Bpl: KY. Bell boy.

CUNNINGHAM, James. Servant. Black. Male. Birthdate: Sept 1864. 35 years old. Birthplace: KY. Father's Bpl: KY. Mother's Bpl: KY. Waiter.

BABBAGE, Henry L. Servant. Black. Male. Birthdate: Sept 1869. 30 years old. Married 7 years. Birthplace: KY. Father's Bpl: KY. Mother's Bpl: KY. Waiter.

CUNNINGHAM, James R. Boarder. Black. Male. Birthdate: July 1848. 51 years old. Married 29 years. Birthplace: West Indies. Father's Bpl: W.I. Mother's Bpl: W.I. Musician.

TURMAN, Lee A. Servant. Black. Male. Birthdate: Oct 1875. 24 years old. Married. Birthplace: KY. Father's Bpl: KY. Mother's Bpl: KY. Bell boy.

DAINNING, Chas. A. Servant. Black. Male. Birthdate: Dec 1876. 23 years old. Married 2 years. Birthplace: IN. Father's Bpl: IN. Mother's Bpl: IN. Bell boy.

LAWSON, James. Servant. Black. Male. Birthdate: Jan 1875. 25 years old. Married 2 years. Birthplace: IN. Father's Bpl: IN. Mother's Bpl: KY. Bell boy.

KENNEDY, Edward. Servant. Black. Male. Birthdate: Oct 1869. 30 years old. Single. Birthplace: KY. Father's Bpl: KY. Mother's Bpl: KY. Bell boy.

CARTER, James. Servant. Black. Male. Birthdate: Mar 1849. 51 years old. Married 31 years. Birthplace: IN. Father's Bpl: OH. Mother's Bpl: KY. Hotel cook.

SHUCK, Fred. Servant. Black. Male. Birthdate: Aug 1877. 22 years old. Single. Birthplace: KY. Father's Bpl: KY.

Mother's Bpl: KY. Waiter.

EDMOND, Oscar. Servant. Black. Male. Birthdate: Feb 1871. 29 years old. Married 3 years. Birthplace: LA. Father's Bpl: LA. Mother's Bpl: LA. Waiter.

EDMUNDS, Mitchel. Servant. Black. Laborer. Birthdate: Feb 1870. 30 years old. Married 3 years. Birthplace: KY. Father's Bpl: KY. Mother's Bpl: KY. Waiter.

SMITH, Frank. Servant. Black. Male. Birthdate: May 1877. 23 years old. Single. Birthplace: KY. Father's Bpl: KY. Mother's Bpl: KY. Waiter.

COLLINS, Albert. Servant. Black. Male. Birthdate: Apr 1866. 34 years old. Widower. Birthplace: TN. Father's Bpl: TN. Mother's Bpl: TN. Waiter.

MCNAIRY, Watts. Servant. Black. Male. Birthdate: Apr 1874. 26 years old. Single. Birthplace: KY. Father's Bpl: KY. Mother's Bpl: KY. Waiter.

CROCK, Millard. Servant. Black. Male. Birthdate: Mar 1874. 26 years old. Married 4 years. Birthplace: KY. Father's Bpl: KY. Mother's Bpl: KY. Waiter.

BACON, Tech. Servant. Black. Male. Birthdate: Dec 1870. 29 years old. Single. Birthplace: KY. Father's Bpl: VA. Mother's Bpl: KY. Waiter.

MURPHY, James D. Servant. Black. Male. Birthdate: 1876. 26 years old. Single. Birthplace: TN. Father's Bpl: TN. Mother's Bpl: TN. Waiter.

THOMAS, Thomas S. Servant. Black. Male. Birthdate: Dec 1875. 24 years old. Single. Birthplace: KY. Father's Bpl: KY. Mother's Bpl: KY. Waiter.

MARTIN, Tyler(?). Servant. Black. Male. Birthdate: Jun 1878. 21 years old. Single. Birthplace: TN. Father's Bpl: TN. Mother's Bpl: TN. Waiter.

LEVELL, William. Servant. Black. Male. Birthdate: Mar 1872. 27 years old. Married 6 years. Birthplace: KY. Father's Bpl: KY. Mother's Bpl: KY. Waiter.

AVERY, John. Servant. Black. Male. Birthdate: Mar 1864. 38 years old. Married 8 years. Birthplace: TN. Father's Bpl: TN. Mother's Bpl: TN. Waiter.

BOARD, Adolphus. Servant. Black. Male. Birthdate: Mar 1864. 38 years old. Married 4 years. Birthplace: KY. Father's Bpl: KY. Mother's Bpl: KY. Waiter.

DUFF, Henry. Servant. Black. Male. Birthdate: Feb 1876. 26 years old. Single. Birthplace: KY. Father's Bpl: KY. Mother's Bpl: KY. Waiter.

WADDY, George. Servant. Black. Male. Birthdate: Feb 1871. 29 years old. Single. Birthplace: TN. Father's Bpl: TN. Mother's Bpl: TN. Waiter.

VANPELT, Walter B. Servant. Black. Male. Birthdate: July 1875. 24 years old. Single. Birthplace: KY. Father's Bpl: KY. Mother's Bpl: KY. Waiter.

MILLER, Henry C. Servant. Black. Male. Birthdate: Jan 1879. 21 years old. Single. Birthplace: TN. Father's Bpl: TN. Mother's Bpl: TN. Waiter.

JACKSON, Sanford. Servant. Black. Male. Birthdate: Sep 1872. 27 years old. Married 5 years. Birthplace: KY. Father's Bpl: KY. Mother's Bpl: KY. Waiter.

PAYNE, William (Dwelling 600, Family 604): Head. Black. Male. Birthdate: Oct 1867. 32 years old. Married 5 years. Birthplace: TN. Father's Bpl: TN. Mother's Bpl: TN. Hotel waiter.

---, Molly E. Black. Female. Birthdate: Mar 1868. 32 years old. Married 5 years. 2 children. Birthplace: GA. Father's Bpl: GA. Mother's Bpl: GA.

---, Gertrude. Step-dau. Black. Female. Birthdate: Jun 1887. 12 years old. Single. Birthplace: GA. Father's Bpl: GA. Mother's Bpl: GA.

---, William C. Son. Black. Male. Birthdate: Mar 1898. 2 years old. Single. Birthplace: IN. Father's Bpl: TN. Mother's Bpl: GA.

SCOTT, George (Dwelling 621, Family 624): Head. Black. Male. Birthdate: Mar 1865. 35 years old. Married 8 years. Birthplace: KY. Father's Bpl: KY. Mother's Bpl: KY. Hotel waiter.

---, Zora. Wife. Black. Female. Birthdate: Mar 1865. 35 years old. Married 8 years. Birthplace: IN. Father's Bpl: KY. Mother's Bpl: KY.

GRIMS(?), Edward (Dwelling 621, Family 625): Head. Black. Male. Birthdate: Mar 1869. 31 years old. Married 4 years. Birthplace: KY. Father's Bpl: KY. Mother's Bpl: KY.

---, Annie (?). Wife. Black. Female. Birthdate: Jun 1871. 28 years old. Married 4 years. Birthplace: KY. Father's Bpl: KY. Mother's Bpl: KY.

---, Carl G. Son. Black. Male. Birthdate: Jan 1897. 3 years old. Birthplace: IN. Father's Bpl: KY. Mother's Bpl: KY.

FIELDS, Andrew J. (Dwelling 638, Family 642): Head. Black. Male. Birthdate: Aug 1858. 41 years old. Married 4 years. Birthplace: KY. Father's Bpl: VA. Mother's Bpl: KY. Hotel porter.

---, Carrie L. Wife. Black. Female. Birthdate: Jun 1863. 36 years old. Married 4 years. Birthplace: KY. Father's Bpl: KY. Mother's Bpl: KY.

SHAFER, Rudolph (Dwelling 639, Family 643): Head. Black. Male. Birthdate: Mar 1873. 27 years old. Married 0 years. Birthplace:

KY. Father's Bpl: KY. Mother's Bpl: KY. Hotel waiter.

---, Jewell A. Wife. Black. Female. Birthdate: May 1873. 27 years old. Married 0 years. Birthplace: MI. Mother's Bpl: AL. Mother's Bpl: AL.

ROGERS, Karl G. Boarder. Black. Black. Male. Birthdate: Sep 1886. 13 years old. Birthplace: MI. Father's Bpl: AR. Mother's Bpl: Canada. Boarder.

FINLEY, Robert (Dwelling 648, Family 652): Black. Male. Birthdate: Mar 1840. 60 years old. Married. Birthplace: AL. Father's Bpl: AL. Mother's Bpl: AL. Hotel cook. (with Hiram Wells, white family)

Jackson Township

STAYTON, Mary A. (Dwelling 96, Family 96): Servant. Black. Female. Birthdate: July 1865. 34 years old. Single. Birthplace: KY. Father's Bpl: KY. Mother's Bpl: KY. House servant.

Orangeville Township

JONES, Liza (Dwelling 32, Family 33): Head. Black. Female. Birthdate: Jan 1846. 54 years old. Widow. 0 children. Birthplace: IN. Father's Bpl: NC. Mother's Bpl: NC. Day laborer.

Orleans Township

BURNETT, Charity. Head. Black. Female. Birthdate: Mar 1826. 74 years old. Widow. 10 children. 4 living. Birthplace: VA. Father's Bpl: VA. Mother's Bpl: VA.

---, James. Son. Black. Male. Birthdate: Apr 1872. 28 years old. Single. Birthplace: IN. Father's Bpl: IN. Mother's Bpl: VA.

ALLEN, Jane. Daughter. Black. Female. Birthdate: Sep 1856. 44 years old. Widow. 0 children. Birthplace: IN. Father's Bpl: IN. Mother's Bpl: VA.

FINLEY, Elijah (Dwelling 94, Family 105): Head. Black. Male. Birthdate: Feb 1864. 36 years old. Married 11 years. Birthplace: IN. Father's Bpl: IN. Mother's Bpl: IN. Stone Mason.

---, Amanda. Wife. Black. Female. Birthdate: Jan 1867. 33 years old. Married 11 years. 1 child living. Birthplace: IN. Father's Bpl: IN. Mother's Bpl: VA.

---, Lester. Son. Black. Male. Birthdate: Jan 1889. 11 years old. Single. Birthplace: IN. Father's Bpl: IN. Mother's Bpl: IN. In school.

TODD, Fred H. (Dwelling 97, Family 108): Head. Black. Male. Birthdate: Feb 1862. 38 years old. Married 13 years. Birthplace: IN. Father's Bpl: KY. Mother's Bpl: KY. Day laborer.

---, Anna. Wife. Black. Female. Birthdate: Apr 1863. 37 years old. Married 13 years. 3 children living. Birthplace: IN. Father's Bpl: IN. Mother's Bpl: VA.

---, Hallie. Daughter. Black. Female. Birthdate: Nov 1882. 17 years old. Single. Birthplace: IN. Father's Bpl: IN. Mother's Bpl: IN. At school.

---, Rolna. Daughter. Black. Female. Birthdate: Nov 1886. 13 years old. Single. Birthplace: IN. Father's Bpl: IN. Mother's Bpl: IN. At school.

---, Edith. Daughter. Black. Female. Birthdate: Sep 1890. 10 years old. Single. Birthplace: IN. Father's Bpl: IN. Mother's Bpl: IN.

PIERCE, Robert (Dwelling 107, Family 107): Head. Black. Male. Birthdate: Mar 1863. 37 years old. Married 17 years. Birthplace: KY. Father's Bpl: KY. Mother's Bpl: KY. Barber.

---, Frances. Wife. Black. Female. Birthdate: Dec 1864. Married 17 years. Birthplace: IN. Father's Bpl: NC. Mother's Bpl: NC.

---, Libbie. Daughter. Black. Female. Birthdate: Nov 1884. Single. Birthplace: IN. Father's Bpl: KY. Mother's Bpl: IN.

---, Nettie. Daughter. Black. Female. Birthdate: Sep 1886. 13 years old. Single. Birthplace: IN. Father's Bpl: KY. Mother's Bpl: IN.

TODD, George (Dwelling 305, Family 332): Head. Black. Male. Birthdate: Nov 1870. 29 years old. Single. Birthplace: IN. Father's Bpl: DK. Mother's Bpl: DK. Day laborer.

Paoli Township

BOWMAN, Oscar (Dwelling 34, Family 34): Head. Black. Male. Birthdate: July 1861. 38 years old. Married 15 years. Birthplace: IN. Father's Bpl: IN. Mother's Bpl: IN. Mail carrier.

---, Allis. Wife. Black. Female. Birthdate: July 1867. 32 years old. Married 15 years. Birthplace: IN. Father's Bpl: IN. Mother's Bpl: IN.

---, Earl. Son. Black. Male. Birthdate: Mar 1886. 14 years old. Single. Birthplace: IN. Father's Bpl: IN. Mother's Bpl:

IN. At school.

---, Olia. Daughter. Black. Female. Birthdate: Aug 1888. 11 years old. Single. Birthplace: IN. Father's Bpl: IN. Mother's Bpl: IN. At school.

---, Hershel. Son. Black. Male. Birthdate: Oct 1892. 7 years old. Single. Birthplace: IN. Father's Bpl: IN. Mother's Bpl: IN.

---, Irean. Daughter. Black. Female. Birthdate: Aug 1894. 5 years old. Single. Birthplace: IN. Father's Bpl: IN. Mother's Bpl: IN.

---, Jessie. Daughter. Black. Female. Birthdate: May 1897. 3 years old. Single. Birthplace: IN. Father's Bpl: IN. Mother's Bpl: IN.

---, Mable. Daughter. Black. Female. Birthdate: May 1899. 1 year old. Single. Birthplace: IN. Father's Bpl: IN. Mother's Bpl: IN.

BURNETT, Archie (Dwelling 35, Family 35): Head. Black. Male. Birthdate: Sep 1844. 55 years old. Widower. Birthplace: IN. Father's Bpl: NC. Mother's Bpl: IN. Day Laborer.

---, Estela. Daughter. Black. Female. Birthdate: Oct 1877. 22 years old. Single. Birthplace: IN. Father's Bpl: IN. Mother's Bpl: IN.

---, Ernest. Son. Black. Male. Birthdate: Aug 1881. 18 years old. Single. Birthplace: IN. Father's Bpl: IN. Mother's Bpl: IN. Day laborer.

---, Claude. Son. Black. Male. Birthdate: Oct 1884. 15 years old. Single. Birthplace: IN. Father's Bpl: IN. Mother's Bpl: IN. At school.

---, Alma. Daughter. Black. Female. Birthdate: Oct 1886. 13 years old. Single. Birthplace: IN. Father's Bpl: IN. Mother's Bpl: IN. At school.

---, Denby. Son. Black. Male. Birthdate: Jun. 1891. 8 years old. Single. Birthplace: IN. Father's Bpl: IN. Mother's Bpl: IN. At school.

PHELPS, Deliah (Dwelling 40, Family 40): Head. Black. Female. Birthdate: May 1825. 75 years old. Widow. 5 children, 1 living. Birthplace: GA. Father's Bpl: GA. Mother's Bpl: GA.

---, James. Son. Black. Male. Birthdate: June 1845. 55 years old. Single. Birthplace: KY. Father's Bpl: GA. Mother's Bpl: GA. Farm Laborer.

TODD, Green (Dwelling 111, Family 114): Boarder. Black. Male. Birthdate: Jun 1880. 20 years old. Single. Birthplace: IN. Father's Bpl: IN. Mother's Bpl: IN. (with Joseph Bell, hotel keeper).

HOWARD, William (Dwelling 163, Family 168): Head. Black. Male. Birthdate: Mar 1847. 53 years old. Married 20 years. Birthplace: KY. Father's Bpl: KY. Mother's Bpl: KY. Day Laborer.

---, Helen. Wife. Black. Female. Birthdate: Mar 1862. 38 years old. Married 20 years. 7 children, 5 living. Birthplace: IN. Father's Bpl: IN. Mother's Bpl: NC.

---, Mary. Daughter. Black. Female. Birthdate: Jul 1880. 19 years old. Single. Birthplace: IN. Father's Bpl: KY. Mother's Bpl: IN.

---, Elmer. Son. Black. Male. Birthdate: Jul 1881. 18 years old. Single. Birthplace: IN. Father's Bpl: KY. Mother's Bpl: IN. Day Laborer.

---, Nannie. Daughter. Black. Female. Birthdate: Feb 1889. 11 years old. Single. Birthplace: IN. Father's Bpl: KY. Mother's Bpl: IN. At school.

---, Jessie. Daughter. Black. Female. Birthdate: Apr 1891. 9 years old. Single. Birthplace: IN. Father's Bpl: KY. Mother's Bpl: IN. At school.

---, Arthur W. Son. Black. Male. Birthdate: Aug 1896. 3 years old. Single. Birthplace: IN. Father's Bpl: KY. Mother's Bpl: IN.

NANCE, John A. (Dwelling 175, Family 181): Head. Black. Male. Birthdate: Apr 1854. 46 years old. Married 7 years. Birthplace: KY. Father's Bpl: WV. Mother's Bpl: KY. Barber.

---, Mary L. Wife. Black. Female. Birthdate: Jun 1868. 31 years old. Married 7 years. 1 child living. Birthplace: AL. Father's Bpl: AL. Mother's Bpl: AL.

---, Alberta. Daughter. Black. Female. Birthdate: Jul 1889. 11 years old. Single. Birthplace: AL. Father's Bpl: AL. Mother's Bpl: AL. At school.

BURNETT, Eli. Porter. Black. Male. Birthdate: Mar 1873. 27 years old. Single. Birthplace: IN. Father's Bpl: IN. Mother's Bpl: IN. Porter.

MITCHELL, Tom. (Dwelling 216, Family 220): Prisoner. Black. Male. Birthdate: June 1862. 37 years old. Single. Birthplace: KY. Father's Bpl: KY. Mother's Bpl: KY. Cook. (in home of County Sheriff Lindley Jones)

WETHERS, Thomas (Dwelling 246, Family 256): Head. Black. Male. Birthdate: Oct 1862. 37 years old. Married 7 years. Birthplace: KY. Father's Bpl: KY. Mother's Bpl: KY. Day Laborer.

---, Anna. Wife. Black. Female. Birthdate: Jan 1881. 29 years old. Married 7 years. Birthplace: IN. Father's Bpl: IN. Mother's Bpl: IN.

BOND, Austin (Dwelling 283, Family 295): Servant. Black. Male. Birthdate: Mar 1871. 29 years old. Single. Birthplace: IN. Father's Bpl: IN. Mother's Bpl: IN. Farm Laborer. (with William Stout, white family)

THOMAS, William (Dwelling 324, Family 336): Head. Black. Male. Birthdate: Apr 1847. 53 years old. Married 2 years. Birthplace: IN. Father's Bpl: UNK. Mother's Bpl: UNK. Day Laborer.

    ---, Snoan(?). Wife. Black. Female. Birthdate: May 1854. 46 years old. Married 2 years. 0 children. Birthplace: KY. Father's Bpl: KY. Mother's Bpl: KY.

    ---, Bertha. Daughter. Black. Female. Birthdate: Nov 1881. 18 years old. Single. Birthplace: IN. Father's Bpl: IN. Mother's Bpl: IN. At school.

    ---, Dessie. Daughter. Black. Female. Birthdate: Dec 1884. 15 years old. Single. Birthplace: IN. Father's Bpl: IN. Mother's Bpl: IN. At school.

    ---, Ada. Daughter. Black. Female. Birthdate: Nov 1886. 13 years old. Single. Birthplace: IN. Father's Bpl: IN. Mother's Bpl: IN. At school.

    ---, Leslie. Son. Black. Male. Birthdate: Jul 1889. 10 years old. Single. Birthplace: IN. Father's Bpl: IN. Mother's Bpl: IN. At school.

    ---, Mary. Daughter. Black. Female. Birthdate: Oct 1881. 8 years old. Single. Birthplace: IN. Father's Bpl: IN. Mother's Bpl: IN. At school.

BURNETT, Winnie (Dwelling 419, Family 425): Head. Black. Female. Birthdate: Aug 1813. 87 years old. Widow. 14 children, 9 living. Birthplace: UNK. Father's Bpl: UNK. Mother's Bpl: UNK. Farmer.

    ---, George. Son. Black. Male. Birthdate: Mar 1850. 50 years old. Single. Birthplace: IN. Father's Bpl: VA. Mother's Bpl: UNK. Farm Laborer.

    ---, Oscar. Son. Black. Male. Birthdate: Dec 1861. 38 years old. Single. Birthplace: IN. Father's Bpl: VA. Mother's Bpl: UNK. Day Laborer.

1910 (13th) U. S. Census

French Lick Township - West Baden Town

GRAHAM, Mintor(?) (Dwelling 9, Family 9): Head. Male. Mulatto. 27 years old. Married 2 years. Birthplace: KY. Father's Bpl: KY. Mother's Bpl: KY. Hotel waiter.

    ---, Minnie. Wife. Female. Mulatto. Birthplace: KY. Father's Bpl: KY. Mother's Bpl: KY.

    WATSON, Everett. Boarder. Male. Black. 24 years old. Single. Birthplace: KY. Father's Bpl: KY. Mother's Bpl: KY. Waiter.

    LANE, Fred. Boarder. Male. Mulatto. 30 years old. Single. Birthplace: VA. Father's Bpl: VA. Mother's Bpl: VA. Waiter.

    MILES, John G. Boarder. Male. Mulatto. 53 years old. Single. Birthplace: VA. Father's Bpl: VA. Mother's Bpl: VA. Waiter.

MILLIKEN, Joseph (Dwelling 10, Family 10): Head. Male. Black. 33 years old. Married 9 years. Birthplace: KY. Father's Bpl: KY. Mother's Bpl: KY. Waiter.

    ---, Mary. Wife. Female. Black. 30 years old. Birthplace: KY. Father's Bpl: KY. Mother's Bpl: KY.

    PORTER, Jefferson. Boarder. Male. Mulatto. 60 years old. Married. Birthplace: KY. Father's Bpl: KY. Mother's Bpl: KY. Waiter.

    MURPHY, James. Boarder. Male. Mulatto. 33 years old. Widower. Birthplace: TN. Father's Bpl: TN. Mother's Bpl: TN. Waiter.

WING, Meadie G. (Dwelling 10, Family 11): Head. Male. Mulatto. 22 years old. Married. Birthplace: KY. Father's Bipl: KY. Mother's Bpl: KY. Bell boy.

    ---, Nannie. Wife. Female. Mulatto. 24 years old. Birthplace: KY. Father's Bpl: KY. Mother's Bpl: KY.

POTTER, Wright (Dwelling 11, Family 12): Head. Male. Black. 52 years old. Married. Birthplace: KY. Father's Bpl: KY. Mother's Bpl: KY. Bell boy.

    ---, Rose. Wife. 50 years old. Birthplace: KY. Father's Bpl: KY. Mother's Bpl: KY. Bath woman, bath house.

    ---, Dan. Brother. Male. Black. 47 years old. Married. Birthplace: KY. Father's Bpl: KY. Mother's Bpl: KY. Hotel porter.

    HALL, John. Boarder. Male. Black. 40 years old. Widower. Birthplace: KY. Father's Bpl: KY. Mother's Bpl: KY. Hotel waiter.

    GILBERT, Bob. Boarder. Male. Black. 33 years old. Single. Birthplace: KY. Father's Bpl: KY. Mother's Bpl: KY. Waiter.

    PEARY, Will. Boarder. Male. Black. 40 years old. Single. Birthplace: KY. Father's Bpl: KY. Mother's Bpl: KY. Waiter.

SEBREE, Dudley (Dwelling 12, Family 13): Head. Male. Black. 50 years old. Birthplace: KY. Father's Bpl: KY. Mother's Bpl: KY. Boot black, own stand.

    ---, Hannah. Wife. Female. Black. 42 years old. Birthplace: KY. Father's Bpl: KY. Mother's Bpl: KY.

    ---, Edward. Son. Male. Black. 24 years old. Single. Birthplace: KY. Father's Bpl: KY. Mother's Bpl: KY. Bell boy.

---, Birdie. Daughter. Female. Black. 19 years old. Single. Father's Bpl: KY. Mother's Bpl: KY. Hairdresser.

---, Marie. Daughter. Female. Black. 16 years old. Single. Birthplace: KY. Father's Bpl: KY. Mother's Bpl: KY.

---, William. Son. Male. Black. 11 years old. Single. Birthplace: KY. Father's Bpl: KY. Mother's Bpl: KY.

DANCIE, George. Boarder. Male. Black. 22 years old. Single. Birthplace: KY. Father's Bpl: KY. Mother's Bpl: KY. Boot black hotel.

KELLEBROO, Leroy. Boarder. Male. Black. 25 years old. Single. Birthplace: TN. Father's Bpl: TN. Mother's Bpl: TN. Waiter.

LANE, Thomas. Boarder. Male. Black. 34 years old. Married. Birthplace: MS. Father's Bpl: MS. Mother's Bpl: MS. Waiter.

---, Amanda. Boarder. Female. Black. 40 years old. Married. Birthplace: KY. Father's Bpl: KY. Mother's Bpl: KY.

CORNISH, Mamie (Dwelling 14, Family 15): Head. Female. Mulatto. 39 years old. Widow. Birthplace: KY. Father's Bpl: KY. Mother's Bpl: KY. Landlady, boarding house.

TAYLOR, Thomas. Boarder. Male. Black. 45 years old. Single. Birthplace: KY. Father's Bpl: KY. Mother's Bpl: KY. Waiter.

EDDINGTON, John. Boarder. Male. Black. 40 years old. Single. Birthplace: TN. Father's Bpl: TN. Mother's Bpl: TN. Waiter.

WILLIAMS, George. Boarder. Male. Black. 45 years old. Single. Birthplace: KY. Father's Bpl: KY. Mother's Bpl: KY. Bath man.

SWANAGAN, George. Boarder. Male. Black. 45 years old. Married. Birthplace: KY. Father's Bpl: KY. Mother's Bpl: KY. Waiter.

MORELAND, Nize. Boarder. Male. Black. 30 years old. Single. Birthplace: IN. Father's Bpl: IN. Mother's Bpl: IN. Porter.

DICKINSON, Sam (Dwelling 15, Family 16): Head. Male. Black. 31 years old. Married. Birthplace: TN. Father's Bpl: TN. Mother's Bpl: TN. Waiter.

---, Novelle. Wife. Female. Black. 25 years old. Birthplace: TN. Father's Bpl: TN. Mother's Bpl: TN.

BRIGGS, Calvella. Boarder. Female. Mulatto. 21 years old. Married. Birthplace: KY. Father's Bpl: KY. Mother's Bpl: KY.

BELL, James (Dwelling 16, Family 17): Head. Male. Black. 36 years old. Married. Birthplace: KY. Father's Bpl: KY. Mother's Bpl: KY. Porter.

---, Jessie. Wife. Female. Black. 26 years old. Birthplace: IN. Father's Bpl: KY. Mother's Bpl: KY.

BURNETT, Louisa. Boarder. Female. Black. 28 years old. Single. Birthplace: KY. Father's Bpl: KY. Mother's Bpl: KY. Hospital nurse.

BLACKWELL, Arthur B. Head. Male. Black. 40 years old. Married. Birthplace: KY. Father's Bpl: KY. Mother's Bpl: KY. Bathman.

---, Alice. Wife. Female. Black. 39 years old. Birthplace: KY. Father's Bpl: KY. Mother's Bpl: KY.

JAMES, Sauick(?). Boarder. Male. Black. 23 years old. Married. Birthplace: CT. Father's Bpl: CT. Mother's Bpl: CT. Hotel clerk.

---, Mabel. Boarder. Female. Mulatto. 20 years old. Birthplace: IN. Father's Bpl: IN. Mother's Bpl: IN.

---, Margaret. Boarder. Female. Mulatto. 1 6/12 year old. Birthplace: IN. Father's Bpl: CT. Mother's Bpl: IN.

BAILEY, Harry. Boarder. Male. Black. 40 years old. Single. Birthplace: KY. Father's Bpl: KY. Mother's Bpl: KY. Bathman.

RICE, Charles P. (Dwelling 21, Family 22): Head. Male. Black. 38 years old. Married. Birthplace: TN. Father's Bpl: TN. Mother's Bpl: TN. Hotel manager.

---, Susie. Wife. Female. Black. 40 years old. Birthplace: KY. Father's Bpl: KY. Mother's Bpl: KY.

RICHARDSON, John. Boarder. Male. Mulatto. 35 years old. Married. Birthplace: VA. Father's Bpl: VA. Mother's Bpl: VA. Waiter.

---, Marie. Boarder. Female. Mulatto. 22 years old. Birthplace: KY. Father's Bpl: KY. Mother's Bpl: KY. Waitress.

SHERROD, Frank. Boarder. Male. Mulatto. 48 years old. Single. Birthplace: AL. Father's Bpl: AL. Mother's Bpl: AL. Bell boy.

HILL, William. Boarder. Male. Mulatto. 22 years old. Married. Birthplace: TN. Father's Bpl: TN. Mother's Bpl: TN. Waiter.

---, Estella. Boarder. Female. Mulatto. 25 years old. Birthplace: KY. Father's Bpl: TN. Mother's Bpl: KY.

POTTER, James. Boarder. Male. Black. 49 years old. Widower. Birthplace: KY. Father's Bpl: KY. Mother's Bpl: KY. Waiter.

DEGABBERT, Jesse. Boarder. Male. Mulatto. 26 years old. Single. Birthplace: KY. Father's Bpl: KY. Mother's Bpl: KY. Porter.

FAULKNER, Burrell (Dwelling 22, Family 23): Head. Female. Black. 57 years old. Married. Birthplace: KY. Father's Bpl: KY. Mother's Bpl: KY. Porter.

---, Mollie. Wife. Female. Black. 43 years old. Birthplace: NY. Father's Bpl: NY. Mother's Bpl: NY. Hotel landlady.

BEECHER, Christopher (Dwelling 24, Family 25): Head. Male. Black. 41 years old. Married. Birthplace: KY. Father's Bpl: KY. Mother's Bpl: KY. Bathman.
   ---, Hattie. Wife. Female. Black. 38 years old. Birthplace: KY. Father's Bpl: KY. Mother's Bpl: KY.
RAY, Lee L. (Dwelling 24, Family 26): Head. Male. Mulatto. 30 years old. Single. Birthplace: KY. Father's Bpl: KY. Mother's Bpl: KY. Harness maker shop.
BEACHAM, Hal (Dwelling 28, Family 31): Head. Male. Black. 27 years old. Married. Birthplace: KY. Father's Bpl: KY. Mother's Bpl: KY. Bellboy.
   ---, Mary L. Wife. Female. Mulatto. Birthplace: KY. Father's Bpl: KY. Mother's Bpl: KY.
   ---, Octavia. Daughter. Female. Mulatto. 5 years old. Birthplace: IN. Father's Bpl: KY. Mother's Bpl: KY.
   ---, Hallie. Daughter. Female. Mulatto. 2 years old. Birthplace: IN. Father's Bpl: KY. Mother's Bpl: KY.
   STOKES, Martha. Mo-in-law. Female. Black. 41 years old. Widow. Birthplace: KY. Father's Bpl: KY. Mother's Bpl: KY. Hotel cook.
WASHINGTON, Stephen G. (Dwelling 29, Family 32): Head. Male. Black. 40 years old. Single. Birthplace: KY. Father's Bpl: VA. Mother's Bpl: VA. Pool room proprietor.
BURNETT, Adis (Dwelling 52, Family 59): Head. Male. Black. 38 years old. Married. Birthplace: KY. Father's Bpl: KY. Mother's Bpl: KY. Porter.
   ---, Lola R. Wife. Male. Black. 35 years old. Birthplace: KY. Father's Bpl: KY. Mother's Bpl: KY.
   ---, Alvin V. Son. Male. Black. 16 years old. Single. Birthplace: KY. Father's Bpl: KY. Mother's Bpl: KY.
   ---, Adis O. Son. Male. Black. Single. 13 years old. Birthplace: IN. Father's Bpl: KY. Mother's Bpl: KY.
   ---, Clarkson. Son. Male. Black. 9 years old. Birthplace: IN. Father's Bpl: KY. Mother's Bpl: KY.
   WHITE, George. Boarder. Male. Mulatto. 35 years old. Married. Birthplace: PA. Father's Bpl: PA. Mother's Bpl: PA. Waiter.
   ---, Arti. Boarder. Wife. Female. Mulatto. 28 years old. Birthplace: GA. Father's Bpl: GA. Mother's Bpl: GA.
AVERITT, John (Dwelling 57, Family 65): Head. Male. Black. 39 years old. Married. Birthplace: TN. Father's Bpl: TN. Mother's Bpl: TN. Waiter.
   ---, Lula. Wife. Female. Mulatto. 34 years old. Birthplace: KY. Father's Bpl: KY. Mother's Bpl: KY.
   KIMDELOW, George. Boarder. Male. Black. 23 years old. Single. Birthplace: TN. Father's Bpl: TN. Mother's Bpl: TN. Hotel pianist.
WADDY, George W. (Dwelling 61, Family 70): Head. Male. Mulatto. 38 years old. Married. Birthplace: TN. Father's Bpl: TN. Mother's Bpl: TN. Bathman.
   ---, Nannie. Wife. Female. Black. 34 years old. Birthplace: TN. Father's Bpl: TN. Mother's Bpl: TN.
   ---, Nicko. Brother. Male. Mulatto. 13 years old. Birthplace: TN. Father's Bpl: TN. Mother's Bpl: TN.
   PRESTON, Ada. Boarder. Female. Black. 30 years old. Single. Birthplace: KY. Father's Bpl: KY. Mother's Bpl: KY. Seamtress.
   SMITH, Erwin. Boarder. Male. Black. 35 years old. Birthplace: MD. Father's Bpl: MD. Mother's Bpl: MD. Solicitor, Insurance Co.
   FITZGERALD, Anthony. Boarder. Male. Black. 25 years old. Birthplace: TN. Father's Bpl: TN. Mother's Bpl: TN. Waiter.
   ---, May. Boarder. Wife. Female. Mulatto. 23 years old. Birthplace: KY. Father's Bpl: KY. Mother's Bpl: KY.
CORNISH, Eliza (Dwelling 65, Family 74): Head. 71 years old. Widow. Birthplace: KY. Father's Bpl: KY. Mother's Bpl: KY.
   LEWIS, Alice. Boarder. Female. Black. 31 years old. Widow. Birthplace: KY. Father's Bpl: KY. Mother's Bpl: KY. Domestic.
   TOSSEN(?), Charles. Boarder. Male. Black. 40 years old. Single. Birthplace: KY. Father's Bpl: KY. Mother's Bpl: KY. Bellboy.
   WEBSTER, Ida. Boarder. Female. Black. 35 years old. Widow. Birthplace: KY. Father's Bpl: KY. Mother's Bpl: KY. Bathlady.
   MASON, Lee. Boarder. Male. Black. 40 years old. Single. Birthplace: KY. Father's Bpl: KY. Mother's Bpl: KY. Minister.
SCOTT, William (Dwelling 66, Family 75): Head. Male. Black. 38 years old. Married. Birthplace: KY. Father's Bpl: KY. Mother's Bpl: KY. Tailor shop worker.
   ---, Ella M. Wife. Female. Black. 32 years old. Birthplace: KY. Father's Bpl: KY. Mother's Bpl: KY. Seamstress.
POLLARD, Harry (Dwelling 67, Family 76): Head. Male. Mulatto. 29 years old. Married. Birthplace: KY. Father's Bpl: KY. Mother's Bpl: KY. Bell boy.
   ---, Azalea. Wife. Female. Mulatto. 27 years old. Birthplace: KY. Father's Bpl: KY. Mother's Bpl: KY.
   ---, Rose E. Daughter. Female. Mulatto. 10 years old. Birthplace: KY. Father's Bpl: KY. Mother's Bpl: KY.
   ---, Harry C. Son. Male. Mulatto. 10 years old. Birthplace: KY. Father's Bpl: KY. Mother's Bpl: KY.
   ---, Lavania E. Daughter. Female. Mulatto. 2 years old. Birthplace: KY. Father's Bpl: KY. Mother's Bpl: KY.
   ---, Willy B. Son. Male. Mulatto. 1 3/12 years old. Birthplace: IN. Father's Bpl: KY. Mother's Bpl: KY.
BURKS, Lula (Dwelling 73, Family 82): Head. Female. Black. 34 years old. Single. Birthplace: KY. Father's Bpl: KY. Mother's

Bpl: KY. Landlady, lodging house.

ROGERS, Ed. Boarder. Male. Black. 26 years old. Single. Birthplace: KY. Father's Bpl: KY. Mother's Bpl: KY. Bathman.

BEE, Will. Boarder. Male. Black. 40 years old. Married. Birthplace: KY. Father's Bpl: KY. Mother's Bpl: KY. Hotel nurse.

SMITH, William. Boarder. Male. Black. 19 years old. Single. Birthplace: KY. Father's Bpl: KY. Mother's Bpl: KY. Bellboy.

HARDIN, George. Boarder. Male. Black. 35 years old. Single. Birthplace: KY. Father's Bpl: KY. Mother's Bpl: KY. Bellboy.

MORGAN, Fern. Boarder. Male. Black. 38 years old. Married. Birthplace: IN. Father's Bpl: KY. Mother's Bpl: IN. Bathman.

---, Mamie. Boarder. Wife. Female. Black. 33 years old. Birthplace: IN. Father's Bpl: KY. Mother's Bpl: IN.

KINCAID, Albert (Dwelling 99, Family 110): Boarder. Male. Black. 25 years old. Married. Birthplace: IN. Father's Bpl: IN. Mother's Bpl: IN. Elevator boy.

---, Flora. Wife. Female. Black. 30 years old. Birthplace: KY. Father's Bpl: KY. Mother's Bpl: KY.

UPTON, Louis (Dwelling 110, Family 121): Servant. Male. Black. 17 years old. Birthplace: KY. Father's Bpl: KY. Mother's Bpl: KY. Bellboy. (with Lester Sutton, white hotel manager)

WILLIAMS, Mattie (Dwelling 147, Family 165): Head. Female. Black. 40 years old. Widow. Birthplace: OH. Father's Bpl: OH. Mother's Bpl: OH. Ticket agent, bathroom.

BEECHAM, William F. Boarder. Male. Black. 23 years old. Single. Birthplace: TN. Father's Bpl: KY. Mother's Bpl: KY. Bathman.

DORSEY, James H. Boarder. Male. Black. 31 years old. Single. Birthplace: KY. Father's Bpl: KY. Mother's Bpl: KY. Bathman.

BELL, James G. Boarder. Male. Black. 41 years old. Single. Birthplace: IN. Father's Bpl: TN. Mother's Bpl: TN. Bathman.

ALEXANDER, Lester. Boarder. Male. Black. 30 years old. Single. Birthplace: KY. Father's Bpl: KY. Mother's Bpl: KY. Bathman.

WILLIAMS, George. Boarder. Male. Black. 37 years old. Single. Birthplace: KY. Father's Bpl: KY. Mother's Bpl: KY. Bathman.

French Lick Town

HUGHES, George S. (Dwelling 7, Family 7): Head. Male. Black. 35 years old. Married. Birthplace: KY. Father's Bpl: KY. Mother's Bpl: KY. Waiter.

---, Alice V. Wife. Female. Mulatto. 36 years old. Birthplace: KY. Father's Bpl: KY. Mother's Bpl: KY.

---, George T. Son. Male. Mulatto. 2 years old. Birthplace: IN. Father's Bpl: KY. Mother's Bpl: KY.

---, Loletta. Daughter. Female. Mulatto. 1/2 year old. Birthplace: IN. Father's Bpl: KY. Mother's Bpl: KY.

TAYLOR, Elizabeth. Mo-in-law. Female. Black. 58 years old. Widow. Birthplace: KY. Father's Bpl: KY. Mother's Bpl: KY. Domestic.

HOLDEN, Willie(?). (Dwelling 8, Family 8): Head. Female. Black. 52 years old. Married. Birthplace: KY. Father's Bpl: KY. Mother's Bpl: KY. Cook.

CLAY, Rosa. Servant. Female. Black. 30 years old. Single. Birthplace: KY. Father's Bpl: KY. Mother's Bpl: KY. Cook. (with William Rhodes, white family).

THOMAS, Dan (Dwelling 14, Family 14): Head. Male. Mulatto. 61 years old. Married. Birthplace: KY. Father's Bpl: KY. Mother's Bpl: KY. Hotel Porter.

---, Mary. Wife. Female. Mulatto. 59 years old. Birthplace: KY. Father's Bpl: KY. Mother's Bpl: KY.

---, Alice M. Daughter. Female. Mulatto. 27 years old. Single. Birthplace: KY. Father's Bpl: KY. Mother's Bpl: KY. Hotel hairdresser.

---, Thomas S. Son. Male. Mulatto. 35 years old. Single. Birthplace: KY. Father's Bpl: KY. Mother's Bpl: KY. Waiter.

HOLDEN, Robert. Son-in-law. Male. Black. 26 years old. Married. Birthplace: KY. Father's Bpl: KY. Mother's Bpl: KY. Owns tailor shop.

---, Carrie S. Daughter. Wife. Female. Mulatto. Married. Birthplace: KY. Father's Bpl: KY. Mother's Bpl: KY.

---, Mayme A. Gr-dau. Female. Mulatto. 4 years old. Birthplace: IN. Father's Bpl: KY. Mother's Bpl: KY.

THOMAS, Ed. Boarder. Male. Black. 30 years old. Married. Birthplace: KY. Father's Bpl: KY. Mother's Bpl: KY.

WHITE, William. Boarder. Male. Black. 30 years old. Married. Birthplace: KY. Father's Bpl: TN. Mother's Bpl: TN. Hotel cook.

MASON, William (Dwelling 15, Family 15): Head. Male. Black. 42 years old. Married. Birthplace: KY. Father's Bpl: KY. Mother's Bpl: KY. Waiter.

---, Anna. Wife. Female. Black. 36 years old. Birthplace: KY. Father's Bpl: KY. Mother's Bpl: KY.

---, Evelyn. Daughter. Female. Black. 14 years old. Birthplace: IN. Father's Bpl: KY. Mother's Bpl: KY.

DIZED(?), Mattie. Sis-in-law. Female. Black. 32 years old. Married. Birthplace: KY. Mother's Bpl: KY.

---, Eugene. Nephew. Male. Black. 17 years old. Single. Birthplace: KY. Father's Bpl: KY. Mother's Bpl: KY. Livery stable driver.

HANDSON, Churchill. Boarder. Male. Black. 27 years old. Single. Birthplace: KY. Father's Bpl: KY. Mother's Bpl: KY. Waiter.

KIMBALL, Georgia. Boarder. Female. Mulatto. 26 years old. Single. Birthplace: KY. Father's Bpl: KY. Mother's Bpl: KY.

JACKSON, Eddie. Boarder. Male. Black. 25 years old. Married. Birthplace: IN. Father's Bpl: IN. Mother's Bpl: IN. Waiter.

---, Bessie. Waiter. Wife. Female. Black. 22 years old. Birthplace: IN. Father's Bpl: IN. Mother's Bpl: IN.

RUST, Oscar (Dwelling 133, Family 141): Head. Male. Black. 30 years old. Married. Birthplace: KY. Father's Bpl: KY. Mother's Bpl: KY. Bellboy.

---, Harriet. Wife. Female. Mulatto. 24 years old. Birthplace: TN. Father's Bpl: TN. Mother's Bpl: TN.

---, Frances M. Daughter. Female. Mulatto. 5 years old. Birthplace: IN. Father's Bpl: KY. Mother's Bpl: TN.

COOK, John P. (Dwelling 175, Family 185): Head. Male. Black. 38 years old. Married. Birthplace: KY. Father's Bpl: KY. Mother's Bpl: KY. Waiter.

---, Lula B. Wife. Female. Black. 32 years old. Birthplace: KY. Father's Bpl: KY. Mother's Bpl: KY.

---, John W. Son. Male. Black. 9 years old. Birthplace: KY. Father's Bpl: KY. Mother's Bpl: KY.

TAYLOR, Henry (Dwelling 176, Family 186): Head. Male. Mulatto. 37 years old. Married. Birthplace: KY. Father's Bpl: KY. Mother's Bpl: KY. Bellboy.

---, Artyl. Wife. Female. Black. 33 years old. Married. Birthplace: IN. Father's Bpl: KY. Mother's Bpl: KY.

---, Margaret. Daughter. Female. Mulatto. 8 years old. Birthplace: CO. Father's Bpl: KY. Mother's Bpl: IN.

---, Helen A. Daughter. Female. Mulatto. 5 years old. Birthplace: IN. Father's Bpl: KY. Mother's Bpl: IN.

---, Jack S. Son. Male. Mulatto. 2 years old. Birthplace: IN. Father's Bpl: KY. Mother's Bpl: IN.

STOCKDALE, Clarence (Dwelling 177, Family 187): Head. Male. Mulatto. 30 years old. Married. Birthplace: KY. Father's Bpl: KY. Mother's Bpl: KY. Hotel hatman.

---, Pearle. Wife. Female. Mulatto. 30 years old. Birthplace: KY. Father's Bpl: KY. Mother's Bpl: KY.

FOSTER, James (Dwelling 178, Family 188): Head. Male. Mulatto. 30 years old. Married. Birthplace: TN. Father's Bpl: TN. Mother's Bpl: TN. Waiter.

---, Anna. Wife. Female. Mulatto. 30 years old. Birthplace: TN. Father's Bpl: TN. Mother's Bpl: TN.

---, Harry W. Son. Male. Mulatto. 14 years old. Birthplace: TN. Father's Bpl: TN. Mother's Bpl: TN. Bellboy.

WHITE, Anna. Boarder. Female. Mulatto. Birthplace: TN. Father's Bpl: TN. Mother's Bpl: TN.

---, Alva. Boarder. Female. Mulatto. 3 years old. Birthplace: TN. Father's Bpl: TN. Mother's Bpl: TN.

---, Anne. Boarder. Female. Mulatto. 2 years old. Birthplace: TN. Father's Bpl: TN. Mother's Bpl: TN.

THURMAN, Clarence (Dwelling 179, Family 189): Head. Male. Black. 27 years old. Married. Birthplace: TN. Father's Bpl: TN. Mother's Bpl: TN. Shoemaker, own store.

---, Madie. Wife. Female. Black. 27 years old. Birthplace: TN. Father's Bpl: KY. Mother's Bpl: TN.

PACE, Edmund (Dwelling 179, Family 190): Head. Male. Black. 26 years old. Married. Birthplace: GA. Father's Bpl: GA. Mother's Bpl: GA. Waiter.

---, Dolcie. Wife. Female. Mulatto. 22 years old. Birthplace: OH. Father's Bpl: IN. Mother's Bpl: IN.

POPER(?), William. Boarder. Male. Black. 38 years old. Widower. Birthplace: FL. Father's Bpl: FL. Mother's Bpl: FL. Proprietor, own saloon.

MCLAWRENCE, Harry (Dwelling 188, Family 199): Head. Male. Black. 25 years old. Married. Birthplace: TN. Father's Bpl: TN. Mother's Bpl: TN. Waiter.

---, Pearl. Wife. Female. Black. 21 years old. Birthplace: TN. Father's Bpl: TN. Mother's Bpl: TN.

WHITE, Marvel. Cousin. Female. Mulatto. 21 years old. Married. KS. Father's Bpl: TN. Mother's Bpl: KS.

MCLAWRENCE, Cary. Brother. Male. Black. 14 years old. Birthplace: TN. Father's Bpl: TN. Mother's Bpl: TN. Porter, barbershop.

DENNY, Ben (Dwelling 190, Family 201): Head. Male. Black. 48 years old. Widower. Birthplace: KY. Father's Bpl: IN. Mother's Bpl: KY. Waiter.

HOLIDAY, James. Boarder. Male. Black. 28 years old. Single. Birthplace: KY. Father's Bpl: KY. Mother's Bpl: KY. Waiter.

RHODES, Andrew. Boarder. Male. Black. 31 years old. Single. Birthplace: TN. Father's Bpl: KY. Mother's Bpl: KY. Waiter.

HAINES, William. Boarder. Male. Black. 43 years old. Single. Birthplace: KY. Father's Bpl: KY. Mother's Bpl: KY. Waiter.

ROLLINS, William. Boarder. Male. Black. 28 years old. Married. Birthplace: KY. Father's Bpl: KY. Mother's Bpl: KY. Waiter.

---, Ola. Boarder. Wife. Female. Black. 25 years old. Birthplace: KY. Father's Bpl: KY. Mother's Bpl: TN.

MILLS, John. Boarder. Male. Black. 34 years old. Married. Birthplace: KY. Father's Bpl: KY. Mother's Bpl: TN. Hotel tailor.

---, Georgia. Boarder. Wife. Female. Black. 30 years old. Birthplace: TN. Father's Bpl: GA. Mother's Bpl: GA.

ALLISTON, George. Boarder. Male. Black. 31 years old. Single. Birthplace: TN. Father's Bpl: GA. Mother's Bpl: TN. Waiter.

BLAKEMAN, James. Boarder. Male. Black. 47 years old. Widower. Birthplace: KY. Father's Bpl: KY. Mother's Bpl: KY. Waiter.

REILLY, William. Boarder. Male. Black. 51 years old. Widower. Birthplace: KY. Father's Bpl: KY. Mother's Bpl: KY. Waiter.

WILLIAMS, Jefferson. Boarder. Male. Black. 40 years old. Single. Birthplace: KY. Father's Bpl: KY. Mother's Bpl: KY. Barber, own shop.

OGLE, William. Boarder. Male. Black. 40 years old. Single. Birthplace: KY. Father's Bpl: KY. Mother's Bpl: KY. Waiter.

PARROTT, John G. (Dwelling 191, Family 202): Head. Male. Black. 40 years old. Married. Birthplace: KY. Father's Bpl: KY. Mother's Bpl: KY. Waiter.

---, Addie. Wife. Female. Black. 37 years old. Birthplace: KY. Father's Bpl: KY. Mother's Bpl: KY.

WHITNEY, Martin. Boarder. Male. Black. 40 years old. Single. Birthplace: KY. Father's Bpl: KY. Mother's Bpl: KY. Waiter.

JORDEN, Grand. Boarder. Male. Black. 40 years old. Single. Birthplace: KY. Father's Bpl: KY. Mother's Bpl: KY. Waiter.

PARKS, Grant. Boarder. Male. Black. 35 years old. Single. Birthplace: KY. Father's Bpl: KY. Mother's Bpl: KY. Waiter.

SMITH, George (Dwelling 192, Family 203): Head. Male. Black. 30 years old. Married. Birthplace: KY. Father's Bpl: KY. Mother's Bpl: KY. Bellboy.

---, Nannie B. Wife. Female. Black. 28 years old. Birthplace: KY. Father's Bpl: KY. Mother's Bpl: NY.

SHOCKENEY, Louis (Dwelling 208, Family 219): Head. Male. Black. 50 years old. Married. Birthplace: KY. Father's Bpl: KY. Mother's Bpl: KY. Bathman.

---, Eva. Wife. Female. Black. 46 years old. Birthplace: KY. Father's Bpl: KY. Mother's Bpl: KY.

ALEXANDER, Lester (Dwelling 209, Family 220): Head. Male. Black. 30 years old. Birthplace: IN. Father's Bpl: KY. Mother's Bpl: KY. Bathman.

---, Mattie. Wife. Female. Black. 30 years old. Birthplace: KY. Father's Bpl: KY. Mother's Bpl: KY.

---, Alliston. Son. Male. Black. 13 years old. Birthplace: KY. Father's Bpl: IN. Mother's Bpl: KY.

PALMER, James (Dwelling 210, Family 221): Head. Male. Black. 45 years old. Birthplace: KY. Father's Bpl: KY. Mother's Bpl: KY. Waiter.

---, Viola. Wife. Female. Black. 38 years old. Birthplace: IL. Father's Bpl: OH. Mother's Bpl: PA.

GLASS, John. Boarder. Male. Black. 34 years old. Widower. Birthplace: KY. Father's Bpl: KY. Mother's Bpl: KY. Waiter.

BLAIN, Ella (Dwelling 211, Family 222): Head. Female. Black. 31 years old. Single. Birthplace: KY. Father's Bpl: KY. Mother's Bpl: KY. Hotel cook.

WASHINGTON, Henry. Boarder. Male. Black. 27 years old. Married. Birthplace: KY. Father's Bpl: KY. Mother's Bpl: KY. Waiter.

---, Cassella. Boarder. Female. Black. 28 years old. Birthplace: IN. Father's Bpl: KY. Mother's Bpl: IN.

HANLEY, Columbus. Boarder. Male. Black. 26 years old. Single. Birthplace: KY. Father's Bpl: KY. Mother's Bpl: KY. Bathman.

BRADFORD, Ella (Dwelling 215, Family 226): Head. Female. Black. 32 years old. Single. Birthplace: LA. Father's Bpl: LA. Mother's Bpl: LA. Bathwoman.

TAYLOR, Joseph. Boarder. Female. Black. 31 years old. Single. Birthplace: KY. Father's Bpl: KY. Mother's Bpl: KY. Bellboy.

DUNCAN, Vernon. Boarder. Male. Black. 27 years old. Single. Birthplace: TN. Father's Bpl: TN. Mother's Bpl: TN. Waiter.

DORSEY, James. Boarder. Male. Black. 40 years old. Single. Birthplace: KY. Father's Bpl: KY. Mother's Bpl: KY. Bathman.

MURPHY, Nick. Boarder. Male. Black. 31 years old. Single. Birthplace: KY. Father's Bpl: KY. Mother's Bpl: KY. Waiter.

WILLIAMS, Elinore. Boarder. Female. Black. 30 years old. Single. Birthplace: KY. Father's Bpl: KY. Mother's Bpl: KY. Dressmaker.

182

LANE, William (Dwelling 235, Family 246): Head. Male. Black. 36 years old. Widower. Birthplace: IN. Father's Bpl: KY. Mother's Bpl: KY. Waiter.

HUNT, David L. (Dwelling 237, Family 248): Head. Male. Black. 30 years old. Married. Birthplace: TN. Father's Bpl: TN. Mother's Bpl: TN. Waiter.

---, Alivia. Wife. Female. Black. 24 years old. Birthplace: LA. Father's Bpl: TN. Mother's Bpl: LA.

---, Katie C. Daughter. Female. Black. 4 years old. Birthplace: TN. Father's Bpl: TN. Mother's Bpl: LA.

KING, Henry (Dwelling 238, Family 249): Head. Male. Black. 40 years old. Married. Birthplace: KY. Father's Bpl: KY. Mother's Bpl: KY. Waiter.

---, Gertrude. Wife. Female. Black. 37 years old. Birthplace: KY. Father's Bpl: KY. Mother's Bpl: KY.

PAYNE, William (Dwelling 261, Family 272): Head. Male. Black. 31 years old. Married. Birthplace: TN. Father's Bpl: TN. Mother's Bpl: VA. Waiter.

---, Mollie. Wife. Female. Black. 22 years old. Birthplace: GA. Father's Bpl: GA. Mother's Bpl: GA.

---, William. Son. Male. Black. 12 years old. Single. Birthplace: IN. Father's Bpl: TN. Mother's Bpl: GA.

---, Daisy. Daughter. Female. Black. 9 years old. Birthplace: IN. Father's Bpl: TN. Mother's Bpl: GA.

---, Othelura. Daughter. Female. Black. 7 years old. Birthplace: IN. Father's Bpl: TN. Mother's Bpl: GA.

---, Walter. Son. Male. Black. 5 years old. Birthplace: IN. Father's Bpl: TN. Mother's Bpl: GA.

---, Vermont. Son. Male. Black. 3 years old. Birthplace: IN. Father's Bpl: TN. Mother's Bpl: GA.

KING, Mansell. Boarder. Male. Black. 31 years old. Single. Birthplace: KY. Father's Bpl: KY. Mother's Bpl: KY. Bellboy.

WATSON, George. Boarder. Male. Mulatto. 34 years old. Single. Birthplace: KY. Father's Bpl: TN. Mother's Bpl: TN. Porter, barbership.

BEAURAGARD, Charles. Boarder. Male. Black. 27 years old. Single. Birthplace: KY. Father's Bpl: KY. Mother's Bpl: KY. Elevator boy.

HOFFMAN, George. Boarder. Male. Black. 40 years old. Single. Birthplace: KY. Father's Bpl: GA. Mother's Bpl: TN. Waiter.

JACKSON, William L. (Dwelling 262, Family 273): Head. Male. Black. 33 years old. Married. Birthplace: KY. Father's Bpl: KY. Mother's Bpl: KY. Waiter.

---, Laura. Wife. Female. Black. 28 years old. Birthplace: KY. Father's Bpl: KY. Mother's Bpl: KY.

BABBAGE, Henry L. (Dwelling 272, Family 283): Head. Male. Black. 41 years old. Married. Birthplace: KY. Father's Bpl: KY. Mother's Bpl: KY. Proprietor, newstand.

---, Sadie. Wife. Female. Black. 38 years old. Birthplace: KY. Father's Bpl: KY. Mother's Bpl: KY.

---, John A. Son. Male. Black. 16 years old. Single. Birthplace: KY. Father's Bpl: KY. Mother's Bpl: KY.

MILLER, William C.(Dwelling 286, Family 300): Head. Male. Black. 34 years old. Married. Birthplace: TN. Father's Bpl: TN. Mother's Bpl: TN. Waiter.

---, Lula. Wife. Female. Black. 37 years old. Birthplace: KY. Father's Bpl: KY. Mother's Bpl: KY.

---, Virginia A. St-dau. Female. Black. 7 years old. Birthplace: KY. Father's Bpl: KY. Mother's Bpl: KY.

RICHARDSON, Maggie. Sis-in-law. Female. Black. 22 years old. Married. Birthplace: KY. Father's Bpl: KY.

---, David. Bro-in-law. Male. Black. 22 years old. Married. Birthplace: KY. Father's Bpl: KY. Mother's Bpl: KY. Bellboy.

LEWIS, Robert. Boarder. Male. Black. 43 years old. Single. Birthplace: KY. Father's Bpl: KY. Mother's Bpl: KY. Waiter.

FIELDS, Carrie L. (Dwelling 281, Family 301): Head. Female. Black. 43 years old. Widow. Birthplace: KY. Father's Bpl: KY. Mother's Bpl: KY.

---, Virginia. Daughter. Female. Black. 9 years old. Birthplace: IN. Father's Bpl: KY. Mother's Bpl: KY.

WIGGINTON, Yarmouth. Boarder. Male. Black. 40 years old. Widower. Birthplace: KY. Father's Bpl: KY. Mother's Bpl: KY. Water dipper, Pluto Spring.

MARTON, Charles. Boarder. Male. Black. 36 years old. Single. Birthplace: KY. Father's Bpl: KY. Mother's Bpl: KY. Fireman, power house.

CAIRO, Samuel. Boarder. Male. Black. 40 years old. Single. Birthplace: NC. Father's Bpl: NC. Mother's Bpl: NC. Waiter.

JONES, William. Boarder. Male. Black. 38 years old. Single. Birthplace: KY. Father's Bpl: KY. Mother's Bpl: KY.

JOHNSON, Theodore. Boarder. Male. Black. 38 years old. Single. Birthplace: CANADA. Father's Bpl: CAN. Mother's Bpl: CAN. Elevator boy.

COOK, James (Dwelling 289, Family 303): Head. Male. Black. 34 years old. Married. Birthplace: TN. Father's Bpl: TN. Mother's Bpl: TN. Waiter.

---, Ouly. Wife. Female. Black. 33 years old. Birthplace: KY. Father's Bpl: KY. Mother's Bpl: KY. Hairdresser.

MOORE, Emma. Servant. Female. Black. 32 years old. Single. Birthplace: KY. Father's Bpl: KY. Mother's Bpl: KY. Housekeeper.

COLEMAN, Bessie. Boarder. Female. Black. 27 years old. Single. Birthplace: KY. Father's Bpl: KY. Mother's Bpl: KY.

183

GIBBS, James. Boarder. Male. Black. 38 years old. Married. Birthplace: KY. Father's Bpl: KY. Mother's Bpl: KY. Waiter.

---, Alma. Boarder. Female. Black. 30 years old. Birthplace: KY. Father's Bpl: KY. Mother's Bpl: KY.

HALL, Gus. Boarder. Male. Black. 30 years old. Single. Birthplace: KY. Father's Bpl: KY. Mother's Bpl: KY. Waiter.

POORE, Sam. Boarder. Male. Black. 18 years old. Single. Birthplace: KY. Father's Bpl: KY. Mother's Bpl: KY. Waiter.

QUALES, (?). Boarder. Male. Black. 18 years old. Single. Birthplace: KY. Father's Bpl: KY. Mother's Bpl: KY. Waiter.

NEEDS, Sam. Boarder. Male. Black. 25 years old. Single. Birthplace: KY. Father's Bpl: KY. Mother's Bpl: KY. Waiter.

MCCOWING, Hulda (Dwelling 290, Family 304): Head. Female. Black. 53 years old. Widow. Birthplace: KY. Father's Bpl: KY. Mother's Bpl: KY.

JACKSON, Sanford. Son. Male. Black. 38 years old. Single. Birthplace: KY. Father's Bpl: KY. Mother's Bpl: KY. Waiter.

SMITH, Richard (Dwelling 306, Family 322): Head. Male. Black. 29 years old. Married. Birthplace: IN. Father's Bpl: KY. Mother's Bpl: KY. Waiter.

---, Mattie. Wife. Female. Black. 23 years old. Birthplace: KY. Father's Bpl: KY. Mother's Bpl: KY.

---, Elizabeth. St-dau. Female. Black. 6 years old. Birthplace: KY. Father's Bpl: KY. Mother's Bpl: KY.

FARRAL, Churchill. Bro-in-law. Male. Black. 36 years old. Married. Birthplace: KY. Father's Bpl: KY. Mother's Bpl: KY. Barber.

---, Hattie. Sister. Wife. Female. Black. 31 years old. Birthplace: KY. Father's Bpl: KY. Mother's Bpl: KY.

MARTIN, William O. (Dwelling 308, Family 325): Head. Male. Black. 36 years old. Married. Birthplace: TN. Father's Bpl: TN. Mother's Bpl: TN. Tailor, own shop.

---, Sarah. Wife. Female. Black. 26 years old. Birthplace: KY. Father's Bpl: KY. Mother's Bpl: KY.

JARLES, ?. Boarder. Male. Black. 24 years old. Married. Birthplace: TN. Father's Bpl: TN. Mother's Bpl: TN. Waiter.

HAINES, James W. (Dwelling 308, Family 326): Head. Male. Black. 25 years old. Single. Birthplace: W INDIES. Father's Bpl: W.I. Mother's Bpl: W.I. Tailor.

SLYE, Erbin (Dwelling 308, Family 327): Head. Male. Mulatto. 38 years old. Single. Birthplace: KY. Father's Bpl: KY. Mother's Bpl: KY. Restaurant owner.

WILLIAMS, Mattie (Dwelling 330, Family 351): Head. Female. Black. 45 years old. Widow. Birthplace: KY. Father's Bpl: KY. Mother's Bpl: KY. Bath woman.

BURDETTE, Mattie. Female. Black. 34 years old. Widow. Birthplace: KY. Father's Bpl: KY. Mother's Bpl: KY. Bath woman.

BEECHAM, William. Boarder. Male. Black. 39 years old. Single. Birthplace: KY. Father's Bpl: KY. Mother's Bpl: KY.

BOARD, Adolph (Dwelling 331, Family 352): Head. Male. Black. 39 years old. Married. Birthplace: KY. Father's Bpl: KY. Mother's Bpl: KY. Waiter.

---, Alice. Wife. Female. Mulatto. 35 years old. Birthplace: KY. Father's Bpl: KY. Mother's Bpl: KY.

---, Dorothy. Daughter. Female. Black. 6 years old. Birthplace: IN. Father's Bpl: KY. Mother's Bpl: KY.

MORGAN, Maggie. Mo-in-law. Female. Black. 53 years old. Widow. Birthplace: KY. Father's Bpl: KY. Mother's Bpl: KY. Nurse.

LOYD, Josephine. Sister. Female. Black. 22 years old. Single. Birthplace: KY. Father's Bpl: KY. Mother's Bpl: KY. Bath lady.

PITTMAN, Solomon (Dwelling 334, Family 356): Head. Male. Mulatto. 53 years old. Married. Birthplace: KY. Father's Bpl: KY. Mother's Bpl: KY. Porter.

---, Carrie. Wife. Female. Black. 33 years old. Birthplace: KY. Father's Bpl: KY. Mother's Bpl: KY.

---, Roy. Son. Male. Black. 12 years old. Birthplace: KY. Father's Bpl: KY. Mother's Bpl: KY.

LAWS, Abraham (Dwelling 335, Family 357): Head. Male. Black. 42 years old. Married. Birthplace: KY. Father's Bpl: KY. Mother's Bpl: KY. Waiter.

---, Hannah. Wife. Female. Mulatto. 47 years old. Birthplace: KY. Father's Bpl: KY. Mother's Bpl: KY.

BROWN, Edward. Boarder. Male. Black. 23 years old. Married. Birthplace: MO. Father's Bpl: MO. Mother's Bpl: MO. Waiter.

---, Nell. Boarder. Female. Black. 25 years old. Birthplace: IL. Father's Bpl: KY. Mother's Bpl: VA.

SHARES, Henry. Boarder. Male. Black. 22 years old. Single. Birthplace: KY. Father's Bpl: KY. Mother's Bpl: KY. Bellboy.

BOBSON, Ernest (Dwelling 336, Family 358): Head. Male. Black. Age: ---. Married. Birthplace: IN. Father's Bpl: IN. Mother's Bpl: IN. Waiter.

---, Susie. Wife. Female. Black. 37 years old. Birthplace: KY. Father's Bpl: KY. Mother's Bpl: KY.

---, Juanita. Daughter. Female. Black. 10 years old. Birthplace: IL. Father's Bpl: IN. KY.

SCAGGS, William. Boarder. Male. Black. 33 years old. Married. Birthplace: TN. Father's Bpl: TN. Mother's Bpl: TN. Waiter.

---, Hannah. Boarder. Female. Black. 22 years old. Birthplace: TN. Father's Bpl: TN. Mother's Bpl: TN.

---, Virginia. Boarder. Female. Black. 1 year old. Birthplace: IN. Father's Bpl: TN. Mother's Bpl: TN.

JACKSON, William R. (Dwelling 337, Family 359): Head. Male. Black. 47 years old. Married. Birthplace: KY. Father's Bpl: KY. Mother's Bpl: KY. Waiter.

---, Mary. Wife. Female. Black. 38 years old. Birthplace: TN. Father's Bpl: TN. Mother's Bpl: TN.

JONES, George. Son-in-law. Male. Black. 28 years old. Birthplace: AR. Father's Bpl: AR. Mother's Bpl: AR. Tailor.

---, Mildred. Daughter. Female. Black. 22 years old. Birthplace: IN. Father's Bpl: KY. Mother's Bpl: KY.

---, George W. Gr-son. Male. Black. 2 years old. Birthplace: IN. Father's Bpl: AR. Mother's Bpl: IN.

RICE, Hugh. Boarder. Male. Black. Single. Birthplace: IN. Father's Bpl: KY. Mother's Bpl: KY. Waiter.

PETERS, Gibson. Boarder. Male. Black. 31 years old. Single. Birthplace: IN. Father's Bpl: KY. Mother's Bpl: KY. Fireman, power house.

BROWN, Gus (Dwelling 343, Family 365): Head. Male. Black. 38 years old. Birthplace: TN. Father's Bpl: TN. Mother's Bpl: TN. Waiter.

---, Irene. Wife. Female. Black. 26 years old. Birthplace: KY. Father's Bpl: KY. Mother's Bpl: KY.

MORGAN, Charles. Boarder. Male. Black. 41 years old. Married. Birthplace: KY. Father's Bpl: KY. Mother's Bpl: KY. Waiter.

---, Anna. Boarder. Female. Black. 37 years old. Married. Birthplace: KY. Father's Bpl: KY. Mother's Bpl: KY.

HAYDEN, William L. (Dwelling 353, Family 376): Head. Male. Black. 25 years old. Married. Birthplace: KY. Father's Bpl: KY. Mother's Bpl: KY. Waiter.

---, Mamie. Wife. Male. Black. 24 years old. Birthplace: KY. Father's Bpl: KY. Mother's Bpl: KY.

All the following were listed with Walter Barnes, white hotel manager, living at Dwelling 366, Family 389):

DAVIS, Isaac B. Servant. Male. Black. 66 years old. Married. Birthplace: KY. Father's Bpl: KY. Mother's Bpl: KY. Kitchen Assistant.

---, Mary. Servant. Female. Black. 57 years old. Birthplace: KY. Father's Bpl: KY. Mother's Bpl: KY. Hotel kitchen asst.

---, Charles A. Servant. Male. Black. 28 years old. Single. Birthplace: KY. Father's Bpl: KY. Mother's Bpl: KY. Waiter.

LANE, William. Servant. Male. Black. 41 years old. Single. Birthplace: KY. Father's Bpl: KY. Mother's Bpl: KY. Waiter.

MARTIN, Tyler. Servant. Male. Black. 38 years old. Widower. Birthplace: KY. Father's Bpl: KY. Mother's Bpl: KY. Waiter.

LEWIS, Joseph. Servant. Male. Black. 27 years old. Widower. Birthplace: KY. Father's Bpl: KY. Mother's Bpl: KY. Waiter.

JONES, William. Servant. Male. Black. 47 years old. Single. Birthplace: IN. Father's Bpl: KY. Mother's Bpl: KY. Waiter.

JOHNSON, William. Servant. Male. Black. 30 years old. Single. Birthplace: KY. Father's Bpl: IN. Mother's Bpl: KY. Waiter.

TODD, John. Servant. Male. Mulatto. 35 years old. Single. Birthplace: KY. Father's Bpl: KY. Mother's Bpl: KY. Bellboy.

---, William. Servant. Male. Mulatto. 28 years old. Single. Birthplace: KY. Father's Bpl: KY. Mother's Bpl: KY. Bellboy.

FIELDS, Charles. Servant. Male. Black. 24 years old. Single. Birthplace: KY. Father's Bpl: KY. Mother's Bpl: KY. Coffee man.

PURNELL, Frank. Servant. Male. Black. 31 years old. Single. Birthplace: KY. Father's Bpl: VA. Father's Bpl: KY. Houseman.

---, Robert. Servant. Male. Black. 27 years old. Single. Birthplace: GA. Father's Bpl: KY. Mother's Bpl: KY. Houseman.

LOWELL, William. Servant. Male. Black. 32 years old. Widower. Birthplace: KY. Father's Bpl: TN. Mother's Bpl: KY. Waiter.

COUCH, Martin. Servant. Male. Black. 41 years old. Single. Birthplace: WV. Father's Bpl: WV. Mother's Bpl: WV. Waiter.

FORD, Samuel. Servant. Male. Black. 30 years old. Single. Birthplace: KY. Father's Bpl: TN. Mother's Bpl: KY. Bellboy.

HOLM(?), Gus. Servant. Male. Black. 29 years old. Single. Birthplace: AL. Father's Bpl: AL. Mother's Bpl: AL. Waiter.

WARAURAC(?), Herman. Servant. Male. Black. 21 years old. Single. Birthplace: AR. Father's Bpl: AR. Mother's Bpl: MS. Waiter.

ALEXANDER, Adam. Servant. Male. Black. 23 years old. Single. Birthplace: MS. Father's Bpl: MS. Mother's Bpl: MS. Waiter.

MILLER, Ollie. Servant. Male. Black. 40 years old. Single. Birthplace: KY. Father's Bpl: TN. Mother's Bpl: TN. Waiter.

---, Pleasant. Servant. Male. Mulatto. 34 years old. Single. Birthplace: KY. Father's Bpl: TN. Mother's Bpl: TN. Waiter.

JACKSON, William. Servant. Male. Black. 36 years old. Single. Birthplace: KY. Father's Bpl: KY. Mother's Bpl: KY. Waiter.

DUFFY, William. Servant. Male. Black. 35 years old. Single. Birthplace: KY. Father's Bpl: KY. Mother's Bpl: IN. Waiter.

WATTS, Jack. Servant. Male. Black. 23 years old. Single. Birthplace: KY. Father's Bpl: KY. Mother's Bpl: TN. Waiter.

WOOD, Burton. Servant. Male. Black. 28 years old. Single. Birthplace: IN. Father's Bpl: IN. Mother's Bpl: KY. Waiter.

WATKINS, Daniel. Servant. Male. Black. 22 years old. Single. Birthplace: KY. Father's Bpl: KY. Mother's Bpl: KY. Waiter.

LEE, Eddie. Servant. Male. Black. 29 years old. Single. Birthplace: KY. Father's Bpl: KY. Mother's Bpl: KY. Waiter.

PACE, Edward. Servant. Male. Black. 27 years old. Single. Birthplace: TN. Father's Bpl: TN. Mother's Bpl: TN. Waiter.

THOMPSON, Ed. Servant. Male. Mulatto. 30 years old. Single. Birthplace: IL. Father's Bpl: TN. Mother's Bpl: TN. Waiter.

WILLIAMS, Andrew. Servant. Male. Mulatto. 31 years old. Single. Birthplace: KY. Father's Bpl: KY. Mother's Bpl: KY. Waiter.

PRATT, Daniel. Servant. Male. Black. 25 years old. Married. Birthplace: KY. Father's Bpl: KY. Mother's Bpl: KY. Waiter.

---, Mollie. Servant. Wife. Female. Black. 27 years old. Birthplace: TN. Father's Bpl: IN. Mother's Bpl: KY. Assistant Cook.

North West Township

CLAY, Dolly (Dwelling 13, Family 16): Head. Female. Black. 53 years old. Widow. Birthplace: KY. Father's Bpl: KY. Mother's Bpl: KY.

Orangeville Township

PINKSTON, Charles J. (Dwelling 112, Family 112): Head. Male. Black. 54 years old. Birthplace: GA. Father's Bpl: GA. Mother's Bpl: GA. Farmer.

---, Mary. Wife. Female. Black. 54 years old. Birthplace: AL. Father's Bpl: VA. Mother's Bpl: VA.

Orleans Township

TODD, Frederick (Dwelling 37, Family 38): Head. Male. Mulatto. 47 years old. Married. Birthplace: IN. Father's Bpl: KY. Mother's Bpl: IN. Driver, livery barn.

---, Anna. Wife. Female. Mulatto. 46 years old. Birthplace: IN. Father's Bpl: NC. Mother's Bpl: NC. Washes at home.

---, Edith. Daughter. Female. Mulatto. 20 years old. Single. Birthplace: IN. Father's Bpl: IN. Mother's Bpl: IN. Washes at home.

THOMAS, Dessie L. Niece. Female. Mulatto. 24 years old. Single. Birthplace: IN. Father's Bpl: IN. Mother's Bpl: IN. Domestic.

BURNETT, Charity (Dwelling 334, Family 335): Head. Female. Mulatto. 85 years old. Widow. Birthplace: VA. Father's Bpl: VA. Mother's Bpl: VA.

---, Jane. Daughter. Female. Mulatto. 52 years old. Widow. Birthplace: IN. Father's Bpl: IN. Mother's Bpl: VA. Laundress at home.

---, James L. Son. Male. Mulatto. 36 years old. Single. Birthplace: IN. Father's Bpl: IN. Mother's Bpl: VA. Laborer.

Paoli Township

PHELPS, James (Dwelling 68, Family 68): Servant. Male. Black. 67 years old. Widower. Birthplace: MS. Father's Bpl: MS. Mother's Bpl: MS. Farm Laborer. (with Laban Lindley, white physician)

HOWARD, William J. (Dwelling 154, Family 155): Head. Male. Black. 61 years old. Married. Birthplace: KY. Father's Bpl: KY. Mother's Bpl: KY. Laborer.

---, Helen M. Wife. Female. Black. 50 years old. Birthplace: IN. Father's Bpl: IN. Mother's Bpl: IN.

---, Mary L. Daughter. Female. Black. 29 years old. Single. Birthplace: IN. Father's Bpl: KY. Mother's Bpl: IN. Laundress.

---, Nancy P. Daughter. Female. Black. 21 years old. Single. Birthplace: IN. Father's Bpl: KY. Mother's Bpl: IN. Laundress.

---, Josephine. Daughter. Female. Black. 19 years old. Single. Birthplace: IN. Father's Bpl: KY. Mother's Bpl: IN.

---, Elmer. Son. Male. Black. 25 years old. Single. Birthplace: IN. Father's Bpl: KY. Mother's Bpl: KY. Carpenter.

---, Arthur. Son. Male. Black. 13 years old. Single. Birthplace: IN. Father's Bpl: KY. Mother's Bpl: IN.

BOWMAN, Sidney (Dwelling 248, Family 249): Head. Male. Mulatto. 47 years old. Birthplace: IN. Father's Bpl: IN. Mother's Bpl: IN. Driver, stage line.

---, Allie. Wife. Female. Mulatto. 41 years old. Birthplace: IN. Father's Bpl: IN. Mother's Bpl: IN.

---, Olia. Daughter. Female. Mulatto. 21 years old. Single. Birthplace: IN. Father's Bpl: IN. Mother's Bpl: IN.

---, Hershel. Son. Male. Mulatto. 17 years old. Single. Birthplace: IN. Father's Bpl: IN. Mother's Bpl: IN. Hotel porter.

---, Irene. Daughter. Female. Mulatto. 15 years old. Single. Birthplace: IN. Father's Bpl: IN. Mother's Bpl: IN.

---, Jesse. Son. Male. Mulatto. 12 years old. Single. Birthplace: IN. Father's Bpl: IN. Mother's Bpl: IN.

---, Mabel. Daughter. Female. Mulatto. 10 years old. Birthplace: IN. Father's Bpl: IN. Mother's Bpl: IN.

---, Elsie. Daughter. Female. Mulatto. 7 years old. Birthplace: IN. Father's Bpl: IN. Mother's Bpl: IN.

---, Lawrence. Son. Male. Mulatto. 4 years old. Single. Birthplace: IN. Father's Bpl: IN. Mother's Bpl: IN.

THOMAS, William (Dwelling 281, Family 282): Head. Male. Black. 63 years old. Married. Birthplace: IN. Father's Bpl: NC. Mother's Bpl: NC. Farm manager.

---, Susan. Wife. Female. Black. 60 years old. Birthplace: KY. Father's Bpl: KY. Mother's Bpl: KY.

---, Dessie. Daughter. Female. Black. 26 years old. Single. Birthplace: IN. Father's Bpl: IN. Mother's Bpl: IN.

---, Addie. Daughter. Female. Black. Single. 23 years old. Birthplace: IN. Father's Bpl: IN. Mother's Bpl: IN. Domestic.

---, Mary. Daughter. Female. Black. 18 years old. Birthplace: IN. Father's Bpl: IN. Mother's Bpl: IN.

---, Leslie. Son. Male. Black. 20 years old. Single. Birthplace: IN. Father's Bpl: IN. Mother's Bpl: IN. Hired hand.

BURNETT, George. Boarder. Male. Black. 60 years old. Single. Birthplace: IN. Father's Bpl: NC. Mother's Bpl: IN. Teamster.

END

APPENDIX C
LANDOWNERS IN LICK CREEK
SETTLEMENT AREA
Based on Land Transactions 1817-1905

(Names of African Americans in CAPITALS)

1. AMOS BAXTER from BENJAMIN ROBERTS 40 acres [NW qr; NE 1/4], Section 28, Township 1 North, Range 1 East between May 15, 1834 and 1853. No actual record of sale yet found.

2. AMOS BAXTER from John Cates and Mary Cates, his wife, 40 acres [SE qr; SE qr] Section 21, Township 1 North, Range 1 East on April 9, 1863; recorded on August 6, 1863. DEED BOOK 21, page 218.

3. AMOS BAXTER and ELEN BAXTER, his wife, to NELSON ROBERTS 40 acres [NW qr; NE qr] Section 28, Township 1 North, Range 1 East on March 24, 1860; recorded June 25, 1860. DEED BOOK 19, page 388.

4. AMOS BAXTER and ELEN E. BAXTER, his wife, to Margory McDonald 40 acres [SE qr; SE qr] Section 21, Township 1 North, Range 1 East on September 12, 1864. Recorded on October 9, 1864. DEED BOOK 22, page 66.

5. THOMAS BUTLER from CALVIN SCOTT 20 acres [N 1/2 SW qr; NW qr] Section 33, Township 1 North, Range 1 East between November 18, 1839 and May 19, 1841. No actual record of sale yet found.

6. THOMAS BUTLER and ANNA BUTLER, his wife, to ALVIN SCOTT 20 acres [N 1/2 SW qr; NW qr] Section 33, Township 1 North, Range 1 East on May 19, 1841. Recorded on June 1, 1841. DEED BOOK H, page 293.

7. MARY A. BONDS inherited an undivided one-fifth interest in the 322 acre estate of MATHEW THOMAS, deceased, when he died in 1870. Other heirs were WILLIAM THOMAS, JEREMIAH THOMAS, ADELINE S. E. WALLS, and GEORGE ETTA THOMAS WADE.

8. MARY A. BONDS purchased an undivided one-fifth interest in the 322 acre estate of MATHEW THOMAS from WILLIAM THOMAS on January 8, 1872. Recorded on January 8, 1872. DEED BOOK 29, page 166.

9. MARY A. BONDS purchased an undivided one-fifth interest in the 322 acre estate of MATHEW THOMAS from JEREMIAH and SETITIA THOMAS (residents of Coles County [Mattoon], Illinois) on September 10, 1873. Recorded on September 12, 1873. DEED BOOK 29, page 502.

10. On March 27, 1875, Hiram Lindley purchased 3/5 interest in the 322 acre estate of MATHEW THOMAS, deceased, at public auction. The property had been auctioned for non-payment of estate expenses by MONROE C. BOND and MARY A. BOND, his wife. Hiram Lindley assigned his interest in the property to Owen Lindley, who was issued a Sheriffs Deed to this property on April 22, 1876. Recorded on April 22, 1876. SHERIFFS DEED BOOK 1, page 38.

11. BANISTER CHAVIS from ELIAS ROBERTS and NANCY ROBERTS, his wife, 80 acres [NE qr; SW qr and SE qr; SW qr] Section 27, Township 1 North, Range 1 East on February 4, 1850. Recorded on April 2, 1850. DEED BOOK 13, page 258.

12. BANISTER CHAVIS from THOMAS ROBERTS and MATILDA ROBERTS, his wife, 80 acres [SE qr; NW qr] and [SW qr; NE qr] Section 27, Township 1 North, Range 1 East on March 10, 1851. Recorded on June 19, 1851. DEED BOOK 14, page 184.

13. BANISTER CHAVIS from SARAH THOMPSON 5 acres of equal width off west side of [SW qr; NE qr], Section 27, Township 1 North, Range 1 East after April 12, 1859, probably about 1870. No record of this sale has yet been found.

14. BANISTER CHAVIS and SARAH CHAVIS, his wife, to ELIAS ROBERTS 80 acres [SW qr; NE qr] Section 27, Township 1 North, Range 1 East on September 25, 1855. Recorded on May 16, 1859. DEED BOOK 19, page 75.

15. JOHN CHAVIS purchased 85 acres in the [NE qr; SW qr] and [SE qr; SW qr] plus 5 acres equal width off west side [SW qr; NE qr], Section 27, Township 1 North, Range 1 East at public auction on May 1, 1905. Property auctioned for non-payment of taxes in 1903 and 1904 by heirs of BANISTER CHAVIS. Deed issued and recorded on May 13, 1907. DEED BOOK 58, page 556.

16. On April 29, 1890, THOMAS CHAVIS and WILLIAM R. CHAVIS of Jackson County, Arkansas, mortgaged their undivided 1/3 interest in the 85 acre estate of BANISTER CHAVIS, deceased, to Morrison and Decker Manufacturing Company. Recorded on June

11, 1890. MORTGAGE BOOK 9, page 347.

17. JOHN CHAVIS and EMMA CHAVIS, his wife, to William Unger 85 acres [NE qr; SW qr and SE qr; NW qr] plus 5 acres equal width off west side [SW qr; NE qr] Section 27, Township 1 North, Range 1 East on January 28, 1911. Recorded on January 30, 1911. DEED BOOK 63, page 422. Comments: JOHN and EMMA CHAVIS were listed as residents of Vermillion County, Illinois.

18. WILLIAM CONSTANT and CHARLES GOIN from United States of America (patented) 160 acres SW quarter, Section 27, Township 2 North, Range 1 East. Recorded date of entry in Tract Book 3, page 89 is August 5, 1817.

19. CHARLES GOIN and ELIZABETH GOIN, his wife, and WILLIAM CONSTANT to Harrison Cornwell 160 SW quarter, Section 27, Township 2 North, Range 1 East on December 28, 1831. Recorded on February 2, 1832. DEED BOOK D, page 271.

20. DAVID DUGGED from United States of America (patented) 40 acres [NE qr; SE qr], Section 10, Township 1 North, Range 1 East. Recorded entry in Tract Book 3, page 77 is October 12, 1832.

21. DAVID DUGGED from Daniel Dawson [NW qr; SE qr] Section 10, Township 1 North, Range 1 East on September 11, 1835. Recorded on March 26, 1836, DEED BOOK E, page 370.

22. DAVID DUGGED and SAVORY DUGGED, his wife, to Robert Hallowell 80 acres [NW qr; SE qr] and [NE qr; SE qr] Section 10, Township 1 North, Range 1 East on February 23, 1841. Recorded on March 8, 1841. DEED BOOK H, page 181.

23. JOHN RICHMOND DUGGED from United States of America (patented) 40 acres [NW qr; SW qr], Section 27, Township 1 North, Range 1 East. Recorded date of entry in Tract Book 3, page 81 is June 19, 1845.

24. JOHN RICHMOND DUGGED from United States of America (patented) 40 acres [NW qr; NE qr], Section 33, Township 1 North, Range 1 East. Recorded date of entry in Tract Book 3, page 83 is January 25, 1847.

25. JOHN RICHMOND DUGGED and JOICY ANN T. DUGGED, his wife, to Robert Hallowell Sr. 40 acres [NW qr; SW qr] Section 27, Township 1 North, Range 1 East on June 23, 1845. Recorded on July 12, 1845. DEED BOOK J, page 407.

26. JOHN RICHMOND DUGGED and JOICY ANN DUGGED, his wife, to ISAAC SCOTT 40 acres [NW qr; NE qr] Section 33, Township 1 North, Range 1 East on June 7, 1851. Recorded on June 7, 1851. DEED BOOK 14, page 168.

27. THOMAS DUGGED from Thomas Lindley and Peggy Lindley, his wife, 30 acres of equal width off north side [NW qr; SE qr] Section 10, Township 1 North, Range 1 East on January 15, 1846. Recorded on March 13, 1846. DEED BOOK J-10, page 635.

28. Sometime between December 28, 1846 and September 16, 1848, THOMAS DUGGED purchased the SW quarter of SE quarter, Section 28 from Eli Lindley. No record of this sale has yet been found.

29. THOMAS DUGGED to Eli Lindley 30 acres of equal width off north side [NW qr; SE qr], Section 10, Township 1 North, Range 1 East on January 5, 1847. Recorded on March 18, 1847. DEED BOOK K, page 356.

30. THOMAS DUGGED died about 1848 while still holding title to 40 acres of land in Section 28. On September 16, 1848, notice was given that John Baker, Esqr. took out letters of administration on the estate of THOMAS DUGGED, deceased. PROBATE ORDER BOOK 3, page 261.

31. John Baker, Esqr., Administrator of the estate of THOMAS DUGGED, deceased, to CALVIN SCOTT [SW qr; SE qr] Section 28, Township 1 North, Range 1 East on February 8, 1851. Recorded on May 20, 1851. DEED BOOK 14, page 144.

The final report on the estate of THOMAS DUGGED, deceased, recorded in Probate Order Book 4, page 164 on November 29, 1851, shows the estate was distributed as follows: (1) 50% to DAVID DUGGED, father of decedent; (2) 50% divided equally between JOHN DUGGED, LEONARD DUGGED, ELLEN WHITE, MARY C. DUGGED, WILLIAM B. DUGGED, and SAMUEL A. DUGGED, who were the brothers and sisters of THOMAS DUGGED, deceased.

32. CHARLES GOIN and WILLIAM CONSTANT from United States of America (patented) 160 acres SW quarter, Township 2 North, Range 1 East. See listings #17 and #18 above for details.

33. JAMES GUTHRIE from United States of America (patented) 40 acres SE quarter, Section 32, Township 1 North, Range 1 East. Recorded date of entry in Tract Book 3, page 83 is June 23, 1847.

34. JAMES GUTHRIE from James Jones and Mary Jones, his wife, 6 acres off north side [SE qr; SE qr], Section 12, Township 1 North, Range 1 West on February 26, 1859. Recorded on March 1, 1859. DEED BOOK 18, page 631.

35. JAMES GUTHRIE died prior to 1868 while still holding title to 40 acres of land. PEGGY GUTHRIE, his widow, deeded 40 acres [SE qr; SE qr] Section 32, Township 1 North, Range 1 East to William Vanzant on February 17, 1868. Recorded on January 1, 1870. DEED BOOK 27, page 255. In this deed PEGGY GUTHRIE was listed as a resident of Howard County, Indiana. Comments: No record found to show how James or Peggy Guthrie disposed of the 6 acres obtained in listing #33.

36. PETER LINDLEY from the United States of America (patented) 40 acres SW quarter, Section 28, Township 1 North, Range 1 East. Recorded date of entry in Tract Book 3, page 82 is October 2, 1832.

37. PETER LINDLEY died circa 1836 while holding title to 40 acres identified in listing #35. At the request of David Lindley, to whom PETER LINDLEY owed money, William Smith, Commissioner of Probate Court, sold the 40 acres to David Lindley. Recorded on October 7, 1836. DEED BOOK E, page 539. Comments: This deed identified the minor heirs of PETER LINDLEY, deceased, as SARAH, MARY and ELIAS LINDLEY.

38. On January 15, 1845, ELI LINDLEY, the son of PETER LINDLEY, deeded his interest in the above mentioned property to David Lindley. Recorded on January 11, 1845. DEED BOOK J-10, page 229.

39. On October 18, 1852, LITTLETON HAMMOND and MARY JANE HAMMOND, his wife and probably the daughter of PETER LINDLEY, deeded their interest in the above mentioned property to ISAAC SCOTT, the next owner on record. Recorded on October 16, 1855. DEED BOOK 17, page 50. It is assumed these two deeds (#37-38) were intended to correct a deficiency in the Commissioner's Deed to David Lindley.

40. MOSES LOCUST from United States of America (patented) 40 acres SW quarter, Section 36, Township 2 North, Range 1 East. Recorded date of entry in Tract Book 3, page 90 is August 20, 1832.

41. MOSES LOCUST from United States of America (patented) 40 acres SW quarter, Section 36, Township 2 North, Range 1 East. Recorded date of entry in Tract Book 3, page 90 is June 14, 1836.

42. MOSES LOCUST from United States of America (patented) 40 acres SE quarter Section 36, Township 2 North, Range 1 East. Recorded date of entry in Tract Book 3, page 90 is October 2, 1838.

43. SIMON LOCUST from John E. Hall and Margaret Hall, his wife, 173 acres [NW corner; NE qr] Section 23, Township 1 North, Range 1 East on March 5, 1870. Recorded on March 23, 1870. DEED BOOK 27, page 325.

44. SIMON LOCUST from James L. Lynd and Millie Lynd, his wife, 200 acres [NW qr; NE qr] Section 23, Township 1 North, Range 1 East on April 19, 1887. Recorded on April 19, 1887. DEED BOOK 37, page 553.

45. James L. Lynd purchased at public auction 200 acres of land in [SE qr] Section 14 and [NW qr; NE qr] Section 23 on January 1, 1886. Property of SIMON LOCUST auctioned for non-payment of debt. Deed issued February 16, 1887. Recorded on March 29, 1887. SHERIFFS DEED BOOK 1, page 530.

46. Charles Edwards purchased at public auction 200 acres of land in [SE qr] Section 14 and [NE qr] Section 23 on March 22, 1897. Property auctioned for non-payment of a Common School Fund Mortgage taken out on April 19, 1887, by SIMON and FLORENCE LOCUST. Recorded on March 22, 1897. DEED BOOK 46, page 354.

47. HARMON LYNCH from United States of America 40 acres [SW qr; Se qr] Section 32, Township 1 North, Range 1 East. Recorded date of entry in Tract Book 3, page 83 is June 20, 1844.

48. HARMON LYNCH from United States of America 40 acres [NW qr; SE qr] Section 32, Township 1 North, Range 1 East. Recorded date of entry in Tract Book 3, page 83 is April 3, 1846.

49. HARMON LYNCH and MARTHA LYNCH, his wife, to Alfred Atkinson 80 acres [SW qr; SE qr] and [NW qr; SE qr] Section 32, Township 1 North, Range 1 East on September 13, 1862. Recorded on September 25, 1862. DEED BOOK 20, page 540.

50. SOLOMON NEWBY from ISHMAEL ROBERTS and LUCRETIA ROBERTS, his wife, 79 acres of the west half of the NW quarter, Section 27, Township 1 North, Range 1 East on December 1, 1846. Recorded on January 12, 1847. DEED BOOK K, page 206.

51. SOLOMON NEWBY and MARGARET NEWBY, his wife, to Jesse Thompson 79 acres of the west half of the NW quarter, Section 27, Township 1 North, Range 1 East on September 17, 1862. Recorded on October 28, 1862. DEED BOOK 21, page 10.

52. JARMON A. RICKMAN from ISAAC SCOTT and JEMIMA SCOTT, his wife, 60 acres S half [SW qr; SE qr Section 28, Township 1 North, Range 1 East on March 4, 1859. Recorded on March 7, 1859. DEED BOOK 18, page 652.

53. JARMON A. RICKMAN and ELIZABETH RICKMAN, his wife, to Lee Hazelwood, 60 acres [NW qr; NE qr] Section 33, and S half [SW qr; SE qr] Section 28, Township 1 North, Range 1 East on September 10, 1862. Recorded on September 25, 1862. DEED BOOK 20, page 543.

54. BENJAMIN ROBERTS from United States of America 40 acres [NE qr; NE qr] Section 28, Township 1 North, Range 1 East. Recorded date of entry in Tract Book 3, page 81 is September 29, 1832.

55. BENJAMIN ROBERTS from United States of America (patented) 40 acres [NW qr; NE qr] Section 28, Township 1 North, Range 1 East. Recorded date of entry in Tract Book 3, page 81 is May 15, 1834.

56. BENJAMIN ROBERTS from William Wilkins 40 acres [SE qr; NE qr] Section 28, Township 1 North, Range 1 East on September 8, 1848. Recorded on October 6, 1848, DEED BOOK 12, page 291. Comments: a second deed signed January 31, 1854 and recorded on February 18, 1854 is believed to be a correction deed, signed and recorded after BENJAMIN ROBERTS had already died.

57. BENJAMIN ROBERTS died in mid-1853 while holding title to 80 acres of land. In his will dated May 16, 1853 and executed September 19, 1853, BENJAMIN ROBERTS left the East half of Section 28 to his wife Sarah. WILL BOOK 2, page 17.

Comments: In his will BENJAMIN ROBERTS mentioned also that he held the power of attorney to sell land [SE qr; SE qr] Section 21 owned by ISHMAEL ROBERTS JR. Also mentioned in the will were a daughter, SENA, and a son, ISHMAEL. No record yet found as to disposition of 40 acres [NW qr; NE qr], Section 28, Township 1 North, Range 1 East.

58. ELIAS ROBERTS from United States of America (patented) 40 acres [NE qr; SW qr] Section 22, Township 1 North, Range 1 East. Recorded date of entry in Tract Book 3, page 80 on November 21, 1832.

59. ELIAS ROBERTS from United States of America (patented) 40 acres [SE qr; NW qr] Section 22, Township 1 North, Range 1 East. Recorded date of entry in Tract Book 3, page 79 is January 9, 1834.

60. ELIAS ROBERTS from JORDON THOMAS and CANDIS THOMAS, his wife, 20 acres west half [SW qr; NE qr] Section 22, Township 1 North, Range 1 East on June 19, 1840. Recorded on April 28, 1845. DEED BOOK J-10, page 344.

61. ELIAS ROBERTS from MATHEW THOMAS and MARY THOMAS, his wife, 20 acres west half [NW qr; SE qr] Section 22, Township 1 North, Range 1 East on February 1, 1845. Recorded on April 28, 1845. DEED BOOK J-10, page 343.

62. ELIAS ROBERTS from United States of America (patented) 40 acres [NE qr; SW qr] Section 27, Township 1 North, Range 1 East. Range 1 East. Recorded date of entry in Tract Book 3, page 81 is February 18, 1845.

63. ELIAS ROBERTS from United States of America (patented) 40 acres [SW qr; SW qr] Section 27, Township 1 North, Range 1 East. Recorded date of entry in Tract Book 3, page 81 is November 21, 1845.

64. ELIAS ROBERTS from United States of America (patented) 40 acres [SE qr;SW qr] Section 27, Township 1 North, Range 1 East. Recorded date of entry in Tract Book 3, page 81 is February 3, 1846.

65. ELIAS ROBERTS from JOSEPH SCOTT and FANY M. SCOTT, his wife, 40 acres [SE qr; SE qr] Section 28, Township 1 North, Range 1 East on February 5, 1847. Recorded on March 13, 1849. DEED BOOK 12, page 434.

66. ELIAS ROBERTS from THOMAS ROBERTS and MATILDA ROBERTS, his wife, 39 acres [NE qr; NW qr] Section 27, Township 1 North, Range 1 East on March 10, 1851 -- except for one acre on the north side of this tract previously conveyed to the trustees of the African Methodist Episcopal Church. Recorded on June 20, 1851. DEED BOOK 14, page 185.

67. ELIAS ROBERTS from Arthur J. Simpson, Commissioner of Court of Common Pleas, 70 acres of equal width south side, SE quarter, Section 20, Township 1 North, Range 1 East on February 16, 1854. Recorded on July 18, 1854. DEED BOOK 16, page 246. Comments: Court of Common Pleas sold property at request of MATHEW THOMAS, guardian of minor heirs of JORDAN THOMAS, deceased.

68. ELIAS ROBERTS from BANISTER CHAVIS and SARAH CHAVIS, his wife, 80 acres [SW qr; NE qr] and [SE qr; SW qr] Section 27 Township 1 North, Range 1 East on September 25, 1855. Recorded on May 16, 1859. DEED BOOK 19, page 75. Comments: Elias Roberts had previously owned the [SE qr; SW qr] Section 27 from February 3, 1846 to February 4, 1850 when he sold 40 acres to BANISTER CHAVIS.

69. ELIAS ROBERTS from CANDIS H. THOMAS 35 acres of equal width on east side of [SW qr; NE qr] Section 27, Township 1 North, Range 1 East on November 4, 1862. Recorded on February 19, 1863. DEED BOOK 21, page 92. Comments: Elias Roberts had previously owned this 35 acres from September 25, 1855 to April 12, 1859 when he sold the property to Candis Thomas.

70. ELIAS ROBERTS and NANCY ROBERTS, his wife, to BANISTER CHAVIS 80 acres [NE qr; SW qr] and [SE qr;SW qr] Section 27, Township 1 North, Range 1 East on February 4, 1850. Recorded on April 2, 1850. DEED BOOK 13, page 258.

71. ELIAS ROBERTS and NANCY ROBERTS, his wife, to John Denham 40 acres [SE qr; SW qr] Section 27, Township 1 North, Range 1 East on June 3, 1857. Recorded on September 1, 1857. DEED BOOK 18, page 181.

72. ELIAS ROBERTS and NANCY ROBERTS, his wife, to CANDIS THOMAS 35 acres of equal width off east side [SW qr; NE qr] Section 27, Township 1 North, Range 1 East on April 12, 1859. Recorded on May 14, 1859. DEED BOOK 19, page 73.

73. ELIAS ROBERTS and NANCY ROBERTS, his wife, to SARAH THOMPSON 5 acres of equal width west side [SW qr; NE qr] Section 27, Township 1 North, Range 1 East on April 12, 1859. Recorded on May 16, 1859. DEED BOOK 19, page 74.

74. ELIAS ROBERTS died in 1866 while holding title to 304 acres of land. On July 31, 1866, notice was given that Harrison Bobbitt took out letters of administration on the estate of ELIAS ROBERTS, deceased. Notice filled on October 29, 1866 in Probate File R.

75. Most of the ELIAS ROBERTS estate was disposed of by the heirs on September 10, 1867 and February 1, 1868: ELI ROBERTS, ELIZA JANE ROBERTS, THOMAS THOMPSON and SARAH THOMPSON, his wife; MATHEW THOMAS; NANCY ROBERTS; ZACHARIAH ROBERTS and CATHERINE ROBERTS (residents of Howard County, Indiana); CANDIS THOMAS (resident of Parke County, Indiana); and JOHN ROBERTS (resident of Marion County, Indiana).

76. Estate of ELIAS ROBERTS to MATHEW THOMAS 38 ACRES: 25 2/3 acres of equal width off north side [SE qr; NW qr] Section 22; 12 1/3 acres of north side of west one-half [SW qr; NE qr] Section 22, Township 1 North, Range 1 East. Recorded on February 26, 1868. DEED BOOK 25, page 114.

77. Estate of ELIAS ROBERTS to David Lindley 70 acres of equal width south side of SE qr Section 20, Township 1 North, Range 1 East. Recorded on February 29, 1858. DEED BOOK 25, page 118.

78. Estate of ELIAS ROBERTS to NANCY ROBERTS 82 acres: 14 1/3 acres of equal width off south side [SE qr; NW qr] Section 22; 7 2/3 acres off south side of west half of [SW qr; NE qr] Section 22; west half of [NW qr; SE qr] Section 22, Township 1 North, Range 1 East. Recorded on April 3, 1868. DEED BOOK 25, page 159.

79. Estate of ELIAS ROBERTS to ELIZA JANE ROBERTS 35 acres in east side of [SW qr; NE qr] Section 27, Township 1 North, Range 1 East. Recorded on April 3, 1868 DEED BOOK 25, page 161.

80. Estate of ELIAS ROBERTS to ELI ROBERTS 39 acres [NE qr; NW qr], Section 27, Township 1 North, Range 1 East, except for 1 acre on the north side of tract previously conveyed to the African Methodist Episcopal Church. Recorded on December 11, 1868. DEED BOOK 25, page 392.

81. In the final report on the estate of ELIAS ROBERTS, deceased, recorded in Probate Order Book 6, page 441 on May 31, 1869, the estate was distributed as follows: (a) 33 1/3 percent to NANCY ROBERTS, widow; (b) 9 2/3 percent each to SALLIE THOMAS, ZACHARIAH ROBERTS, ELIZABETH ROBERTS, ELI ROBERTS, CANDIS THOMAS, and JOHN ROBERTS, assumed to be the surviving children of ELIAS and NANCY ROBERTS; and (c) 1 11/18 percent each to WILLIAM THOMAS, JOICE THOMAS, JERRY THOMAS, MARY BOND, ADALINE THOMAS, and JOHN THOMAS, assumed to be the surviving children of MATHEW THOMAS and MARY ROBERTS THOMAS, the deceased daughter of ELIAS and NANCY ROBERTS.

82. It was recorded in Probate Order Book 7, page 364 on February 5, 1873 that JOHN THOMAS died before receiving his 1 11/18 percent share of the ELIAS ROBERTS estate. This share was then divided equally between his five surviving brothers and sisters.

83. On March 6, 1882 ELI ROBERTS purchased at public auction 40 acres in the [SE qr; SE qr] Section 28, Township 1 North, Range 1 East. Property was auctioned for non-payment of taxes by ELIAS ROBERTS for the years 1879 and 1880. Recorded on March 30,

1885. DEED BOOK 36, page 267.

84. No record has yet been found for how ELIAS ROBERTS disposed of 40 acres [SW qr; SW qr], Section 27, Township 1 North, Range 1 East.

85. ISHMAEL ROBERTS from United States of America (patented) 80 acres in the west half of NW quarter Section 27, Township 1 North, Range 1 East. Recorded date of entry in Tract Book 3, page 81 is March 28, 1836.

86. ISHMAEL ROBERTS and his wife, LUCRETIA ROBERTS, to the Union Meeting House Trustees, namely DAVID DUGGED and MARTIN SCOTT one (1) acre of land in the NE corner of [NW qr; NW qr] Section 27, Township 1 North, Range 1 East on April 27, 1837. Recorded on May 4, 1837. DEED BOOK F, page 140.

87. ISHMAEL ROBERTS and his wife, LUCRETIA ROBERTS, to SOLOMAN NEWBY 79 acres of the west half of the NW quarter, Section 27, Township 1 North, Range 1 East on December 1, 1846. Recorded on January 12, 1847. DEED BOOK K, page 266.

88. ISHMAEL ROBERTS JR. from United States of America (patented) 40 acres [SE qr; SE qr] Section 21, Township 1 North, Range 1 East. Recorded date of entry in Tract Book 3, page 79 is March 28, 1836.

89. ISHMAEL ROBERTS and DELENA ROBERTS, residents of Hamilton County, Indiana, to John Cates 40 acres in [SE qr; SE qr] Section 21, Township 1 North, Range 1 East on April 24, 1854. Recorded on May 20, 1854. DEED BOOK 16, page 178.

90. THOMAS ROBERTS from Samuel Chambers lot #42 in the town of Chambersburg on May 3, 1841. Recorded on September 3, 1846. DEED BOOK K, page 142.

91. THOMAS ROBERTS from William and Grace Wilkins 120 acres in [SW qr; NE qr] Section 27, Township 1 North, Range 1 East on May 17, 1841. Recorded on May 18, 1841. DEED BOOK H, page 287.

92. THOMAS ROBERTS to Peter Cornwell one lot #42 in Chambersburg on May 20, 1841. Recorded on October 9, 1841. DEED BOOK H, page 473.

93. THOMAS ROBERTS and his wife, MATILDA ROBERTS, to the Trustees of the African American Episcopal Church. namely ELIAS ROBERTS, MATHEW THOMAS, THOMAS ROBERTS, ISAAC SCOTT and SAMUEL CHANDLER, one (1) acre of land on the north side of [NE qr; NW qr] Section 27, Township 1 North, Range 1 East on December 14, 1843. Recorded on January 9, 1845. DEED BOOK J-10, page 225.

94. THOMAS ROBERTS and his wife, MATILDA ROBERTS, to BANISTER CHAVIS 80 acres of land in [SE qr; NW qr] Section 27, Township 1 North, Range 1 East on March 10, 1851. Recorded on June 19, 1851. DEED BOOK 14, page 184.

95. THOMAS ROBERTS and his wife, MATILDA ROBERTS, to ELIAS ROBERTS on March 10, 1851, 39 acres in the [NE qr; NW qr], Section 27, Township 1 North, Range 1 East except for one acre on north side of tract previously conveyed to the African Methodist Episcopal Church. Recorded on June 20, 1851. DEED BOOK 14, page 185.

96. ZACHARIAH ROBERTS from Robert Hollowell 40 acres in [NW qr; SW qr] Section 27, Township 1 North, Range 1 East on April 27, 1848. Recorded on August 23, 1848. DEED BOOK 12, page 251.

97. ZACHARIAH ROBERTS to MATHEW THOMAS 40 acres in [NW qr; SW qr] Section 27, Township 1 North, Range 1 East on August 16, 1853. Recorded on August 31, 1853. DEED BOOK 15, page 472.

98. SARAH ROBERTS from her late husband, BENJAMIN ROBERTS, 80 acres in east half of NE quarter Section 28, Township 1 North, Range 1 East. Will dated May 16, 1853 and executed on September 19, 1853. Recorded in Will Book 2, page 17.

99. SARAH ROBERTS to Granville P. Peyton 80 acres east half of NE quarter Section 28, Township 1 North, Range 1 East on October 31, 1859. Recorded on April 2, 1860. DEED BOOK 19, page 306.

100. NELSON ROBERTS from AMOS and ELEN BAXTER 40 acres in the [NW qr; NE qr] Section 28, Township 1 North, Range 1 East on March 24, 1860. Recorded on June 25, 1860. DEED BOOK 19, page 388.

101. NELSON ROBERTS and his wife, MARY ROBERTS, both residents of Wayne County, Indiana, to ANNY ROBERTS 40 acres in [NW qr; NE qr] Section 28, Township 1 North, Range 1 East on December 6, 1869. Recorded on December 31, 1869. DEED BOOK

26, page 133.

102. NANCY ROBERTS from the heirs of the late ELIAS ROBERTS 82 acres: 14 1/3 acres of equal width of south side [SE qr; NW qr]; 7 2/3 acres of equal width of south side, west half of [SW qr; NE qr]; 40 acres [NE qr; SW qr]; 20 acres, west half [NW qr; SE qr]; all in Section 22, Township 1 North, Range 1 East on September 10, 1867. Recorded on April 3, 1868. DEED BOOK 25, page 159.

103. In 1876 NANCY ROBERTS died while still holding title to 82 acres of land. The heirs -- THOMAS THOMPSON and SARAH THOMPSON, his wife; ELIZA J. ROBERTS; ADALINE S. E. WALLS; MARY A. BONDS; WILLIAM THOMAS; JOHN ROBERTS (resident of Marion County, Indiana); JEREMIAH THOMAS (resident of Illinois); ZACHARIAH ROBERTS; and CANDIS THOMAS - - (resident of Boone County, Indiana) deeded the 82 acres to James W. Montgomery on September 27, 1876, by ZACHARIAH ROBERTS on November 7, 1876 and by CANDIS THOMAS on December 5, 1876. Recorded on January 10, 1902. DEED BOOK 52, pages 92, 105, and 110.

104. ELI ROBERTS from WILLIAM PAUL QUINN, Bishop of the African Methodist Episcopal Church, the one acre church lot along the north side of [NE qr; NW qr] Section 27, Township 1 North, Range 1 East on December 14, 1863. Recorded on March 25, 1869. DEED BOOK 25, page 547.

105. ELI ROBERTS from heirs of late ELIAS ROBERTS 39 acres [NE QR; NW qr], except for one acre on north side of this tract conveyed previously to the African Methodist Episcopal Church, Section 27, Township 1 North, Range 1 East on September 10, 1867. Recorded on December 11, 1868. DEED BOOK 25, page 392.

106. ELI ROBERTS at public auction 40 acres [SE qr; SE qr] Section 27, Township 1 North, Range 1 East on March 30, 1885. Property auctioned for non-payment of taxes for the years 1879 and 1885. Recorded on March 30, 1885. DEED BOOK 36, page 267.

107. In 1887 ELI ROBERTS died while holding title to 80 acres of land. In 1887 and 1888, the heirs deeded the 80 acres in [SE qr; SE qr] Section 28, Township 1 North, Range 1 East to the Studebaker Brothers Manufacturing Company.

Heirs were: WILLIAM THOMAS, and his wife, DELILAH THOMAS; MARY A BONDS; JOHN ROBERTS JR.; ADALINE WILSON, and her husband, JOHN T. WILSON (residents of Owen County, Indiana); SARAH THOMPSON (Parke County, Indiana resident); JOHN ROBERTS (Parke County, Indiana resident); CANDIS H. THOMAS (Parke County, Indiana resident); and ZACHARIAH ROBERTS (resident of Lawrence County, Indiana).

108. The Bank of Mitchell, Indiana purchased at public auction 40 acres [NE qr; NW qr] Section 27, Township 1 North, Range 1 East on February 10, 1902. Property auctioned for non-payment of taxes by the ELI ROBERTS heirs. Deed issued to Milton N. Moore on February 23, 1904. Recorded in DEED BOOK 55, page 45.

109. ELIZA JANE ROBERTS from heirs of late ELIAS ROBERTS 35 acres of equal width of east side [SW qr; NE qr] Section 27, Township 1 North, Range 1 East on September 10, 1867. Recorded on April 3, 1868. DEED BOOK 25, page 161.

110. ELIZA JANE ROBERTS to J. N. Walker and A. D. Topping 35 acres on east side [SW qr; NE qr], Section 27, Township 1 North, Range 1 East on June 14, 1884. Recorded on March 1, 1886. DEED BOOK 37, page 35.

111. ANNY ROBERTS from NELSON ROBERTS and his wife, MARY ROBERTS, 40 acres [NW qr; NE qr], Section 28, Township 1 North, Range 1 East on December 6, 1869. Recorded on December 31, 1869. DEED BOOK 26, page 133.

112. ANNA [ROBERTS] BURNETT and her husband, OLIVER BURNETT, to Samuel Lindley 40 acres in [NW qr; NE qr] Section 28, Township 1 North, Range 1 East on October 16, 1883. Recorded on October 25, 1883. DEED BOOK 35, page 330.

113. ALVIN SCOTT from THOMAS and ANNA BUTLER 20 acres north half [SW qr; NW qr] Section Township 1 North, Range 1 East on May 19, 1841. Recorded on June 1, 1841. DEED BOOK H, page 293.

114. ALVIN SCOTT from MARTIN and MARY SCOTT 40 acres [NW qr; NW qr] Section 33, Township 1 North, Range 1 East on April 17, 1844. Recorded on June 11, 1844. DEED BOOK J-10, page 89.

115. ALVIN SCOTT from United States of America (patented) 80 acres north half of NW quarter Section 4, Township 1 South, Range 1 East. Recorded date of entry in Tract Book 3, page 103 is October 10, 1847.

116. ALVIN SCOTT and his wife, Jane, to MARTIN SCOTT 20 acres in the north half of [SW qr; NW qr], Section 33, Township 1 North, Range 1 East on April 17, 1844. Recorded on July 8, 1844. DEED BOOK J-10, page 100.

117. ALVIN SCOTT and his wife, Mary Jane, to JORDAN THOMAS 40 acres [NW qr; NW qr] Section 33, Township 1 North, Range 1 East on September 27, 1847. Recorded on January 31, 1849. DEED BOOK 12, page 404.

118. ALVIN SCOTT and his wife, ELIZABETH, to John Lindley and Alfred Atkinson 80 acres north half of NW quarter Section 4, Township 1 South, Range 1 East on September 16, 1862. Recorded on October 28, 1862. DEED BOOK 21, page 12.

119. CALVIN SCOTT from United States of America (patented) 40 acres [SE qr; SE qr] Section 28. Recorded date of entry in Tract Book 3, page 81 is November 1, 1838.

120. CALVIN SCOTT from David Lindley 20 acres [SW qr; NW qr] Section 33, Township 1 North, Range 1 East on December 26, 1836.

Mortgage held by David Lindley to be paid off by September 4, 1838.
Mortgage Deed recorded in DEED BOOK F, page 54 on January 11, 1837.

David and Ruth Lindley deeded these 20 acres to CALVIN SCOTT on November 18, 1839. Recorded on December 25, 1839. DEED BOOK G, page 272.

CALVIN SCOTT and his wife, POLLY, mortgaged this property to THOMAS BUTLER to be paid off November 16, 1840. Mortgage Deed recorded in DEED BOOK G, page 263 on December 9, 1839.

121. CALVIN SCOTT to JOSEPH SCOTT 40 acres [SE qr; SE qr] Section 28, Township 1 North, Range 1 East on October 31, 1842. Recorded on December 14, 1842. DEED BOOK I, page 285. Comments: CALVIN SCOTT was listed as a resident of Clark County (Clarksville), Indiana in this deed.

122. There appears to be no record of how CALVIN SCOTT disposed of the 20 acres in the north half of [SW qr; NW qr] Section 33. It is likely that he was unable to pay off the mortgage to THOMAS BUTLER, because the next deed of record for this property is to ALVIN SCOTT from THOMAS and ANNA BUTLER on May 19, 1841 and recorded in DEED BOOK H, page 293 on June 1, 1841.

123. ISAAC SCOTT from United States of America (patented) 40 acres [NE qr; NW qr] Section 33, Township 1 North, Range 1 East. Recorded date of entry in Tract Book 3, page 83 is September 16, 1835.

124. ISAAC SCOTT from United States of America (patented) 40 acres [SE qr; SW qr] Section 28, Township 1 North, Range 1 East. Recorded date of entry in Tract Book 3, page 82 is January 26, 1837.

125. ISAAC SCOTT from John Baker, Administrator of estate of THOMAS DUGGED, 40 acres [SW qr; SE qr] Section 28, Township 1 North, Range 1 East on February 8, 1851. Recorded on May 20, 1851. DEED BOOK 14, page 144.

126. ISAAC SCOTT from J. R. DUGGED and his wife, JOICY ANN, 40 acres [NW qr; NE qr] Section 33, Township 1 North, Range 1 East on June 7, 1851. Recorded on June 9, 1851. DEED BOOK 14, page 168.

127. ISAAC SCOTT from David Lindley and his wife, Ruth, 40 acres [NE qr; SW qr] Section 28, Township 1 North, Range 1 East on October 20, 1851. Recorded on November 10, 1851. DEED BOOK 14, page 291.

128. ISAAC SCOTT from David Lindley and his wife, Ami, 160 acres in the west half of east half of SE quarter, Section 29, Township 1 North, Range 1 East on February 16, 1852. Recorded on February 27, 1852. DEED BOOK 14, page 406.

129. ISAAC SCOTT from JORDAN THOMAS and his wife, CANDIS, 40 acres in [NW qr; NW qr], Section 33, Township 1 North, Range 1 East on February 25, 1852. Recorded on February 27, 1852. DEED BOOK 14, page 414. Comments: In this deed Isaac Scott is referred to as a "man of color."

130. ISAAC SCOTT from Samuel D. Bosley and his wife, Martha J., Lot #158 in the town of Chambersburg on October 13, 1855. Recorded on October 15, 1855. DEED BOOK 17, page 49.

131. ISAAC SCOTT and his wife, JAMIMA, to Samuel Bosley 160 acres west half of SW quarter, Section 28, and east half of SE quarter Section 29, Township 1 North, Range 1 East on October 13, 1855. Recorded on October 15, 1855. DEED BOOK 17, page 52.

132. ISAAC SCOTT and his wife, JAMIMA, to Joseph W. Cox Lot #158 in Chambersburg on March 24, 1854. Recorded on August 18, 1856. DEED BOOK 17, page 349.

133. ISAAC SCOTT and his wife, JAMIMA, to JARMON A. RICKMAN 60 acres [NW qr; NE qr] Section 33, and South half of [SW qr; SE qr], Section 28, Township 1 North, Range 1 East on March 4, 1859. Recorded on March 7, 1859. DEED BOOK 18, page 652.

134. ISAAC SCOTT and his wife, JAMIMA, to David Lindley 180 acres in the north half of NW quarter of Section 33, the east half of SW quarter of Section 28, the north half of [SW qr; SE qr] Section 28 on September 29, 1862. Recorded on December 10, 1862. DEED BOOK 21, page 32.

135. JOSEPH SCOTT from CALVIN SCOTT 40 acres [SE qr; SE qr] Section 28, Township 1 North, Range 1 East on October 31, 1842. Recorded on December 14, 1842. DEED BOOK I, page 285.

136. JOSEPH SCOTT from United States of America (patented) 40 acres [SW qr; SW qr] Section 33, Township 1 North, Range 1 East. Recorded date of entry in Tract Book 3, page 83 is February 9, 1847.

137. JOSEPH SCOTT and his wife, FANY M., to ELIAS ROBERTS 40 acres [SE qr; SE qr] Section 28, Township 1 North, Range 1 East on February 5, 1847. Recorded on March 13, 1849. DEED BOOK 12, page 434.

138. JOSEPH SCOTT and his wife, FANY, to Lee Hazelwood 40 acres [SW qr; SW qr] Section 33, Township 1 North, Range 1 East on September 10, 1862. Recorded on October 25, 1862. DEED BOOK 20, page 542.

139. MARTIN SCOTT from United States of America (patented) 40 acres [NW qr; NW qr] Section 33, Township 1 North, Range 1 East. Recorded date of entry in Tract Book 3, page 83 is August 24, 1835.

140. MARTIN SCOTT from United States of America (patented) 40 acres [SE qr; NW qr] Section 33, Township 1 North, Range 1 East. Recorded date of entry in Tract Book 3, page 83 is April 4, 1836.

141. MARTIN SCOTT from ALVIN SCOTT and his wife, JANE, 20 acres in the north half of [SW qr; NW qr] Section 33, Township 1 North, Range 1 East on April 17, 1844. Recorded on July 8, 1844. DEED BOOK J-10, page 100.

142. MARTIN SCOTT and his wife, MARY, to ALVIN SCOTT 40 acres in [NW qr; NW qr] Section 33, Township 1 North, Range 1 East on April 17, 1844. Recorded on June 11, 1844. DEED BOOK J-10, page 89.

143. MARTIN SCOTT and his wife, MARY, to George Dolts 13 acres out of north half of [SW qr; NW qr] Section 33, Township 1 North, Range 1 East on December 29, 1854. Recorded on December 29, 1854. DEED BOOK 16, page 513.

144. MARTIN SCOTT and his wife, MARY, to John Williams 47 acres: [SE qr; NW qr] Section 33; 7 acres off east side of north half of [SW qr; NW qr] Section 33, Township 1 North, Range 1 East on July 4, 1857. Recorded on November 23, 1857. DEED BOOK 18, page 197.

145. There appears to be no record of how MARTIN SCOTT disposed of Lot 178 on the town of Chambersburg.

146. ANDERSON SMITH from William and Miriam Halladay 80 acres in the [SE qr; NE qr] Section 33, and [NE qr; SE qr] Section 33 Township 1 North, Range 1 East on August 14, 1841. Recorded on July 22, 1844. DEED BOOK J-10, page 104.

147. ANDERSON SMITH from United States of America (patented) 40 acres, [SW qr; NE qr] Section 33, Township 1 North, Range 1 East. Recorded date of entry in Tract Book 3, page 83 is May 5, 1846.

148. ANDERSON SMITH from Masson and Sarah Glasson 20 acres in the east half of [NW qr; SE qr] Section 33, Township 1 North, Range 1 East on June 14, 1848. Recorded on October 4, 1848. DEED BOOK 12, page 290.

149. ANDERSON SMITH and his wife, LENNE, to Vincent Moore 140 acres: [SE qr; NE qr] Section 33; [NE qr; SE qr] Section 33; [SW qr; NE qr] Section 33; and the east half of [NW qr; SE qr] Section 33, Township 1 North, Range 1 East on February 18, 1853. Recorded on February 22, 1853. DEED BOOK 15, page 256.

150. CANDIS THOMAS from ELIAS ROBERTS and his wife, NANCY, 35 acres of equal width off east side of [SW qr; NE qr] Section 27, Township 1 North, Range 1 East on April 12, 1859. Recorded on May 14, 1859. DEED BOOK 19, page 73.

151. CANDIS H. THOMAS to ELIAS ROBERTS 35 acres of equal width off east side of [SW qr; NE qr] Section 27, Township 1 North, Range 1 East on November 4, 1862. Recorded on February 19, 1863. DEED BOOK 21, page 92.

152. JORDAN THOMAS from United States of America (patented) 40 acres [SW qr; NE qr] Section 22, Township 1 North, Range 1 East. Recorded date of entry in Tract Book 3, page 79 is February 1, 1836.

153. JORDAN THOMAS from ALVIN and MARY JANE SCOTT 40 acres [NW qr; NW qr] Section 33, Township 1 North, Range 1 East on September 27, 1847. Recorded on January 31, 1849. DEED BOOK 12, page 404.

154. JORDAN THOMAS purchased 70 acres of equal width off south side of SE quarter, Section 20, at public auction on January 1, 1853. Arthur J. Simpson, Commissioner of Commons Pleas Court deeded the land to Jordan Thomas. Recorded on August 8, 1854. DEED BOOK 16, page 244.

155. JORDAN THOMAS to MATHEW THOMAS 20 acres in east half [SW qr; NE qr] Section 22, Township 1 North, Range 1 East on January 11, 1838. Recorded on December 15, 1838. DEED BOOK F, page 542.

156. JORDAN THOMAS and his wife, CANDIS, to ELIAS ROBERTS 20 acres in west half of [SW qr; NE qr] Section 22, Township 1 North, Range 1 East on June 19, 1840. Recorded on April 26, 1845. DEED BOOK J-10, page 344.

157. JORDAN THOMAS and his wife, CANDIS, to ISAAC SCOTT 40 acres in [NW qr; NW qr] Section 33, Township 1 North, Range 1 East on February 25, 1852. Recorded on March 2, 1852. DEED BOOK 14, page 414.

158. JORDAN THOMAS died about 1853 holding title to 70 acres in Section 20. At the request of MATHEW THOMAS, guardian of the minor children of the late JORDAN THOMAS, Commissioner of Common Pleas Court sold 70 acres of the south side of SE quarter to ELIAS ROBERTS on February 16, 1854. Recorded on August 8, 1854. DEED BOOK 16, page 246. Comments: Minor heirs of JORDAN THOMAS, deceased, were: SAMIRA, NANCY, ELIAS, WILLIAM, HELEN, SARAH, and JORDAN JR.

159. MATHEW THOMAS from Zachariah and Margaret Lindley 80 acres in south half of NW quarter, Section 14, Township 1 North, Range 1 East on May 21, 1831. Recorded on June 18, 1831. DEED BOOK D, page 186.

160. MATHEW THOMAS from United States of America (patented) 40 acres [SE qr; NE qr] Section 22, Township 1 North, Range 1 East. Recorded date of entry in Tract Book 3, 79 is June 3, 1834.

161. MATHEW THOMAS from United States of America (patented) 40 acres [SW qr; SE qr] Section 22, Township 1 North, Range 1 East. Recorded date of entry in Tract Book 3, page 80 is October 29, 1835.

162. MATHEW THOMAS from United States of America (patented) 40 acres [NW qr; SE qr] Section 22, Township 1 North, Range 1 East. Recorded date of entry in Tract Book 3, page 80 is February 24, 1837.

163. MATHEW THOMAS from JORDAN THOMAS 20 acres east half of [SE qr; NE qr] Section 22, Township 1 North, Range 1 East on January 11, 1838. Recorded on December 15, 1838. DEED BOOK F, page 542.

164. MATHEW THOMAS from ZACHARIAH ROBERTS 40 acres [NW qr; SW qr] Section 27, Township 1 North, Range 1 East on August 16, 1853. Recorded on August 31, 1853. DEED BOOK 15, page 472.

165. MATHEW THOMAS from James and Sarah A. Danner 40 acres [NE qr; SE qr] Section 22, Township 1 North, Range 1 East on March 20, 1858. Recorded on May 22, 1853. DEED BOOK 18, page 390.

166. MATHEW THOMAS from James and Sarah A. Danner 5 acres equal width off of north side of east half of [SE qr; SE qr], Section 22, Township 1 North, Range 1 East on October 14, 1863. Recorded on November 7, 1863. DEED BOOK 21, page 261.

167. MATHEW THOMAS from David and Catherine Cates 19 acres of equal width of south side of [NW qr; SW qr] Section 22 and south half of SW quarter Section 22 -- totaling 99 acres -- Township 1 North, Range 1 East on November 13, 1864. Recorded on December 20, 1864. DEED BOOK 22, page 168.

168. MATHEW THOMAS from James and Sarah A. Danner 20 acres west half of [SE qr; SE qr] Section 22, Township 1 North, Range 1 East on April 4, 1865. Recorded on June 19, 1865. DEED BOOK 22, page 468.

169. MATHEW THOMAS from the heirs of ELIAS ROBERTS 25 2/3 acres of equal width of the north side of [SE qr; NE qr] Section 22, and 12 1/3 acres of equal width of north side of west half [SW qr; NE qr] Section 22 totaling 38 acres on September 10, 1867. Recorded on February 26, 1868. DEED BOOK 25, page 114.

170. MATHEW THOMAS to William F. Bracy 80 acres south half of the NW quarter of Section 14, Township 1 North, Range 1 East on December 14, 1833. Recorded on March 4, 1834. DEED BOOK E, page 113.

171. MATHEW THOMAS and his wife, MARY, to ELIAS ROBERTS 20 acres in the west half of [NW qr; SE qr] Section 22, Township 1 North, Range 1 East on February 1, 1845. Recorded on April 28, 1845. DEED BOOK J-10, page 343.

172. MATHEW THOMAS and his wife, MARY, to Mary Hallowell 40 acres in the [NW qr; SW qr] Section 27, Township 1 North, Range 1 East on March 20, 1858. Recorded on November 29, 1858. DEED BOOK 18, page 516.

173. MATHEW THOMAS died in 1870 while still holding title to 322 acres of land in Section 22. Hiram Lindley was named Administrator of the estate of Mathew Thomas on January 3, 1871 and recorded in Probate Order Book 7, page 66 on January 30, 1871. The heirs were: WILLIAM THOMAS, JEREMIAH THOMAS, MARY BOND, ADALINE WALLS, and GEORGE E. THOMAS WADE.

174. THOMAS THOMPSON was named guardian of the minor heirs of MATHEW THOMAS, deceased, on April 2, 1872 and recorded in Probate Order Book 7, page 215 on June 3, 1872.

175. WILLIAM THOMAS to MARY A. BOND his undivided one-fifth interest in the 322 acres owned by the late MATHEW THOMAS on January 8, 1872. Recorded on January 8, 1872. DEED BOOK 29, page 166.

176. JEREMIAH THOMAS and his wife, LETITIA, (residents of Coles County, Illinois) to MARY A. BOND their undivided interest in the 322 acres owned by the late MATHEW THOMAS on September 10, 1873. Recorded on September 12, 1873. DEED BOOK 29, page 502.

MARY A. BONDS, ADALINE WALLS, and GEORGE ETTA THOMAS WADE evidently retained their individual undivided one-fifth interests in the 322 acres owned by the late MATHEW THOMAS. Hiram Lindley, Administrator, filed the final report on the estate of MATHEW THOMAS on April 11, 1876, Probate Order Book 9, page 29.

177. WILLIAM THOMAS from Owen and Emily C. Lindley the undivided 3/5 interest in [NE qr;SE qr], in [SE qr; NE qr], in [SW qr; SE qr], the north half of [NE qr; SE qr; SE qr], 6 1/3 acres out of the SW corner of [SW qr; NE qr], 12 2/3 acres in the SW corner of [SE qr; NW qr] -- all totaling 144 acres in Section 22, Township 1 North, Range 1 East on August 10, 1880. Recorded on August 11, 1880. DEED BOOK 33, page 440.

178. WILLIAM THOMAS from ADALINE WILSON and her husband, JOHN T. WILSON and GEORGE ETTA COLE and her husband, DANIEL COLE the undivided 2/5 interest in the 144 acres of land in Section 22, Township 1 North, Range 1 East as described in item #175 on August 12, 1880. Recorded on September 4, 1880. DEED BOOK 33, page 450.

179. WILLIAM THOMAS to Charles W. Heard 204 acres in Section 22, Township 1 North, Range 1 East on March 18, 1902. Recorded on March 25, 1902. DEED BOOK 52, page 258.

180. JONATHAN B. THOMPSON from Isaac and Rebecca Hickman 40 acres in [NE qr; SE qr] Section 32, Township 1 North, Range 1 East on November 4, 1851. Recorded on November 11, 1851. DEED BOOK 14, page 297.

181. JONATHAN B. THOMPSON and his wife, PRISCILLA, to Lee Hazelwood 40 acres [NE qr; SE qr] Section 32, Township 1 North, Range 1 East on September 10, 1862. Recorded on October 25, 1862. DEED BOOK 20, page 541.

182. SARAH THOMPSON from ELIAS and NANCY ROBERTS 5 acres of equal width off of the west side of [SW qr; NE qr] Section 27, Township 1 North, Range 1 East on April 12, 1859. Recorded on May 16, 1859. DEED BOOK 19, page 74.

183. There appears to be no record as to how SARAH THOMPSON disposed of the 5 acres of equal width in Section 27 as described in item #180. The next mention of this property is in a mortgage deed from THOMAS and WILLIAM R. CHAVIS, heirs of the estate of BANISTER CHAVIS, deceased, to Morrison and Decker Manufacturing Company recorded in Mortgage Book 9, page 347 on June 11, 1890.

184. THOMAS THOMPSON from Alexander H. Tuell 40 acres [SW qr; SW qr] Section 27, Township 1 North, Range 1 East between 1868 and 1873. Records searched but none found for this transaction. Tax duplicates show the property in the name of THOMAS THOMPSON or his heirs continuously between 1873 and 1906.

Deeds distributing the estates of NANCY ROBERTS, deceased, and ELI ROBERTS, deceased, indicate THOMAS THOMPSON died between 1876 and 1888. THOMAS THOMPSON was heir to these estates because his wife, SARAH THOMPSON, was a daughter of Nancy and a sister to Eli.

185. Bayles Harvey purchased 40 acres at public auction (estate of THOMAS THOMPSON) [SW qr; SW qr] Section 27, Township 1 North, Range 1 East on February 15, 1906. Property was auctioned for non-payment of taxes. Recorded on April 10, 1908. DEED BOOK 60, page 121.

186. GEORGE ETTA THOMAS WADE inherited an undivided one-fifth interest in the 322 acre estate of MATHEW THOMAS, when he died in 1870. Other heirs were: WILLIAM THOMAS, JEREMIAH THOMAS, MARY A. BONDS, and ADALINE WALLS [WILSON].

ADALINE WILSON and her husband, JOHN T. WILSON, and GEORGE ETTA COLE and her husband, DANIEL COLE, purchased from Owen and Emily Lindley an undivided 3/5 interest in the south half of SW quarter Section 22; 13 acres of equal width off of south side on [NW qr; SW qr] Section 22; 12 1/6 acres in north part of west half of [SW qr; NE qr] Section 22; 12 1/2 acres in west half of north part of [SE qr; NW qr] Section 22, Township 1 North, Range 1 East on August 10, 1880. Recorded on August 10, 1880. DEED BOOK 33, page 439.
       Comments: DANIEL and GEORGE ETTA COLE were listed as residents of Barber County, Kansas. Last two descriptions in this deed appear to be in error. They should be replaced by "6 2/3 acres of equal width off the east side of north part of [SE qr; NW qr] Section 22, and 12 1/3 acres of equal width off of north side of west half of [SW qr; NE qr] Section 22."

187. ADALINE WILSON, and her husband, JOHN T. WILSON, and GEORGIA COLE, and her husband, DANIEL COLE, to Laura A. Harlan 99 acres in south half of SW quarter Section 22 and 19 acres of equal width off north side of [NW qr; SW qr] Section 22 Township 1 North, Range 1 East on June 22, 1885. Recorded on June 25, 1885. DEED BOOK 36, page 387. Comments: DANIEL and GEORGE ETTA COLE listed as residents of Barber County, Kansas.

188. No record found for how GEORGE ETTA COLE disposed of her undivided 1/2 interest in 19 acres of equal width off of west side of north part of [SE qr; NW qr] Section 22. Next deed of record is to William Wineman from Sarah E. Hill and her husband, James A. Hill, on February 28, 1912. DEED BOOK 65, page 228.

189. ADALINE S. E. WALLS inherited an undivided one-fifth interest in the 322 acre estate of MATHEW THOMAS, after he died in 1870. ADALINE WILSON and GEORGE ETTA COLE from Owen and Emily Lindley an undivided interest in south 1/2 of SW quarter of Section 22, 19 acres of equal width off south side of [NW qr; SW qr] Section 22, 12 1/6 acres in the west half of north part of [SE qr; NW qr] Section 22, 12 1/2 acres in west half of north part of [SE qr; NW qr] Section 22, Township 1 North, Range 1 East on August 10, 1880. DEED BOOK 33, page 439. See comments for item #184. ADALINE and JOHN T. WILSON listed as residents of Owen County, Indiana.

190. ADALINE WILSON and her husband, JOHN T. WILSON, and GEORGIA COLE, and her husband, DANIEL COLE, to Laura A. Harlan 99 acres in the south half of SW quarter of Section 22, and 19 acres of equal width off of south side of [NWqr; SW qr] of Section 22, Township 1 North, Range 1 East on June 22, 1885. Recorded on June 25, 1885. DEED BOOK 36, page 387.

191. ADALINE WILSON and her husband, JOHN T. WILSON, to Rudolphius S. Dillinger an undivided 1/2 interest in 19 acres of equal width off of west sdide of north part of [SE qr; NW qr] Section 22, Township 1 North, Range 1 East on January 19, 1888. Recorded on January 24, 1888. DEED BOOK 38, page 434.

192. ELIAS WASHINGTON from Samuel and Eleanor Chambers lots 123, 124, 125 and 178 in the town of Chambersburg on January 14, 1841. Recorded on September 10, 1842. DEED BOOK I, page 204.

193. ELIAS WASHINGTON and his wife, SALLEY WASHINGTON, to Peter Coppley lots 123, 124, and 125 in Chambersburg on November 2, 1846. Recorded on December 28, 1846. DEED BOOK K, page 241.

194. ELIAS WASHINGTON and his wife, SALLEY WASHINGTON, to MARTIN SCOTT Lot #178 in the town of Chambersburg on February 22, 1847. Recorded on May 27, 1847. DEED BOOK K, page 439.

END

APPENDIX D
EARLY U. S. CENSUS DATA
ROBERTS FAMILIES

1790 North Carolina: Roberts Heads of Free Colored Families. Name, County, Number in Family.

1. Roberts, Elias, Northampton Co., 4.
2. Roberds, Ishmael, Chatham Co.,, 10.
3. Roberts, James, Northampton Co., 4.
4. Roberts, James Jr., Northampton Co., 7.
5. Roberts, John, Northampton Co., 8.
6. Roberts, Jonathan, Northampton Co., 5.
7. Roberts, William, Northampton Co., 1.

1800 North Carolina: Roberts Heads of Free Colored Families. (partial listing)

1. Roberts, Claxton, Northampton Co.
2. Roberts, Ishmael, Robeson Co.
3. Roberts, James Sr., Northampton Co.
4. Roberts, James Jr., Northampton Co.
5. Roberts, Jonathan, Northampton Co.
6. Roberts, William, Northampton Co.

1810 North Carolina: Roberts Heads of Free Colored Families (partial listing)

1. Roberts, Claxton, Northampton Co.
2. Roberts, Elias, Northampton Co.
3. Roberts, Ishmael, Chatham Co.
4. Roberts, James, Northampton Co.
5. Roberts, Jonathan, Northampton Co.
6. Roberts, Kinchen I, Northampton Co.
7. Roberts, Kinchen II, Northampton Co.
8. Roberts, Richard, Northampton Co.
9. Roberts, William, Northampton Co.
10. Roberts, Willis, Northampton Co.

1820 North Carolina: Roberts Heads of Free Colored Families

1. Robards [Roberts], Nathaniel, Granville Co.
2. Roberds [Roberts], Joseph, Person Co.
3. Roberts, Benjamin, Chatham Co.
4. Roberts, David, Hertford Co.
5. Roberts, Anthony, Northampton Co.
6. Roberts, Claxton, Northampton Co.
7. Roberts, Dick, Northampton Co.
8. Roberts, Henry, Northampton Co.
9. Roberts, James, Northampton Co.
10. Roberts, James Jr., Northampton Co.
11. Roberts, Mary, Northampton Co.
12. Roberts, Rachel, Northampton Co.
13. Roberts, Ransom, Northampton Co.
14. Roberts, Watson, Northampton Co.
15. Roberts, Willis, Northampton Co.

16. Roberts, Ethelread, Robeson Co.

1830 North Carolina: Roberts Heads of Free Colored Families, Age range, and Total Number in Household

1. Roberts, Tom, Beaufort Co., 36-55, 1.
2. Roberts, Zachariah, Chatham Co., 24-36, 5.
3. Roberts, John, Chatham Co., 55-100, 3.
4. Roberts, Jonathan, Cumberland Co., 36-55, 8.
5. Roberts, John, Northampton Co., 24-36, 3.
6. Roberts, Willis, Northampton Co., 24-36, 4.
7. Roberts, Hansel, Northampton Co., 36-55, 10.
8. Roberts, Elias, Northampton Co., 55-100, 9.
9. Roberts, James, Northampton Co., 55-100, 3.
10. Roberts, Richard, Northampton Co., 36-55, 10.
11. Roberts, Hamil, Northampton Co., 36-55, 10.
12. Roberts, Ransom, Northampton Co., 36-55, 8.
13. Roberts, Sarah, Pasquotank Co., 36-55, 3.
14. Roberts, Ishmael, Robeson Co., 10-24, 1.
15. Roberts, Ethelread, Robeson Co., 55-100, 12.

1830 Indiana: Roberts Heads of Free Colored Families and Total Number in Household

1. Roberts, Aaron, Owen Co., 3.
2. Roberts, Anthony, Rush Co., 7.
3. Robards [Roberts], Benjamin, Orange Co., 5.
4. Robards [Roberts], Elias, Orange Co., 9.
5. Roberts, Elijah, Rush Co., 8.
6. Robards [Roberts], Ishmael, Orange Co., 8.
7. Roberts, James, Rush Co., 7.
8. Roberts, Joe, Union Co., 8.
9. Roberts, Joseph, Union Co., 12.
10. Roberts, John, Monroe Co., 11.
11. Robards [Roberts], Kitchen [Kinchen], Orange Co., 7.
12. Roberts, Parden B., Owen Co., 5.
13. Robards,[Roberts], Richard, Orange Co., 4.
14. Roberts, Willis, Rush Co., 10.

1830 Ohio: Roberts Heads of Free Colored Families Age range and Total in Household

1. Roberts, Joseph, Fairfield Co., 36-55, 6.
2. Roberts, John, Greene Co., 36-55, 2.
3. Roberts, Robert, Highland Co., 55-100, 3.
4. Roberts, Leander(?), Highland Co.,55-100, 7.
5. Roberts, Robert, Highland Co., 55-100, 2.
6. Roberts, Plesents, (f), Lawrence Co., 55-100, 6.
7. Roberts, Molly, 36-55, Lawrence Co., 36-55, 3.
8. Roberts, Isaac, Miami Co., 55-100, 3.
9. Roberts, Isaac, Ross Co., 36-55, 2.
10. Roberts, Jonathan, Ross Co., 24-36, 2.

APPENDIX D: ROBERTS FAMILIES

<u>1830 Kentucky</u>: Roberts Heads of Free Colored Families:
None.

<u>1840 Indiana</u>: Roberts Heads of Free Colored Families
Total in Household

1. Roberts, Lucy, Clarke Co., 1.
2. Roberts, Milton, Fayette Co., 4.
3. Roberts, Hansel, Hamilton Co., 8.
4. Roberts, Wade, Hamilton Co., 2.
5. Roberts, Elijah, Hamilton Co., 11.
6. Roberts, Bo[w]en, Lawrence Co., 3.
7. Roberts, Benjamin, Orange Co., 6.
8. Roberts, Elias, Orange Co., 8.
9. Roberts, Ishmael, Orange Co., 5.
10. Roberts, Wiley, Orange Co., 7.
11. Roberts, Thomas, Orange Co., 4.
12. Roberts, Aaron, Owen Co., 5.
13. Roberts, Ellizabeth, Randolph Co., 6.
14. Roberts, James S., Rush Co., 6.
15. Roberts, James A., Rush Co., 3.
16. Roberts, Anthony, Rush Co., 11.
17. Roberts, Willis, Rush Co., 8.
18. Roberts, Stephen, Rush Co., 4.
19. Roberts, Richard, Rush Co., 5.
20. Roberts, James D., Rush Co., 5.
21. Roberts, John, Rush Co., 6.
22. Roberts, Willis, Rush Co., 3.
23. Roberts, Joseph, Union Co., 8.
24. Roberts, Elias, Vigo Co., 3.
25. Roberts, Jas., Vigo Co., 10.
26. Roberts, K[inchen], Vigo Co., 4.
27. Roberts, R., Vigo Co., 9.

SELECTED BIBLIOGRAPHY

Basic Genealogy Books

Cromm, Emily A. *Unpuzzling Your Past: A Basic Guide to Genealogy.* 2nd ed. White Hall, VA: Betterway Publications, Inc. 1989.

Doane, Gilbert H. *Searching For Your Ancestors.* New York: Bantam Books, 1974.

Greenwood, Val D. *The Researcher's Guide to American Genealogy.* Baltimore, MD: Genealogical Publishing Co., Inc., 1973.

Jacobus, Donald L. *Genealogy as Pastime and Profession*, 2nd ed. rev. Baltimore: Genealogical Publishing Co., 1968.

African American Genealogy

Blockson, Charles L. *Black Genealogy.* Englewood Cliffs, NJ: Prentice-Hall, Inc., 1977; reprint, Black Classic Press, 1991.

Lawson, Sandra M. *Generations Past: A Selected List of Sources for Afro-American Genealogical Research.* Washington, DC: Library of Congress, 1988.

Newman, Debra L., comp. *List of Free Black Heads of Families in the First Census of the United States--1790.* Washington, D.C.: National Archives Record Service, 1973.

Robbins, Coy D. *Source Book: African American Genealogy in Indiana.* Bloomington, IN.: Indiana African American Historical and Genealogical Society, 1989.

Streets, David H. *Slave Genealogy: A Research Guide With Case Studies.* Bowie, MD: Heritage Books, Inc., 1986.

Witcher, Curt C. *A Bibliography of Sources for Black Family History in the Allen County Public Library Genealogy Department.* Ft. Wayne, IN: Allen County Public Library, 1983.

African Canadian Genealogy and History

Henson, Josiah. *The Life of Josiah Henson: Formerly A Slave.* Boston: Arthur D. Phelps, 1849; reprint Dresden, Ontario: Uncle Tom's Cabin Museum. 1984.

Hill, Daniel G. *The Freedom Seekers: Blacks in Early Canada.* Agincourt, Canada: The Book Society, 1981.

Landon, Fred. "The Negro Migration to Canada After the Passing of the Fugitive Slave Act." *The Journal of Negro History,* V (1920), 22-36.

Robbins, Arlie C. *Legacy to Buxton.* Chatham, Canada: Ideal Printing, 1983.

Robinson, Gwendolyn and John W. Robinson. *Seek the Truth: A Story of Chatham's Black Community.* Chatham, Canada: Privately printed, 1989.

Shreve, Dorothy Shadd. *The AfriCanadian Church: A Stabilizer.* Jordan Station, Ontario: Paideia Press, 1983.

History of Africans in the United States

Balesi, Charles J. *The Time of the French in the Heart of North America 1673-1818.* Chicago: Alliance Francaise Chicago, 1992.

Barclay, Wade Crawford. "The Church and Interracial Relations" in *Early American Methodism: 1769-1844.* New York: The Board of Missions and Church Extension of The Methodist Church. 1950.

Baugham, Samuel Glenn. *The Town of Rich Square [N.C.]: A History 1717-1983.* North Carolina: Privately printed, 1983.

Berlin, Ira. *Slaves Without Masters. The Free Negro in the Antebellum South.* New York: Vintage Books, 1976.

"Condition of the Free Colored People of the United States," *The Christian Examiner.* Boston: The Proprietor, 24 Bromfield St., 1859), 5th Series, Vol. IV (Jan, Feb, and Mar), 256-7.

Cornish, Dudley Taylor. *The Sable Arm: Negro Troops in the Union Army, 1861-1865.* New York: W. W. Norton & Co., 1956; Norton Library ed. 1966.

Crow, Jeffrey J. and Flora J. Hadley, eds. *Black Americans in North Carolina and the South.* Chapel Hill: University of North Carolina Press, 1984.

Davis, F. James. *Who is Black? One Nation's Definition.* University Park, PA., The Pennsylvania State University Press, 1991.

Department of Commerce, U. S. Bureau of Census. *Negro Population 1790-1915.* Washington, D.C.: Government Printing Office, 1918.

Department of Defense. *Black Americans in Defense of our Nation.* Washington, DC.: U. S. Government Printing Office. 1985.

Dodge, David. "The Free Negroes of North Carolina," *Atlantic Monthly,* VVII (1886), 20-30.

Fitts, Leroy. *A History of Black Baptists.* Nashville, TN: Broadman Press, 1985.

Foner, Eric. *Nothing But Freedom: Emancipation and Its Legacy.* Baton Rouge: Louisiana State University Press, 1983.

_____. *Free Soil, Free Labor, Free Men: The Ideology of the Republican Party before the Civil War.* New York: Oxford University Press, 1970.

Foner, Jack D. *Blacks and the Military in American History.* New York: Praeger Publishers, 1974.

Foner, Philip S. *Blacks in the American Revolution.* Westport: Greenwood Press, 1976.

Franklin, John Hope. *The Free Negro in North Carolina, 1790-1860.* (Chapel Hill: University of North Carolina Press, 1943).

_____. *From Slavery to Freedom: A History of Negro Americans.* New York: Alfred A. Knopf; Fifth Edition, 1980.

Glattharr, Joseph T. *Forged in Battle: The Civil War Alliance of Black Soldiers and White Officers.* New York: Free Press, 1990, reprint Meridian Books, 1991.

Greene, Lorenzo J. *The Negro in Colonial New England.* New York: Athenum, 1969.

Greene, Robert Ewell. *Black Defenders of America, 1775-1973: A Reference and Pictorial History.* Chicago: Johnson Publishing Co. 1974.

Heinegg, Paul. *Free African Americans of North Carolina.* Saudi Arabia: By the author, c/o ARAMCO Box 7030, Udhailiyah, 1992.

Higginson, Thomas Wentworth. *Army life in a Black Regiment.* Boston: Beacon Press, 1869; 1970 edition.

Hilty, Hiram H. *Toward Freedom For All: North Carolina Quakers and Slavery.* Richmond, IN.: Friends United Press, 1984.

Jackson, Luther P. "Free Negroes of Petersburg, Virginia." *Journal of Negro History,* XII (1927), 378.

Johnson, Daniel M. and Campbell, Rex R. *Black Migration in America.* Durham: Duke University Press, second printing 1982.

Jordan, Winthrop D. *White Over Black: American Attitudes Toward the Negro 1550-1812.* Chapel Hill: University of North Carolina Press, 1968.

Kaplan, Sidney. *The Black Presence in the Era of the American Revolution: 1770-1800.* Washington, D.C.: Smithsonian Institution Press, 1973.

Katz, William Loren. *Black Indians: A Hidden Heritage.* New York: Athenum, 1986.

--------. *The Black West.* Seattle: Open Hand Publishing Inc., Third Edition, 1987.

Lakey, Othal Hawthorne. *The History of the CME Church.* Memphis: Publishing House, 1985.

Leech, Margaret. Chapter XII "Black, Copper and Bright" in *Reveille in Washington 1860-1865.* Alexandria, Va.: Time-Life Books, Inc. 1980.

Litwack, Leon F. "The Federal Government and the Free Negro, 1790-1860." *The Journal of Negro History (1958),* 43: 261-2.

_____. *North of Slavery: The Negro in the Free States, 1790-1869.* Chicago: University of Chicago Press, 1961.

McPherson, James M. *The Negro's Civil War.* Urbana: University of Illinois Press. 1982.

Meyer, Duane. *The Highland Scots of North Carolina, 1732-1776.* Chapel Hill: University of North Carolina Press, 1987.

"Minutes of the Indiana Conference of the A. M. E. Church, 1848-1912 (incomplete)." Bishop Arnett Papers and Collection, Archives, Rembert E. Stokes Learning Center, Wilberforce University, Ohio.

Nell, William C. *The Colored Patriots of the American Revolution.* Boston: Robert F. Wallcutt, publisher, 1855; reprint 1986.

Payne, Daniel A. *History of the African American Methodist Episcopal Church.* Nashville: A.M.E. Sunday School Union, 1891; repr., New York: Arno Press, 1969.

Quarles, Benjamin. *The Negro in the American Revolution.* Chapel Hill: University of North Carolina Press, 1961.

_____. *The Negro in the Civil War.* Boston: Little Brown and Co., 1969.

_____. "The Nonslave Negro (1800-1860)," *The Negro in the Making of America.* New York: Collier Books, revised edition 1969.

Redding, Saunders. *They Came in Chains: Americans from Africa.* New York: J. B. Lippincott Co., 1950.

Reuter, Edward B. *Race Mixture: Studies in Intermarriage and Miscegenation.* New York: Whittlesey House, 1931; reprint Negro Universities Press, 1969.

Richardson, Clement ed. *The National Cyclopedia of the Colored Race.* Montgomery, AL: National Publishing Co., 1919. S.v. "The Knights of Pythias of North America, South America, Europe, Asia, Africa an Australia," by John J. Jones.

Roydhouse, Marion. "Manumission" in *Dictionary of Afro-American Slavery* edited by Randall M. Miller and John David Smith. Westport: Greenwood Press, 1988, 214-216.

Russell, John M. *The Free Negro in Virginia, 1619-1865,* Series XXXI, No. 3, John Hopkins University Studies in Historical and Political Science. Baltimore, 1913.

Sernett, Milton C. ed. *Afro-American Religious History: A Documentary Witness.* Durham: Duke University Press, 1985.

Taylor, R. H. *The Free Negro in North Carolina.* Chapel Hill: North Carolina Historical Society, 1920.

The Role and Contribution of American Negroes in the History of the United States and of Illinois: A Guide for Teachers and Curriculum Planners. Springfield, IL: Office of Superintendent of Public Instruction, 1970.

Van Sertima, Ivan. *They Came Before Columbus.* New York: Random House, 1976.

Voegeli, J. Jacque. *Free but Not Equal: The Midwest and the Negro in the Civil War.* Chicago: University of Chicago Press, 1967.

Walls, William J. *The African Methodist Episcopal Zion Church: Reality of the Black Church.* Charlotte, N.C.: A.M.E.Z. Publishing House, 1974.

Walters, Ronald G. *The Antislavery Appeal: American Abolitionism After 1830.* New York: W. W. Norton & Co., 1978.

Williams, George W. *History of the Negro Race in America 1619-1880.* 2 vols. New York: G. P. Putnam's Sons, 1883; Arno Press reprint 1968.

Wilson, Benjamin C. *The Rural Black Heritage Between Chicago and Detroit: 1850-1929.* Kalmazoo, MI: Western Michigan University New Issues Press, 1985.

Woodson, Carter G. *A Century of Negro Migration.* Washington, D.C.: The Association for the Study of Negro Life and History, 1918.

_____. *The Education of the Negro Prior to 1861.* Washington, D.C., The Association for the Study of Negro Life and History, 2nd ed., 1919.

_____. *The History of the Negro Church.* Washington, D.C.: The Associated Publishers, 1921.

_____. *Free Negro Owners of Slaves in the United States in 1830.* Washington, D.C.: Association for the Study of Negro Life and History, 1924.

_____. *Free Negro Heads of Families in the United States in 1830...* Washington, D. C.: The Association for the Study of Negro Life and History, 1925.

Wright, James M. *The Free Negro in Maryland, 1634-1860*. New York: Columbia University, 1921.

Wright Jr., Richard R. *The Bishops of The African Methodist Episcopal Church*. Nashville, TN., The A.M.E. Sunday School Union, 1963.

Yancey, Mary E. *Rocked in the Cradle of the Deep*. Harrisburg, PA.: By the author, 1844 Forester Street, 1989.

African American History in Indiana

"An Act to enforce the 13th article of the Constitution." in *The Statutes of the State of Indiana*. James Gavin and Oscar B. Hord, eds.; 2nd ed. Indianapolis: 1870. I; 443-44.

Barnhart, John D. and Carmony, Donald F. *Indiana: From Frontier to Industrial Commonwealth* (2 vols.). New York, 1954; reprint, Indiana Historical Bureau, 1979.

Bigham, Darrel E. *We Ask Only A Fair Trial: A History of the Black Community of Evansville, Indiana*. Bloomington, IN: Indiana University Press, 1987.

Blanchard, Charles ed. *Counties of Morgan, Monroe and Brown, Indiana*. Chicago: F. A. Battey & Co., 1884.

Boone, Richard G. *A History of Education in Indiana*. New York: D. E. Appleton and Co.; reprint, Indiana Historical Bureau, 1941.

Bowers, Frank. *A History of the Order of Knights of Pythias in Indiana, with the Story of Damon and Pythias*. Indianapolis: Carlon & Hollenbeck, printers, 1885.

Civil Rights Laws in Indiana. Indianapolis: Indiana Civil Rights Commission Publication, 1965, 4-5.

Clifford, Eth and McDowell, John. *Freedom's Road: A History of the Black People in Indiana*. Indianapolis, IN: David-Stewart Publishing Co., 1970.

Conkling, Edgar C. "Roberts Settlement--A Mixed-Blood Agricultural Community in Indiana." M.A. diss., University of Chicago, 1957.

Cortez, Jacqueline Y. *Contributions in Black and Red: Local History of Negro Settlement in Southwestern Indiana and Illinois*. VIncennes, IN: Vincennes University Printing Center, 1976.

Crenshaw, Gwendolyn J. *Bury Me in a Free Land: The Abolitionist Movement in Indiana, 1816-1865*. Indianapolis, IN: Indiana Historical Bureau, 1986.

Edwards, Beulah Ross. "History of Lost Creek Township." *Our Community Roots*. Terre Haute: Published privately, Lost Creek Community Club, 1979.

Ferguson, Earline Rae. "In Pursuit of the Full Enjoyment of Liberty and Happiness: Blacks in Antebellum Indianapolis, 1820-1860." *Black History News & Notes*, 32 (1988), 4-8.

Finkelman, Paul. "A Constitution for an Empire of Liberty," *Pathways to the Old Northwest: An Observance of the Bicentennial of the Northwest Ordinance*. Indianapolis: Indianapolis: Indiana Historical Society, 1988, 1-18.

Gilliam, Frances V. Haskell. *A Time To Speak: A Brief History of the Afro-Americans in Bloomington, Indiana 1865-1965*. Bloomington, IN: Pincus Strobus Press, 1985.

Heller, Herbert Lynn. "Negro Education in Indiana from 1816 to 1869." Ph.D., diss., Indiana University, 1951.

Journal of Proceedings of the Fifteenth Annual Conference of the African Methodist Episcopal Church, for the District of Indiana, held at Indianapolis, September 6, 1854. Indianapolis: Printed by Rawson Vaile, 1854.

Lyda, John D. "History of Terre Haute, Indiana." *The Indiana Negro History Society Bulletin*, (mimeographed) January, 1944.

_____. *The Negro in the History of Indiana*. Coatesville, Ind.: Hathaway Printery, 1953.

Lyles, Carl C. Sr. *Lyles Station, Indiana: Yesterday and Today*. Evansville, IN: Burkert-Walton, Inc., 1984.

Mather, George R. *Frontier Faith: The Story of the Pioneer Congregations of Fort Wayne, Indiana 1820-1860*. Ft. Wayne, IN: The Allen-County-Fort Wayne Historical Society, 1992; chap. 12, "African Methodists."

"Minutes of the Indiana Annual Conference, African Methodist Episcopal Church" in the *African Methodist Episcopal Church Magazine*, [Rev.] George Hogarth, editor, for the years 1840-1845.

Minutes of the 64th Annual Communication of the Grand Lodge of the Free and Accepted Masons of the State of Indiana held at Noblesville, Indiana August 18, 19, and 20, 1920." Printed by Graessle-Mercer Co., Seymour, Ind.

Money, Charles H. "The Fugitive Slave Law of 1850 in Indiana." *Indiana Magazine of History*, 17, (1921), 159-98 and 257-97.

Ralston, Penny A. "The Cabin Creek Settlement: The Historical Study of a Black Community in Randolph County, Indiana." Honors Thesis, Ball State University, 1971.

Robbins, Coy D. "Black Heritage in Westfield, Indiana" in *Our Westfield (1834-1984): A History of Westfield and Washington Township*. Leanna K. Roberts, ed. Noblesville, IN: Rowland Printing Co., 1984, 70-73.

_____. "Sesquicentennial of the Indiana A. M. E. Church: 1840-1990." *Ebony Lines* (Fall and Winter, 1990).

_____. *African American Soldiers from Indiana with the Union Army in the Civil War 1863-1865*. Bloomington: Indiana African American Historical and Genealogical Society, 1989.

_____. *African Heritage in Morgan County, Indiana*. Bloomington, Ind.: Indiana African American Historical and Genealogical Society, 1991.

_____. "Civil War Letters (1864-1865)." *Ebony Lines* 4 (Fall-Winter 1992): 20-26.

Rohrbough, Malcolm J. "Diversity and Unity in the Old Northwest" *Pathways to the Old Northwest: An Observance of the Bicentennial of the Northwest Ordinance*. Indianapolis: Indiana Historical Society, 1988, 71-87.

Sweet, William W. "Early Methodist Churches in Indiana." *Indiana Magazine of History*, 10 (1914), 359-368.

Taylor, Jr., Robert M. "Soaking, Sluicing, and Stewing in Hoosier Mineral Waters." *Traces*, 4, (Winter 1992), 4-9.

Terrell, William H. H. *Report of the Adjutant General of the State of Indiana*. Indianapolis: Samuel M. Douglas, State Printer, 1866. 3:379-383.

The Revised Laws of Indiana... "An Act concerning Free Negroes and Mulattoes, Servants and Slaves" approved by the Indiana Assembly, February 10, 1831." Indianapolis: Printed by Douglas and Maguire, 1831, 375-376.

Thornbrough, Emma L. "Indiana and Fugitive Slave Legislation." Indiana Magazine of History, L-3, (September 1954), 201-228.

_____. *Since Emancipation: A Short History of Indiana Negroes*, 1863-1963. Indianapolis: Indiana Division American Negro Emancipation Centennial Authority, 1963, 4.

Thornbury, W. D. "The Mineral Waters and Health Resorts of Indiana: A Study in Historical Geography." *Indiana Academy of Science Proceedings*, L (1940), 154-164.

Vincent, Stephen A. "The Robertses and Roberts Settlement: Emergence of a Black Rural Community." B. A. Honors Thesis, History Dept., Indiana University, Bloomington, 1981.

_____. "African-Americans in the Rural Midwest: The Origins and Evolution of Beech and Roberts Settlements, ca., 1760-1900." Ph. D. diss., Brown University, 1991.

Voyles, June. "Guardianships 1820-1859 Washington County, Indiana." Salem: Washington County Historical Society, 1989.

Werle, Audrey. "Thomas Malston: Indiana Pioneer, 1771-1867," *Black History News & Notes*, (November 1988), 4-7.

Orange County, Indiana

Armstrong, Nellie C. *Indiana Boundaries: Territory, State, and County*. Indianapollis: Indiana Historical Bureau, 1933; repr., 1967.

Bridgwaters, Rev. Elizabeth. Interviews by author between October, 1991 and February, 1992, Bloomington, IN.

Dillard, Arthur L., comp. *History of the Orange County Courthouse*. Paoli, Ind.: By the author; undated.

French Lick Centennial 1857-1957, Historical Souvenir Program. French Lick, IN.: Privately printed, 1957.

French Lick (Indiana) High School. *Plutonian Year Book*, 1930.

Gatsos, Gregory S. *History of the West Baden Springs Hotel*. Paoli, Ind. Private printing, 1985.

History of Orange, Lawrence and Washington Counties, Indiana. Chicago: Goodspeed Bros. & Co., 1884; repr., 1986.

Robbins, Coy D. "Lick Creek Settlement: An Early Black Community in Orange County." *Black History News & Notes*, (February and May, 1982).

Sieber, Ellen and Cheryl A. Munson. *Looking at History: Indiana's Hoosier National Forest Region, 1600 to 1950*. Bedford, IN: U.S. Dept. of Agriculture, Forest Service, 1992.

"Scouts Unearth History Chapter at County's Dense Little Africa." *The Paoli (Indiana) News*. December 31, 1970.

Vanausdall, Jeanette. "'A Miracle of Rare Devices': Images of the West Baden Springs Hotel," *Traces*, 4, (Winter 1992) 10-19.

Williams, Wanda G. "Little Africa Cemetery." "Page in History Is Uncovered; Little Africa Cemetery Found." "Negroes Unsecure in Early Indiana." "Negro Count Was Taken." *Bloomington (Indiana) Sunday Herald-Times*. January 3, 1971.

INDEX

M

Made in the USA
Las Vegas, NV
30 January 2021

16804991R00131